HEALING
DOGS THEIR WAY

The real solutions your dog deserves.

Marijke van de Water

B.Sc., DHMS

SAPPHIRE PUBLISHING
OKANAGAN VALLEY, BC

Healing Dogs Their Way: The Real Solutions Your Dog Deserves
Published by: Sapphire Publishing   ISBN: 978-0-9810492-3-6
Editor: Warren Layberry
Illustrator: Warren Layberry
Book & Cover Design: Jill Veitch, WebbPublishing.ca
Printed in Canada

Disclaimer

Dedication

This book is dedicated to the tens of millions of dogs around the world who offer unconditional love and devotion every day, sharing with us their open hearts, despite our shortcomings. Their time has now come. Let us seek to finally grasp their profound wisdom, recognize them as true teachers and healers, and explore their spiritual consciousness on a much broader scale.

Contents

Prologue:

Kava, the hound who became a healer

Let me tell you about Kava.

He arrived on Christmas Day 2001, wearing a big, shiny red bow around his neck. The most handsome Catahoula hound you ever did see, with his sleek black and white coat, a white tip on his tail, four white majestic paws and two different coloured eyes, one blue and one brown. As pleasantly surprised as we were, we were also completely unsure how we were going to manage this young, rambunctious one-year-old joining the growing pack; we already had two dogs, both seniors – a twelve-year-old golden spaniel and a fifteen-year-old saluki. We had no intentions of owning or needing a third dog. But Kava was determined.

One month prior to him moving in, I was asked to assess a couple of horses by a local dog groomer and trainer. When I picked her up at her shop with my truck, she asked if her dog – then named Gator – could come along.

"Sure," I said.

I *assumed* that he would jump into the truck box like most farm dogs do, but no. The minute the cab doors were open, he leaped into the back seat behind me with his big muddy paws and sat right down. So off we went to the nearby pasture where he jumped out upon arrival and, true to the Catahoula lineage, promptly started to herd the running horses.

All went well, and when it was time to go home, we all piled back into the truck, and Gator claimed his already familiar spot in the back seat. I pulled into the yard, and my friend and I got out. She opened the back door to call Gator, and much to both our surprise, he didn't come. In fact, he didn't even move, he just stared ahead. She reached in to pull him out, and quick as a seventy-five-pound jack rabbit he jumped into the front seat behind the steering wheel and sucked himself up against the driver's door. It was clear that he wasn't going anywhere! At least not voluntarily. Long story short, Gator had to be physically removed from my truck that day. But never mind, he had already made up his mind.

And so, he arrived to our home soon after on that Christmas Day and started his life on Riva's Ranch as a proud guardian over the land and the horses. He came to be known as Kava. He was so called not because kava is a herb used for stress and anxiety – in which case everyone could use a dog named Kava – but because Kava is a short version of a Portuguese word "kavorka" which means to have charisma and to attract others to you with your prowess and sense of success and abundance.

Kava not only had the charisma, but he also had an incredible sensitivity, intuition, and inherent wisdom on all matters that were important. He was a gentle soul although, if he perceived that another dog tried to threaten us, one of the horses, or even the chickens, he would grab them by the back of the neck and pin them to the ground until they apologized. He never once in his lifetime hurt another living being except for the occasional mouse.

Kava became nothing less than a colleague as he shadowed my every career move in the healing and health industry. Over his lifetime, he sat in on every one of my thousands of healings and hundreds of classes with his incredible presence. Kava may have begun his life as a herder, but he ended it as a healer.

It was not until Kava passed over the rainbow bridge at the age of fifteen that I truly understood how much of a legacy he'd created. He wasn't just a dog; he was a guardian, a greeter, a friend, a healer, a steward of the Earth, and a spirit guide. He opened the hearts of thousands of people who were touched by his healing energy during office appointments, distance consultations, workshops,

fire ceremonies, and retreats. He was calm, kind, respectful and very, very special. On Saturday May 16, 2015, at just after three o'clock in the afternoon, Kava made a beautifully sacred transition and passed into another dimension of consciousness – a place of peace, love and reverence.

Kava's healing spirit lives on to help thousands more dogs as he continues to grace our labels and approve of all our products. Kava never left the ranch or Riva's Remedies and never will; his beautiful spirit flows everywhere – every tree, blade of grass, leaf, blossom and gentle breeze. He's the dog that knew (and still knows) it all.

Kava, the hound who became a healer.

Introduction

Healing Dogs Their Way

There are hundreds of breeds of dogs and countless breed mixes. Some are so small they fit inside a teacup while others are as large as a pony; their weights range from half a kilogram to over 120 kilograms! There is no other sub-species of animal on the planet with that kind of phenotypical variation. People have bred and in-bred dogs for centuries. Most of this breeding was unselective and based on human needs (as opposed to the needs of the dogs themselves). The lack of comprehensive foresight as to the ultimate outcome of this breeding has led to numerous congenital problems for our beloved dogs, many of them serious. Furthermore, our domestication practices have contributed to endemic canine health issues arising from modern diets, unbalanced nutrition, unnatural lifestyles, and the transference of emotional problems from human families to our dogs. All of this has eroded the quality of life and longevity of our dogs. It's time now for us increase our awareness of what our dogs are really all about, why they are in our lives, and what it is that they need for optimum health and wellness.

I originally started my natural health practice for people, but as an animal lover and a lifelong pet parent (dogs, cats, and horses) it was a natural progression to build on my foundation of common-sense health practices and apply it first to my own animals, and then to my clients' animals. Healing had always been my "calling", and I can remember as a child holding sick animals in my lap with compassionate hands to ease their pains or to twist the ticks out from the skin of the feral dogs. Even though I was a youngster, I had an intuitive sense that there was an underlying *cause* for every health condition and that disease and unwellness were not merely random events, as many believed and still believe. Of course, I did not have enough knowledge as a ten-year-old to fully comprehend the details. Therefore, when my childhood dog Timmy – a black cocker spaniel cross – began to have epileptic seizures, I could only sit and hold and stroke him until his nervous system calmed and he was once again ready to run happily behind me in the pastures and sit in my canoe on the lake. I did not know that, if I had changed up his food, added extra nutrients such as magnesium and vitamin B12, visited a homeopath and understood the parallels between his health and mine, the seizures would have stopped, and he would have lived a healthier and longer life. Ultimately, his life ended prematurely. By then I was a teenager, and my priorities shifted – for a time.

A decade later, I began studying seriously and started my career as a human health practitioner. A few years later, I branched out into horses. Horses were in desperate need of health modalities based on what was good for the horse, ones that diverged significantly from existing mainstream practices which included high sugar grains, unlimited grass grazing, full-time shoeing, confinement, isolation, annual vaccines, excess medications and barbaric training methods. My first experience was with my own horse, a beautiful palomino named Nugget. He colicked one morning on his hay after eating green corn husks the night before, compliments of his "green" owner. He immediately began to bloat and cramp and repeatedly laid down to roll in an effort to ease his discomfort. I kept him on his feet, encouraged him to walk (movement is best for almost everything) and tried him on two homeopathic medicines carefully selected based on his symptoms. Remarkably this thousand-pound animal responded to three tiny low-potency pellets of *C. colocynthis* (bitter cucumber) licked right off my hand! Within minutes, he relaxed, took in a big drink of water, and headed for the hay. I was astounded! From that day forward, I never looked back. I became one of North America's most well-known experts in natural equine healthcare, helping thousands of horses and presenting talks, workshops, and lectures across Canada and the U.S. Then I wrote the bestselling *Healing Horses Their Way* which continues to be a leading reference book for thousands of concerned horse owners. As one reader exclaimed, "I use your horse-keeping book like a bible!"

Dogs came next (and a few cats too) into my practice, and after working on tens of thousands of people, horses and dogs it was clear that my practices were far more than an alternative; in fact, they were rapidly becoming mainstream in most of my client's households. I had proved, time and time again, by way of results, that drugs and surgery ought to be considered the alternative and not the other way around.

Yes, we all understand that emergency medicine and extreme acute conditions belong in mainstream veterinary care, but what many of us don't understand is that conventional practices, for chronic ailments and the modern epidemic of health problems, have fallen far behind and have little success in dealing with modern canine conditions. Why? Because the veterinary industry is not expanding its continuing education program to keep up with a fast-moving industry that is developing successful health modalities outside the scope of drugs and surgery. Rather, it's preoccupied with carefully defending its borders along with its limited practices to protect itself from competition. In fact, in most provinces and states, veterinary powers have made it *illegal* – under the guise of protecting your animals – for anyone, including other health professionals, to work on your animals whether it is massage therapy, nutrition, chiropractic, acupuncture, energy work or homeopathy. But what is even more disturbing is the fact that, while it is not legal for you to help your dog with holistic therapies, it *is* legal for you to kill your dog should you decide to shoot it. Does this sound like an animal protection plan to you? Does your dog need to be protected from acupuncture, reiki, homeopathy or improved nutrition but not from guns? Clearly this archaic system is self-serving, confused and broken.

In addition, although not surprising, Big Pharma is highly motivated to maintain this status quo for their moneyed interests. They have a powerful and strategic marketing plan in place – in fact, much of a veterinarian's education comes *directly* from the pharmaceutical companies teaching them to espouse the drug and vaccine industry and condemn other therapies, *especially* homeopathy. These big wheels have a lot to gain with this dogma as they conspire to convince all pet owners that there is nowhere else to turn and that all other therapies outside of their paradigm are not "evidence-based". In fact, when veterinarians take my classes and request continuing education credits for the course from their colleges, the requests are always denied.

This monopoly on animal healthcare has not served our dogs well, and as members of our family, they deserve so much more. There are eighty-four million dogs in North America, and of those, at least half of them have health problems. That's a lot of sick dogs! Dogs are itching, scratching, losing hair, biting themselves, vomiting, limping, shaking, trembling, sleeping, reacting to food, and suffering major breakdowns of the immune system like never before. Conventional treatment methods are helpless in the face of millions of food allergies, multiple immune disorders, sore joints, skin ailments, the "plastic cone" epidemic, anxiety and rising deaths due to cancer. And still, the masses of pet lovers are told that there are no cures. What that *really* means is that they have exhausted their options with no further drugs or surgery available at their disposal that could help.

In other words, they haven't identified the underlying problem.

Early on in my practice, I realized that holistic health had another difficulty, namely, that our animals lacked appropriate quality herbs, nutritional supplements, and natural medicines that were specifically created for them, and not for people. I needed products that were precisely directed at their individual requirements, their nutritional needs, and their unique disease states. To meet that demand, I formulated two product lines – one for horses and one for dogs. The new product launch was called Riva's Remedies, named after my very own special mare. She is from the Riva Ridge lineage – the famed Secretariat's barn and running mate. Each product line has three categories: herbal blends, homeopathic remedies, and specialized nutrients. They are all intended to address the many animal health issues and nutrient deficiencies that have crossed my desk over many years. I like to say that the animals themselves created these products with their constant feedback on what they need.

So, the time has never been more right to provide our much-loved dogs with a new paradigm based on a deeper understanding of their physical, emotional, mental and spiritual needs. As a homeopathic practitioner, holistic nutritional consultant, and medical intuitive who has worked with tens of thousands of animals and their people for over twenty-five years, I have witnessed thousands of success cases based on solid nutritional principles, the effectiveness of natural medicines, and a sensitive understanding of the emotional relationship between dogs and their human parents.

It was this experience that compelled me to write *Healing Dogs Their Way*. Readers will learn detailed information on how diet causes disease, the benefits of therapeutic nutrition, food allergies and intolerances, natural medicines, canine emotions, animal communication, the human-canine relationship, and most importantly, a variety of natural health programs that dogs now demand. I have personally formulated these programs with consistently outstanding results, and every reader can easily apply these programs at home. Despite its depth and comprehensive information, *Healing Dogs Their Way* is user-friendly, easy-to-follow, focused, and rigorously organized. Read it cover to cover (you eventually will anyway) or start with the chapter that interests you or applies to your dog's health condition. Refer to it time and time again.

Healing Dogs Their Way is a book that bridges science, natural health, and the intuitive healing arts to provide concrete solutions, not merely *alternatives* or *explorations into other health options*. It is based on extensive experience, on-going research, cutting-edge information, proven results, and *thousands* of happy dogs and their happy parents. It provides an opportunity for dog lovers everywhere to reward their dogs for their steadfast and unconditional love and devotion by helping them feel better than they have ever felt before!

Honest and holistic healthcare modalities belong smack-dab in the middle of primary animal healthcare. Our dogs deserve better than they've been getting. And it's up to us to make the change.

1. Are We Feeding Dogs or Wolves?

DNA vs Lifestyle

Let's be clear on this. Dogs are neither similar nor dissimilar *to* wolves, nor did they evolve *from* wolves. Dogs are, in fact, wolves themselves. They are a subspecies. All wolves are considered subspecies of *Canis lupus* also known as the timber wolf or gray wolf. Dogs are one of thirty-seven such subspecies, so for example, the red wolf is *Canis lupus rufus*; the Arctic wolf is *Canis lupus arctos*; and modern dog is *Canis lupus familiaris*.

Animal researchers once thought that dogs descended from gray wolves approximately 15,000 years ago in Central Asia. However, with the advent of modern genetic techniques, scientists have discovered that both share a common ancestor, rather than a direct lineage. As such, dogs share approximately 98.9 percent of their DNA with gray wolves.

By contrast, wolves (*Canis lupus*) and coyotes (*Canis latrans*) share only 94 percent of their DNA.

Wolf and dog.

Canis lupus

Canis lupus familiaris

Interestingly enough, though dogs vary greatly in terms of size and build, those differences arise as a result of a very small number of genes. In other words, all dogs, from Pomeranians to Great Danes, are virtually identical from a genetic standpoint, hard though that may be to believe.

Given the genetic similarities within *Canis lupus*, if we are to fully understand our dogs including their diets, behaviour, and instincts, it only makes sense to look to wolves such as the gray wolf in their natural element.

Dogs, of course, are not gray wolves. If they were, they wouldn't merit their own subspecies. But it is important to recognize that the most fundamental distinction between dogs and other wolf subspecies is not genetic at all but rather springs from the fact that *Canis lupus familiaris* has, for thousands of years, been half of a profound relationship with another species altogether, namely, *Homo sapiens*. And for thousands of years, we people have been calling the shots and making decisions based on what *we* felt was best for our dogs—or as often as not, what worked for us.

However, while thousands of years seems like a long time, it's the blink of an eye from an evolutionary standpoint. In other words, there is a lot we can learn about our dogs from studying other wolves.

For the sake of simplicity, from this point forward, when I talk about "wolves" it should be understood that I am talking about *other* subspecies of wolves, such as gray wolves; and, of course, when I talk about dogs I am talking about that most remarkable subspecies of wolf, *Canis lupus familiaris*. And when I talk about "all wolves", I am talking about both.

Why study wolves?

Without the context gained by studying wolves, we are at risk of drawing erroneous and perhaps self-serving conclusions about the feeding habits and lifestyle requirements of our dogs. By comparing the wolf's diet with knowledge of the canine intestinal anatomy, dog experts

have assumed that the normal healthy domestic dog excels on a high protein diet, with raw or cooked meat as the primary staple. Now that's a very reasonable statement founded on solid biological facts, and is, at the very least, a highly intelligent construct. But nature too has an innate intelligence – often beyond our current understanding – which allows her to make a variety of adaptations to any evolutionary circumstance. She is, therefore, completely capable of over-riding the original biology and making any modification necessary to sustain health and life in the event that the environment or circumstance becomes drastically altered.

This is a pivotal point as we discuss just how much impact the domestication process has had on dogs: quality and quantity of foods available, living arrangements, exercise levels, indiscriminate breeding, stress levels, and modern diseases have played a significant role in canine DNA development and expression. Let's find out how these insights can help us to maintain healthy, happy, disease-free companions with appropriate diets and nutritional therapies specific to modern dog.

What a Wolf Eats

Healthy adult gray wolves weigh between 36 and 45 kilograms with males weighing on average 20 percent more than females. They can bring down prey weighing up to 1,000 kilograms and eat up to 9 kilograms in one meal. A lone wolf is a very efficient hunter who eats mostly beavers, raccoons, rabbits, fish, snakes, gophers, squirrels, small rodents (such as rats, mice, and moles) and even insects – all served raw.

They also prey on ungulates (such as elk, deer, bison, moose, caribou or other hoofed mammals), but these larger prey animals can only be hunted successfully by a pack, which normally consists of six to seven wolves. Unfortunately for the wolves, the pack hunt has become increasingly scarce because loss of habitat has affected the food availability, making it difficult to sustain a group of wolves in one area. When thinning a herd of animals, wolves prey first on the vulnerable meaning that young, old, and weak animals will be preferentially targeted.

During times of shortage, wolves will often turn to livestock or even domestic dogs and cats in order to survive. Note that the wolf's usual prey is mostly herbivorous meaning that their prey only eats plant material. It is thought that wolves do not eat carnivorous prey simply because carnivores are more difficult to hunt down as

they are predators themselves. A wolf's exceptional hunting and tracking skills owe much to an acute sense of smell, able to pick up scents up to 2.5 kilometres away, and excellent hearing capable of picking up sounds up to 16 kilometres away across open ground. With their keen senses, wolves will track their prey all day if necessary.

With these changing environments, wolves have adapted to a feast-or-famine foraging pattern, and they often only consume a kill every two or three days depending on wolf density, prey density, season, snow levels and vulnerability of the prey. In the absence of fresh meat, wolves scavenge from old carcasses that consist mostly of bone and hide. Wolves have also been observed to cache their food. After a large prey has been taken down, the so-called alpha wolves eat first, along with their offspring, eating as much as they want. The other wolves then join in the feast. In times when food is scarce, the other adults in the pack may have to disperse and fend for themselves. However, wolves tend to feed amicably when food is ample. In either situation, we can assume that the subservient wolves have a somewhat different diet with consistently less choice organ meats and muscle meat and more scraps to choose from. And a wolf who is physically unable to hunt must either rely on a picked over carcass or succumb to its weakened state.

Wolves take down prey and eviscerate carcasses with jaws that can exert pressure of 1,500 psi – roughly equivalent to the compacting strength of a garbage truck. They eat the organs first, such as the liver, kidneys, lungs and heart followed by the muscle meat. As far as we know, when wolves eat large herbivorous prey, they do not intentionally eat any vegetation present in the chambers of the stomach or small intestine, but they are known to eat the stomach and intestinal linings. Wolves in captivity eat everything except the stomach, its contents, and the fur. However, when consuming smaller prey, the intestinal contents will be consumed as well since the contents are more difficult to separate from the intestines themselves.

The wolf also eats fatty tissue, bone marrow (by crushing the bone) and eventually the hide, which is to say fragments of skin with or without the hair attached. Some hair is ingested with the meat which may serve the purpose of facilitating intestinal transit time. Wolf scat contains bones and fur. Wolves must also feed their young by storing chewed up food in their stomachs which they regurgitate for the pups back at the den.

Why does the wolf ingest organ meats first? Because

organs and organ meats, especially the liver, are nutritional powerhouses packed with a variety of nutrients, including high-quality protein, saturated fats, essential fatty acids, vitamins and minerals; B vitamins especially folic acid and B12, coenzyme Q10, vitamin A, vitamin E, vitamin D, vitamin K, choline, iron, copper and zinc are abundant nutrients in organ meats. Levels of vitamin A and K are particularly high in herbivorous animals who consume fresh green grass.

Interestingly, the wolves living in one Canadian sanctuary are provided with a raw meal every two to three days but do not care to eat the smaller animals such as gophers, mice, or rabbit. Nor do they like pork, bear, or beaver. They prefer to eat what must be choice delicacies for them: beef, elk, deer, and veal. They will eat some poultry, although it's not a favourite. They will also eat fresh fish, but they will not eat any fish that has been frozen. And, even if the fish is fresh, they will first eat the head and then the remainder of the fish over one or two days – obviously not a favourite. Captive wolves who do not care to eat a particular meat will still defend it as a meal and normally bury it.

Unlike most cats, such as cougars, wolves are not obligate carnivores meaning that they are not limited to meat. Wild wolves will eat berries, plant material, grasses, leafy greens, and even fruit if available, but in much lesser quantities than meat. Seasonal grass and plant material are found in wolf scat, and a wolf's stomach contents can on occasion contain up to 74 percent plant matter; berries can account for up to 20 percent depending on the season. In summertime, wolves eat more vegetation and fewer ungulates because their energy requirements are lower thus this increased ingestion of plant material appears to be intentional. Ungulates are also more difficult to hunt in the summer since the snow- and ice-free ground gives these larger animals an advantage when it comes to outrunning wolves. Aside from convenience, wolves may rely on seasonal vegetation for an added source of roughage, vitamins, minerals and essential fatty acids. It is also likely that they rely on plants, grasses, and herbs as natural medicines to address issues such as indigestion, and detoxification from acid-rich meat and/or parasite infections. Grasses can purge parasites by wrapping the worms and increasing intestinal peristalsis which expels parasites as well as their eggs. Many plants also contain natural anti-parasitic activity which can paralyze or kill worms before elimination. Grasses also induce vomiting.

What Does This Mean for the Modern Dog?

The genetic similarity between the wolves and dogs would suggest that wolf diets can inform a healthy, viable dietary framework for modern dogs. However, we need to realize that the lifestyle of a wolf, including feeding behaviours, are vastly different than the lifestyle of a modern dog. These lifestyle changes make a difference because lifestyle determines not only changes in physical appearance, behaviours, and abilities but also the changes in physiology including digestive inabilities and capabilities. The physical, behavioral, and ecological characteristics of wolves are directly related to several variables: predation abilities, hunting environment, prey availability, prey population density, prey vulnerability, climate, and the wolf population density itself. In the face of change – the only universal constant – wolves have shown themselves to be highly flexible with a great capacity to evolve and adapt their predation and feeding behaviours according to their habitat, their environmental conditions, and the ecology. Let's call it a genetic toughness for survival. Dogs have the same biological talents, of course, but they have not yet been fully recognized and credited for these abilities. Until now.

So let's take a closer look at the distinct lifestyle differences between the wolf and dog so we can gain a better understanding of what adaptations may have already occurred, which ones must occur to optimize health and lifestyle, and most importantly, how our awareness of these lifestyle differences can be used to optimize their health.

Wolf and Dog: Lifestyle Differences

Family Dynamics

Wolves generally live in a "pack" of six or more animals all related by blood. They are very social, and they travel, hunt, and play together. They have a strict hierarchy, with a dominant or alpha male and female pair at the top of the group that have bred and produced offspring. The female wolf only heat-cycles once per year and gives birth to an average of six puppies. The other members of the wolf pack are also their offspring and are inferior to the mating pair. The whole pack assists in the upbringing of the youngsters, however, to help feed both the mother and her puppies. They act as "nursemaids" when the mother herself goes hunting and protect the area from other predators like grizzly bears. Wolves are known to have very complex patterns of communication and behaviour – they yip, whine, growl and howl to express happiness, joy, play, sadness or just to sing. But wolves never bark.

Modern dog typically lives in a doghouse or in a human house on a cushion. There is no naturally occurring pack, usually no mate, and no natural biological ability to have offspring. A sexually-mature, unspayed female dog heat cycles twice per year. There is usually no canine hierarchy – other than a single human or human family who may consider themselves "alpha" to a lone dog. Or perhaps two lone dogs. A dog's family is, and had been for generations beyond counting, another species entirely, namely, *Homo sapiens* with entirely different physical bodies, ancestors, languages, communication rules, and definitely a different perspective on life and its priorities and realities. Like all wolves, dogs are carnivores, but their instincts have been curtailed somewhat since falling into line with the most successful omnivores on the planet. Like wolves, dogs howl, whine and growl to express all the same feelings and emotions. But dogs do a lot more barking! Is this a result of the demands and the hidden frustrations of living with a foreign pack in confined areas?

~~~~~~~~~~ 🐾 ~~~~~~~~~~

Modern dog typically lives in a doghouse or in a human house on a cushion. There is no naturally occuring pack, usually no mate, and no natural biological ability to have offspring.

~~~~~~~~~~~~~~~~~~~~~~~~~~~

Food Availability

The wolf habitat can vary between grasslands, forests, desert, wetlands, and tundra. Living in the wild is a very different experience and not easy as they literally fight and kill for their lives. A pack uses a distinct territory that can be up to eighty square kilometres which it defends against other wolves. There are many obstructions and disruptions in the daily struggle for food including the weather (snow, rain, storms, floods, fires, and unbearable heat or cold), hunting competition (bears, cougars, humans and other wolves); loss of habitat, and long periods of hunger. Wolf packs must also provide food for their young family.

Wolves rarely feast on bigger game such as bison, for a coordinated hunt on large prey is only successful once out of every seven to ten hunts, and there is always risk involved expending energy when the result is in question.

Perhaps this is why wolves in captivity prefer the large animal meat – it's normally rare! Wolves hunt more ungulates in the winter because they have a speed advantage to outrun deer and caribou who have more difficulty in the deep snow. Despite this seasonal hunting advantage, meat, organs or bones from large prey animals are not the mainstay of their diet. Wolves more often hunt birds, rodents, goats – especially in the summer – and sometimes deer. This is a critical point when feeding dogs since, despite popular opinion, they don't do all that well on large animal meats.

> A notable exception to the typical feeding patterns of wolves exists in Wood Buffalo National Park in northern Alberta, a sanctuary to thousands of wood bison set up in an effort to save the species. The wolf packs in this national park are the only wolves in the world that specialize in hunting bison ten times their size. Primarily hunting these buffalo in the winter with the advantage of the deep snow, they have grown to be the largest and most powerful wolves on earth. The herds are critical to the survival of the wolves, as eight-five percent of their diet is comprised of bison meat.

In a normal, caring household dogs have all their food provided. Fed once or twice daily, dogs simply need walk across the room or come in from outside – no chasing, no fighting, no killing, no injuries, and no competition aside from the occasional snarl at another household dog or cat who might have dared a sideways glance at the food dish. There are no other pack members or youngsters to look after; they need only feed themselves, and they can do so with little effort. But it's not all a piece of cake; the biggest stressor for the modern dog is that they are at the mercy of their people to determine how and when they will be fed and, more to the point, *what* they will be fed.

Most of us are more likely to feed our beloved dogs according to the agenda of the dog food companies, rather than what is best for our dogs. The concept of feeding the same dog food for the rest of a dog's life simply because it is complete and balanced is highly unreasonable and very unhealthy. A dog's physiological needs are in a constant state of change as determined by both her internal and her external environment; and dogs appreciate food variety just as much as we do. The human pack frequently misses specific nutrient requirements and frequently feeds large animal meats, which are not a permanent or regular staple of other wolf subspecies. Furthermore, most dog parents are not feeding the whole carcass but rather parts of the carcass – raw, cooked, or commercially processed. Dogs are also frequently being fed a mixture of different meat proteins all in the same meal. It is not unusual to see dogs feeding on bison, lamb or chicken all at once. Or turkey, salmon and duck; or lamb, duck and fish. No wolf has ever had this kind of opportunity for a feast. And then there's the whole issue of understanding how to feed *other* food groups such as fats and carbohydrates. We are also feeding our dogs a cocktail of chemicals, preservatives and additives, which at one time, were not a part of their wolf environment, at least not in their food. As we shall see, all these dietary indiscretions in the domestic household are a significant cause of a variety of diseases.

> The concept of feeding the same dog food for the rest of a dog's life simply because it is reported to be complete and balanced is highly unreasonable and very unhealthy.

On the plus side, when wolves and other wild animals cease to thrive on their existing diet, they begin to decline rather quickly because the wild doesn't furnish a lot of viable alternatives. Our domestic dogs, on the other hand, have a plethora of food choices and programs available to them if their current diet isn't supporting health and wellness.

Feeding Behaviours

When a wolf devours an animal, she eats as much as she can hold in her stomach because she doesn't know when or where the next meal might come from. She is also driven to eat as much as she can before another pack member or predator steals her food. The wolf's stomach can accommodate a large volume of food because the stomach membranes can stretch and increases its size. Wolves can eat up to as much as 25 percent of their bodyweight.

A dog also 'wolfs' down her food because she has the same biological instincts and anatomy as her forbearers. But she can only consume up to 7 to 8 percent of her bodyweight in one meal. However, it is generally recommended to feed a dog only 2 to 3 percent of her total bodyweight daily.

> Given that dietary requirements, especially the quantity of meat protein intake, is very much dependent upon exercise, physical lifestyle should be a significant factor in our choices of dog food.

Exercise

Wolves expend a tremendous amount of energy stalking, chasing, and killing their prey. Wolves are known to travel up to 35 kilometres per day at a walk or trot and can swim over 20 kilometres. They can run up to 65 kilometres per hour when chasing prey and maintain these speeds for up to 20 kilometres. Packs are known to travel up to 100 kilometres in one night. During winter, wolves may travel long distances, especially when the main prey is a migratory species such as caribou. The lifestyle of the pack is all about the hunt.

The exercise program of dogs, on the other hand, is subject to the whims or priorities of the dog guardian, and exercise can range from regular to sporadic. Many dog owners feel that their dogs get adequate exercise in the backyard and studies show that approximately 40 percent of dog owners do not intentionally exercise their dogs. Given that dietary requirements, *especially* the quantity of meat protein intake, is very much dependent upon exercise, physical lifestyle should be a significant factor in our choices of dog food.

Stress

Wolves, at least from the human perspective, live a life of constant stress – the hunting ground, territory defence, the elements, disease, predators, thirst, hunger, starvation, injuries, altercations, and loss of loved ones. These pressures are very likely the reason that wolves have a shorter lifespan. A wild wolf lives, on average, five or six years while a wolf in captivity can live anywhere from thirteen to fifteen years. It is worth noting, too, that the long-term survival rates for lone wolves in the wild is dramatically reduced. Only the wolf knows which life she would consider most qualitative and fulfilling.

The biggest stressor in a modern dog's life is her human pack. The human pack can be guilty of abuse, neglect, abandonment, poor nutrition, confinement, loneliness, and lack of protection. And even when all physical and mental needs are kindly provided, the human family itself almost always suffers its own hardships of emotional distress, disease, trauma and/or abuse which is then, without exception, transferred over and energetically absorbed by the family pet (see Chapter 17 for more information on "sponging").

Would you rather be a wolf or a dog?

Breeding

Wolves have very little breeding variation resulting in a very consistent genotype. Compare this to modern dogs who can range from a giant Newfoundlander or Great Dane to a miniature poodle to a fast-running greyhound. In addition, due to unselective and random breeding, many of our dog breeds have been afflicted with horrendous health problems, but no longer have the genetic diversity required to reintroduce healthier traits back into the breed. Most of these diseases are unheard of in wolves (see Chapter 16 for more information on the effects of indiscriminate breeding).

Health and Disease

Wild wolves are susceptible to and can suffer from a wide variety of health problems including viral and bacterial infections although it is difficult to predict the actual incidence of these diseases. Reportedly, the most common causes of death in wolves are poisonous plants (hunger?) and respiratory diseases. Viral diseases can include distemper, parvovirus, infectious canine hepatitis, papillomatosis, canine coronavirus, and rarely rabies. Bacterial diseases include brucellosis, Lyme disease, leptospirosis, tularemia, listeriosis, and anthrax. It's very interesting to note that those wolves living near farms and ranches are more vulnerable to bacterial and viral diseases, likely due to exposure to infected domestic animals and their waste. Wolves are often affected by different parasites, including tapeworms, roundworms, and hookworms although their frequent forced winter fasts serve to keep the parasite loads under control. They are also plagued by fleas, ticks, lice, mites, and mange. Wolves must also endure injuries and wounds with no medical care other than exercise and perhaps foraging medicinal plants.

Most dogs don't have it any better. They suffer from all these pathogenic diseases, with the addition of genetic diseases caused by careless breeding and other "modern" diseases sponged from humans. Arthritis, obesity, insulin resistance, diabetes, cancer, cataracts, heart conditions, hormone imbalances, digestive conditions, vaccinosis, immunity problems, and allergies are endemic. And while wolves have been known to develop common dog diseases such as arthritis or cancer, these types of diseases are not common occurrences in the wild. However, our increasingly toxic environment with our air, food, water and soil rife with chemicals, toxins, and pollutants are a serious concern for both species. And given the tremendous differences in feeding patterns and food choices, it is likely that the microflora in the colonic ecosystem between the two species is vastly different.

Epigenetics and the Ability to Adapt

Now if we can accept that the wolf has adapted and altered her own characteristics over time to optimize her living conditions and chances for survival in response to her environment, then we must also accept that modern dogs are not only capable of similar biological strategies, but have already accomplished this and more.

So the question is have modern dogs, over the years, strayed from the original DNA blueprint in order to survive the new and unfamiliar domain. Yes. Of course, it has. Hard to believe? Not according to DNA scientists who have now discovered a new and exciting branch of science known as epigenetics. These scientists have learned that each chromosome (chromosomes contain the DNA) within each cell has chemical annotations attached to it. These annotations tell the cellular machinery how to read the DNA code so it knows how to act and function. But there's more! These annotations are altered, re-written, or deleted according to all environmental conditions: climate, emotions, events, the adverse effects of vaccines, traumas, and of course, food and diet all dictate how the DNA re-organizes itself. This means that all external and internal influences impact life on a cellular level, and can not only alter the information on the genes but to also affect their expression. All of this is done in the name of survival. Now, this does not mean that you can transform a dog into a monkey just by feeding it and treating it like a monkey – at least not yet anyway. But it does mean that your dog has an incredible ability to adapt and transform her behaviour and physiology in order to tolerate the ever-changing surroundings including, but not limited to, the contents of the dogfood dish!

For example, according to genetic research, the genes of domestic dogs indicate that they are better able to digest starches than wolves are. (And, it is also true that

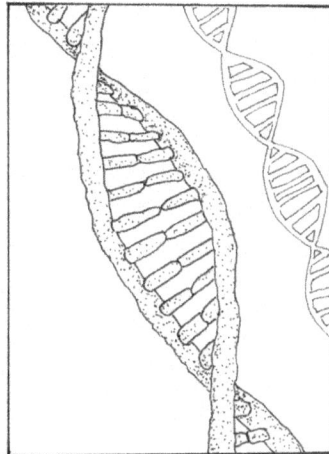

Strands of deoxyribonucleic acid, also known as DNA

humans who eat more grains and starches than meat show genetic changes different from their hunter-gatherer ancestors.) Degrees of adaptation vary, of course, depending on breed types, strength of constitution, geography, and ancestral health history. But because dogs have lived in the human environment for thousands of years, it is clear they have become more omnivorous, proving that they are versatile and fully capable of thriving on a variety of different foods. Dogs living with humans over thousands of years evolved to survive on meat scraps, non-meat scraps, and human food throwaways. A hungry dog cannot afford to be selective.

Now again, this does not mean that a horse can be fed like a dog or a dog like a horse; we must keep sight of the genetic background because it is the origins of specific genes that are responsible for having determined the original biological construct in the first place. And we also cannot use these canine survival strategies of adaptation as an excuse to sustain dogs on poor quality grain-based diets and/or to feed wheat and corn as staples any more than we can use the excuse that horses can eat beef and people can survive on bread, coffee, and alcohol diets because they have adapted to it. It does, however, explain why so many dogs are so forgiving with our canine dietary faults – they have provided us with a very large window of error. Thankfully.

Thus, the canine genetic ability to adapt to the environment, no matter what that may look like, has served them well. And it is also very much in our favour because it allows us to feed our dogs with the dietary variations and modifications necessary in today's world to resist toxic foods (including meat), contaminated environments, and disease. Diet can help maintain optimum health levels in what is now a less than an optimal environment.

But no matter what our dogs eat, the primary purpose of a dog's diet is to maximize health – not to satisfy the human agenda. Animal nutrition is a complex study, and too often experts and the pet parents alike try to apply the same principles to all dogs. Dogs each have individual needs and requirements. What works for your dog, might not work for many others and vice-versa. Listen to your dog; don't get stuck listening to others. Feeding dogs is not a cult nor a religion. If what you're doing isn't working, simply change up the program. Dog owners tend to be very passionate about what they feed their dogs, but open minds are happy minds that lead to happy dogs.

Nutrigenomics

Before we start feeding our dogs, we need to know one more thing. And that is the science of how diet affects gene expression. For years, I have observed in my human health practice that those people who took good care of themselves never seemed to succumb to any genetic diseases to which they were predisposed. The better they ate and the more they exercised, the stronger they became, no matter how old they were or what health problems were in the family. There's a new word for it now; it's *nutrigenomics*. This is the study of how food, diet, and nutrition interacts with DNA to either increase or decrease the risk of disease. Nutrigenomics tells us that no matter what information is coded on the genes, it is the external environment, including diet and nutrition, which ultimately determines how the genes will express themselves. This gives us an exciting amount of control not just over our own health, but our dogs' health as well.

Nutrigenomics tells us that no matter what information is coded on the genes, it is the external environment, including diet and nutrition, which ultimately determines how the genes will express themselves.

2. How Dogs Eat

Down the Hatch

We have established the importance of diet and nutrition in both the prevention and treatment of all diseases in all dogs. Now we need a basic understanding of the intestinal anatomy of a dog in order to determine how foods are processed and metabolized so that the food is able to nourish the dog's body in a most optimum way.

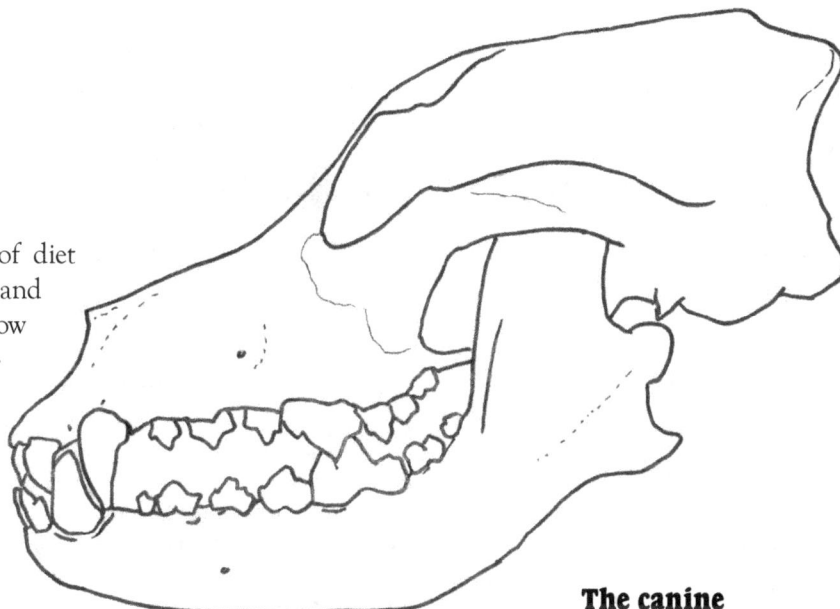

How Canis lupus Digests Its Food

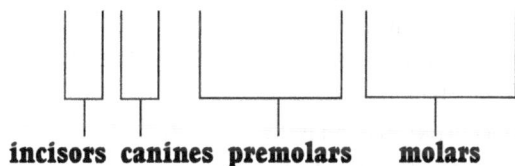

The canine skull and dental structure.

incisors canines premolars molars

The Mouth and Teeth

The word carnivore derives from the Latin words *caro* (meat) and *vorare* (to devour). Carnivores devour meat and are very effective hunters. In the case of the wolves (including dogs) this means that they have binocular vision, a highly-evolved sense of smell and hearing, strong claws that grant them traction when running down prey, long sharp teeth which grab, cut, tear, crush, and scrape meat off bones; a strong tongue; and hinged jaws which cannot move from side to side and are, therefore, designed for tearing and shredding rather than chewing and/or grinding.

Carnivores are also anatomically designed to digest meat as a primary food source and efficiently extract the most important nutrients for absorption. In wolves, the sight and smell of food stimulates the flow of saliva, which causes the dribbling of saliva on cue. Since dogs can't chew their food and must "wolf" it down, there is no need for any enzymatic activity (such as amylase, a starch digesting enzyme common in the saliva of omnivores) in the mouth; their food isn't there long enough for any effective digestion to take place anyway. Saliva does, however, have other important functions. It lubricates food for easier swallowing, aids oral hygiene by continually flushing and cleaning the mouth, and buffers acidity. It also contains lysozyme, a powerful anti-pathogenic that controls bacteria overgrowths, which is how dogs can heal wounds by licking them. In fact, I have a miniature cross donkey named Bo who bonded with my Catahoula hound Kava right after he was gelded because Kava insisted on licking his surgery site for several days after. Truth be told though, the hound's intention of licking him in the first place was motivated by a nervous reaction to his jealousy over the attention that Bo received during and after his gelding procedure. After that time, Kava ran to lick - but not bite - Bo's underbelly whenever the horses were getting too much attention. But that's a whole other story...

Bo and Kava.

The Stomach Digests Meat

Once the meat is torn into small enough pieces to swallow, it travels down the esophagus and through the cardiac sphincter into the stomach as a bolus (small, rounded mass of food) where the first stage of digestion can begin as the lining of the stomach contains glands that produce enzymes and digestive acids. The stomach only digests protein; it does not digest fats, fibre or carbohydrates including sugars. The acid levels in the gastric juice of a carnivore are much stronger than that of an herbivore and contain very high concentrations of HCl (hydrochloric acid) and pepsin which are critical for digesting meat. These powerful acids, combined with the natural antibiotics in the saliva, means that a dog can eat septic meat, and thirty minutes later the foul or rotten meat in the stomach will be copletely sterile. That's an amazing process. HCl lowers the pH (a measure of acid levels) to at least a value of one, meaning that the stomach is a very acidic environment which is inhospitable for not only bacteria, such as *E. coli*, *Salmonella*, *Campylobacter* and strains of *Helicobacter* but also kills off yeast, various viruses, and parasites and their eggs. A healthy stomach is safe from the destructive acid itself because the glands of the stomach also produce mucous, which protects the stomach from being digested by its own acid and enzymes. An unhealthy stomach is a completely different matter - as we shall see.

The stomach of *Canis lupus* represents approximately 65 percent of the entire gastro-intestinal tract. Compare that with the stomach of a horse which represents only 8 percent of its entire gastrointestinal tract. This large gastric representation in the dog is required to digest large quantities of protein - namely meat.

Once the food contents of the stomach are mixed and ground, it forms a liquid mass called chyme which is a blend of partly digested protein and gastric juices that is now delivered through the pyloric sphincter into the small intestine. The emptying of the stomach contents is initiated by the volume.

The Small Intestine Digests Meat, Grains, Plants and Fats

The small intestine (also called small colon) is longer than the large intestine (also called large colon) but is referred to as small because its diameter is smaller than the large intestine. It consists of three parts - the duodenum, the jejunum and the ileum (in that order) - and is usually two and a half times the length of the animal's body. The small intestine of a carnivore is relatively short compared to that of an herbivore (vegetarian) since it is designed to digest food quickly, absorbing critical nutrients and avoiding putrefaction of raw meat as could be caused by mal-digestion and/or a slow transit time. Because animal meat is high in protein and fat, it must be digested and eliminated quickly to prevent toxicity.

The interior membranes of the small intestine are lined with microscopic capillaries in the shape of finger-like projections called villi. In the small intestine, the partly digested meat, to complete the digestive process, is now exposed to more protein-digestive enzymes - produced by the pancreas this time and delivered through the pancreatic duct. The primary pancreatic enzyme for digesting meat is protease, which is responsible for breaking up the proteins into amino acids which are the building blocks of all protein. Other pancreatic protein digestive enzymes include trypsin and chymotrypsin. These molecules of amino acids are now small enough to be absorbed directly through the villi and into the bloodstream. These villi protrude out towards the center of the intestine and greatly increase the surface area available for digestion and absorption.

All wolves are carnivores, but they are what's known as facultative carnivores. Which means they subsist primarily but not entirely on meat. There are, among land mammals, in fact, very few "true" or obligate carnivores that subsist solely on meat – cats being the best example. Then there are omnivores, like *Homo sapiens*, who subsist on both meat and plant matter based on environment and opportunity. In obligate carnivores, the enzyme for protein digestion is always active, but in omnivores and non-obligate carnivores like wolves that enzyme is only activated if meat has been eaten.

After leaving the stomach, dietary carbohydrates and fats and oils now begin the digestive process in the small intestine. Carbohydrates such as grains, plant materials, and sugars are digested by pancreatic amylase, the enzyme produced by the pancreas. Dogs produce adequate amylase for carbohydrate digestion and have four times more

~~~~~~~~ 🐾 ~~~~~~~~

There are, among land mammals,
in fact, very few "true" or obligate
carnivores that subsist solely on meat
– cats being the best example.

~~~~~~~~

than cats. However, like all carnivores, the ingestion of excess or inappropriate starches can cause a variety of health problems for many dogs.

Fats are digested by lipase, a fat digesting enzyme also produced by the pancreas. However, dietary fats must first be emulsified by bile which is produced by the liver and then stored and concentrated in the gallbladder. Bile is composed of bile acids which are derived from cholesterol. Bile is transported from the gallbladder into the small intestine when notified by specific hormones (cholecystokinin and secretin) to contract. Bile then emulsifies fats through a "detergent" process that breaks the fat globules into microscopic droplets whereby it greatly increases the surface area of the fats, making them more digestible and water soluble. This makes it possible for the pancreatic enzyme lipase to access the inside of the droplets and digest them. Then the particles are absorbed into the villi and/or delivered to the liver for further decongestion.

But fat globules that are too large will not be able to be absorbed by the villi. In this case absorption will

occur by the lymphatic capillaries (lacteals) in the small intestine and they will be delivered to the liver via the lymphatic system instead of the bloodstream. Fats absorbed by the lymph system are known as chyle. And considering how critical the lymphatic system is for immune-related diseases, including cancer, it is very important that our dogs eat healthy, fresh (i.e., non-rancid) fats to prevent damage to the lymphatic system.

Bile is also responsible for transporting fat-soluble vitamins into the villi for absorption into the blood. From there, the vitamins are delivered to the organs and tissues in need.

And it's not just the fat-soluble vitamins and minerals that are absorbed here; *all* other vitamins and minerals are absorbed into the blood from different areas of the small intestine as well.

Once food is passed out of the small intestine, all the digestible food which the dog has eaten in this one meal should (ideally) be fully digested with only undigested matter, electrolytes, and water left in the chyme. The chyme now moves through the ileocecal valve, which regulates the speed and volume of the contents, and into the large intestine or colon.

The Pancreas Produces Digestive Enzymes and Insulin

In the previous section, we learned that the pancreas produces and secretes a variety of different enzymes transported in pancreatic juice through the common bile duct to the small intestine. This is an exocrine function. Enzymes such as lipase, protease, amylase and cellulose digest fats, proteins, starches, and fibre respectively. The pancreas also produces sodium bicarbonate (baking soda) to help buffer the strong acidity in the small intestine, as does the bile; both are transported through the common bile duct.

The pancreas has another important function, and that is to manufacture hormones to regulate blood sugar. This is the endocrine function of the pancreas where small islands of cells (islets of Langerhans) produce insulin and glucagon which are released into the bloodstream rather than into the pancreatic ducts as the enzymes are. When blood sugar rises, these cells detect an increase in blood sugar concentration and then release insulin, which acts to lower the blood sugar by opening up receptors in the muscles and liver to allow the uptake of sugar for energy or for storage.

The Large Intestine Ferments Undigested Food and Eliminates Waste

The large intestine (colon) has thinner walls than the small intestine. It also is shorter and has a larger diameter (thus the name) than the small intestine and comprises the entire colon, cecum, rectum, and anal canal. Once the liquid and undigested food matter arrives, the large intestine recovers all the water and electrolytes and reabsorbs it back into the tissues. This reabsorption of fluids and electrolytes including salt is performed in the cecum – a comma shaped pouch that lies at the junction of the ileum and colon. The cecum will also mix the contents with mucus for lubrication purposes for a smoother transit. The cecum will also now make use of millions of colony-forming units from hundreds of species of friendly bacteria (probiotics) to ferment any non-digestible carbohydrates (grains) and plant material. This fermentation of non-digestible starch and fibre produces volatile fatty acids which are also reabsorbed and are important for energy, colon health, and immunity.

The reabsorption process is aided by the churning movements of the large intestine (peristalsis), which expose more digestive material and residue to the absorbing walls. The contents are then moved through the colon with gastro-colic reflexes that then form and store feces in the rectum and anal canal until defecation.

For a carnivore one of the most important functions of the liver is the production of bile, which is stored in the gallbladder, a small sac or bladder attached to the bottom part of the liver. Meat diets contain or produce a lot of acids including uric acid. Such acids, when in excess, can be destructive. Thus the liver of a carnivore has the capacity to eliminate far more uric acid than the liver of an omnivore or herbivore. However, while this is a necessary carnivorous trait, it does not mean that dogs are exempt from health problems induced by or caused by high meat/protein diets.

Are Dogs Perfectly Designed?

Well, yes and no. Canine evolution has crafted a digestive system that is still very similar to the wolf and is highly efficient and functional; it is equipped to do exactly what it is supposed to do – eat and digest a high protein diet. The digestive organs are designed and calibrated to work together to sustain life by breaking food into small and useable components, extracting nutrients, and eliminating waste. But despite its perfection, it can and often does break down, not just due to external factors but also due to faulty and less than perfect breeding (see Chapter 16). Nevertheless, these breakdowns are not random events over which we have no control (as the scientific community would have us believe). No, not at all. These events are precipitated by underlying factors that are more obvious to the holistically trained eye. And armed with this information, we can more easily prevent and address most health conditions. Let's start with the first and very important factor. Diet.

3. How to Feed Your Dog

The Age of Choice

Today, the dogfood marketplace abounds with an amazing abundance of foods – most of them fit for dogs – and a few not so fit for dogs. Meat, bones, organs, cereal grains, vegetables, fruit, plants and even legumes can be found in every pet-food store in a variety of different forms and packages. Sales of commercial pet food in North America topped $48 billion in 2016, and most of this is sold as dry dog food (including treats) weighing 22.6 million metric tons. This is serious production. On behalf of dogs everywhere, I do not advocate for pet-food companies and suppliers whether they sell dry kibble, canned meat, freeze-dried packages or raw. I am here to advocate for the dogs, and each dog has unique dietary and nutritional needs based on a variety of factors. So, let's take a close and objective look at the amazing array of choices that we have available to us now to feed our dogs. And always keep in mind that one dog's meat can be another dog's poison; what works for your dog may have nothing to do with what works for your neighbour's dog.

Commercial Dog food

There are several ways to feed commercially prepared dog food: dry kibble, wet or canned, frozen, dehydrated, freeze-dried or fresh-prepared.

Dry Kibble

Many pet health practitioners, caretakers, and dog guardians are taught that a scientifically-designed commercial diet provides a balanced diet with all the protein, carbohydrates, fats and nutrients that a dog needs to maintain health – not *optimum* health, just health. Fortunately, the variety of dry dog food has rapidly increased over the last decade, and there are now many good quality dog foods to choose from; dogs can now benefit from grain-free kibble and/or higher quality grains, as well as fruits and vegetables, fibre, and the addition of vitamins and minerals. However, for many dry dog foods, including some prescription dog foods, this one-bag-feeds-all paradigm is definitely *not* going to work. And it doesn't always work for the high-quality feeds either. Remember, every dog is unique, and if your feeding program isn't working, try something else. Diet and nutrition is not simple especially for complicated dogs. And furthermore, there are several variables which can dramatically alter nutrition requirements – breed, lifestyle, stress, exercise levels, disease, biochemistry, and specific health conditions.

Having multiple feed options is important because, as we have learned, there is not one kind of dog food that suits every dog. We cannot ask what the best dog food is out there because it is dependent on the dog.

So, let's take a look at quality. Protein sources can vary from a low of 18 to 20 percent to a high of 37 percent. Fats content ranges from 10 to 20 percent and fibre from 3 to 8 percent. Moisture content is low at 6 to 10 percent and is the downside of feeding dry kibble since dogs can find themselves in a dehydrated state if they don't drink adequate water.

Lower-protein kibbles contain more grains, and the higher-protein foods contain little to no grains. Higher-quality commercial foods will name the specific protein, e.g. beef, salmon, lamb, and chicken – meaning that it contains *real* meat. Look for meat that is listed as the first ingredient in the dog food since they are listed in descending order by weight from the largest amount to the smallest amount. Beef and bison proteins come from striated muscle, tongue, heart, esophagus, fat, skin, and nerve and blood vessels found within the flesh. Poultry sources will include a combination of meat and skin and sometimes bone and is derived from the whole carcass of the bird. Poultry meat should not include by-products such as feathers, heads, necks, feet, immature eggs or entrails which are intestines or internal organs. And sources from beef/bison should not include these by-products: lung, spleen, kidney, brain, liver, blood, stomachs and intestines.

The use of generic words such as *meat, poultry* or *fish* leaves the pet-food manufacturer open to using meat rendered from sources such road kill, dead farm animals (possibly diseased), dead zoo animals (also possibly diseased) and even euthanized dogs and cats (often diseased) as well as the presence of by-products. These are known as the 4D animals – dead, diseased, disabled or dying. This is not the kind of energy that any animal should eat!

Rendering is a process whereby the meat and/or the leftover parts of the animal not suitable for human consumption are taken from livestock, poultry, and fish carcasses. These are crushed and ground up in huge vats and cooked for hours. Rendering removes water, separates the fats, and kills various pathogens including bacteria, viruses and parasites. The leftover fats can then be added to dog food as beef fat or chicken fat for example. The remaining solids—now a dry powder and highly concentrated in protein—become *meal* or *by-product meal* if the by-products have been included. Choose meals labelled as specific animals (e.g., chicken meal) rather than simply *meat meal*. All meal is derived from all the animal parts added to the vat except for blood, hair, hooves, horns, hide, intestinal contents, and manure. Meal is frequently added to pet food and labelled accordingly. The quality of meals can vary greatly from brand to brand. Some dogs don't like the taste, so quite often artificial flavours or fats are added to the rendering process. Most kibble is sprayed with highly preserved animal fat mixed with vitamin supplements to replace nutrients destroyed during processing.

Many commercial foods of lower quality also use non-rendered by-products. These also consist of leftover parts and can include bone, necks, blood, spleen, kidneys, lungs, fatty tissue and intestines without their contents. Adding by-products to dog food is a cheaper way to maintain protein levels and thus keeps the production costs down, but the savings may or may not be passed down to the consumer's final product. Again, look for the name of the real animal, e.g. *chicken* by-products or *lamb* by-products as opposed to *poultry* by-products or *meat* by-products. Remember, it's not always just a choice of animal parts used for food, but it is the energy of the animals from where the food comes from. Never feed the meat from sick or suffering animals. Dogs, like most animals, are extremely sensitive and vulnerable to these type of energies – more than most owners will ever be aware.

The rendering plant is nothing short of gruesome; however, rendered or non-rendered, the meat has the same toxic issues as all other meat no matter how it is prepared. Contaminants, insecticides, nitrates, radiation, heavy metals, drugs and synthetic chemicals are present in ALL meat intended for human or animal consumption.

Most of the meats and the by-products in pet food contain quite a lot of bone. *Deboned meats* have had the bone removed mechanically and *boneless meat* indicates that the bones have been separated from the flesh manually with knives. Thus, if the label specifies either boneless or deboned the product contains more meat.

Many lower-quality feeds use cheaper protein substitutes or extenders such as corn gluten, wheat gluten and/or soybean meal. Corn, wheat, and soy products are highly undesirable foods for dogs (see Feeding Grains section, below). And some not-so-low-quality kibbles may also include legumes as proteins sources or extenders such as peas, garbanzo beans, and red lentils. Legumes are high in fibre, and low in fat and protein. While a small quantity might pass the grade, legumes are a common cause of gas, bloating, and digestive upset in sensitive dogs. Like soybeans, legumes can contain varying levels of lectins, a highly toxic food protein that can disrupt membrane function contributing to leaky gut and immune problems. However, legumes can have value for a short-term vegetarian diet or cleanse. Many dog foods also use rice protein or brewer's rice. Brewer's rice is a by-product of rice milling and is the small milled fragments of rice kernels that have been separated from the larger kernels of rice – these rice bits are not as nutritious as a whole ground rice kernel. It is used exclusively for animal food, and is also often found in canine *prescription* diets.

Fillers in lower-quality dog foods are common and usually lacking in valuable nutrition: corn bran, cereal by-products, soybean hulls, cottonseed hulls, peanut hulls, rice hulls, wheat middlings and/or citrus pulp add little value to the daily diet.

The fat content of a dog food is created by adding the meat fat which is separated during the rendering process. Believe it or not, this fat is a healthier choice than the canola oil or cottonseed oils used commercially as a primary fat source. In addition, these fats are often hydrogenated but are not listed on the label (see Feeding Fats section, below). However, often more fat is added than is necessary because fat increases the calories, changes the texture, and improves palatability.

Other ingredients may include a variety of fruits and vegetables – parsley, carrots, celery, beets, pears, tomatoes and a variety of berries. Chicory, yucca and/or beet pulp can be added for their value as a prebiotic. Probiotics are often added as well, but they are sprayed on and cannot survive the storage conditions. Thus, the long-term potency of a room-temperature probiotic mixed in with numerous other ingredients is questionable.

Beet pulp is the fibrous pulp material left over after the sugar has been extracted from sugar beets. It is a well-tolerated and very digestible source of 18 percent crude fiber, a natural prebiotic and very low in sugar. Beet pulp contains both soluble and insoluble fibre which is mostly pectin. Added fibre is very important in kibble because of the low moisture content – 10 percent compared to the 70 percent in a raw food or wet food diet. Beet pulp also contains 10 percent protein and is high in calcium. I frequently feed a beet pulp, wheat bran, wheat germ mix to the horses in the morning and my hound begged for the pail to lick it clean.

Vegetarian dog foods are also now available – this can be a very useful option for those dogs that are specifically suffering from conditions caused by excess dietary protein and/or multiple food allergies. They contain ingredients such as oatmeal, pea protein, lentils and potatoes instead of meat to supply protein. A vegetarian diet can be very helpful for detoxifying, cleansing and to attain or regain dietary balance, but it should be monitored carefully for protein levels.

Avoiding foods that contain toxins, preservatives, and chemicals goes without saying. The grains used in low-quality pet foods are purchased for their low cost not for their quality. Crops in this market sector are grown based on high yield, and that is usually accomplished with heavy applications of pesticides and herbicides. Preservatives are important to prevent fats from going rancid and meat from spoiling; however, common preservatives used can include BHA (butylated hydroxyanisole), BHT (butylated hydroxytoluene), TBHQ (tertiary butylhydroquinone), or ethoxyquine. All these have been implicated in immune disorders, liver and kidney issues, thyroid problems, and cancer. Choose dog foods that are naturally preserved with vitamin E (d-Tocopherol) or vitamin C (ascorbic acid). In addition, artificial colourings can contribute to allergies and cancer.

Digests are the waste and digested debris from an animal's intestine which are treated with heat and enzymes to form concentrated natural flavours, and is then added as a meat flavouring. Digests have no nutritive value and should be avoided.

Avoid prescription diet kibbles claiming to be *hypoallergenic*. Many people are under the impression that prescription pet foods are somehow superior and better regulated. This is completely false. The pet food industry is poorly regulated, and the prescription pet foods are no exception. Furthermore, these so-called prescription foods cost up to four times as much even though they are variations of the same formula as the manufacturer's regular pet food. These prescription kibbles often contain corn, wheat, feathers, fillers and/or hydrolyzed protein from either chicken liver or soy beans. All hydrolyzed proteins contain MSG (monosodium glutamate) which is not mentioned on the label. MSG can cause headaches, sweating, heart flutter, chest pain, and nausea.

~~~~~~~~ 🐾 ~~~~~~~~

Avoid prescription diet kibbles claiming to be hypoallergenic. Many people are under the impression that prescription pet foods are somehow superior and better regulated. This is completely false.

~~~~~~~~~~~~~~~~

No matter what kind of dry kibble your dog is eating, it is likely that she is not getting the same volume of water compared to dogs on raw meat. Fresh or frozen meat provides a lot of water, whereas dry kibble is essentially a water-depleted diet with very low moisture content. This can be problematic for dogs who are prone to kidney and bladder problems because the minerals from the food build up in the urinary tract or bladder as crystals. This is a result of the reduced frequency of urination which then over-concentrates the urine. So, if you are feeding kibble, it is beneficial to add broth to the dish.

Wet Food

Wet or canned dog food normally contains the same cooked ingredients as dry dog food (with chicken, turkey or beef broth included) therefore the same label precautions apply. Wet food is higher in protein and fat compared to a similar kibble on a dry matter basis, meaning that in order to compare dry kibble to wet food, the wet food must be measured without its water content. Wet food is significantly higher in moisture than dry kibble. Whereas kibble might contain 6 to 10 percent water, canned food contains 60 to 90 percent.

In order to compare protein percentage between wet and dry foods, you must first factor out the water of the wet food. Once this is done, you then divide the protein percentage by the dry matter percentage to get the protein percentage of the dry matter. Sounds confusing, but it's not.

A simple example:

A wet food is 80% water and 10% protein.

If this food is 80% water that means it is 20% dry matter.

If 20% of what is in the can of wet food is dry matter, and 10% of what's in the can is protein, then clearly half the dry matter is protein; i.e., 10 (protein)/20 (all dry matter) = 0.5 (or 50%).

Thus the protein and fat contents in the wet food is, in reality, much higher than dry kibble. Also, if a dog is fed only canned food, they must eat a larger quantity than kibble due to the water content, but this, in turn, may push the dietary protein intake to excess. For this reason, many dog owners feed wet food with kibble.

Many canned dog foods also contain what is known as *fabricated* meat. These meat chunks have the texture of real meat but rather than 100 percent meat, they are a meat product made with some animal protein to which gums or vegetable thickeners have been added; the entire mixture is then extruded to resemble a real meat. And since there are no labelling regulations watch for labels that include gums or vegetable binders which likely indicates that the product is made of fabricated meats.

Corn or wheat gluten is sometimes used in wet dog food to create artificial meaty chunks. Canned wet food is commercially sterilized by cooking before canning.

Frozen or Fresh-Prepared

Frozen food can come in raw or cooked form, but the cooked meat is not processed or modified. This is useful for those dog lovers who want the high quality of a food program similar to home-cooked meals but do not have the time or the information to make it themselves. Meals can consist of meat, ground bone, vegetables, and some vitamins and minerals. Protein content is normally 78 to 87 percent raw meat, organs, and bone with the remainder consisting of vegetables and/or supplements. Various vegetables are used and can include kale, zucchini, seeds, pumpkin, squash, carrots, spinach, apples, pears, sweet potatoes, and organic vegetable juice.

Freezing raw meat inactivates the bacteria into dormancy, but it does *not* eliminate them. Therefore, once raw meat or fish is thawed, it must be cooked or used within the best before date to avoid contaminating your pet.

One might wonder why I am suggesting that dogs require the safeguard of cooking, for clearly wolves get along just fine without it, and didn't I start off the book talking about basing dog nutrition on wolf nutrition? The difference here is not genetic but *environmental*. Wolves are consuming wild meat and are generally (though not always) eating it fresh. Commercial meats are subject to a different subset of diseases and maladies not found in the wild. Commercial meats are also processed in slaughterhouses, and a product off an enormous assembly line is very different than an animal that has fallen to a predator. Finally, and most importantly, dogs have not built up the same robust set of immunities that come from eating raw meat by default, nor have they had any such immunities passed down from their parents.

Dogs will normally tolerate eating either cooked meat or a mix of a good quality kibble with raw food in the same diet, but I would recommend feeding them at different meals.

Dehydrated or Freeze-Dried

These products can be raw or cooked and are either air-dried or frozen and then dehydrated to reduce the moisture to levels, which in turn inhibits the growth of microbes and bacteria. They do not need to be refrigerated. Dehydrated dog food looks like dry kibble, but it needs the addition of water before serving. There is a little nutrient value lost due to the air and heat exposure.

When freeze-drying, the dehydration temperatures are kept lower so that the overall nutrient loss is even less. As a result, freeze-dried foods are a nutritionally valuable way to feed your dog and are becoming very popular. Unlike dehydrated dog food, freeze-dried dog food does not need to be rehydrated.

Fresh or Refrigerated

Fresh food can be raw or lightly cooked. They can be pasteurized with heat or HPP (high pressure processing) and then sealed in a vacuum package. These foods are kept refrigerated until served. This type of dog food is extremely vulnerable to bacteria if *not* properly refrigerated and has a shelf life of two to four months, unopened.

Brand Names and Labels

- All pet food has a guaranteed analysis which informs the buyer as to what percentage of protein, fats, fibre, moisture and some essential fatty acids. A guaranteed analysis does *not*, however, indicate the sources of these food groups.

- When looking at brands, terms like premium, super-premium, ultra-premium, or gourmet are basically marketing labels and thus meaningless.

- Pet foods labeled as natural must only contain ingredients from plant, animal, or mineral sources and cannot be highly processed or contain chemically synthetic ingredients. Nevertheless, the word natural still leaves a lot of leeway for unhealthy ingredients.

- If a pet food contains at least 90 percent (by weight) of a single ingredient, then that ingredient can be named without a qualifier in the brand, e.g., Farmer Joe's Chicken Dog Food, or Ocean Harvest Salmon Dog Food.

- If a pet food contains between 25 and 90 percent (by weight) of a single ingredient, then that ingredient can be named in the brand only with a qualifying descriptive term, e.g., Uncle Bob's Beef Dinner for Dogs.

- If a pet food contains between 3 and 25 percent (by weight) of a single ingredient, then that ingredient can only be mentioned in the brand as an addition, e.g., Frisky Fella's Dog Food with Lamb.

- If a pet food contains less than 3 percent (by weight) of a single ingredient, then that ingredient may only appear in the brand as flavouring, e.g., Happy Hound Beef Flavour Dog food. It's also worth noting that something called Mama Lioni's Ultra-Premium Gourmet Filet Mignon Flavour Kibble might not contain any filet mignon beef whatsoever, but it would require 3 percent beef.

- If a meat protein is named in the label, this does not mean that it is the only protein ingredient in the bag, so use caution if, for example, your dog has chicken or fish allergies since any other meat ingredients may be used.

- Organic pet foods are made without the use of conventional pesticides and artificial fertilizers and are processed without ionizing radiation or food additives. Meat must be raised without the routine use of antibiotics and growth hormones. Manufacturers must have special certification and follow specific production standards in order to market the food as organic. On labels "100% Organic" means just that; "Organic" means it contains at least 95 percent certified organic ingredients; and "made with organic ingredients" means it contains at least 70 percent certified organic ingredients.

Nutraceuticals Added to the Dog Food

Nutraceuticals such as MSM, chondroitin and glucosamine have been so widely marketed for arthritis and musculo-skeletal problems that they are now being used for every ache, pain and joint discomfort imaginable, including even symptoms that are completely unrelated. There are thousands of different arthritis products available for both people and their pets that contain these nutraceuticals. It's even now routinely added to the dog food! Such is the power of marketing. But panaceas don't exist - even though we are often sold on the promise that they do - and frequently cause other health problems. It turns out that nutraceuticals have a number of side-effects particularly with long-term use. See Chapter 14 for more information.

Feeding Grains

What Is a Grain?

All grains are a type of carbohydrate, which means any food that contains sugars, starches, or cellulose. All grains begin life in their original or natural state as the seed of a plant. Common grains include wheat, rice, barley or rye and the kernels on a corn cob (which are actually seeds). Seeds consist of the bran as the outer skin, the endosperm which makes up the bulk of the seed and provides energy to the young growing plant, and the germ which is the inner embryo which gives life to the new plant. All these parts are edible but are protected from heat, light, rain, wind, insects and disease by an inedible husk. The edible parts are highly nutritious and contain B-vitamins, minerals, proteins, essential fatty acids, antioxidants and always the all-important fibre. Whole grains are known as complex carbohydrates such as brown rice, oatmeal, and dried beans (legumes).

We can assume that the wolf ingests seeds in their whole state as part of their seasonal foraging behaviour when their dietary intake of plant material increases. And some dogs, including my late hound, absolutely love a handful of seeds (especially with nuts) as a treat. It all sounds pretty good so far.

When Does a Grain Become Unhealthy?

Grains become unhealthy when refined and "partial". As we see, plant-based carbohydrates are not bad for dogs; to the contrary, they can be an important and useful source of energy and nutrients. But it largely depends on what form we choose to feed it and how much we choose to feed. In general, a grain becomes unhealthy when it is refined, that is when the bran and the germ are removed and only the endosperm remains. From there, the grain may be ground, pounded, puffed, flaked, rolled, milled and beat into another form to produce flours, pastas, cereals, breads and all other refined carbohydrates. Refinement decreases the protein content by up to 25 percent, results in a loss of almost all the fibre, reduces a substantial number of key nutrients and raises the glycemic index or GI. Human food manufacturers normally *enrich* or *fortify* these refined products by adding back some vitamins and minerals in unnatural proportions, but this so-called enrichment never makes up for the loss, and the whole grains continue to provide significantly more protein, more fibre, and more vitamins and minerals. This is an important point considering that cereal by-products are frequently used in the manufacturing of commercial dog foods.

For dogs, refined grains are unhealthy, *especially* when they are used as a staple, when fed in excess, and more importantly, when they are used as fillers in commercial dog food. Adding grain either as a meat substitute or as a filler is a common practice to provide a convenient and cheaper-than-meat form of protein to fill the bag. Refined grains are easily obtained, have a long shelf life, and are convenient for forming kibble. This is why many cheaper versions of dry dog food are still grain based and why manufacturers, practitioners, and anyone with a vested interest, are still arguing in favour of feeding dogs starches, such as white rice, corn, and wheat.

The digestive system breaks carbohydrates into smaller units of sugars which are then absorbed into the bloodstream and used for energy by muscles and organs, including the brain. But once grains have been refined and their fibre stripped away, it raises the glycemic index, which is a measure of the rate of absorption of sugar from the intestines into the bloodstream. A high glycemic index, or a rapid absorption rate, combined with a depletion of key vitamins and minerals is the most common cause of weight gain, obesity, insulin resistance, diabetes, intestinal conditions, liver stress, and heart problems.

The lectins in grains can also present a problem for some dogs. Lectins are strong food proteins, which are toxins that invoke immune responses by causing damage to tissues through antibody attacks. Lectins can bind to membranes on the surface of arteries, intestines, organs, and glands, including the thyroid, pituitary, pancreas, kidneys, liver, brain and adrenals. The subsequent inflammation and cell damage leads to food reactions, intestinal problems, hormone imbalances (even if spayed or neutered), auto-immune disorders, and degenerative diseases. Lectins are found in all grains except for wild rice and white rice. They are also found in all dairy products, eggs, potatoes, tomatoes, nuts, seeds and legumes. For sensitive dogs, the most problematic lectin-containing foods seem to be the grains, dairy products, legumes and sometimes potatoes.

Corn Gluten

Corn is a common staple in poor-quality dry dog foods. Corn kernels on a cob of sweet corn are quite nutritious, delivering B vitamins, beta-carotene, vitamin C, protein and anti-oxidants. Corn is 8 percent protein, 10 percent fat and 82 percent carbohydrates in the form of starch. But while corn on or off the cob is classified as a nutritious vegetable, it is considered a grain as soon as it is processed, even if popped.

Corn that is labelled as cornmeal is made by grinding dried corn kernels. However, the cornmeal used for pet food is made from the less nutritious and barely-edible grain corn as opposed to the corn on the cob corn known as sweet or sugar corn. Field corn is harvested much later when the kernels are dry and hard and all the sugar has been converted to starch. The kernels from field corn are, therefore, not as sweet but are nevertheless used to manufacture high-fructose corn syrup, cornmeal, ethanol, cooking oils, human corn chips, and animal feed. More than 95 percent of the corn grown in North America is classified as field corn.

Corn gluten meal is a processed wet-milled corn that is first soaked in hot water and sulphur dioxide then ground and run through a centrifuge which separates it into starch, oil (from the germ), and fibre as well as gluten which is the fraction that is used in the pet food. Corn gluten meal is, therefore, low in carbohydrates, fibre, and oil and higher in protein. Corn gluten meal contains 50 to 60 percent protein although corn protein is an incomplete protein because it is low in several amino acids and lacks lysine and tryptophan. For these reasons corn is considered a low-quality protein with lower biological value. Biological value compares the nutritional worth of the protein's ability to supply amino acids, especially the essential ones, in the appropriate proportions. Meat protein on the other hand is a complete protein containing all 10 essential and 13 non-essential amino acids for a total of 23. For most dogs, plant protein of any kind is a poor long-term substitution for meat protein on its own and must always be combined with other foods. Even then plant-based proteins used as a meat substitute on a permanent basis is rarely successful. Protein from animal sources are the only proteins that have both high biological value and high digestibility; the higher the biologic value of a protein, the less the amount of that protein is needed in a diet.

In addition, Mother Nature did not intend for us to chop up her plant foods into fractions, re-structure the ratios, and then modify them through processing. Once the synergy of a plant is lost, so are all its health benefits. At this point, the food can no longer provide any long-term or quality sustenance to an animal or a human.

In its defence, corn does has a relatively low allergenic potential as a food, and the gluten protein is not a real gluten in that it does not have the same amino-acid structure as the highly intolerant and symptom-causing wheat gluten. However, these credits are overridden by the fact that virtually all field corn is now GMO (genetically modified organism). This is a critical consideration, and unless the dog food claims to be organic, you can be sure that your dog is eating GMO corn. GMO or GE (genetically engineered) refers to any plants created with biotechnology – in other words foods that are produced by merging DNA from a different species into another. The process is typically intended to develop pesticide and herbicide resistant crops. But in fact, the pests and weeds have become increasingly resistant to the chemicals – even *with* GMO crops – thus more spraying is required anyway. GMO foods are highly controversial and have been linked to impaired immunity, cancer, growth abnormalities, liver atrophy, organ abnormalities, poor digestion, blood sugar problems, infertility, generalized inflammation and neurological problems. Over twenty countries have banned GMO crops in various regions. GMO can be found in corn, soya products, sugar beets and canola oil.

Corn can also be a source of aflatoxins, which are naturally occurring mycotoxins that could be found in corn, wheat, barley, peanuts and sugar. Small amounts of aflatoxins can be metabolized or detoxified; however, regular ingestion can lead to toxic levels resulting in liver toxicity, liver cancer, immune disorder, and infectious diseases.

Relative Protein Content

Eggs	100
Poultry	79
Beef	78
Fish	70
Corn	60
Brown Rice	57
Whole Wheat	49
Soybeans	47

Soybean Meal

Soybean meal is commercially prepared by removing the oil and grinding the dried beans, and it is used as a cheaper meat substitute or a meat extender. Soybeans can be labeled as soybean meal, flour, grits, hulls, concentrate, isolates and textured vegetable protein or TVP, which converts into MSG (monosodium glutamate) in the body. While pet food manufacturers argue that soybeans are an excellent protein source with high digestibility, soybeans are a major GMO crop, are poorly tolerated, can cause gastric symptoms and can interfere with hormone balance including thyroid function. In addition, just because something has been processed to improve digestibility it does not mean that it is necessarily high in nutrition.

Soybeans are also high in lectins - lectins are very strong proteins that can damage cells and disrupt membrane function. Unlike food allergies or intolerances, lectins are toxins that invoke immune responses by causing damage to tissues through antibody attacks leading to degeneration and inflammation in any body system including a leaky gut. Lectins are also found in regular potatoes, nuts, seeds and some legumes. Normally small/moderate amounts are not a problem, but if soybean and/or legumes are used as major staples, lectins can become problematic - especially in sensitive dogs.

Glutens

Wheat gluten, like corn gluten, is the protein part of the plant, but unlike corn, it is highly allergenic. Wheat is what I consider a food intolerance rather than a food allergy. A food intolerance means that there is a problem with the food, whereas a food allergy means that there is a problem with the immune system. Gluten-containing grains include wheat, rye, and barley however barley is very well tolerated. Wheat has the highest level of glutens and is, therefore, the most problematic, resulting in a myriad of symptoms including fatigue, skin problems, joint pain, behavioural issues, constipation, diarrhea, irritable bowel, colitis, gas, ulcers, leaky gut, blood sugar imbalances, diabetes, weight gain and obesity. This is a significant problem for the dogs who are being fed dry dog food that contain wheat or wheat gluten as a meat substitute. What is shocking is that wheat, combined with corn, is often a primary protein ingredient in so-called "hypoallergenic" dry dog food. These so-called prescription diets contain corn gluten, wheat gluten, unhealthy oils, inorganic minerals, and synthetic vitamins. Wheat gluten is manufactured commercially by centrifuging a gluten mass (collected by mechanical kneading), removing the water, and milling it into a powder.

Feeding Healthy Grains

Clearly, there is a vast difference between feeding your dog home-cooked grains as part of a healthy, whole, and balanced diet and feeding your dog the unsuitable grains found in many commercial dog foods. Somewhere along the way, refined, processed, and unhealthy grains became synonymous with all grains, thus "grain-free" dog food has become the rage. It's time to clarify this with healthy facts on good nutrition.

Healthy grains can be tolerated by many dogs (remember the epigenetics factor) and can be a useful addition to the homemade diet. Grains can provide an important source of carbohydrates; without adequate carbohydrates (as well as fats) the body must use up meat protein to convert into sugars as an energy source. And if there is not enough bioavailable protein, the body may lack the proteins necessary for tissue building and repair as well as maintaining a healthy immune system.

> Clearly, there is a vast difference between feeding your dog the unsuitable grains found in many commercial dog foods and feeding your dog home-cooked grains as part of a healthy, whole, and balanced diet.

Grains should always be cooked, and I would recommend feeding them in a separate meal from meat protein. This strengthens the capabilities of the digestive system and allows for more complete digestion. It also increases the absorption of nutrients and lessens the possibility of allergies. As much as possible, feed grains that are grown organically. A well-digested grain will provide a number of important vitamins and minerals. But bear in mind that not all dogs will handle all grains; one dog's grain is another dog's poison.

- **Barley** does not contain the same levels of gluten as wheat, and is, therefore quite well tolerated. Some dogs with very sensitive immune systems will react to all gluten-containing grains, but this is not usually the case. Barley is high in fibre and rich in important minerals such as manganese, molybdenum, selenium and copper. Cooked barley is normally well digested and is a good source of beta-glucan, a type of fibre that proves beneficial for a number of health conditions by reducing the absorption of sugars. Slow sugar absorption from the small intestine into the blood helps control diabetes, insulin resistance, cholesterol levels, and weight gain. Beta-glucans also form a gel-like solution in the intestines which is very soothing and healing to the intestinal membranes. Barley also acts as a prebiotic which promotes the production of natural probiotics, i.e. friendly bacteria.

- **Bulgur** wheat is a light, nutty flavoured grain which is made by grinding the wheat kernels. But bulgur has no allergenic potential and is extremely well tolerated probably because it is so easy to digest. Remember, any food that is not well digested will eventually become an intestinal toxin. Bulgur is very high in fibre as well as potassium, magnesium, and iron.

- **Brown rice** can be fed as a rich source of fibre and is also an excellent source of minerals including manganese, selenium, copper, magnesium and B-vitamins. By contrast, white rice is stripped of most of its nutrition including all its fibre and most of the B-vitamins. Despite this, some dogs have trouble digesting brown rice but can digest white rice in small amounts.

- **Oats** do not contain any gluten and are a rich source of protein as well as fibre. They are a good source of manganese, magnesium, iron, zinc, potassium, vitamin E and B vitamins. Oats also aid weight reduction, blood sugar imbalances and satiety and can help prevent colon cancer and heart/circulation problems.

- **Brans** include wheat bran, oat bran, and rice bran, all of which are the outer layers of the grain and are thus a good source of fibre, high in certain nutrients and contain natural anti-oxidants. Rice bran is very high in fat (approximately 20%) which is not always a good thing depending on the dog. High fat diets can decrease appetite, hamper digestion, and clog the liver and lymph system.

- **Quinoa** is an ancient grain originating from South America, and in the last few years it has become very popular in North America. Not all dogs tolerate quinoa – perhaps because of the processing that is necessary to remove the outer layer of the seed that contains the bitter tasting saponins. It is also high in lectins. Quinoa can, therefore, cause digestive problems and/or fatigue.

Can We Feed Too Much Grain?

Yes, we can, especially if they are unhealthy grains which should not be fed at all and/or if any grains are used as a dietary staple long-term. This is often the case with poor quality dry dog food and many prescription dog foods. Here's what to know about feeding grains:

- Some dogs are sensitive to grains and tolerate very little resulting in digestive symptoms and conditions

- Some dogs do very well on healthy grains which helps them to reduce the levels of dietary toxic meat

- Grains provide energy as carbohydrates that is more easily stored as fat than meat proteins

- Unhealthy grains fed long-term can predispose dogs to metabolic disorders including insulin resistance and Cushing's disease.

- The proteins in grain do not have the same bio-availability as meat proteins.

Beneficial Grains†	Grains to Avoid
Bulgur	Wheat
Oats	Wheat gluten
Barley	Corn gluten
Brans	Soybeans
Rice, brown	Quinoa (unless tolerated)

†*Always choose organic grains*

Feeding Fats

Based on our ancestral model, meat protein and fats are the most important food groups necessary for dogs. The average canine diet consists of 10 to 20 percent fat. Fats are concentrated and dense and are important sources of energy and nutrition. Inadequate dietary fat can result in fatigue, slow growth, weight loss, and reduced fertility. They also facilitate the digestion and absorption of fat-soluble vitamins such as A, D and E.

All meat fat is saturated fat. It is solid at room temperature and is very stable in the presence of high heat and strong light; saturated fats have single bonds between the molecules. Saturated fats are safe when cooked, help to stabilize blood sugar, and are beneficial for weight loss as they promote satiety, meaning they make one feel fuller and for longer periods of time. It is best to feed saturated fat as naturally found on meat rather than feeding tallow or lard which are exceptionally dense forms of saturated fats.

Monounsaturated fats have single bonds between the molecules as well except for one double bond. This still gives them relative stability for cooking and heating and retaining the health properties. Monounsaturated fats are found in nuts, avocados, grapeseed oil, sesame oil, and olive oil. Olive oil is a natural anti-oxidant, anti-inflammatory, and is beneficial for the heart, liver, and colon. Grapeseed oil is a light nutty flavoured oil helpful for the prevention of heart problems, cancer, arthritis, poor circulation, and allergies.

Unsaturated or polyunsaturated fats are found in fish, seeds, nut oil, corn oils, canola, and all vegetable oils. Unsaturated fats are not stable because of their chemical bond structure with double bonds between the molecules. They are therefore very reactive and unstable in the presence of heat, light, and processing which denatures them. Refined oils are exposed to solvents and are bleached, winterized (removing parts of the oil that have a high melting point) and deodorized. Once they are denatured, they are toxic to animals and people because the broken chemical bonds release free electrons, i.e. free radical damage. Free radical damage is responsible for tissue and DNA damage, causing disease to the cardiovascular system, immune system, skin, connective tissue, brain and nervous system. It is also a major culprit in degenerative diseases including cancer. This is a significant problem when feeding commercial dog foods, many of which contain polyunsaturated vegetable oils such as canola or soy oils.

Dietary free radicals can be difficult to avoid completely, but we can help protect our pets from damage with the use of anti-oxidants, which are substances that neutralize the free electrons by donating an electron of their own. Controlling free radical damage is the key to preventing DNA damage, premature aging, cancer, and degenerative diseases. Anti-oxidants include vitamin E, vitamin C, beta-carotene, coenzyme Q10 and selenium – these and others are found in abundance in fruits and vegetables.

Essential fatty acids (EFAs) are special types of polyunsaturated fats that are essential to life and good health; EFAs have to be provided for in the diet since the body cannot manufacture them on its own. There are two main types of essential fatty acids: linoleic (omega-6) and linolenic (omega-3). Omega-6s are found in meat, eggs, nuts and beans, rice bran oil and almost all vegetable oils while omega-3s are provided by leafy greens, spirulina, seeds, nuts, and cold water fish. Omega-3s convert into gamma-linolenic acid or GLA, which then converts into prostaglandins which are natural hormone-like substances important for liver health, metabolism, the cardiovascular system, circulation, skin health, hormone balance, the nervous system and the immune system. They are, therefore, very beneficial for allergies, inflammation, and arthritis.

Omegas-6s, on the other hand, convert to unhealthy prostaglandins if they are fed in excess usually via vegetable oils. These are inflammatory prostaglandins that will compete with the health benefits of the omega-3s and cause inflammatory conditions – arthritis, weak bones, skin infections, dry skin and hair, dull coats, cancer, weight gain and behavioural problems. Strike two for polyunsaturated vegetables oils, rancid and processed, containing high levels of omega-6 and low levels of omega-3. Soybean oil, corn oil and sunflower oil are the usual culprits used in our cooking or in our dog foods. And while canola oil comparatively has the lowest quantities of omega-6, canola oil presents *other* significant problems for our dogs (and for us).

Don't let the fields of beautiful bright yellow flowers fool you. Canola oil (named for low oil acid) is produced from the rapeseed plant (there is no such thing as a canola plant) which is part of the mustard family. The oil is pressed from the seeds, and aside from now being used as food, it is also used as industrial oil for soap, candles, lubricants and biodiesel fuel. Rapeseed oil, in the past, was used in limited quantities due to high levels of erucic acid (over 50%), which is damaging to the heart and respiratory system. Today's food grade canola oil now contains between 2 and 5 percent erucic acid. Over 90 percent of canola seeds are GMO (Genetically Modified Organisms – see "Feeding Grains, Corn" below for more information) which has resulted in an extremely disease- and drought-resistant canola. Despite this, canola crops are still heavily sprayed with chemicals, putting the field workers and the consumers at high risk. Equally troubling is that canola oil is also partially hydrogenated – along with sunflower oil, and soybean oils – over 90 percent of all soybeans are now GMO as well.

Avoid all hydrogenated fats and oils; hydrogenation of oils is done when food manufacturers start with a poor quality and usually already rancid liquid vegetable oil and want to make it into a solid. They do so by subjecting the oils to high heat and pressure with hydrogen gas. The hydrogen atoms destroy the double bonds and thus harden the oil from a liquid to a solid. This is a convenient form for manufacturers to use in processed and/or commercial foods (think margarine). This change in molecular structure is drastic; vital organs such as the liver, heart and brain have no idea how to metabolize these artificial fats, and thus hydrogenated oils are implicated in heart problems, diabetes, cancer, obesity, liver diseases, neurological conditions, behavioural changes and degenerative diseases.

Feeding Healthy Oils as Supplements

It is clear that fats are an important part of a dog's healthcare program. As we see, saturated fats are the healthiest fats for our dogs but must be balanced with the addition of essential fatty acids which are not produced by the body but are necessary to attract oxygen to the cells producing energy and preventing diseases that thrive in an oxygen-free environment: cancer, heart disease, arthritis, obesity and aging. It's interesting to note here that the only way that wolves can benefit from the omega-3s is to eat plant material, particularly the seeds unless they are fortunate enough to catch a fish. This means that their intake of these healthy oils is determined by the season and one can only wonder how their health could improve with omega-3s available to them year-round.

The best source of all oils for dogs is *food*, not supplemental oils, including the omega oils. But we must also recognize that the unique requirements of many dogs according to health history, diet, breed, age, stress levels, and disease necessitate the use of therapeutic nutrition. Thus, many benefits can be had by making use of the therapeutic dosages of oils to restore optimum health. However, the choice of oils should be carefully considered, and the supplementation of oils should never be administered indefinitely. Why? Because we need to always be mindful of the liver, which is the primary organ for fat decongestion. And if the liver gets over-congested or backed up, the blood will become "fatty", and the liver will not be able to efficiently perform the other very important functions including detoxification of chemicals and foods, metabolism of sugars, carbohydrates, fat-soluble vitamins and proteins, and supporting the immune system. Furthermore, if the liver gets over-congested, the kidneys must increase their detoxification functions, which they are not designed to do over long periods of time. And despite their carnivorous anatomy, I also see a variety of other symptoms and health conditions attributable to the overfeeding or overdosing of fats and oils. This is true for humans too.

So, let's take a look at some very healthy oil supplements containing essential fatty acids. But remember, let's not overdo a good thing – feed sparingly and short-term as required. Balance + moderation = good health.

Flaxseed oil is a very rich source (58%) of a specific omega-3 called alpha-linolenic acid or ALA and can be therefore beneficial for circulation, skin, joint inflammation, allergies, hormone balance, heart health and cancer. However, to be of maximum benefit the ALA must be converted into other omega-3 fats, i.e. eicosapentaenoic acid (EPA) and docosahexaenoic acid (DHA) which not all dogs (nor people) can easily do, especially dogs that have liver problems, are overweight, have insulin resistance, or have Cushing's disease and/or a poor immune system. In these cases, it is better to use evening primrose oil which is a direct source of another Omega-3 known as gamma-linolenic acid (GLA).

Hempseed oil has the highest quantity of EFAs at 80%. It is considered to be a nutritionally balanced oil because it contains a perfect ratio of omega-6, omega-3 and GLA: 55% omega-6, 22% omega-3 (ALA), and 2 to 4% GLA. The oil also contains a unique protein called edestin, which is a factor in DNA repair making it useful for cancer. Hempseed oil is an excellent choice for inflammation, allergies, immunity, oxidation, skin conditions, heart health and cancer.

Evening Primrose oil (EPO) contains up to 15% gamma linolenic acid (GLA) making it a very therapeutic remedy in small doses without any chemical conversions required. EPO is beneficial for brittle nails and hair, skin allergies, immunity, joint inflammation, nerve problems and hormone imbalances. EPO can be used externally as well.

Olive oil is a natural anti-oxidant and anti-inflammatory and is beneficial for the heart, liver, colon and gallbladder. It aids digestion and is soothing and healing to dry skin when applied externally.

Fish oils contain eicosapentaenoic acid or EPA and docosahexaenoic acid or DHA which have been studied for their beneficial effects on heart health, circulation, brain function, immunity, arthritis and skin conditions – fish oils are natural anti-inflammatories. Sources of fish oil include salmon, cod, halibut, tuna and krill although, energetically, I have not found the krill to be suitable. However, supplemental fish oils are also subjected to and damaged by light and heat during the manufacturing and packaging of capsules, so unless the fish oil is of a very high quality, it is better to feed fresh fish. But not all dogs like fish, nor do all dogs tolerate it. I would therefore recommend the higher quality fresh vegetable oils that are organic and bottled, rather than capsuled.

And don't be fooled by pet foods that claim to contain healthy Omega-3s – the instability of these oils means that the light, heat and processing completely degrades these oils long before they reach the dog dish, at which point they are detrimental to health, not beneficial.

Coconut oil has received a bounty of good press in the last few years. Coconut oil is a saturated fat chemically different from meat fats but still very stable and resistant to heat and light. Coconut oil has been shown to have numerous health benefits. It is a natural antifungal, antibacterial, and antiviral; it benefits the skin and hair coat and can help with weight loss as it promotes satiety. And yet I still get the sense that the coconut oil marketing is somewhat out of proportion to the actual benefits. It's better to feed the coconut rather than the oil since coconut is a very heavy saturated oil and much more concentrated in oil form. Coconut is also not found in the natural canine food chain. However, if you do prefer to feed the straight oil, keep the quantities to a minimum and over short-term and, as with all supplements, only continue if the benefits are obvious.

Beneficial Oils†	Oils to Avoid
Evening Primrose oil	Canola oil
Olive oil	Soybean oil
Hempseed oil	Corn oil
Fish oil (high quality only)	Hydrogenated oils
Flaxseed oil	

†*Always choose organic oils*

Can Dogs Get Too Much Fat?

Yes, they can. Aside from the health problems that unhealthy fats can cause, some dogs don't tolerate a lot of saturated fat content in meat (or coconut) which can cause problems with digestion, diarrhea, and immunity. Caution is also required with pancreatitis, an inflammation of the pancreas that effects digestive enzyme production. To reduce overall fat, eliminate beef, pork, poultry skin, and excess fat on meat and bones. White poultry meat, which is lower in fat, can be fed in place of dark meat. Dogs with higher and/or more intense exercise levels are more likely to tolerate higher fat intake. Dogs prone to weight gain, insulin resistance, Cushing's disease, and immobility or a sedentary lifestyle should be limited in their intake of saturated fat. It may also be beneficial to switch them to a primary vegetarian diet for a few weeks until their health is restored.

It is estimated that close to half of all dogs are overweight, and even although this is correctly attributed to an overload of carbohydrates, many dogs on low-carbohydrate diets are still struggling with weight gain. Fat can be a cause of weight gain in these cases, especially if the diet is too high in fat compared to the dog's exercise level and/or natural metabolic rate. Slow moving, sedentary dogs do not need much fat. For fat-sensitive dogs, it is prudent to reduce the dietary fat and increase the dietary fibre with whole grains and vegetables. Fibre helps to detoxify and eliminate fats, improve satiety, and prevent disease.

In addition, large fat globules are not absorbed by the small intestine but are delivered to the liver for detoxification by the lymphatic system instead. This is how they contribute to various immune diseases including cancer – by directly interfering with immune function in the lymphatic system. It is very important that our dogs eat healthy, fresh, and non-rancid fats to prevent contamination to the lymphatic system.

Fats and **Oils Summary**

- Where possible, rely on fat-containing natural foods rather than concentrated oils.

- Use caution with supplemental fish oils which are often rancid from processing

- Ensure an adequate intake of linolenic acid (omega-3s).

- Avoid hydrogenated oils such as canola, soybean, and vegetable.

- Avoid GMO oils such as canola, soybean, corn

- Healthy oils include olive, grapeseed, flaxseed, and sometimes coconut.

- Don't use fat and oil supplements long-term unless benefits are clearly observable.

- Reduce fat intake for dogs that are sedentary, overweight, have diabetes, insulin resistance, Cushing's disease or any kidney or liver problems

Feeding Meat

For the average dog of normal health, meat protein is, and *should* be, the primary staple. However, it must be pointed out that many dogs now are in a state of protein excess, leading to a variety of health problems as discussed below. But first let's learn about protein.

Proteins consist of long chains of amino acids that contain carbon, hydrogen, oxygen, nitrogen, and usually sulphur. Protein is a main constituent of muscles, bone, cartilage, skin, hair, and blood. Twenty percent of the bone matrix is also composed of protein. Proteins are essential in the diet of animals for the growth and repair of tissue. They are also required for many different body functions including enzyme, hormone, and antibody production. The proteins consumed in the diet must be broken down into their individual amino acids by the digestive system so the body can then reassemble them to build and re-build all the body's tissues. Dogs can manufacture eleven of the twenty-one amino acids required for health if their diet is relatively balanced, these are alanine, asparagine, aspartic acid, cysteine, glutamic acid, glutamine, tyrosine, glycine, ornithine, proline, and serine. However, like humans, they need a dietary source for the ten others amino acids, namely, arginine, methionine, histidine, phenylalanine, isoleucine, threonine, leucine, tryptophan, lysine and valine.

Low dietary protein can result in deficiency symptoms causing poor appetite, slow growth, weight loss, dull coat, increased incidence of physical injuries, sluggish cognitive skills and/or poor immune function.

There are many different types of meat staples including beef, bison, venison, pork, lamb, chicken, turkey, duck, fish (salmon and white fish), eggs, and more exotic foods such as kangaroo, alpaca, quail, pheasant, elk and rabbit. These meats can be provided as a raw food diet, a cooked food diet, or commercial dog foods as dry kibble or canned wet food. How a food is prepared can be as important as the quality of the ingredient itself.

Raw Meat

Raw food diets for dogs were previously known as BARF (Bones and Raw Food) and now more commonly referred to as Biologically Appropriate Raw Food. Raw food proponents advocate feeding dogs a raw meat diet which includes fresh meat, organ meats, bones (whole or ground) and fats – or they may feed the entire carcass.

Raw food can also include offal, which means the pieces that *fall off* a carcass when it's butchered. This includes the heart, liver, lungs, kidneys, pancreas and all other abdominal organs, as well as the tails, feet, brains, tongue, and reproductive organs. Tripe refers to the stomach of a grazing animal such as a cow or bison.

Raw diets provide wholesome nutrition, containing naturally occurring proteins, vitamins and minerals. Raw meats are not subjected to high heat and/or processing and are also digested much quicker than processed food, which allows for increased nutrient absorption in the small intestine. High protein meat diets – raw or cooked – also result in less protein degradation and fermentation in the intestinal tract, which in turn, results in less toxicity, less acidity, improved immunity, and less damage to the intestinal walls. It's also interesting to note that the saliva of dogs on a raw meat diet contains more mucus than a dog on dry kibble whose mucus is predominantly serous, meaning that it contains more water and fluids.

Raw food in its natural uncooked state also provides its own enzymes, known as "live" enzymes. Enzymes are organic catalysts made from amino acids (proteins) that accelerate all chemical reactions in the body including tissue repair, hormone activity, energy production and the digestive processes. The digestive enzymes produced by the stomach and pancreas (as discussed in Chapter 2) make it possible for the body to digest its food and extract nutrients from this food. But all food in its natural state contains live enzymes which, when ingested as an unprocessed food, aids in the digestive process and are credited for a variety of different health benefits for the digestive system, immune system, musculoskeletal system, the absorption of nutrients and general detoxification.

However, live food enzymes are very sensitive proteins and can be inactivated by high heat as in cooking as well as certain chemicals and preservatives in commercial food. It is believed that, if live enzymes in the food have been destroyed, the body itself must then produce more of its own digestive enzymes to digest the cooked food thus creating more work for the body. Studies have indicated that food enzymes are destroyed when wet-heated above 48°C (118°F) or dry-heated above 66°C (150°F). However, enzymes are also destroyed in highly acidic environments such as the stomach, so raw food opponents state that food enzymes are all destroyed in the stomach anyway before they can be of benefit. This process would be, of course, dependent on how long the food material remains in the stomach which is dependent on everything that is eaten at any given time. But what may not be so commonly known is that plant enzymes are much more stable in acidic environments and are, therefore, *not* destroyed. This is another important benefit for feeding our dogs plant material, in the way of fruits and vegetables (more on this later).

~~~~~~~ 🐾 ~~~~~~~

Nature is neither perfect nor imperfect; nature is merely natural and, even in the wild that often means supplemental strategies and workarounds to counteract natural nutritional shortfalls.

~~~~~~~~~~~~~~~~~~~~~

Because raw food diets provide a tremendous amount of protein and wholesome nutrition, many people are under the impression that all a dog's nutritional requirements are satisfied. This is true to a point as many raw dogs are certainly receiving comparatively superior nutrition; but we only need to look at the lifestyle differences between dogs and other wolf species, as previously discussed, to understand that dogs are under the influence of many different pressures, stressors, behaviours, and diseases which have all altered homeostasis and ancestral nutritional requirements. And remember too that the wolf is not in perfect health herself many times, nor is the wolf's environment perfect. "Natural" and "perfect" are not synonymous. Let us then understand that there is no perfect diet for either the wolf or dog. We only need to observe the feeding habits of wolves, their behaviours, and incidence of various diseases, to see that this is so. Nature is neither perfect nor imperfect; nature is merely *natural* and, even in the wild that often means supplemental strategies and workarounds to counteract natural nutritional shortfalls. Whole health is not about simplicity, it's about balance and the ability to adapt.

Preparation of Raw Meat

Most commercial pre-made raw meat is preserved by freezing. Freezing, also called fresh-prepared, does not go through any kind of processing thereby retaining more nutritional integrity. However, pre-made raw meat and the bones may be ground up for ease of swallowing and prevention of choking, and proponents of grinding raw meat point out that the dogs are unable to rip and tear their food apart as a wolf would in the wild. Non-ground meat is fed as carcasses and raw meaty bones or RMB.

Many dog owners opt to prepare their own raw meat and bones by acquiring fresh meat from the local butcher which they may chop up, depending on the size of the carcass or carcass parts, and then freeze. Raw meat and bones can be fed frozen but is normally thawed out before feeding. However, frozen meat should always be thawed *in the refrigerator*, not at room-temperature. Homemade raw meat diets should not be considered a balanced diet if meat is the only food group in the diet. Dogs – like wolves – will also require fibre and fruit and vegetables for optimum nutrition. Dogs who receive a wide variety of foods over several days – rather than only one day – can still be eating a balanced diet. Home-prepared dog food gives the dog owner total control over what is included in the dog food and where those ingredients come from.

Raw food is also available in dehydrated or in freeze-dried form. Dehydrated foods are air dried and then dehydrated to reduce moisture levels which helps to inhibit bacterial growth. The appearance is very like kibble but warm water is added before serving. Freeze dried foods are frozen and then dehydrated through an evaporation process. Freeze dried foods do not need to be rehydrated. Dehydrated foods only lose 3 to 5 percent of nutrients because the temperatures used are much lower than those used for preparing commercial kibble.

Then there are concerns over bacterial contamination such as *Salmonella*, *Listeria*, and *E. coli*. Of course, wolves ingest prey foods in the wild that have putrefied and are therefore infected with microorganisms. But the wolves have adapted their immune systems to build up a natural resistance to most of these strains of bacteria. Dogs on the other hand function in a completely different environment and have not been exposed to as many strains of bacteria as the wolf in the wild and, therefore, do not have the same resistance. Dogs are also threatened by very tenacious antibiotic resistant strains of bacteria created by humans and now omnipresent in the modern world.

As such many pet parents and pet food manufacturers are becoming increasingly more diligent in order to avoid contaminated food and product recalls. Dogs on any kind of diets can be at risk for bacteria, but the highest risk to dogs is the bacteria found in raw salmon (*Nanophyetus salmincola*), and the bacteria found in raw pork and wild game (*Trichinella spiralis*) which is resistant to freezing.

Freezing raw food at appropriate temperatures inactivates the bacteria into dormancy, but it does not eliminate them. Therefore, some large producers of raw pet food have incorporated what is known as a kill-step into production that is designed to eliminate pathogens while maintaining the integrity of enzymes, proteins and other nutrients. This is known as high-pressure processing or HPP and uses extremely high pressure – up to 90,000 psi – to crush the outer membrane of all prokaryotes (single celled organisms). In this way, the high pressure should kill all harmful strains of bacteria, but there are a number of other concerns, for HPP will *also* kill beneficial strains of bacteria, alter the natural pH (acidity levels), and in fact denatures the proteins of the meat itself which could render the protein incapable of functioning. And perhaps more importantly, the killing of *beneficial* bacteria means that the meat is more likely to be re-infected by pathogenic bacteria at home in the kitchen. There has also been some evidence that raw meat containing calcium-rich bone provides protection for *E. coli* bacteria, making this strain more resistant to the high-pressure process. Perhaps this is why some HPP-processed food batches have already been voluntarily recalled. In any case, the uncertain effects of all processing methods negates the reason for feeding raw in the first place - high quality proteins, active enzymes, and the presence of friendly bacteria.

While we must always take precautions against feeding contaminated food to our pets (and ourselves, of course) I must point out that the holistic health model does not subscribe to what is known as *germ theory* – the overly simplistic belief that the best way to treat a disease is to target the pathogen responsible for it. Rather, we focus on the health of the terrain which ultimately determines the resistance to all bacteria, yeast, viruses and parasites. For example, 36 percent of all healthy dogs carry live *Salmonella* bacteria in their intestines without falling ill, which illustrates a fundamental flaw in the germ theory. Dogs that *do* succumb to naturally-occurring bacterial or viral infections - and the same is true with humans - usually have underlying problems such as poor digestion, poor diet, poor immunity, nutrient deficiencies and/or high stress levels.

Cooked Meat

Countless dog guardians have regained their dogs' health and vigor by switching from commercial food diets to raw meat diets. Raw food diets often result in optimized nutrition, improved digestion, improved immunity, higher energy levels, reduced allergies, effective eliminations, healthier coats and skin, and balanced blood sugar levels. Although, to be fair, some dogs who improve after switching to a raw meat diet have improved due to the elimination of *processed* foods, chemicals, preservatives and inorganic minerals in their previous kibble. They have gone to eating human-grade food from eating intensely processed commercial pet foods. It is therefore entirely possible that these dogs would have reaped the same benefits by switching to a diet of unprocessed cooked meat rather than unprocessed raw meats.

Many raw food advocates believe that a dog can *only* be healthy if it is on a raw food diet. We have already established that raw food provides a tremendous amount of nutrition; however, the fact remains that many dogs do *not* tolerate raw meat, and there are also many dogs on cooked food - homemade or commercial - who are not only very healthy but have lived a very long life. The real key is whether the dog is being nourished with balanced amounts of protein, fats, fibre and vitamins and minerals on a regular basis, and, perhaps more importantly, where these food groups are coming from. And since these requirements can vary tremendously between individual breeds, sizes, and lifestyle, choices should be based on the dogs rather than dogma.

The meat in homemade dog meals can also be fed cooked. When meat is cooked, the protein molecules unwind, the muscle fibres shrink, and the protein molecules coagulate. This process of unwinding, shrinking, and coagulating is called denaturing and can make the proteins more available to digestive enzymes. This is beneficial for certain dogs such as those with sensitive digestive systems or digestive health conditions.

The opposite argument is that these denatured proteins are not quite as bioavailable and/or could be identified and targeted as foreign invaders which cause the immune system to react. This premise was derived from research on humans observed to have digestive leukocytosis, a term used to explain certain immune-system reactions after eating cooked meat. Studies showed that white blood cell counts increased resembling a stress response to infection or trauma. But on closer review, we learn that this immune reaction is only triggered by foods cooked at *very* high heat or food that is processed and refined which also often produce carcinogens. The strongest triggers were not initiated by cooked foods but by processed foods – cooked or not. These foods included those that were homogenized and pasteurized (e.g. dairy products) as well as all refined sugars and carbohydrates. Therefore, this information cannot be used as an added argument against feeding lightly cooked meats to dogs. Overcooked meat is not recommended because it produces 4-hydroxynonenal or HNE, a toxic chemical linked to chronic inflammation, blood-sugar problems, and cancer.

Simmer, stew, or put in the slow cooker but keep your dogs (and yourself) away from the BBQ. Cooking meat at lower temperatures also helps to reduce loss of nutrients.

As for my own health practice, I have not seen any evidence that healthy and lightly cooked meat causes digestive problems, toxicity problems, or any immune conditions in dogs.

Cooked meat is easier to pull apart and this can be an advantage for those dogs with poor teeth, compromised jaw movement, or less strength to tear apart raw meat and bones. Lightly cooked meats are also beneficial for senior dogs and arthritic dogs as well as dogs with weakened digestive conditions including intestinal ulcers, colon problems, and low levels of probiotics, unbalanced intestinal ecosystems and pancreatitis. Also, for dogs with suppressed immunity and/or certain immune diseases, cooking the meat kills off food bacteria which is particularly important for the immune-compromised dog. For this reason alone, many dog owners choose cooked meat over raw. In any event, families that make their own dog food – raw or cooked – should follow common sense hygienic procedures to avoid potential contamination of utensils and surfaces in the human household.

Raw or cooked? If in doubt, let your dog be the judge: offer her a piece of cooked meat beside a piece of raw meat and see which one she chooses – consistently. She might choose one or the other, or she might choose both or either depending on the type of protein it is, the time of day or on her present mood.

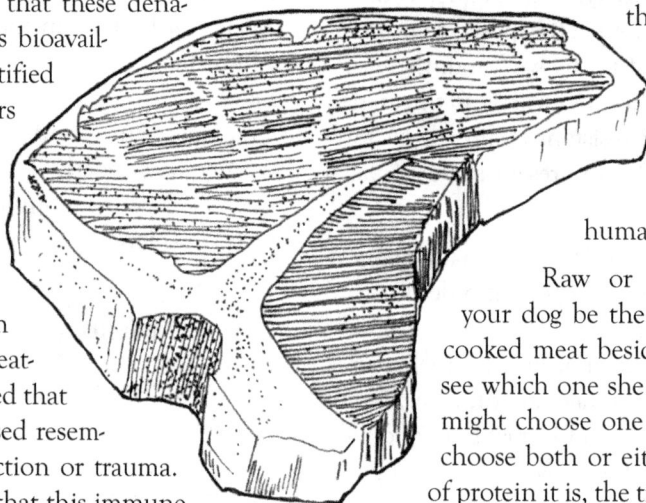

Raw and Cooked Meat Together

There is no reason to make an uncompromising choice between raw and cooked meat whereby you only feed raw or you only feed cooked. In fact, many dog parents rotate their dogs' meals to feed cooked meat for two or three days, then raw meat for two or three days, or whatever cycle your dog prefers. Not only does this offer variety to your dog, but it also helps you learn what kind of meat your dog prefers and how they like it cooked. I don't recommend feeding raw and cooked meat in the same meal since each form requires different chewing and digestive processes. And whether or not it's raw or cooked it is not advisable to feed more than one meat protein in the same meal which can upset dogs who have a more sensitive digestive system. For example, don't mix together chicken and lamb, or chicken and beef, or venison and turkey in the same meals. Also avoid kibbles with mixed meats if possible - buy kibble which only contains one meat protein and change it up frequently. You may want to feed raw or cooked meat as the primary food or to alternate with a good quality kibble.

Not every pet parent is able to provide raw or cooked meat or expensive dog food, but they can learn to make healthier choices.

Are We Poisoning Our Dogs with Meat?

We know how important meat protein is for canines, but balance is the key, and excess meat *can* be a problem just like any other food group fed in excess. In addition, dogs are frequently fed meat, organ meats, and bone all sourced from large animals even though, as discussed in Chapter 2, beef, bison, and elk are not a regular part of the wolf's diet – the season, terrain, wolf-pack size, and hunting opportunities are major limiting obstacles to a successful hunt for large prey. Should the wolf hunt be fortunate enough to eat ungulates (mammals with hooves), you can be very sure that they have earned it by running hard for days. A wolf only eats any kind of meat every two to three days at best, and it's comparatively clean meat.

By contrast dogs feast at least once per day, usually twice, and never have to work for it. They may share 98.9 percent of their genetic material with other wolf species but what they share in terms of lifestyle is another matter altogether. When the output doesn't equal the input, or if a dog does not efficiently digest meat, then general health and wellness is sure to deteriorate. And that's exactly what we are seeing. Whether meat is raw, cooked, or fed as a high-protein or grain-free kibble, many dogs are now suffering from conditions caused by excess meat consumption including the accumulative toxicity from chemicals, pollutants, and drug residue. I have worked with many dogs of all breeds with very challenging health conditions where significant improvements were accomplished by changing protein types, reducing dietary protein levels, or even transitioning them to vegetarian diets for a period of time.

Senior dogs, chronically ill dogs, dogs with digestive conditions, sore and arthritic dogs, dogs with specific nutrient deficiencies and/or sedentary dogs are examples of at-risk dogs that may be compromised with inefficient protein digestion, slower rates of metabolism and an inability to efficiently eliminate acids produced from protein. Caution is also required for puppies, especially large breed puppies, where excessive protein intake can result in skeletal problems, now or later in life.

As a rule, dogs with high exercise levels, high rates of metabolism, and/or higher intensity workouts can be fed higher protein levels as well as fat without destructive effects. The harder the muscles work, the higher the requirement for protein and the more efficient the metabolism.

Whether meat is raw, cooked, or fed as a high-protein or grain-free kibble, many dogs are now suffering from conditions caused by excess meat consumption including the accumulative toxicity from chemicals, pollutants, and drug residue.

So What's Wrong with Meat?

1. If meat is not fully digested with enzymes in the stomach and small intestine before it reaches the colon, the mal-digested protein will be fermented or putrefied since the colon is unable to enzymatically digest it. This results in the production of toxic substances such as ammonia, amines, phenols and sulphides – these compounds are major contributing factors to "leaky gut" (see Chapter 4) which is a common colon condition that results in a variety of health problems including sore joints, arthritis, skin conditions, allergies and behavioural problems.

2. Excess protein can overwhelm the digestive processes since the body will try to oxidize any excess protein in the liver (unlike fats which are a clean burn). Oxidized proteins in the liver will form toxins such as HNE (4-hydroxynonenal) and MDA (malondialdehyde), both of which can damage the DNA as well as the mitochondria which are the power plants of the cells where biochemical processes, oxygen processing, and the metabolism of foods take place. HNE is actually a derivative of omega-6 fats found in all meat, particularly meat that is from soy and corn-fed animals, such as cattle from feed lots. Interestingly enough, blood tests can show low protein even though the dogs are on very high protein diets. This is evidence that the proteins are not efficiently digested nor assimilated.

3. Excess protein consumption can put the body into a state of inflammation, which then interferes with fat metabolism. This increases HNE production and overwhelms the cells' detoxification pathways.

4. The nitrogen molecules in protein are converted to ammonia in the colon, which is how it is delivered to the liver where, through a number of chemical processes, it is converted to less toxic urea. Urea is then eliminated through the kidneys and is what gives urine a strong smell – especially in big meat eaters. However, in the case of excessive intake of meat (or faulty metabolism) the kidney filters become saturated, and the ammonia begins to deposit into the joints, muscles, and connective tissue causing inflammation, soreness and arthritis. Excess ammonia is toxic to the liver (inhibiting other detoxification processes), the kidneys, the heart, the brain and other major organs. If urea levels are consistently high, the kidneys will eventually become damaged as the tiny filtration tubules clog up. Furthermore, any excess nitrogen that cannot be handled by the liver and converted into urea will convert into uric acid instead, which then deposit into the joints, muscles, and connective tissue causing inflammation, soreness and arthritis as well as immune conditions. Organ meats are particularly high in uric acid.

5. Beef, bison, and all other red meats are high in arachidonic and lactic acids, which if accumulated in the system – as often happens with senior and/or sedentary dogs – will deposit into the joints, muscles, and connective tissue causing inflammation, soreness and arthritis. It's worth reiterating here that the average lifespan of wolves in the wild is only five to six years. Most dogs however, have an expected longevity well beyond the six-year mark which creates a new stage of senior dog years.

6. Almost all beef is now fed GMO-concentrated dried corn, which is nutritionally void. Thus the fats in beef products are poor quality, the meat less nutritious, the nutrients are more difficult to absorb, and the beef itself is more difficult to digest. The corn in the beef is why many dogs feel over-full and bloated.

7. High acid conditions affect bone density and strength since the bones, including cartilage, are then forced to give up calcium – which is alkaline – to buffer the acidic blood conditions. This results in bone loss and possible kidney stones. An acidic (or low pH) body also causes liver and kidney toxicity, skin conditions, immune issues, a higher incidence of allergies, heart symptoms, hormone imbalances and fatigue. Calcium supplements are often required for dogs with high acidity even if they are chewing bones and eating eggshells, which may not provide the required therapeutic dosages to offset the pH imbalance.

8. When a wolf eats a freshly killed animal, it not only ingests the muscles, organs and other tissues, but it also takes in a considerable amount of glycogen. Glycogen is a starch and is the storage form of sugar whereby sugar is transported into the muscles and liver from the blood where it is converted into glycogen, which is then converted back into sugar when the body requires energy. Glycogen is a complex carbohydrate that provides quick and efficient energy for the wolf. However, when a dog eats raw meat, the meat is not a fresh kill, and the glycogen converts to lactic acid during storage. Aside from the higher acid levels, the dogs must use the meat protein instead for immediate energy which is a slower and less efficient form of energy. Good thing most of our dogs don't have to travel 30 to 50 kilometres per day – they would never make it!

9. Use caution with feeding too much head meat and necks containing thyroid tissue since raw thyroid tissue can initiate hyperthyroidism resulting in increased appetite and/or weight loss, excessive thirst and urination, and nervousness. Thyroid tissue can also be found in raw dog treats.

10. No matter what quantity of meat a dog is being fed, raw or cooked, the incidence of toxicity, intolerances, and allergies to meat continues to rise. It is, therefore, prudent to rotate the various meat proteins by feeding a different type of meat every few weeks or even every few days depending on the condition of the immune system. In other words, you might feed chicken for a few days or weeks, then switch to fish, then switch to duck and so on. This is particularly helpful to prevent and/or treat food allergies and intolerances in dogs that are immune compromised and, therefore, prone to food allergies and intolerances. And, similar to the wild wolf, dogs will benefit from two-three days of cleansing without meat.

11. Senior dogs, immune-compromised dogs and those who are more sedentary, are particularly prone to the effects of excess meat protein and acids which often results in digestive problems and/or general inflammation. Bear in mind that the wild wolf with a life expectancy of 5 to 6 years does not make it into the so-called senior dog years since once they can no longer eat raw meat – due to various circumstances

including age – they die. So we have no comparisons here to draw with our own senior dogs who continue to be fed like kings and queens no matter how slow, sleepy or decrepit they are.

12. A major concern is the chemical and toxic overloads found in meat - this is an increasingly significant problem for both the health of the dogs, the health of the people and the health of the planet. Mother Nature continues to be exploited by humans, and meat, being at the top of the food chain, is now completely contaminated with chemicals (preservatives, colourings and flavourings), pesticide run-off, insecticides, nitrates, radiation, GMO, climate change, heavy metals, fluoride, and medication residue i n c l u d i n g antibiotics, hormones and anaesthetics. There are thousands of synthetic chemicals now found in the environment, most of which are unrecognizable by the liver, lymph, or kidneys. These incredible organs are responsible for detoxifying and eliminating all foreign particles and toxins. But when these organs are not even able to recognize these invaders, they will accumulate in the tissues where they can reside for years or even for the lifetime of the animal. These are serious health concerns for all animals: livestock, domestic pets, wildlife, and humans. DDT (dichlorodiphenyltrichloroethane), PCBs (polychlorinated biphenyls), dioxins, hormones, and herbicides are all known carcinogens, and there are over 80,000 chemicals in commercial use which can all contribute to immune disorders, neurological disorders, heart conditions, digestive problems, and various inflammations. Meat is a front-running cause of all types of cancer.

For all the reasons mentioned above, it is more important than ever to make use of plants and herbs in your pet's diet. Plants and herbs afford your dog the benefit of the rich nutrients, added fibre, and natural detoxifiers. The medicinal effects of plants and herbs, so necessary in the modern world of dogs far overrides any arguments against them. No animal of any kind can escape the omnipresent toxicity of the external environment. As such there are no perfect foods. Organic meats, when available, are the best choice we have but we must also be conscious of over-feeding meat and reducing our overall consumption - organic or not.

Halle's Remarkable Recovery

"Halle is a six-and-a-half-year-old Doberman who was suffering very poor health. She had blister-like sores on her chin which often bled, skin bumps all over her body, goopy infected eyes, and bad breath. She also had trouble bearing weight on her left rear leg and was extremely lethargic. I honestly thought I was going to have to put Halle down since she had been fighting poor health for over two years. And I had spent $11,000 trying to resolve her health problems. So I asked Marijke to do a full health session on Halle, and as a result she was put on a completely different diet program - low meat protein and high fibre. Halle was also put on several B-vitamins including B12 and folic acid as well as the Immune Boost Herbal Blend. Halle is now completely recovered. I cannot thank Marijke enough for helping me with her. She is back to playing with our other two dogs and is up for anything once again. It's sure nice to have her back!"

–Darlene W.

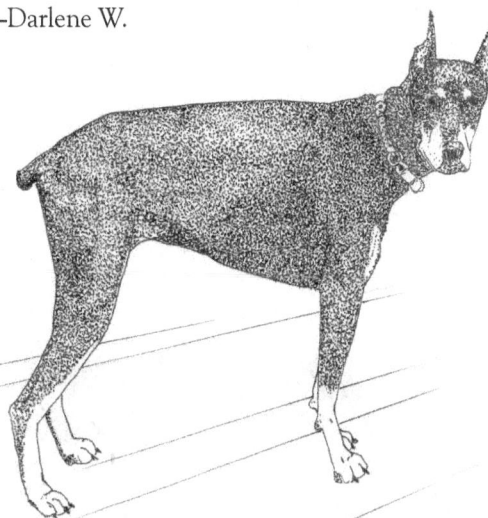

Ethical Meat

We are in a painful conundrum. Most dog owners are passionate about all animals, not just dogs. So how do we rationalize the horrific lives of factory farmed animals and the pain and suffering that they endure - confinement, isolation, emotional deprivation, illness, disease, toxic food, toxic water and toxic drugs? And the energy of this unpleasant scenario is passed down with every bite of meat that you and your dog take. The energy fields of happier and healthier animals that wolves eat is vastly different from the energy fields of suffering and unhealthy factory animals. Truly we are the energy that we eat.

The impact of raising animals instead of crops is staggering: more than 51 percent of global greenhouse-gas emissions are caused by animal agriculture. One kilogram of beef requires more than 20,000 litres of water for drinking and for flushing out factory farms. And our water supplies everywhere are becoming polluted with nitrates, bacteria, and viruses. The transportation of meat is also a major draw on resources as it requires a tremendous amount of fuel and refrigeration equipment.

It is estimated that there are 525 million dogs worldwide. Granted that many of these dogs are also scavengers but the global consumption of animal meat just to feed dogs is beyond our comprehension.

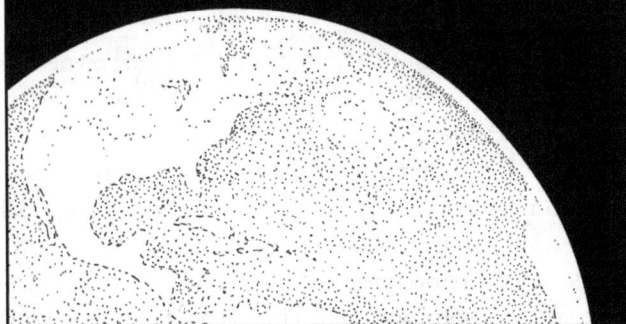

If we are serious about ever healing the Earth – and all the resident animals and people that Mother Earth provides for – we must honour our land, our water, and all living beings without delay. We need to treat all animals with dignity and kindness and feed them with clean and nutritious food in a humane environment. Our dogs would not have it any other way; underneath the primal and biological behaviour of every teeth baring, growling, meat-eating predator is found an open heart with an astounding amount of compassion for all species and a sense of stewardship for their land. Perhaps the cruel hierarchy inside the world of the prey and predator, solely intended for survival, was not the evolutionary journey our animals expected.

> **It is estimated that there are 525 million dogs worldwide... the global consumption of animal meat just to feed dogs is beyond our comprehension.**

Here's what you can do to help the planet and ALL of her animals, not just dogs:

1. Eat organic
2. Support pasture-fed and free-range meat
3. Adopt a Meatless Monday or more for the entire family – canine and human
4. Do not own more than one or two dogs
5. Do not support indiscriminate breeding, puppy mills or the breeding of genetically sick dogs (see Chapter 16)
6. Rescue dogs instead of breeding them

Feeding Bones

Raw meaty bones or RMB are an excellent source of minerals with a balance of calcium and phosphorus, essential fatty acids, proteins, and enzymes as well as natural levels of cartilage and marrow for healthy teeth and bones. In addition, chewing on bones help to give dogs a natural outlet for their chewing instincts, and the right bones can help keep your dog's teeth clean through the abrasive action.

While feeding RMB is generally safe, there are some important considerations to follow to make it even safer:

- Never feed cooked bones as they can splinter during chewing resulting in choke or intestinal damage.
- Don't feed smaller pieces of bone such as chicken wings or necks, or cut bones unless attached to the whole bird. This prevents the gulping or swallowing of small bones which can damage the esophagus, stomach and/or intestine resulting in expensive surgeries or worse.
- Always supervise a dog that is chewing bone. As safe as chewing bone normally is for dogs, dogs have been known to fatally choke, particularly on smaller bones.
- Pork and/or rib bones are more likely to splinter than other bone types.
- Large bones such as shank bones from beef or bison are harder than dogs' teeth and can therefore result in a cracked tooth
- Bones require very strong stomach acid to dissolve into smaller pieces before they move into the intestines. Hold the bones if your dog has difficulties with gastric digestion, chewing and/or dental problems.

- Too much bone can constipate dogs; conversely dietary bone can also help firm up stool, and a firmer stool can also help press out anal gland impactions.

- Not all dogs like bones, and that's okay.

- Feed bones once or twice per week. Dogs that chew bones too often may develop excess tension in the chewing muscles.

- Small dogs who chew on big bones won't naturally scale their teeth because they can't chew through them.

- Frozen bones are safe and slow down the rate of chewing.

- Good RMB include whole beef bones, chicken leg quarters, turkey thighs or whole birds. For added safety, bones can also be ground (rather than fed whole) and added to the food once or twice weekly.

- While bones are a good thing, don't assume that dogs chewing on RMB with or without a raw meat diet will provide adequate mineral intake. Hair analysis results indicate that dogs that get bones can still be deficient in minerals. No matter what kind of diet dogs are on or in what proportions, we cannot *assume* that the dietary intake of minerals is adequate, including calcium, which remains one of the most important supplements for many dogs. Aside from the various nutritional requirements necessary for dogs, it is possible that the bones themselves are less nutritious now because of depleted soils and improperly fed animals. And while some experts believe that adult dogs need less calcium than puppies, I have not found this to be true especially with dogs on high meat diets (whether raw or cooked), immune-compromised dogs or arthritic dogs.

- Meat diets are mostly combined with organ meats and bones to ensure nutritional balance; however, a high meat diet will very often require added calcium supplementation, especially to buffer excess acidity.

- Avoid any commercial dental bones that contain any chemical preservatives, artificial flavourings, sulfites and/or unhealthy oils. Also avoid rawhide, which is the inner layer of the livestock hide, for it may contain residual drugs, heavy metals and/or hormones. Many dogs are hypersensitive to rawhide and/or the substances in it, and rawhide can also cause choking if large pieces are swallowed.

Feeding Vegetables and Fruit

Whether to feed our dogs fruit and vegetables is still a debate in the raw crowd, but it really shouldn't be debated in any crowd. We all know or have known dogs that love apples, dig carrots out of the garden, crave beets, and beg for vegetable stew. Study after study and testimony after testimony have proved the human health results for eating an abundance of fruit, vegetables and their juices. Dogs are no different and they have much to benefit from eating these nutrient-rich foods. In fact, there is no reason to limit their intake of fruit and vegetables – let them choose. Fruit and vegetables are high in fibre, contain many anti-oxidants, are rich in vitamins and minerals, and contain live enzymes. This high nutritive value works to detoxify all body systems, enhance digestion, maintain a healthy colon, support the heart, nourish endocrine gland function and provide nutrition for the brain and neurological system. Vegetables promote longevity and prevent cancer – again numerous studies have shown that feeding cruciferous vegetables, for example, stops the growth of cancer cells. A variety of vegetables and herbs promote apoptosis within cancer cells, meaning that the unhealthy cancerous cells die off normally without inflammation, allowing the healthy cells to flourish. If cancerous cells do not die off naturally, they continue to proliferate and form tumours.

Dogs may enjoy eating fruits and vegetables raw as well as cooked although raw vegetables are more difficult for them to digest. Lightly cooking the vegetables opens the plant cellulose, making it easier to digest, and also improves access to water-soluble vitamins such as the B vitamins and vitamin C. Raw or cooked vegetables still provide the benefits of fibre and enzymes. If your dog, small or large, refuses a piece of raw fruit or vegetable as a treat, it's often because they find the pieces too large and they prefer smaller easy-to-chew pieces. When adding raw vegetables to a meal chop, mince, grate or cut into small pieces. Freshly made vegetable and fruit juices can also be added to the diet. Raw fruit and vegetables contain many live enzymes and, unlike the live enzymes from raw meat, the enzymes from plant material are not destroyed in the high acid environment in the stomach.

Healthy vegetables include carrots, greens (kale, spinach, carrot tops, bok choy, beet tops), green beans, broccoli, corn scraped off the cob, beets, squash, pumpkin, parsley, potatoes, and sweet potatoes. Don't overcook them unless you are making a stew or a soup where the liquid is retained. Simmer briefly, par-boil, or steam. Regular potatoes do not need to be avoided but are best fed organic with the skins for the added potassium and fibre which helps counter the starch content. Both regular potatoes and sweet potatoes are nutritious and high in fibre and sweet potatoes are high in beta-carotene (as are all yellow vegetables) and more soothing for the digestion. Neither one of them should be fed in excess – twice per week is ample. The sugars in sweet potatoes can aggravate some dogs who are more sugar sensitive.

Dogs can enjoy all fruits including berries (no grapes or raisins), apples, tomatoes, peaches, melons, bananas and pears. Plums can also be offered as they are high in beta-carotene, vitamin C and zeaxanthin, a carotenoid which is excellent for the eyes.

I was amazed one early morning just after dawn when I was awakened by a ruckus outside my bedroom window in the fruit tree orchard. I quietly tip-toed to the window so as to not to step on or wake up the hound (who slept on a big cushion on the floor at the end of the bed) and was surprised to see three coyotes under the plum tree. They were taking turns leaping high into the air to grab the plums that they couldn't reach from the ground. It was a beautiful sunny summer morning and plants, seeds, and prey were abundant in the area. I was very impressed with how far they were going to fetch a high fibre, high fructose snack. The poor plum tree though – it's been a favourite in the past for other wildlife too and had been seriously pruned the year before by bears who were too heavy for the branches. That year I was left with a total of three plums at the very top of the tree that the bears couldn't reach (nor could I) before they came tumbling down to the ground on the broken branches. So obviously, plums are a big hit with the wildlife. Coyotes and bears also feast on the field corn crops to the point where I find vomit piles in the yard as a result of them gorging on corn starch!

Dogs don't normally care for citrus, which should be avoided anyway due to the high acid and allergenic potential. Although lemon juice can be used therapeutically as a digestive aid, to decongest the kidneys and/or drain the lymph system.

Feed all vegetables and fruits organic.

The Importance of Fibre

Fibre is the starchy part of the plant that cannot be digested enzymatically. Different types of plants contain different types of fibre, including cellulose, hemicellulose, lignins and pectins. There are two types of fibre: soluble and insoluble. Soluble fibres are found in grains and dissolve in water, while insoluble fibres don't dissolve in water and come from grains, seeds, and legumes and include the woody, stalky part of the plant. However, insoluble fibres absorb water which bulks up the stool, making it softer and bulkier and increasing intestinal transit time which is good; constipation increases the colon's exposure to toxic substances. A bulkier stool will also correct diarrhea.

All toxic chemicals – environmental, food, medications, and pollutants – as well as fats must be metabolized and processed by the liver and then dumped into the bile for excretion. Bile transports all the wastes and toxins from the liver and delivers them to the small intestine where it binds with dietary fibre and is then carried out of the body through the colon via the waste. A lack of dietary fibre results in the re-absorption of these toxins along with the fatty bile back into the bloodstream and again into the liver. These circulating toxins cause damage to the blood vessels, tissues and organs. They also form cancer-producing compounds. Now this might not have been as big of a problem for our ancestral wolf with its very different and very rural lifestyle which does not regularly subject them to medications, food toxins and indoor pollutants – although outdoor pollutants are sure to be a bigger problem for them now than ever before. Thus, perhaps wolves now too are craving fibre as part of their survival instinct to reduce the effects of their forced exposure to increasing levels of environmental toxins. Coyotes in the plum trees... physical intelligence?

Over half of all dogs regularly ingest fibrous grass although this habit is more common with the younger dogs. Overall, there does not seem to be any correlation between a low fibre diet and dogs compelled to seek out grass. Grass does provide nutrition though, for it is high in chlorophyll and anti-oxidants. In addition, dogs often seek out the indigestible grasses as a digestive aid or cleanser since they can eat grass to induce vomiting; presumably to cleanse/purge the stomach of toxins and mal-digested food; wolves do the same thing. It has also been suggested that dogs may use grass, especially sharp-leafed grasses as a natural anti-parasitic since grass helps to immobilize and then purge parasites.

For those of you who like preparing fresh vegetable juices in the kitchen juicer, the leftover pulp is very fibrous and can be added to your dog's diet one to three times per week. You may have to experiment with which fruit and vegetable fibres your dog likes the best – also don't feed it as one big ball but break it into smaller pieces. And if your dogs don't eat it, the chickens and the horses surely will.

Table Scraps

What on earth are table scraps? Food that is not fit for human consumption after the meal is finished? Leftover food where the nutritional quality has somehow been degraded just after being spooned into the dog dish? The prevailing myth on table scraps is just that; table scraps will *not* upset the balance of whatever else the dog is eating. In fact, it might add to it depending on what kind of food they are already getting. Nor will table scraps make them fat. To the contrary, table scraps will add extra nutrition and could work wonders – so long as the humans in the house are eating healthy and nutritious meals.

Dogs can be given some very nutritious food out of the kitchen including meats, fish, eggs, cooked grains, vegetables and fruit. Too many times do people throw perfectly good food away while the dog watches with anxious eyes and a drooling mouth, and owners ignore all this salivation because they are convinced that the kibble is all that their dog needs. Rarely does dried kibble fulfill all nutritional requirements. Listen to your dog; can you imagine what they must be thinking? Use your healthy leftovers as a top-dressing on the dog's meal or as a complete meal if there is enough of it. Obviously, we need to find a new name for table scraps – how about "real meal food"?

Do not feed dairy products, processed meats, wheat, bread, quinoa, sugar, large beans, soy products or junk food including cookies, chips, cheezies, chocolate, French fries or deep fried foods. Junk foods are not table scraps, and pet parents shouldn't be eating them either. Also avoid any kind of moldy foods, raw bread dough and/or alcohol. As well, there are certain foods which are specifically toxic to dogs (see Feeding Dogs at Home – Foods to Avoid).

Making Dog Food at Home

There are general guidelines, but these should *only* be considered guidelines. Every breed is unique, every dog is unique, and every lifestyle and situation is unique. And no matter what kind of diet your dog is on – raw, cooked, homemade, commercial, vegan – if it's not working for your dog, then it's not working, so change it.

Mother nature, as always, is very forgiving and provides a lot of latitude before things go wrong, so don't be afraid to experiment. It's hard to kill a dog with real food, and dogs don't need every specific food group every day to maintain health. And give yourself credit for knowing your dog better than anyone else knows your dog.

Choose a variety of different and healthy foods from the food groups as previously discussed and bear in mind that, when making any major diet changes, it is always in the best interest of the dog to transition slowly. As a rule, and this is just a general one, an adult dog will require 2 to 3 percent of its bodyweight as total food per day. Thus a dog that weighs 18 kilograms will require from 360 to 540 grams of food per day. Or a 40-pound dog will require 0.8 to 1.2 pounds of food per day.

Guidelines for Daily Protein Requirements:

Find below a handy chart for optimum protein percent of meal (by weight) to be fed by way of meat, fish and/or egg protein.

†Note: puppies will also require over twice as many calories as adult dogs to support optimum growth.

Puppies†	22-30%
Adult dogs with typical activity levels	15-30%
Performance or hard-working dogs	25-35%
Lactating/pregnant dogs	25-35%
Senior or sedentary dogs	15 20%

Guidelines for Healthy Daily Fat Requirements:

Find below a handy chart for optimum fat percent of meal (by weight) to be fed primarily as saturated meat fat although healthy oils should be included as discussed previously such as light olive oil and essential fatty acids.

Puppies	10-15%
Adult dogs with typical activity levels	10-20%
Performance or hard-working dogs	20-30%
Lactating/pregnant dogs	20-25%
Senior or sedentary dogs	10-15%

Guidelines for Daily Carbohydrate Requirements:

Carbohydrate requirements are sourced from grains, fruit, potatoes and sweet potatoes. Dietary requirements for dogs are extremely difficult to predict, and the reason that experts have such a hard time agreeing on dietary requirements is because requirements vary widely depending on the dog and their state of health or other nutritional requirements. Carbohydrates are a readily available source of energy, thus, when low levels of carbohydrates are fed, the dog's body draws more heavily on its protein supplies to meet its energy needs. However, so long as the protein intake is adequate, less energy is required from other dietary sources. Conversely, dogs do have a glucose requirement to fuel the brain and maintain metabolic functions. Dogs, like humans, can metabolize glucose from proteins and fats in a process known as gluconeogenesis; however, if carbohydrates are available, they will be converted to energy first because they are easier to convert. If carbohydrates are not available, then fats will convert to glucose before protein. A starving animal or a wolf with infrequent feedings will thus use up their fat reserves first, but in the face of further starvation they will metabolize muscle for energy eventually resulting in an emaciated appearance.

So aside from the fact that there no commonly acceptable levels, we can consider the intake as low (20-25% by weight), moderate (25-40%), or high (40-60%). Dogs that have difficulty digesting fats, dogs with pancreatitis or other fat-related health conditions, and even some overweight dogs may benefit from a higher carbohydrate diet because it is lower in fats. On the other hand, some overweight dogs will require fewer carbohydrates to make room for more healthy fats. For more information refer to the specific diets recommended in the health program chapters.

If you are a diehard raw foodist, you won't be considering grains anyway, but as we have already established there is no reason to - indeed you *shouldn't* - withhold fruit and vegetables (raw or cooked) as part of a healthy dog diet. If your dog likes cooked meat or a combination of raw or cooked meat, there can still be a nutritional benefit from feeding cooked grains, but feed them in separate meals away from the meat meals. In other words, feed grains by themselves and meat by itself. And some dogs simply *prefer* producing energy from the easy-to-convert carbohydrates. Read your dog and see what they prefer. Dogs should know best. In any case, don't rely on grains as a primary protein source over long-term unless your dog is on a cleansing or therapeutic vegetarian diet as discussed below.

Guidelines for Feeding Fruit and Vegetables

Include your dog's favourite fruit and vegetables raw or cooked - whatever she likes the most and however much she wants to eat. Refer to the previous section on Fruits and Vegetables for selections. Fruit and vegetables provide fibre, optimum nutrition, disease-prevention compounds, healthy enzymes and natural medicinals.

Include Soups, Stews and Broths

These are easy to make or to prepare ahead and maybe freeze thus making them very convenient. Liquid foods provide a lot of nutrition and are excellent for dogs who have problems eating due to dental issues and/or digestive conditions. They can also be used as a healthy gravy to top other foods making them more palatable. Broths can be vegetarian or bone broth with the bones strained off before feeding.

Force-Feeding

No matter how nutritious you may think a food is for your dog, don't mix or hide foods that they don't like into their meals - this is true for all food groups including meat, grains, fats and fruit and vegetables. I've seen many well-intentioned dog parents try to find ways to make their dogs eat foods such as a specific meat because it is organic, exotic meats, fish, corn, wheat, extra fat, etc. There's a reason why dogs don't like certain foods, and their physical intelligence should be considered higher than our mental intelligence when it comes to food.

Foods to Avoid

Avocado. If the skin or flesh is fed in large quantities it may cause mild stomach upset. Small amounts of avocado added to the food is not a problem. Do not feed the pit.

Caffeine in chocolate, coffee and/or pop. Caffeine is a strong stimulant which can cause anxiety, agitation, nausea, thirst, urination, heart palpitations and/or seizures and (in extreme cases) death. Many a dog has snuck into the holiday chocolate without adverse effects; however, caffeine-sensitive dogs should be monitored closely. It's interesting to note that these same symptoms are common in people as well, yet many people continue to drink the highly addictive coffee without making a connection between their caffeine habit and the many health symptoms that it causes.

Grapes and Raisins. Most dogs can eat a few grapes/raisins without suffering any ill effects; however, a few can experience life-threatening problems within twelve hours after ingestion. Even dogs that have had no problems previously can sometimes find themselves in peril. Symptoms are related to kidney dysfunction and may include vomiting, fatigue, loss of appetite, dehydration and/or changes in urination.

Macadamia Nuts. Symptoms are mild, non-life-threatening, and will subside within 48 hours. Toxicity symptoms may include hind end weakness, discomfort, possible tremors, and/or a low-grade fever.

Onions and garlic. Small amounts of cooked onions and/or garlic in the food is not a problem. In fact, garlic has many health benefits. However, if a dog happens to ingest large amounts of concentrated forms as found in dry mixes, powders or salts, it may cause temporary anemia by damaging the red blood cells. Symptoms of anemia may surface within a few days and can include fatigue, lethargy, loss of concentration, and/or poor immunity.

Water Quality

Tap water and/or well water can be high in chlorine, fluoride, nitrates, iron, sulphur, arsenic, manganese, lead and/or copper. Any of these elements can cause problems for certain sensitive dogs or health conditions, so if you suspect that your dog's drinking water contains unhealthy minerals or chemicals, either install a high-quality filtration system or purchase bottled water - preferably spring water rather than purified or reverse osmosis. Dogs on dry dog food *must* drink more water than dogs on fresh meat diets, especially raw meat diets. And dogs frequently don't like drinking out of metal or plastic water bowls, which sends them to the water trough or the toilet bowl.

To determine mineral status or levels of toxic heavy metals in the dog have a Hair Tissue Mineral Analysis conducted. See the Appendix for more information.

The Vegetarian Dog

Many of our modern and domestic dogs, particularly senior dogs and immune-compromised dogs, have meat-protein intolerances, which are resulting in chronic immune problems, allergies, skin conditions, poor digestive function, joint problems, anxiety, and some conditions of the nervous system. As discussed, this is due to the high protein levels which our dogs can no longer metabolise, for accumulations of meat result in toxic levels of ammonia, urea and various acids. Certain health conditions will interfere with efficient protein digestion, and these dogs will also show signs of protein toxicity and/or maldigestion. And as we know, the consumption of excess meat by both humans and animals has become a frighteningly major problem that threatens our health, the health of our pets, our water supplies and our planet too. But perhaps the most troubling aspect is that it degrades the welfare of animals everywhere that are raised for food commercially. So even if your dog is not requiring a vegetarian diet for health reasons, millions will benefit if dog owners adopted more reasonable diet strategies.

In any case, after working on thousands of dogs with challenging and persistent problems over many years, I have found that the toxic effects of excess protein is a major culprit in many pet health conditions. When meat consumption is reduced or temporarily eliminated, most of these pets improve dramatically. A meat-free cleanse increases nutrient intake and detoxifies the major elimination organs: intestines, liver, kidneys and skin.

Dogs will not perish or become ill if deprived of meat for a few weeks. Granted, a permanent vegetarian diet is not the solution for most dogs, nor will it maintain optimum health levels in the long run - but neither will toxic meat diets; and our dogs can and *do* benefit from occasional meat-free cleanses just like their canine wild ancestors who also cleanse on a regular basis, albeit mostly due to difficult hunting circumstances which makes it hard to find prey at certain times. Subsequently, wolves and coyotes do not suffer the symptoms of an excess meat diet.

Plant-based proteins have a lower biological value than meat, but dogs are quite adept at making the intestinal and digestive adaptions (epigenetics) to sustain themselves on more plant-based foods. However, when first increasing the quantity of healthy grains and vegetables in your dog's diet, the volume of fibre increases as well. Some dogs will need time to adjust to the higher dietary fibre and may experience some bloating and/or diarrhea due to the transition. To ease the transition, give a daily dose of the Pro-Colon probiotics (Riva's Remedies) to aid the intestinal fermentation of fibre.

Vegetarian diets may also be a philosophical choice since some pet parents themselves have adopted a vegetarian lifestyle and philosophy and are loath to feed their dogs meat of any kind. There are many accounts of dogs doing well on vegetarian diets, and there are many variables that account for this: food choices, epigenetics, nutrigenomics, lifestyle, stress levels and most importantly the intention of the dog parent who is very often a vegetarian herself. And as we shall see in Chapter 17, when we explore the *sponging* or *mirroring* concepts that occur between animals and humans on a regular basis, pets easily take on our identity including our food choices and diets. However, dogs will not thrive on a vegetarian diet long-term and must be carefully monitored for signs of a protein deficiency.

After 6 to 8 weeks on the program, be mindful and watch for protein deficiencies as could be indicated by: constant hunger, weight loss, dull hair coat, fatigue, poor coordination, sluggish cognitive skills and/or poor immune function. Depending on the complexity and variety of a new diet symptoms of deficiency usually do not occur in the first 3 to 4 weeks. Any health problems during this time are more often signs of detoxification and/or continuing food reactions.

When re-introducing meat proteins - as necessary - do so gradually one protein at a time to ensure that there are no adverse or immune reactions. Dietary toxins and food allergies/intolerances can take anywhere from 6 to 12 weeks to clear. Avoid feeding beef, bison, venison, other red meats and organ meats. And avoid mixing meat protein types together in the same meal, including fish.

Ideally, try and strike a balance between a vegetarian diet and supplementing with meat protein as needed.

The Vegetarian Cleanse: 6 to 8 Weeks

1) **Protein.** One-third to one-half of every meal should consist of a protein source including:

- **Eggs** (if tolerated) can be included every day or two. Eggs should be free-range, organic, and laid by happy hens.

- **Salmon** (if tolerated) raw or cooked, preferably wild (with the skin on if they like it) can be included twice weekly if tolerated. Do not combine eggs with salmon in the same meal.

- **Legumes.** Small beans such as lentils, split peas, black beans, adzuki beans, pinto beans and chick peas can be fed. Avoid lima beans, navy beans, and kidney beans. All beans except lentils and peas need to be soaked before cooking to break down starches. Ensure that all beans are well cooked and cook them twice to improve digestibility and reduce the gas-producing oligosaccharides which are found in all beans. Canned beans will generally be more gas-producing. A healthy digestive system free of wheat, corn gluten, excess meat and unhealthy oils can digest legumes more easily. Not every meal has to include beans.

- NOTE: To make the beans more digestible, drain off the wash water and the soaking water, then simmer beans for ten minutes in fresh water. Then skim the foam and drain off this cooking water as well. And finally cook in clean fresh water until well done. Then grind or mash the well-cooked beans before adding them to the meal.

- **Seeds.** Hemp, chia, flax, pumpkin and sesame seeds provide protein, fibre, essential fatty acids and nutrition.

- **Nuts.** Almonds, cashews, pistachios (raw only and without the shell). Crush or grind and feed in small amounts no more than twice per week. Nuts can also be mixed into a trail mix with seeds and dried fruit. No macadamia nuts. Use nut butters sparingly.

- **Spirulina.** A blue-green algae that contains 60 percent protein by weight and contains all the essential amino acids.

2) **Grains and Vegetables.** The non-protein portion of every meal (i.e. from half to two thirds of the meal) should be made up of a mix of both grains and vegetables/fruit

Grains may include oats, brown rice, wild rice, wheat germ, buckwheat, barley, millet, bulgur, rye. NOTE: Cook all grains before feeding. Avoid all forms of wheat.

Fruit and vegetables may include carrots, greens (kale, spinach, carrot tops, bok choy, beet tops), corn on the cob or canned corn, beets, squash, pumpkin, parsley, potatoes with skins, and sweet potatoes. Many dogs enjoy apples, cucumbers, watermelon, berries, peaches, pears, etc. NOTE: avoid avocados, grapes, raisins or onions.

- Baked potatoes (regular or sweet) with beans, vegetables, and oil.

- Lentil and barley casserole.

- Cooked barley or brown rice with lentils.

- Rice, beans and corn.

- Homemade soup broths with fresh bones which are strained off before serving.

- Thick soups, such as vegetable barley, vegetable rice, lentil soup, black bean or pea soup. Wild rice makes a nutritional addition as well.

- Vegetable stews made with any variety of vegetables, grains or legumes.

- Stir fries – vegetables, rice and egg (if egg is allowed).

- Salads – many dogs like a variety of raw greens – chop into small pieces.

Thick soups, such as vegetable barley, vegetable rice, lentil soup, black bean or pea soup.

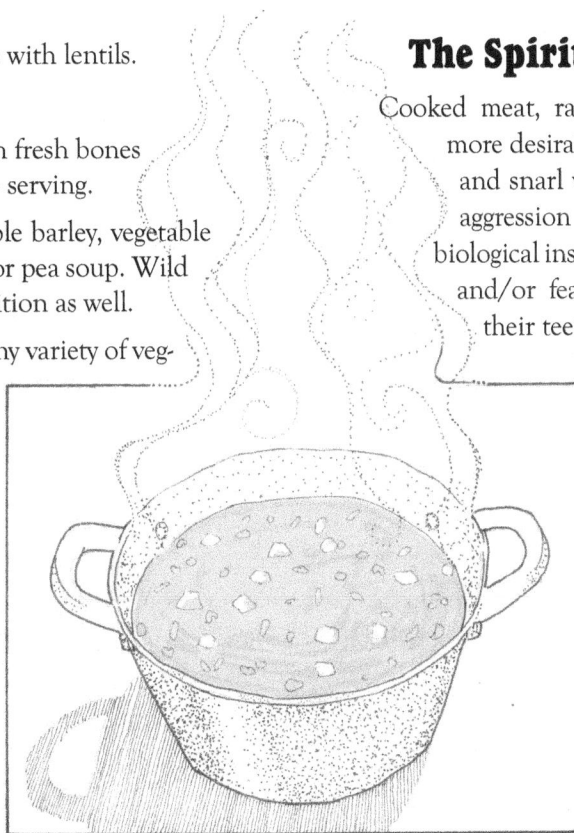

3) Fats. Include a dose of olive oil, flaxseed oil, evening primrose oil or hemp seed oil added to their food every day.

Further Diet Notes

- If your dog tolerates salmon and/or egg you may add to any dish.

- Ensure that your dog gets a variety of vegetables every day – vegetables help with satiety and are a rich source of fibre, vitamins, minerals and anti-oxidants.

- Hemp, buckwheat and spirulina are vegetarian sources of complete proteins

- A combination meal of rice, beans and corn (as a vegetable) will provide a complete protein with all amino acids

- Nutrients that may need supplementation: iron, calcium, zinc, vitamin B12, folic acid, vitamin A, taurine and/or carnitine

- Vegetarian dogs, even if they eat eggs, will need extra salt – add an appropriate amount (based on weight) of sea salt to their food daily.

- Commercial brands of vegetarian foods are available in many pet health outlets; if possible to choose a freeze-dried brand over a kibble.

The Spiritual Dog

Cooked meat, rather than raw meat, could be more desirable for aggressive dogs who snap and snarl whenever food is involved since aggression is very often based on a strong biological instinct of protection, guardianship and/or fear. Wolves don't growl or bare their teeth at their prey – they run down and kill their prey. But they will sometimes get aggressive *protecting* a kill. The smell of blood and the tearing of raw meat can sometimes trigger inherent aggressive instincts around food protection. Think of raw meat as a powerful forceful *yang* food, while on the opposite end of the spectrum plants are a more passive *yin* food.

Parents of vegetarian dogs report that the temperament of their dogs change as they slowly lose their taste for flesh and blood and, therefore, their desire to hunt and kill. This, they will tell you, makes dogs friendlier and gentler companions with all animals, large or small.

Thus diet, in a peaceful environment, can be beneficial for calming an emotional or biological imbalance back to a state of increased harmony and cooperation. Should this be your intention, the very yin canine vegetarian diet can serve to re-connect and align your dog's state of consciousness with your own as you both seek higher ground on a blessed journey of enlightenment.

Ten Ways Your Dog Can Tell You That She Needs a Food Change

1. Excessive hunger – your dog can't wait to be fed and may even wake you up in middle of the night so she can eat. This can also indicate a blood-sugar problem.

2. Skipping meals. If you offer meals twice per day, your dog may not eat until supper or, conversely will only eat breakfast.

3. Your dog looks at the meal, walks away and comes back later – in other words, she will only eat it when feeling really hungry.

4. Your dog looks up at you before starting to eat, often reluctantly. This can mean that your dog doesn't like the food, but is too hungry too refuse it – there are no other options.

5. Your dog picks through the food and eats very slowly, but will wolf down treats or food offered from the kitchen.

6. Burying the food before eating it. Now this may be interpreted as the dog liking it SO much they are saving it for later, but most often if a hungry dog buries its food it means that they don't have enough interest in it to eat it right away. It's the same as skipping a meal.

7. Your dog scavenges anything she can find – scraps, dog poop, horse poop, chicken food and leftover garbage.

8. Frequent vomiting after eating, either immediately or 2 to 3 hours later.

9. Frequent digestive symptoms – bloating, gas, constipation and/or diarrhea.

10. Your dog is suffering poor health including allergies, immune issues, panting, fatigue and/or anxiety, despite the current diet.

Understanding Health Problems

The next few chapters will detail various body systems and address the most common health conditions with diet, nutrition, and natural health programs. These programs are based on over two decades of clinical experience, extensive knowledge, and a common-sense and practical approach. The emphasis is always on the underlying cause of the condition, rather than suppressing symptoms. The wisdom and practicality within this holistic approach leads us to effective health solutions and solid natural health programs to benefit all dogs.

4. Gastrointestinal Health

Digestion & Elimination

The gastrointestinal tract is responsible for breaking down, digesting, and extracting all nutrients – including amino acids, fats, sugars, vitamins and minerals – from ingested food. Any food material that is not digested is collected as waste and is eliminated as feces. The gastrointestinal tract is a long hollow tube starting with the mouth (where food is torn and then swallowed) and ending at the anus where undigested food material is released. The GI tract therefore includes the teeth, mouth, esophagus, stomach, small intestine, large intestine and rectum.

In general, larger breeds have a proportionately smaller gastrointestinal tract, comprising 3 to 4 percent of total bodyweight compared to 6 to 7 percent of total bodyweight in smaller breeds.

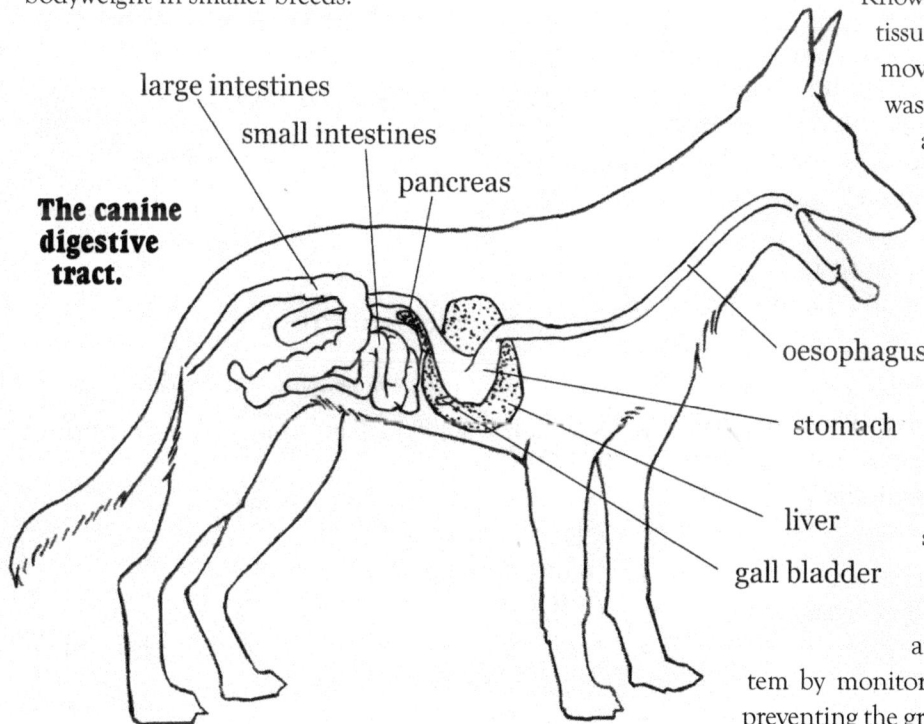

The Intestinal Immune System

The intestinal immune system is the primary reason that an unhealthy or toxic diet is a major contributor to most diseases.

Over 70 percent of a dog's immune system is found throughout the small and large intestine which contains the largest volume of lymphoid tissue in the entire body. Known as GALT (gut-associated lymphoid tissue) this amazing system filters and removes mal-digested feed material, debris, waste products and toxins – all of which are often too large to be removed by the bloodstream. GALT also helps to absorb fluids and fats and transport proteins. The intestinal lymph produces antibodies and stores important white blood cells to attack foreign invaders, foreign proteins and pathogens. The small intestine itself houses the Peyer's patches or PP, which are small masses of lymphatic tissue containing hundreds of lymph nodes found throughout the ileum. They produce lymphocytes and form an important part of the immune system by monitoring intestinal bacteria populations, preventing the growth of disease-causing bacteria, and

The canine digestive tract.

large intestines
small intestines
pancreas
oesophagus
stomach
liver
gall bladder

promoting the growth of friendly bacteria and probiotics.

Considering the volume of digestive waste that must be processed and detoxified in the intestines every day, the optimum function of GALT is not only critical to digestive health, but to the health of every other body system and their diseases. Thus, the intestinal immune system is the primary reason that an unhealthy or toxic diet is a major contributor to most diseases.

The Importance of Probiotics

Probiotics are defined as live microorganisms that, when administered in adequate amounts, confer a health benefit on the host. Most friendly bacteria are found in the large intestine with the lowest number found in the stomach, where few bacterial species are adapted to the acidic environment, and in the small intestine, where food passes through quickly and where there are higher levels of bile acids. Probiotics are not only required for efficient fermentation of starches, sugars and fibre in the large intestine but they are also critical for keeping balance within the colonic ecosystem.

Probiotic Deficiencies

The most common cause of a probiotic deficiency is diet.

Hard to digest foods – usually wheat, corn, sugars, and/or unhealthy grains – will not be efficiently digested in the small intestine and will, therefore, be forced into the large intestine as an incomplete food mass. Since the large intestine cannot enzymatically digest food, it must ferment it by using large numbers of probiotics. But the large intestine is not anatomically designed to ferment large quantities of undigested starches, and thus the probiotic levels are easily depleted.

The mal-digestion of excess meat protein will cause putrefaction by bacteria in the large colon creating very toxic waste products that require high quantities of probiotics for control. We need to know that the meat our dogs are eating is being digested.

Food intolerances and/or allergies create inflammation and encourage the proliferation of more pathogenic bacteria in the intestinal walls. Probiotics protect the intestinal walls by adhering to the membranes, and if problem foods continue to be ingested, the probiotics will be rapidly used up. However, this doesn't mean that supplemental probiotics alone will neutralize the effects of negative foods – these foods must be eliminated from the diet.

The Benefits of Supplementing Probiotics

Probiotic supplements are beneficial for a variety of different intestinal conditions:

- Limit the action of putrefactive microbes
- Discourage the growth of unfriendly bacteria, yeast, and viruses
- Support weight loss through fat metabolism
- Support weight gain through increased nutrient absorption from food
- Improve appetite
- Reduce diarrhea
- Promote gut motility and peristalsis
- Promote the production of intestinal vitamin K, vitamin B1, B2, B12 and folic acid; probiotics synthesize *several* important vitamins – which are then reabsorbed back into the body through the colon walls
- Have a protective effect on the liver
- Stimulate the immune system
- Produce volatile fatty acids – acetic, butyric, and propionic – which generate energy, support a healthy intestinal barrier, and have a positive impact on the immune system
- Reduce the incidence of allergies
- Prevent intestinal cancers
- Metabolize and regulate the balance of hormones including estrogen and testosterone, enabling them to be re-absorbed from the colon, converted by the liver into useable form, and then excreted if in excess. This is a critical process for hormone-related diseases.

When to Supplement Probiotics

Use probiotics for the following health conditions:
- Symptoms of indigestion, ulcers, gas, and/or bloating
- Diarrhea or constipation
- Weight loss and/or poor appetite
- Obesity or weight gain
- Insulin resistance
- Cushing's disease
- Medication use – antibiotics, steroids, chemical dewormers, and/or antacids
- Prolonged periods of stress

- A history of poor nutrition and/or starvation
- A history of diets using wheat, corn, or other grains as staples
- Allergies
- Immune conditions
- Senior dogs

How to Supplement Probiotics

From numerous studies - as well as the results from dog owners - it is clear that supplementing high-quality probiotics to dogs is beneficial to intestinal health, the immune system, and more. A healthy probiotic supplement should contain live active cultures, meaning that the microorganisms are alive. Therefore, to ensure maximum potency, a good live probiotic should require refrigeration and never be stored on the shelf at room temperature, whether at home or in the store. This is also a problem for probiotics which have been added to dog food or herbal supplements. Probiotics are frequently stabilized with freeze drying for storing at room temperature with a longer shelf life, but these types of probiotics always have a lower potency than live bacteria which is refrigerated.

Probiotics should also not be exposed to moisture, for both heat and moisture will kill off bacteria. Therefore, probiotics should not be heated after the fermentation process during production. Probiotics should also not be added to commercial food or an herbal supplement before it has undergone the manufacturing process since this will also kill off the bacteria.

Note that even though the probiotics in yoghurt can be live, dogs should not be fed yoghurt since most of them will react negatively to the lactose and/or the milk protein.

Depending on the size of the dog, an average dosage should provide between 2.5 and 7 billion colony-forming units or CFUs. This should be given with food, rather than on an empty stomach. Despite the widespread marketing of probiotics more is not necessarily better, and there have been some cases where an overgrowth of even healthy bacteria has caused an increase of gas and/or bloating. Remember, the colon functions best in a healthy, balanced environment with an ecosystem containing a varied community of biological organisms - both friendly and pathogenic - designed to work together. It's all about the terrain.

No matter how prime the probiotic supplement is, it is best not to rely on permanent or indefinite supplementation; this is the case with *any* supplement. Nutritional supplements such as probiotics should be used as a cure to *correct* the problem, not as a crutch that, when discontinued, causes the same problem to reappear. Use probiotics to replenish a depleted colon, aid the digestion, and contribute to the improvement of a particular health condition. From there, a sensible and appropriate diet with food that contains adequate fibre and prebiotics will allow your dog to manufacture their own microflora for optimum health. Most dogs in reasonable health, and without remarkable or severe health symptoms, normally require three to four weeks of daily supplementation to replenish depleted levels. However, if your dog demonstrates obvious benefits beyond that time, then it is safe to do so.

Do Probiotics Survive the Intestinal Tract?

There is much discussion as to whether probiotics can survive the acidic environment of the stomach (in both dogs and humans) before reaching the large intestine which contains most of the probiotic colonies. Acidity is measured by pH levels (a measure of the concentration of hydrogen atoms) the lower the number the higher the acidity. A dog's normal stomach pH is between 1 and 1.5. Although there are differences in acid resistance and survival rates between strains and species of friendly bacteria, generally bacteria will become sensitive to a pH lower than 3, meaning that they will start to die off in this highly acidic environment. And although the studies are not exactly clear on whether a dog's pH is higher on an empty or full stomach, we do know that saliva has a high pH of between 8.5 and 9 and functions to buffer acidity. Food lubricated by the saliva before entering the stomach, will neutralize the gastric acid by raising the pH and thus allow the passing of any transient microflora such as probiotics. In addition, once the food remains have entered the small intestine, the secretions of bile (from the gallbladder) as well as sodium bicarbonate (from the pancreas) alkalizes the acidity even further. Gastric acidity is also affected by the type of food eaten, for example, a dog on a meat diet produces more mucous in the saliva than a dog on a dry food diet. Either way, it's a delicate balance, for the stomach must be acidic enough to kill pathogenic bacteria but still allow for healthy probiotics - either in food or as a supplement - to make its way intact to the ever-important large intestine.

What about Prebiotics?

Prebiotics are a component of fibre that is non-digestible in both the stomach and intestines, but which can be fermented by probiotics in the large intestine to generate energy. In turn, prebiotics stimulate the growth and activity of these same probiotics thus increasing the overall benefits of the microflora and their ecosystem. In addition, prebiotics have a favourable effect on GALT, improve mineral absorption (particularly calcium), address diarrhea and constipation, and prevent growths in the colon, including tumours. Prebiotics include foods such as inulin and oligosaccharides including fructo-oligosaccharides and galacto-oligosaccharides.

Prebiotics are found in many foods including Jerusalem artichoke (which is rich in inulin), cooked barley, garlic (yes, dogs can eat garlic), dandelion greens, sweet potato, chicory root, and beet pulp. This is the reason that many dog foods include chicory and/or beet pulp in their ingredients.

Probiotics and Wolves

Depending on geography and seasonal variations, it is likely that wolves ingest a fair amount of prebiotic fiber in their indigenous diets since it is available year-around in wild roots, tubers, and fibrous foods which are found nearly everywhere. However, their predominantly meat diets combined with drastically different lifestyles determines that their species, strains, and counts of intestinal microflora will differ dramatically from the domestic dog. Or should I say that the domestic dogs' lifestyles differ drastically from the wolf as discussed in Chapter One.

Natural Health Programs for Stomach Health

~~~~~~~~~~~~~~~~~~ 🐾 ~~~~~~~~~~~~~~~~~~

Heartburn, Reflux, Bloating and Ulcers

Symptoms

Symptoms of gastric indigestion are similar those in humans, even though your dog may not be able to display or express specific symptoms. Burning, discomfort, tightness and bloating are the symptoms that the pet parent cannot easily observe; however, gas, bloating, constipation, and bad breath are more easily detected. Dogs with digestive discomfort may also groan in their sleep.

Causes

The most common physical causes of stomach indigestion are either a production of excess acids from fermentation and/or the inability to break down meat protein mostly due to a lack of HCl (hydrochloric acid) required for all protein digestion. The stomach is only intended to break down protein. So, if a dog eats too many starches or carbohydrates, these foods can become contained in the stomach where they will begin to ferment before being passed into the small intestine where they should be enzymatically digested. Fermentation in the stomach promotes the production of various strains of unfriendly bacteria including *Lactobacillus* and *Helicobacter pylori*. Destructive bacteria produce acids such as lactic and organic acids (volatile fatty acids or VFAs) which lower the pH, inflame the stomach lining (gastritis), cause indigestion, favour the production of more unfriendly bacteria, inhibit HCl production, and delay stomach emptying. A delay in stomach emptying will create more fermentation since the undigested food remains in the stomach for too long. While it is true that excess acid causes heartburn, reflux, and ulcers, it is not the excess HCl levels that are the culprit; rather it is these destructive organic acids produced by fermentation and bad bacteria. Healthy levels of HCl are an absolute necessity for digesting proteins and overall digestion. The resulting soup pot of mal-digested feed, bacteria, and acid – combined with the mechanical overload – can force the mal-digested feed back up into the esophagus in an effort to alleviate the pressure. This reflux causes burning, indigestion and nausea, and ultimately, these continuing cycles of irritation and damage to the stomach lining (mucosa) will eventually create ulcers.

Many more dogs now are also having problems digesting meat protein, usually caused by low HCl levels (hypochlorhydria). Low HCl acid levels can result from nutrient deficiencies, long-term antacid medication, bacteria over-growths, poor diets, excess meat, inappropriate food combinations, and/or stress. Undigested meat lying in the stomach for delayed periods of time can make dogs very uncomfortable with burning, bloating, tightness, nausea, vomiting and much discomfort. Eventually the poorly digested protein will also affect the small and large intestines, and you may see gas, diarrhea and constipation as the result. A leaky gut may also develop.

The common practice of using antacid medication may give temporary relief of burning acids, but over the long-term it will deplete the HCl levels and adversely affect digestive function in the process. The lower the HCl levels, the higher the production of destructive organic acids.

Ulcers are also commonly caused by the overuse of non-steroidal anti-inflammatories which cause a decrease in the production of prostaglandins, substances that protect the stomach and intestinal linings.

Natural Health Program

Diet

- Identify and eliminate any food allergies or intolerances causing irritation and inflammation. Common problem foods include wheat, corn, beef, and fish (and chicken if they have become intolerant to it).

- No wheat, corn gluten, soy and/or legumes.

- No dairy products.

- Use caution with raw meat and organ meat since the HCl levels must be strong to digest these foods.

- Ensure that any meat including raw meat is bacteria-free.

- Don't feed too much food in one meal as this may cause discomfort and bloating.

- Don't feed added fats, and discontinue all fat supplements (e.g. essential fatty acids), for fats will slow down the transit time delaying the emptying of the stomach.

- With acute, challenging, or chronic stomach problems, eliminate all meat protein until their symptoms have improved. Eggs are normally tolerated, but use caution.

- Identify and discontinue any supplements that could be irritating the stomach\

Nutrients

- **folic acid** [*one dose daily*][†]– protein digestion and metabolism, supports the production of HCl, promotes the natural production of probiotics; tissue repair

- **potassium citrate** [*one dose daily*][†]– regulates acidity (pH), eliminates waste, supports normal stomach contractions

Herbal & Home Remedies

- **red wine vinegar** [*feed with meals*][†]– aids protein digestion, aids the relief of heartburn and reflux, contains anti-oxidants to aid digestion

- **aloe vera juice** [one dose daily][†] – supports intestinal membranes and promotes healthy stomach function; relieves heartburn and ulcers

Riva's Remedies

- **Five Herb Digest, herbal blend** [*one dose daily*][†] – soothes indigestion, gas, and bloating; relieves heartburn and reflux; toxicity from meat protein

- **Pro-Dygest, herbal blend** [*one dose daily*][†] – protects healthy stomach membranes in an acidic environment

- **Gastricol, homeopathic** [*one dose twice daily or as needed*][†] – fast-acting relief for gas, bloating, and colic symptoms; liver support

- **Pro-Colon, probiotic** [*one dose daily*][†] – probiotics and prebiotics, supports nutrient absorption and intestinal immunity

[†]See Appendix for recommended dosages and duration for all supplements.

Nausea and Vomiting

Symptoms

Dogs frequently experience nausea, which may or may not cause them to vomit. Vomiting is a good thing from the perspective that it not only helps to empty the stomach of the irritants, but it also alerts the pet parent to a problem with the stomach. Nausea by itself may also be indicated by loss of appetite, drooling, lip-licking, excess salivation, and/or an increase in thirst.

Causes

Diet and food is the most common cause of nausea and vomiting, including recent diet changes, introduction of new foods, an increasing intolerance to the existing diet (most common), and bolting down dry dog food - often a result of poor satiety caused by the feed choice. Other causes include ingestion of a poison including tick/flea control products and medications, parasites (particularly in puppies), supplements that are not agreeing with the dog, and/or motion sickness from riding in cars.

Natural Treatment Program

Diet

- Be cautious of any recent food changes or introduction of new foods, and eliminate any suspected problems.
- If the nausea/vomiting persists, change the existing food and ensure that they are feeling satisfied on their diet and not going hungry.
- Eliminate wheat and corn gluten.
- Don't overfeed; keep meals smaller and more frequent if necessary.
- Don't feed added fats, and discontinue all fat supplements (e.g., essential fatty acids). Fats will slow down the transit time, delaying the emptying of the stomach.

- Identify and discontinue any supplements that could be irritating to the stomach.
- Ensure that drinking water is available at all times to cleanse the stomach and replenish any lost fluids and/or prevent dehydration from vomiting.

Nutrients

- **folic acid** [*one dose daily*][†] - protein digestion and metabolism, supports HCl production, promotes the natural production of probiotics
- **potassium citrate** [*one dose daily*][†] - regulates acidity (pH), eliminates waste, supports stomach contractions

Herbal & Home Remedies

- **ginger, powdered or fresh** [*one dose once or twice daily as needed*][†] - aids nausea and vomiting and relaxes the stomach
- **peppermint, fresh or dried** [*one dose once or twice daily as needed*][†] - digestive stimulant, improves digestion

Riva's Remedies

- **Five Herb Digest, herbal blend** [*one dose once or twice daily as needed*][†] - soothes indigestion and nausea, intestinal detoxification
- **Gastricol, homeopathic** [*one dose twice daily or as needed*][†] - use for nausea, vomiting, and bloating; liver toxicity
- **Calm-aid, homeopathic** [*one dose twice daily or as needed*][†] - promotes calm behaviour in dogs with stress, anxiety, motion sickness and/or a nervous stomach
- **Pro-Colon, probiotic** [*one dose daily*][†] - probiotics, prebiotics, digestive support, maintains a healthy intestinal ecosystem

[†] See Appendix for recommended dosages and duration for all supplements.

Natural Health Programs for Small Colon and Pancreas Health

Malabsorption Syndrome

Symptoms

Malabsorption syndrome is not technically a disease, but rather a condition that results from other intestinal health problems that interfere with efficient digestion and absorption of food. The absorption processes then are not able to absorb specific nutrients from food such as protein, carbohydrates, fats and/or vitamins and minerals. Symptoms can include an increased or voracious appetite, pica (eating non-food substances), coprophagia (eating their own stool), gas, greasy stools and/or weight loss.

Causes

Malabsorption syndrome can be caused by bacterial, viral or parasitic infections as well as IBD (inflammatory bowel disease), and/or EPI (exocrine pancreatic insufficiency). EPI is commonly found in German Shepherds but can occur in other breeds as well. EPI is the inability of the pancreas to secrete the digestive enzymes necessary to digest all food. Eventually the body becomes deprived of the nutrients needed for growth, repair, and metabolism. Ongoing or chronic indigestion can also result in overgrowths of unfriendly bacteria and/or yeast as the intestinal ecosystem becomes unbalanced from the over-fermentation of mal-digested food.

Natural Health Program

For bacterial and/or viral infections or IBD follow Treatments for Small Intestine Diarrhea.

Exocrine Pancreas Insufficiency:

Diet

- If you were feeding cooked meat, go with raw food.
- If you were feeding raw, go with cooked food, preferably homemade.
- If you were feeding grains, go with grain-free.
- If you were feeding all meat, go vegetarian.
- No beef, bison, pork or venison.
- No raw bones – meaty or not.
- No wheat or corn gluten.
- No dairy products.
- No excess fats; and no canola, vegetable, or coconut oils whatsoever.

Nutrients

- **digestive enzymes** [*feed with each meal*]† – digests food groups and improves nutrient absorption – Note that vegetarian digestive enzymes can be used if the dog is sensitive to enzymes containing animal products including pancreatin.
- **folic acid** [*one dose daily*]† – protein digestion and metabolism; supports intestinal immunity, promotes the natural production of probiotics
- **vitamin B12** [*one dose daily*]†* – immunity; supports intestinal ecosystem and energy levels; liver detoxifier
- **vitamin E** [*one dose daily*]†* – aids circulation, fat metabolism; benefits immunity and supports muscle function

Herbal & Home Remedies

- **aloe vera juice** [*one dose daily*]† – nutrition, anti-inflammatory, enzyme activity, nutrient absorption; supports the intestinal immune system

Riva's Remedies

- **Pro-Colon, probiotic** [*one dose daily for 3 to 4 weeks or longer if needed*]† – probiotics and prebiotics, intestinal support; discourages the growth of unfriendly bacteria and yeast, absorption of nutrients, promotes a healthy intestinal immune system
- **Digestive Drops, homeopathic** [*one dose twice daily for 7 to 10 days*]† – healthy digestion and nutrient absorption
- **Detox Dog herbal blend** – [*one dose daily*] – colon, liver and kidney support. Natural detoxifier
- **Happy Pets or Happy Pets Senior, herbal blend** [*one dose daily for maximum nutrition*]† – plant-based source

of over 65 minerals, vitamins, and anti-oxidants; highly absorbable superior nutrients for coat, skin, immunity, and all body functions

†See Appendix for recommended dosages and duration for all supplements.
*Also available as a Riva's Remedy

Lymphangiectasia

Symptoms

Any fat particles that are too large for absorption directly through the villi will pass through the lacteals (also found in the villi) into a lymph vessel for transport to the liver. These fats will mix with lymph fluid to form chyle, and the lacteals will turn white when they fill up with fats. Lymphangiectasia occurs when the lymph vessels become inflamed and then enlarge and dilate. Eventually the lymph fluid will be obstructed, and the lacteals may rupture and spill their contents – lymph fluid, inflammatory toxins, undigested fats and proteins – back into the small intestine. However, the small intestine may not be able to reabsorb the contents including the nutrients. At this point, one of the primary problems is that proteins are either not absorbed or are eliminated before digestion, and the dog may become malnourished and protein deficient. This is known as protein-losing enteropathy, which simply means that proteins are being lost including albumin, antibodies, certain enzymes, and blood-clotting proteins.

In addition, any time that the lymph system becomes congested, the intestinal immune system is adversely affected and unable to efficiently protect the intestines from other toxins and pathogens.

Symptoms may include vomiting, diarrhea, gas, weight loss, fatigue, abdominal fluid, and sometimes fluid build-up in the chest which can affect breathing. Blood tests will show a low lymphocyte count, low cholesterol levels, and low albumin. Albumin is the protein produced by the liver that acts as a carrier for important biochemicals in the body. Albumin also acts to prevent water from leaking out of the tissues.

Causes

Any kind of malabsorption due to chronic inflammation in the intestines, including the lacteals and the lymph system, are due to diet, nutrient deficiencies, depleted probiotics, pathogens and sluggish peristalsis (the wave-like muscle contractions that move food through the digestive tract). Lymph fluid flows within the intestines and travels throughout the body due to muscular activity, it is not pumped (like blood by the heart). It is likely that either IBD (Inflammatory Bowel Disease) or IBS (Irritable Bowel Syndrome) is present, which predisposes the intestines to further problems including lymph problems. As well, all fat digestion relies on adequate levels of bile, which is produced by the liver then stored in and released by the gallbladder. Bile is necessary for emulsifying all the fats and oils in the small intestine.

Natural Health Program

Diet

- Identify any food allergies/intolerances, for these are a common cause of chronic inflammation and malabsorption. Food intolerances can also include any staple food such as beef, chicken, and/or rice for example.

- No added oils of any kind nor commercial dog food containing *these* oils: canola, vegetable, sunflower, safflower, flax, hemp, soy, fish, olive or coconut. Inappropriate or excess oils can congest the liver, impede bile flow, and plug the lacteals. Note that even though coconut oil is a medium-chain triglyceride and, therefore, easier to absorb, it is still not part of the natural canine food chain.

- No fish of any kind.

- Rely on the natural saturated fats from poultry, lamb, and/or eggs, but keep the saturated fats low as well until healed.

- No wheat and corn gluten.

- No dairy products.

- Identify and discontinue any supplements that could be causing intestinal inflammation and irritation.

Nutrients

- **folic acid** [*one dose daily*]† – aids protein digestion, supports intestinal immune system and tissue repair, promotes the natural production of probiotics

- **vitamin B12** [*one dose daily*]†* – balances colon ecosystem; nutrition for diarrhea; supports liver function

- **vitamin C** [*one dose daily*]†* – supports immunity, promotes a healthy lymphatic system; liver support

- **potassium citrate** [*one dose daily*]† – regulates water levels, helps to eliminate intestinal waste, and aids protein digestion

Herbal & Home Remedies

- **dandelion root, tincture** [*one dose once or twice daily*]† – stimulates bile flow, aids liver function; digestive aid

Riva's Remedies

- **Pro-Colon, probiotic** [*one dose daily for 3 to 4 weeks, or longer if needed*]† – probiotics and prebiotics for optimum digestion; improves absorption of nutrients, aids intestinal immune system
- **Detox Dog herbal blend** – [*one dose daily*] – colon, liver and kidney support; natural detoxifier and immune support
- **Digestive Drops, homeopathic** [*one dose twice daily for 7 to 10 days*]† – promotes healthy digestion, liver support; maintains healthy function of the lymph system
- **Gastricol, homeopathic** [*one dose twice daily or as needed*]† – formulated to promote the elimination of toxins and poisons; relieves bloating and gas

†See Appendix for recommended dosages and duration for all supplements.
*Also available as a Riva's Remedy

Pancreatitis

Symptoms

Pancreatitis means that the pancreas is inflamed as caused by prematurely activated enzymes. Or conversely, the pancreas becomes inflamed, which then causes the enzymes to behave abnormally. Normally, pancreatic enzymes are inactive until they reach the small intestine. In pancreatitis, the enzymes are activated while they are still in the pancreas, and they start to "digest" and irritate the pancreas (instead of food) causing pain and more inflammation. Repeated bouts can cause more serious damage to the pancreas with the formation of scar tissue, which adversely affects its ability to produce enzymes and/or insulin, resulting in blood sugar abnormalities.

Symptoms of acute pancreatitis may come on suddenly (even though it has been in the development stage before hitting the crisis point) and can range from acute to severe with a lack of appetite, vomiting, fatigue, and a painful abdomen and/or a "hunched" up posture. Suffering animals will also usually appear weak or listless and may have a fever. Pancreatitis can also present as a chronic condition whereby the symptoms are milder or even absent but could also include a "greasy" stool and depression.

Causes

The primary cause of pancreatitis is diet. Whereas pancreatitis is typically thought to be caused by a high fat diet, it can also be caused by a number of dietary other imbalances: high fat, unhealthy fats, high carbohydrates (grains), excessive protein, and/or any foods that are irritating and difficult to digest. Over time, the repeated demands on the pancreas to digest problematic foods will cause irritation and inflammation. Older overweight dogs are most at risk not always because they are eating more fat (although they might be) but because the pancreas has been adversely affected over the years by one or more of the aforementioned food groups.

Natural Health Program

Diet

- In the acute phase, don't feed any solid food for 2 to 3 days. You may offer clean water or strained soup broth. A short fast helps take the load off the pancreas to reduce inflammation.
- Introduce foods one food at a time, starting with vegetable soup and/or cooked vegetables.
- Analyze the current diet and determine where the excesses are; a diet high in grains should go grain-free, a high-fat diet should go low-fat, a high-protein diet should go low protein.
- Don't feed grains and meat proteins in the same meal.
- Try to feed as much organic food as possible.
- Feed as many cooked vegetables and vegetable soups as your dog will eat.
- Some dogs may have to go on a low-fat, vegetarian cleanse to restore pancreatic function and reduce inflammation.
- No added fats other than naturally occurring fats in the diet.

- No canola, vegetable, soy, or coconut oil.

- No beef, bison, pork, venison, lamb, or duck.

- No wheat or corn gluten.

- No dairy products.

- No processed food or kibble.

- No artificial additives, flavourings, or chemicals.

Nutrients

- **folic acid** [*one dose daily*]† – protein digestion and metabolism; supports intestinal immune system, aids the natural production of probiotics

- **vitamin B12** [*one dose daily*]†* – immunity; supports intestinal ecosystem, maintains energy levels

- **digestive enzymes** [*feed with each meal*]† – helps to digest various food groups, improves nutrient absorption, and relieves the pancreas. Vegetarian digestive enzymes can be used if the dog is sensitive to enzymes containing animal products including pancreatin

Herbal & Home Remedies

- **dandelion root, tincture or dried leaf** [*one dose twice daily*]† – improves bile flow, aids the release of pancreatic enzymes, and acts as a digestive stimulant

Riva's Remedies

- **Gastricol, homeopathic** [*one dose twice daily for 7 to 10 days*]† – supports digestive processes, relieves discomfort; supports healthy pancreas function

- **Five Herb Digest, herbal blend** [*one dose once or twice daily as needed*]† – calms and soothes digestion, supports healthy function of pancreatic enzymes

†See Appendix for recommended dosages and duration for all supplements.
*Also available as a Riva's Remedy

Health Programs for Intestinal Health

〰〰〰〰〰〰〰〰〰〰 ❧ 〰〰〰〰〰〰〰〰〰〰

Diarrhea – Inflammatory Bowel Disease and Irritable Bowel Syndrome

Symptoms

Diarrhea means that a dog is passing liquid and/or loose stools and is passing stool more often than normal. Most dogs have had diarrhea at least once in their lives, but for some it can either be a long-term problem or a reoccurring one. Diarrhea is the most common intestinal symptom and can indicate that there are problems in either the small intestine or the large intestine; however, each one can have different causes.

A problem in the small intestine results in a larger volume of stool with approximately 3 to 4 bowel movements per day. There can be excess gas rumbling in the belly, and if the small intestine is bleeding, the blood will show up as black in the stool. Very often there is a foul odor to it and there can be an increase in gas. There is normally no straining or difficulty in passing stool. Chronic diarrhea originating in the small intestine can

result in dehydration, listlessness, depression and weight loss as they cannot absorb important nutrients.

Diarrhea caused by a problem in the large intestine also has an increase of volume in stool passed as well as an increase in frequency – often up to 5 or more times per day. Any blood in the stool will usually be red, and the stool frequently has mucus in it. There is usually no straining and no weight loss although the dog can become dehydrated, thirsty, tired and sometimes depressed. There can be bloating with the passage of gas.

Bacterial infections can cause a fever; however, viruses often do not. Intestinal infections can range from a mild case with complete recovery within 2 to 3 days to more serious cases that can linger for 2 to 3 weeks or longer if the treatment program isn't working.

Causes

There are a variety of common causes of small intestine diarrhea including infections, parasites, yeast, ingestion of toxins or poisons, eating rotten food, food allergies/intolerances, and/or reactions to medication. All of these can cause chronic intestinal inflammation often referred to as IBD (inflammatory bowel disease) with diarrhea and/or gas. Many dogs are diagnosed with IBD although it is mostly caused by an allergic reaction to food or a reaction to bacteria, yeast, and/or parasites. IBD is also often referred to as IBS (irritable bowel syndrome) in the large colon; however, both names are important sounding labels that simply mean that the intestines are irritated and inflamed – which we already know. Chronic inflammation in the small intestine interferes with enzyme production thus forcing mal-digested food into the colon, eventually resulting in leaky gut as well.

Infections of the small intestine is known as enteritis, which is a term used to describe infections as caused by bacteria and viruses. Viruses include parvovirus, coronavirus, rotavirus and distemper. Bacteria include *Salmonella*, *E. coli*, *clostridia* and *Campylobacter* and can also inhabit the large intestine (see Food Poisoning below). Diarrhea of large intestinal origin is also caused by food intolerances and infections of unfriendly viruses and/or parasites.

Undiagnosed yeast overgrowths are often treated as infections with antibiotics. The antibiotics work for a short time only to be followed by a repeat of the same symptoms at which point the antibiotics may be repeated again. Some of these dogs are prescribed two or three courses or more of antibiotics with no lasting relief – in fact symptoms can exacerbate because the levels of yeast continue to increase due to the medication.

Diarrhea of all kinds can also be caused by a hyper (overactive) thyroid or by pancreatitis.

Natural Health Program

Diet

- For cases of severe diarrhea or cases that last longer than a couple of days, discontinue the regular diet.

- Offer small amounts of cooked brown rice, cooked pumpkin, cooked sweet potatoes and/or soup broth (no meat or bones in the broth). However, if the dog prefers not to eat anything, it is perfectly safe and even beneficial for them to "fast" for 2 or 3 days.

- Once the diarrhea stops, introduce one food at a time instead of a mix of foods such as might be found in dry kibble for example. This way you can determine what your dog can and cannot tolerate. Increase quantities of food slowly.

- Eliminate wheat and corn gluten permanently.

- Be mindful of any food allergies/intolerances as these are a common cause of IBD/IBS and can include any staple in their diet such as beef, chicken, fish and/or rice for example.

- Eliminate all food additives, flavourings, and preservatives as commonly found in commercial dog treats.

- No dairy products.

- No legumes.

- Identify and discontinue any supplements that could be causing intestinal inflammation and irritation.

- Ensure that drinking water is always available to replenish lost fluids and prevent dehydration, which is a serious concern if the diarrhea persists.

Nutrients

- **folic acid** [*one dose daily*][†] – supports intestinal immune system, aids the natural production of probiotics, tissue repair, parasite resistance

- **vitamin B12** [*one dose daily*][†*] – supports a healthy colon ecosystem and liver function; can be depleted with diarrhea

- **iodine, liquid** [*one dose daily*][†] – bacteria and yeast, supports immune system

- **potassium citrate** [*one dose daily*][†] – regulates water levels, balances pH, eliminates waste, and aids digestion

Herbal and Home Remedies

- **grapefruit seed extract** [*one dose daily for one month*][†] – bacteria and yeast; supports normal digestive function

- **psyllium seed** [*one dose daily*][†] – extra fibre, absorbs excess water

Riva's Remedies

- **Pro-Colon, probiotics** [*one dose daily for 3 to 4 weeks or longer if needed*][†] – probiotics and prebiotics for intestinal support; discourages the growth of unfriendly bacteria and viruses, improves absorption of nutrients, and aids intestinal immune system

- **Pro-Dygest, herbal blend** [*one dose daily for 4 to 6 weeks*]† – intestinal detoxifier and cleanser; protects intestinal membranes; supports healthy colon function

- **Para+Plus, tincture** [*one dose daily for 3 to 4 weeks*]† – bacteria, yeast and parasites; promotes healthy liver function

- **Detox Dog, herbal blend** [*one dose daily for 4 to 6 weeks*] – promotes the detoxification of elimination organs: skin, liver, kidneys and colon. Supports the immune system.

- **Infection Drops, homeopathic** [*one dose twice daily for 3 to 4 days*]† – for symptoms of diarrhea due to intestinal infections

- **Digestive Drops, homeopathic** [*one dose, twice daily for 7 to 10 days*]† – chronic diarrhea, promotes healthy digestion and nutrient absorption

- **Gastricol, homeopathic** [*one dose twice daily or as needed*]† – liver toxicity; relieves bloating, gas, and colic

†See Appendix for recommended dosages and duration for all supplements.
*Also available as a Riva's Remedy

Food Poisoning - Acute

Symptoms

Despite the fact that a dog, as a carnivore, has very strong stomach acids and natural antibiotics in the saliva which kills off many more bacteria and toxins than the stomach of an herbivore, dogs can still ingest enough bacteria by eating rotten food and meat, raw meat, raw eggs, carrion, compost, and/or garbage to overwhelm this built-in protective mechanism. Many dogs are not very selective – especially if they are not satisfied with their current diet – and will wolf almost anything down. If a dog ingests more bacteria than it can kill, food poisoning can result with symptoms showing up within a few hours after ingestion. Diarrhea is almost always present because the bacteria produces toxins which adversely affects or damages the intestinal walls causing excess fluids to leak into the intestine. Other symptoms vary and depend on the type of bacteria involved, but can include vomiting, diarrhea, blood or mucus in the stool, abdominal pain, poor or no appetite, dehydration through fluid loss from diarrhea and vomiting, fatigue, and/or fever. Because bacteria also produce endotoxins, the liver will work harder to detoxify the entire body.

Causes

Common strains of intestinal bacteria responsible for food poisoning include *E. coli*, *Clostridium* and *Salmonella*. *Salmonella* is one of the most common bacteria in food poisoning cases and is often ingested through raw meat, particularly chicken, or raw eggs. Symptoms appear within 6 to 72 hours with a high fever, nausea, vomiting and diarrhea. And while the dogs can get very ill with *Salmonella*, it is not usually fatal.

Dog most predisposed to bacterial poisoning include young dogs, senior dogs, and/or any dog with a compromised digestive or immune system. However, the most significant risk factor is the health of the digestive and intestinal system including the intestinal immune system. If the stomach acid levels are low and/or the intestinal probiotic levels are depleted – as is the case with dogs who have been on or *are* on antibiotics or steroids – the ability to resist pathogens is weakened. For example, 80 percent of all dogs harbor *Clostridium perfringens* whether they have diarrhea or not, thus the majority of dogs remain unaffected by the presence of this bacteria. This is also the case with other bacteria as well including *E. coli* and *Salmonella* – the intestinal ecosystem is not *meant* to be sterile but the organisms should always be in balance. Overgrowths of pathogens, acids, and toxins can cripple the intestinal immune system and damage the permeability of the intestinal membranes resulting in leaky gut which then allows all colon toxins to migrate into other tissues and body systems, resulting in further health problems.

Reactions to mycotoxins from moldy foods can occur as well but these reactions are not very common.

Natural Health Program

Diet

- Offer small amounts of cooked pumpkin, cooked sweet potatoes, and/or soup broth (no meat or bones in the broth). However, if the dog prefers not to eat anything it is perfectly safe and even beneficial for them to fast for 2 or 3 days.

- No fats, meat or dairy products.

- Ensure that drinking water is always available to replenish lost fluids and prevent dehydration, which is a concern if the diarrhea persists.

Nutrients

- **folic acid** [*one dose daily*]† – supports intestinal immune system, aids the natural production of probiotics; promotes tissue repair; parasite resistance

- **vitamin B12** [*one dose daily*]†* – promotes a healthy colon ecosystem; B12 can be depleted with diarrhea, promotes healthy appetite

- **iodine, liquid** [*one dose daily*]† – bacteria and yeast; supports immunity

- **potassium citrate** [*one dose daily*]† – balances pH, promotes the elimination of waste products, aids protein digestion

Herbal & Home Remedies

- **arsenicum 30C, homeopathic** [*one dose (3 pellets) twice daily for 3 to 4 days or sooner if symptoms disappear*] – give pellets directly into a clean mouth without food; symptoms of unhealthy bacteria from meat including diarrhea, weakness, thirst, nausea and vomiting, restlessness, and anxiety.

Riva's Remedies

- **Pro-Colon, probiotic** [*one dose daily for 3 to 4 weeks after symptoms disappear*]† – probiotics and prebiotics for intestinal support; discourages the growth of unfriendly bacteria, supports a healthy intestinal immune system

- **Pro-Dygest, herbal blend** [*one dose daily for 3 to 4 weeks after symptoms disappear*]† –colon cleanser and detoxifier; protects intestinal membranes from toxicity

- **Para+Plus, tincture** [*one dose daily for 2 weeks*]† –bacteria and yeast, supports immunity and healthy liver function

- **Detox Dog, herbal blend** [*one dose daily for 4 to 6 weeks*] – promotes the detoxification of elimination organs: skin, liver, kidneys and colon. Supports the immune system.

- **Gastricol, homeopathic** [*one dose twice daily or as needed*]† –liver toxicity; relieves bloating, gas, and colic

- **Infection Drops, homeopathic** [*one dose twice daily for 3 to 4 days*]† – acute diarrhea due to intestinal bacteria

†See Appendix for recommended dosages and duration for all supplements.
*Also available as a Riva's Remedy

NOTE: To ensure a complete recovery of the intestinal membranes and to re-balance the colonic ecosystem the residual toxicity from a case of food poisoning should be addressed as well. Therefore, continue with folic acid, vitamin B12, Pro-Colon, and Pro-Dygest for up to one month afterward – or longer if your dog is demonstrating benefit.

Natural Health Programs for Large Colon Health

Constipation, Gas, and Bloating

Symptoms

Constipation occurs when dogs are having difficulty or are straining to pass stool or if they are passing stool too infrequently - less than once every day. The stool may also appear as dry and hard, darker in colour or be abnormally shaped, e.g., pencil-shaped, pellets or pieces smaller than normal. A dry stool means that the transit time is slow and that the feces is being held for too long with too much water absorbed. If constipation continues, the colon will become increasingly toxic as food waste ferments in the colon rather than being eliminated. Colon toxicity attracts more bacteria, viruses, yeast and parasites. Constipation can also be accompanied by bloating and gas and unusual crouching postures. Some dogs with digestive discomfort will groan in their sleep.

Causes

Most cases of constipation are due to the diet. A lack of fibre can be a contributor, but it is also commonly caused by the inability to digest certain foods - constipation is a common symptom of food intolerances, either a particular meat or a grain. Dogs must also be drinking enough water to keep the stool hydrated for easy passage. Sometimes constipation is caused by the ingestion of foreign objects such as stones, wood or plastic or from specific injuries. Constipation can be a side effect of medication and can also be an indicator of low thyroid function. Gas, bloating, and feelings of "over-fullness" can also be caused by eating too much, especially in one meal.

Natural Health Program

Diet

- No corn gluten, wheat, soy or excess grains.
- No legumes.
- No dairy products.
- No raw bones.
- Be alert to food intolerances – often found in foods that the dog has been eating for a long time without a break such as chicken, beef, corn, wheat and/or rice.
- Switch from dry kibble if necessary to raw, homemade or canned since dry kibble has very little moisture.
- Ensure clean drinking water that tastes good.
- Increase fibre intake by adding more vegetables including pumpkin, potatoes, and sweet potatoes with the skin on. Cooked barley is well tolerated by many dogs as well.
- Don't overfeed your dog by portioning out too much food in one meal.

Nutrients

- **folic acid** [*one dose daily*]† – supports digestion and the intestinal immune system, promotes the natural production of probiotics
- **vitamin B12** [*one dose daily*]†* – balances colon ecosystem, supports metabolism and liver function
- **iodine, liquid** [*one dose daily*]† – thyroid nutrient, supports metabolism and symptoms from bacteria and yeast

Herbal & Home Remedies

- **flaxseed oil** or **light olive oil** [*one dose daily*]† – natural intestinal lubricant, natural anti-inflammatory

NOTE: Don't use laxatives of any kind since these do not address the underlying problem and can irritate the colon.

Riva's Remedies

- **Pro-Colon, probiotic** [*one dose daily as needed*]†

– probiotics and prebiotics for intestinal support; discourages the growth of unfriendly bacteria and viruses, supports absorption of nutrients and a healthy intestinal immune system
- **Pro-Dygest, herbal blend** [*one dose daily as needed*]† – constipation relief, colon cleanser, added fibre
- **Digestive Drops, homeopathic** [*one dose daily for 7 to 10 days*]† – for constipation or diarrhea; supports nutrient absorption and overall digestion
- **Gastricol, homeopathic** [*one dose 2 to 3 times daily as needed*]† – gas, bloating, intestinal discomfort, and colic; liver toxicity

†See Appendix for recommended dosages and duration for all supplements.
*Also available as a Riva's Remedy

Leaky Gut

Symptoms

Leaky gut (cecal acidosis) is a condition which results from the toxic by-products of food digestion and can be considered an epidemic among dogs (and their people). Any foods that are mal-digested will produce fermentative acids, toxins, heat, and pathogenic bacteria, all of which eventually damage the colon membranes. These damaged membranes then become overly permeable, allowing the acids, toxins and mal-digested food proteins to leak through the membranes and migrate into the general body, resulting in a process known as auto-intoxication. This toxicity originating from the colon frequently damages or interferes with the normal physiological function of organs and body systems. Skin conditions, fatigue, immune problems, increased incidence of food allergies, liver toxicity, and joint pain are common conditions associated with leaky gut. Colon toxins also affect brain chemistry and can, therefore, exacerbate behavioural issues such as depression, anxiety, and hyperactivity. Digestive symptoms such as gas, bloating, and diarrhea can also be present, but leaky gut can intoxicate the body without digestive problems being present.

———— ❧ ————

Leaky gut is a condition which results from the toxic by-products of food digestion and can be considered an epidemic among dogs.

————————

Causes

Poor digestion, hard-to-digest foods, and repeated antibiotic or steroid prescriptions are the most common problems contributing to leaky gut. Food culprits are usually wheat, corn, and white rice and/or soy products. These carbohydrates should be completely and efficiently digested in the small intestine, and any food material which is not thoroughly digested there will pass into the large colon where it will ferment releasing excessive amounts of hydrogen, carbon dioxide, and methane gases which damage the intestinal membranes. The resulting imbalance in the colon ecosystem creates an environment of acids and toxins that kill off friendly bacteria (probiotics) which subsequently encourages the growth of unfriendly bacteria, yeas, and parasites. In addition, probiotics are required to protect the intestinal membranes from damage.

Poorly digested meat can also cause colon toxicity, whereby excess protein is fermented in the colon producing ammonia, amines, phenols and sulfides. These are highly toxic chemicals that intoxicate the colon and stress the liver and kidneys.

In addition, all the blood supply from the colon is passed through the liver for detoxification, therefore, the more toxic the colon, the harder the liver must work. A toxic colon = a toxic liver.

Natural Health Program

Diet

- No corn gluten, wheat, white rice, soy or excess grains.
- No legumes.
- No dairy products.
- Senior dogs should decrease overall meat consumption
- Increase fibre intake by adding cooked vegetables including leafy greens, carrots, beets, peas, potatoes, sweet potatoes, vegetable soups and stews. Fibre is a very effective detoxifier, and nutrient-dense vegetables contain a number of compounds that soothe and heal the intestinal membranes.

Nutrients

- **folic acid** [one dose daily]† – promotes a healthy digestive system, supports intestinal immunity, promotes the natural production of probiotics; tissue repair
- **vitamin B12** [one dose daily]†* – balances the intestinal ecosystem and supports liver function; metabolism

Herbal & Home Remedies

- aloe vera juice [once daily for 2 to 3 weeks]† – excellent for intestinal membranes; aids digestion – NOTE: in rare cases aloe vera can cause diarrhea, in which case it should be stopped

Riva's Remedies

- **Pro-Colon, probiotic** [one dose daily for 3 to 4 weeks]† – probiotics and prebiotics for intestinal support; discourages the growth of unfriendly bacteria and viruses, supports absorption of nutrients and a healthy intestinal immune system
- **Pro-Dygest, herbal blend** [one dose daily for 3 to 4 weeks]† – colon cleanser and detoxifier; soothes intestinal membranes; maintains a healthy digestive system
- **Detox Dog, herbal blend** [one dose daily for 4 to 6 weeks] – promotes the detoxification of elimination organs: skin, liver, kidneys and colon; supports the immune system

†See Appendix for recommended dosages and duration for all supplements.
*Also available as a Riva's Remedy

Parasites

There are a variety of parasites which affect dogs. Parasites do their damage by interfering with digestive function, robbing the host of nutrients, depressing the immune system, and intoxicating the system by excreting waste products and toxic chemicals such as ammonia, which affect the liver, kidneys and brain function.

Symptoms

Symptoms of parasitic infection can range from none whatsoever to mild to gravely ill. Common observable symptoms are: diarrhea, vomiting, pot bellies, coughing, increased appetite, weight loss, dull hair coat, fatigue, anxiety, and lack of focus and/or poor immunity. Other symptoms include heart abnormalities and anemia which further depresses the immune system predisposing them to more infections – parasites or otherwise. Symptoms can be a result of encysted larvae and/or adult worms.

Causes

Common parasites affecting dogs include: roundworms, hookworms, whipworms, and tapeworms. Dogs do not contract pinworms.

Roundworms (ascarids) are the most common, especially in puppies. They are round, white to light brown and can be up to 13 centimetres long. Adult dogs ingest larvae from contaminated soil or from infected mice or other small mammals. Roundworms eggs are protected by a hard shell and can, therefore, exist in the soil several years. Puppies can be born with roundworms if the larvae cross the placenta before birth. Nursing puppies can also ingest the larvae from milk. Puppies will have a pot-bellied appearance and poor growth. Roundworms live in the intestines and consume the food that the dog eats. Larvae can encyst to the liver and can also travel to the lungs causing respiratory symptoms and are then coughed up and/or swallowed again where they hatch out in the intestines. Roundworms can be seen in stool or vomit.

Hookworms are smaller than roundworms and are not usually seen in the stool or the vomit. The hookworm lives in the intestines and attaches itself to the intestinal membranes with sharp teeth and suck the host's blood resulting in blood loss and anemia. They live and reproduce in the small intestine and, like roundworms, can encyst to the liver and/or travel to the lungs. Adult dogs can ingest or contact contaminated soil whereby the larvae can burrow through the skin or feet. Hookworms are also passed to puppies through nursing. Hookworms can be a common cause of illness in older dogs, resulting in low energy levels, weakness, poor immunity and weight loss. Unfortunately, we often erroneously blame these symptoms on old age.

Whipworms are wide at one end and taper off to a narrow head. They live in the large intestine where they bite the intestinal membranes and suck the host's blood. They can cause bloody diarrhea in the dog but anemia is not as common as with hookworms. Whipworms are even smaller than roundworms and are also not often seen in the stool. However, the stool can be covered in mucus. Whipworms are also contracted from soil where they can lay dormant for years until consumed by a host. Whipworms can cause intermittent diarrhea and weight loss. They are difficult to detect in the stool since they shed very few eggs.

Tapeworms are long, flat worms that can grow up to 10 to 15 centimetres in length and attach themselves to the small intestine of the host. They consist of multiple segments that grow onto the head and neck of the worm. Each segment has a reproductive section. Dogs get tapeworms from ingesting fleas or eating animals such as rodents that are infested with fleas since tapeworm eggs develop inside the fleas. Tapeworm infections do not commonly cause observable symptoms but can appear as flat, rice-like segments around the anus. The tapeworm itself is still inside the intestines since it is not shed into the stool.

Heartworms are a variety of roundworm that are only spread by mosquitos, but not *all* mosquitos – only certain female mosquitos and under very specific conditions. The larvae slowly mature into worms as they migrate from the muscles to the pulmonary artery, heart, and lungs, a process which can take up 6 to 8 months. The heartworm lifecycle is very much dependent on temperature whereby the temperature has to be above 27°C (80°F) for over two weeks and over 14°C (57°F) for over six weeks. Thus, the only areas with a high incidence of heartworm is Florida and parts of Texas and Hawaii. And despite the hot temperatures in the Okanagan Valley in British Columbia the incidence of heartworm is extremely low. Symptoms may not appear for months until the heart is infected and can include coughing, fatigue, shortness of breath and poor immunity.

Detection

Roundworm and hookworm are detected by a fecal flotation test where the eggs can be observed and counted. However, the fecal flotation is not a reliable test for either whipworms or tapeworm nor for encysted larvae. Encysted larvae are larvae that have migrated to other organs and encapsulated. Larvae can migrate to any other tissues or organs where they encapsulate themselves until they hatch into adult worms.

The common test to detect heartworms involves checking a blood sample for worm protein; however, there is also a DNA test now available which is more accurate. If your dog lives in a high-risk area test for heartworms every 3 to 4 months. But do *not* be duped into giving your dog monthly preventative drugs for a lifetime. Despite the fear-mongering by the pharmaceutical industry, heartworms have a low incidence of killing dogs. But the drug industry has marketed to thousands of veterinarians (and, therefore, *millions* of dog owners) to convince them that all healthy dogs are at risk – even in low-risk areas – unless they use preventative medication. And this so-called preventative medication is the same as the treatment medication that is used on horses as a chemical dewormer. It is an insecticide that kills larvae and has multiple side effects including digestive symptoms and skin reactions.

As with all intestinal diseases the best treatment of all parasites is prevention. Weaker, unhealthy dogs attract illness and parasites while healthy dogs with strong digestion and a strong immune system have a much greater resistance to all pathogens and parasites. A healthy intestinal immune system can destroy parasitic larvae, including heartworm larvae, before they hatch out into mature worms and/or migrate into other organs. Research has also shown that a healthy colon ecosystem with healthy levels of probiotics can influence the lifespan of intestinal worms.

Natural Health Program

Diet

- No wheat or corn gluten.
- Ensure that all meat is "clean" and free of bacteria and other contaminants.
- Be mindful of any food allergies/intolerances present in the diet that are continually weakening the digestive system and/or immune system which predisposes them to and attracts parasite loads.
- Add fresh vegetables every day for extra fibre and roughage. Many vegetables are also a natural prebiotic – prebiotics help to produce more probiotics.

Nutrients

- **folic acid** [*one dose daily*]† – supports intestinal immune system, promotes the natural production of probiotics; tissue repair; parasite resistance
- **iodine, liquid** [*one dose daily*]† – bacteria and parasites; supports immune system and colon function
- **vitamin B12** [*one dose daily*]†* – anemia, colon and liver support; energy and immunity
- **vitamin C (ascorbic acid)** [*one dose daily*] †* – intestinal parasite resistance; immune nutrient; liver support
- **Iron-Up (iron gluconate)** [*one dose daily*]†* – anemia; support for immune system, circulation and energy

Herbal & Home Remedies

- **red wine vinegar** [*one dose once or twice daily with meals*]† – helps to acidify the intestines thus discouraging parasites; aids protein digestion
- **black walnut hulls, tincture** [*once daily for 3 to 4 weeks*]† – natural anti-parasitic
- **pumpkin seeds, crushed** [*one teaspoon for every 4.5 kilograms of bodyweight*]† – natural anti-parasitic, source of fibre and essential fatty acids

Riva's Remedies

- **Para+Plus, tincture** [*one dose daily for 3 to 4 weeks*]† – bacteria, yeast and parasites; natural detoxifier, supports liver function and immunity
- **Pro-Colon, probiotic** [*one dose daily for 3 to 4 weeks*]† – probiotics and prebiotics for intestinal support; discourages the growth of unfriendly bacteria and viruses, supports absorption of nutrients and a healthy intestinal immune system
- **Pro-Dygest, herbal blend** [*one dose daily for 3 to 4 weeks*]† – supports intestinal membranes; intestinal cleanser and detoxifier
- **Detox Dog, herbal blend** [*one dose daily for 4-6 weeks*] – promotes the detoxification of elimination organs: skin, liver, kidneys and colon; supports the immune system.

†See Appendix for recommended dosages and duration for all supplements.
*Also available as a Riva's Remedy

NOTE: The de-worming of encysted larvae and/or an abnormally heavy load of parasites may require chemical de-wormers since larvae which have encysted to other organs and tissues can be very resilient and tenacious. For encysted larvae, it is best to use between 2 to 4 small dosages of chemicals every 4 to 7 days rather than one large dose used once.

Anal Gland Impaction

Symptoms

Two anal glands are located at the anal opening, one sac on each side. They are small nut-sized glands that produce a pungent or strong smelling yellow-brown fluid. When feces are passed through the anus, the glands are squeezed from the pressure and the fluid is released. Fluid can also be released when a dog is marking territory, identifying herself to other dogs or when experiencing acute anxiety. Anal gland fluid also aids the body in releasing toxins.

Problems occur when the anal sac fluid thickens and then become impacted at which point they do not drain during a bowel movement. If the anal sacs remain impacted for too long, the toxicity attracts overgrowth of bacteria leading to an infection. Eventually, an abscess may form in an effort to contain the toxicity, pus, and infection, at which point it becomes inflamed and painful. The abscess may rupture which then releases the foul smelling toxic fluid.

Dogs will lick the anus, strain to poop, or scoot along the floor in attempt to relieve the discomfort or pressure.

Causes

Anal gland impactions are mostly caused by an inappropriate and/or toxic diet - low fibre, too much meat, and specific food intolerances; all of which may cause constipation and/or chronic inflammatory reactions in the anal glands. Smaller dog breeds, such as Chihuahuas and poodles, seem more prone to anal gland problems. Impactions are also seen more commonly with overweight dogs, too little exercise, and dogs with a soft stool or diarrhea - since there is not enough fecal pressure to push the fluid out. For overweight dogs the anal glands are pressed into fat tissue making it more difficult for them to empty naturally.

Natural Health Program

Diet

- No wheat or corn gluten.
- Identify any food allergies/intolerances present in the diet that could contribute to chronic inflammation. These foods can include chicken, beef, fish or rice for example.
- If the dog is on a high protein diet, reduce the meat and add more fibre. Senior dogs may have to eliminate meat completely. If the dog is eating a lot of grains, reduce the grains, and increase the protein.
- Eliminate bones and/or calcium supplements.
- Add more fresh vegetables and healthy cooked grains such as barley and oatmeal for extra fibre and roughage and to bulk up a soft stool if necessary.

Nutrients

- **folic acid** [*one dose daily*]† - supports intestinal immune system and promotes the natural production of probiotics; tissue repair
- **iodine, liquid** [*one dose daily*]† - natural antibiotic; supports immunity

Herbal & Home Remedies

- **Epsom salts** - If possible, encourage your pet to sit in a little warm water with magnesium sulphate (Epsom salts) added. Magnesium sulphate relaxes the muscles, reduces inflammation, and encourages the elimination of toxins. Add ¼ cup salts to 4 cups of warm water. You can also dissolve the salts into a little warm water, soak a cloth in it and hold it over the rectum.

Riva's Remedies

- **Pro-Colon, probiotic** [*one dose daily for 3 to 4 weeks or longer if needed*]† - probiotics and prebiotics for intestinal support; discourages the growth of unfriendly bacteria, supports a healthy intestinal immune system
- **Pro-Dygest, herbal blend** [*one dose daily for 3 to 4 weeks or as needed*]† - colon cleanser and detoxifier; promotes healthy bowel function and encourages regularity
- **Infection Drops, homeopathic** [*one dose twice daily as needed for up to 4 days*]† - symptoms of infections and abscesses
- **Kava's Healing Oil** [*Apply topically to the glands as needed*] - reduces abscessing, maintains healthy tissues, wound care

†See Appendix for recommended dosages and duration for all supplements.

NOTE: Anal glands should not have to be mechanically expressed on a regular basis. Chronic anal problems indicate that the underlying cause has not been addressed. Never have anal glands surgically removed; this invasive procedure does *nothing* to resolve the cause which will then simply cause health problems somewhere else in the body. First do no harm.

An Important Word about Stress and Digestion

Stress affects every dog (and wolf for that matter) in the world. No animal, humans included, can escape the physical and emotional pressures of survival and the inherent biological responses to stressful events. And stress of all kinds has a direct effect on the digestive system including the stomach, pancreas, and the small and large colon. First, stress causes an increase in the production of cortisol, a steroid-like hormone produced by the adrenal glands. Cortisol helps regulate various stress reactions including inflammation, but it also inhibits the synthesis of prostaglandins. Prostaglandins are complex hormones that stimulate the production of protective mucus and the repair of tissues in the stomach and intestines. And they also regulate HCl and bicarbonate levels in the stomach and control intestinal inflammation. Without the protective effects and enzyme activity of prostaglandins, the digestive system is at risk for heartburn, reflux, ulcers, and the mal-digestion of most foods.

Emotionally, the large colon corresponds to the second chakra which is the energy centre that processes emotions due to personal relationships. Dogs, like most animals, are highly emotional, thus any distress or conflict with another dog or relationships within the pet's human family can result in gas, bloating, diarrhea, constipation or other various mal-functions.

❖

Emotionally, the large colon corresponds to the second chakra which is the energy centre that processes emotions due to personal relationships.

Teddy Recovers Without Meat

Ten-year-old Teddy was in very poor health. His pet parent wrote that he had quit eating, had lost weight, and was getting increasingly weak and lethargic with chronic diarrhea. This had been going on already for three to four months, and the medications were not improving his condition, so his health continued to decline. Upon review of his case, it was clear that the first intention for this Yorkie would have to be an increase in appetite without causing more diarrhea, which was being caused by the mal-digestion of food. Teddy already knew this, which is why he didn't feel like eating. But his lack of nutrition, when he stopped eating, caused him further fatigue and lethargy. In addition, Teddy had a previous episode of pancreatitis – a sure sign that he had many digestive problems combined with food toxicity for quite some time.

The first step was to eliminate all the foods that Teddy could not digest. In this case, it was all the meat protein including red meats, poultry, fowl and fish. Teddy simply no longer had the digestive strength to fully and efficiently break down meat for absorption and metabolism. And furthermore, Teddy's hair analysis showed high levels of aluminum; one of the most common dietary sources of high aluminum is table salt. All meat is naturally (or artificially) high in salt. Aluminum toxicity can cause mal-digestion, heartburn, diarrhea, and an aversion to meat. Teddy's hair analysis also revealed poor metabolism of calcium, an important mineral for buffering acids from excess meat.

Teddy.

Teddy's new health program eliminated *all* the raw meat, raw fish and cooked poultry and organ meats from his diet. Instead, he was switched over to a high-fibre, vegetarian diet. High-fibre vegetarian diets are better when cooked and prepared at home; however, some dogs can tolerate a vegetarian kibble during the recovery stage. When Teddy's symptoms

improved, Teddy's pet parent was instructed to slowly and cautiously introduce more protein in the form of eggs (raw or cooked) and small amounts of fish.

Teddy was then given Pro-Colon probiotics for improving fermentation and nutrient absorption, the Riva's Kidney Care Herbal Blend to decrease acids and support liver and kidney function, and homeopathic Digestive Drops to improve nutrient absorption and ease the diarrhea. Organic selenium was also added since this is an aluminum antagonist.

Teddy's parent reported that Teddy made a complete turnaround within a few weeks with a robust appetite, no diarrhea, and much improved energy levels. Not bad for a senior Yorkie!

Diego Finds Love

Diego was a four-year-old brown border collie who represented quite a few challenging problems for his pet parent, Darlene. He had a very sensitive nervous system as collies can, and if he got overexcited, scared, or touched by a stranger he liked to curl his lip, growl and then nip. I even had to be careful doing the surrogate energy testing with him – he was so sensitive, he could feel my hand zeroing in on a particular organ even when my hand was several inches away. Diego also felt his emotions on a very deep level. Darlene brought him in one day because he had lost his appetite and had barely eaten for four to five days. He wouldn't even lick water, and he looked very depressed. He even threw up some yellow bile. Diego's veterinarian had prescribed antibiotics and anti-nausea medication, however; Diego was not responding well. She thought perhaps that he had an intestinal blockage or pancreatitis, but the tests were not conclusive.

I could tell that Diego was having an emotional reaction, not a physical one, so I asked more questions. It turned out that Darlene and Diego had been visiting family out of town for Christmas, and there were two other dogs there, one of which Diego absolutely adored. She was a lovely and attractive golden retriever named Rosie. No one noticed how deeply the bond had developed, but by the time the visit was over, Diego was in love. And the last thing he wanted to do was go home. So, of course, he did what we all do when we can't be with our beloveds – he pined. So he lost his appetite and quit eating; he felt like life wasn't worth living without his new friend. Many of us can relate, can we not? But life isn't always sensible, especially with matters of the heart. The whole ordeal exhausted his adrenal glands so we put him on a program to help him balance his emotions and get through his heartache. Homeopathic Aurum 1M, Calm & Cool herbal blend, and a little probiotic to stimulate his digestion was all that he needed. The whole ordeal lasted just over a week; all was well again, and Diego went back to a healthy appetite and a good life.

Diego.

Healing Dogs Their Way

5. Liver & Kidney Health

Cleansing & Detoxification

The ability of the body to detoxify is critical to maintaining a body free of waste, toxins, acids, and pathogens such as bacteria, yeast, fungus, viruses and parasites. Unlike the conventional veterinary model which focuses on the "germ theory" leading them to prescribe millions of prescriptions of antibiotics every year, the holistic model prudently focuses on the *whole* body and its ability to not only manage toxicity but to prevent the overgrowth of pathogens by maintaining its ability to cleanse, detoxify, and eliminate. It is, therefore, very important to support the health of the liver and kidneys to optimize their function as high-performance cleansing organs that decontaminate the entire body of pathogens, toxins and waste.

Unlike the conventional veterinary model which focuses on the "germ theory"… the holistic model prudently focuses on the whole body and its ability to… prevent the overgrowth of pathogens by maintaining its ability to cleanse, detoxify, and eliminate.

Natural Health Programs for Liver Health

The liver is the second largest organ in the body (after the skin). It draws a massive blood supply and weighs anywhere from less than a hundred grams to more than a kilogram depending on the size of the dog. The liver is responsible for numerous critical functions: detoxification of all chemicals and toxins, the production of energy, regulating immunity, and metabolizing fats, protein, and carbohydrates. The liver also plays an active role in digestion by producing bile, a fluid which is a mixture of water, bile salts, cholesterol and bilirubin. Bile is stored in the gallbladder, a small sac or bladder attached to the bottom part of the liver from where it is transported as needed. Bile helps to digest fats and carries toxins and debris out of the liver for elimination.

Chronic Liver Toxicity

Symptoms

Our dogs' livers are more often affected now by *accumulated* toxins than acute poisonings. Over time liver toxicity can result in toxic liver, fatty liver disease, hepatitis, virus infections, insulin resistance, gallbladder congestion (mucocele) and immune related liver conditions. Watch for chronic liver symptoms such as: poor digestion, poor appetite, nausea and/or vomiting, weight loss or gain, insulin resistance, fatigue, depression, dull hair coat, skin rashes and/or chronically itchy skin. Liver health is also affected by a toxic colon since all of the blood supply from the colon is directed to the liver for detoxification. This is how diet, digestion and colon toxicity affects liver health.

Causes

Liver toxins are mostly sourced from meat, hormones, commercial diets, pesticides, second hand smoke, heavy metals, preservatives, additives, and artificial flavour and colour. Air pollution, gases, fumes or toxic sprays also contribute to liver toxicity. Medications are a significant cause of toxic liver problems and immune suppression including non-steroidal anti-inflammatories, steroids, antibiotics, anticonvulsants, frequent use of anti-parasitics, and long-term use of pain killers. Avoid chemical flea and tick repellants and treatments, for they contain highly toxic insecticides and pesticides which many dogs cannot tolerate.

Natural Health Program

Diet

- Ensure a low-fat diet.
- Avoid canola oil, soya oil, and excessive saturated fats from meat/eggs.
- Discontinue all fat supplements including fish oils and omega oils.
- Rely on natural foods for healthy fats, e.g., vegetables, seeds and fresh fish (if your dog tolerates fish).
- No red meat such as beef, pork, bison, elk or venison.
- No organ meats.
- Choose organic meats where possible.
- No dairy products.
- No wheat or corn gluten.
- No artificial colourings, flavourings or preservatives.
- Emphasize dietary vegetables.
- Increase dietary fibre.

Nutrients

- **vitamin B12** [*one dose daily*]†* – liver detoxification, metabolic function, appetite, and energy
- **vitamin C** [*one dose daily*]†* – liver support; anti-oxidant and immunity
- **selenium, organic** [*one dose daily*]† – liver detoxifier, anti-oxidant; chelates chemicals and toxins

Herbal & Home Remedies

- **milk thistle seed, tincture** [*one dose daily for 4 to 6 weeks*]† – liver detoxifier; supports liver function, blocks allergy reactions
- **dandelion root, tincture or dried leaf** [*one dose daily for 4 to 6 weeks*]† – liver support stimulates liver function to encourage the elimination of toxins; supports digestion

Riva's Remedies

- **Pro-Colon, probiotic** [*one dose daily for 2 months*]† – probiotics and prebiotics discourages the growth of unfriendly bacteria and viruses, supports digestion and absorption of nutrients, and maintains a healthy intestinal immune system
- **Gastricol, homeopathic** [*one dose twice daily or as needed*]† – toxicity and liver support; nausea, vomiting, and bloating
- **Detox Dog, herbal blend** [*one dose daily for 4 to 6 weeks*]† – promotes the detoxification of elimination organs: skin, liver, kidneys and colon; supports the immune system
- **Para+Plus, tincture** [*one dose daily as required for parasites*]† – bacteria, yeast and parasites; liver support.

†See Appendix for recommended dosages and duration for all supplements.
*Also available as a Riva's Remedy

Acute Poisons

Symptoms

Any toxic substance that interferes with liver function is considered a poison. There are many kinds of poisons that a dog's liver can be exposed to. Some of the more obvious symptoms that a pet parent would notice include difficulty breathing, diarrhea, drooling, unexplained skin conditions, loss of appetite, vomiting, lethargy, weakness, lack of coordination, seizures and/or neurological changes.

Causes

Acute reactions can be caused by chemicals such as antifreeze, insect repellants, cleaning products, rat poison, poisonous plants, herbicides, snake venom and medications. Dogs may also experience food poisoning.

NOTE: for cases of *acute poisoning*, follow the protocol for treating the specific poison as recommended by a veterinarian.

Natural Health Program

Diet

- Avoid all added oils
- Discontinue all fat supplements including fish oils and omega oils.

- No meat of any kind
- No wheat or corn.
- No artificial colourings, flavourings or preservatives.

Nutrients

- **vitamin B12** [*one dose daily*]† - liver detoxification and colon support

Herbal & Home Remedies

- **Nux-vomica**, 200C or 1M - one dose (3 to 4 pellets) every 2 hours for all poisons.
- **Ipecac** 200C or 1M - one dose (3 to 4 pellets) every 2 hours as needed for nausea and vomiting

Riva's Remedies

- **Pro-Colon, probiotic** [*one dose daily for 2 months*]† - probiotics and prebiotics discourages the growth of unfriendly bacteria and viruses, supports digestion and absorption of nutrients, and maintains a healthy intestinal immune system
- **Gastricol, homeopathic** [*one dose twice daily or as needed*]† - toxicity and liver support; nausea, vomiting, and bloating

†See Appendix for recommended dosages and duration for all supplements.
*Also available as a Riva's Remedy

Liver Cancer

Symptoms

Primary liver cancer, meaning that the cancer starts in the liver, is relatively rare in dogs. It is much more common for dogs to have secondary or metastatic liver cancer, meaning that the cancer was spread to the liver from other organs such as the spleen and pancreas via the bloodstream or the lymphatic system. Metastatic liver tumours are usually multiple nodules. Because the liver is so resilient and can continue to function with up to 30 percent organ damage, symptoms often don't appear until the cancer is in the advanced stages. It is, therefore, important to know your dog's habits, movements, and behavior well enough that you can detect any changes early on which may identify a more serious health problem. In addition, if an animal has a health problem, despite the lack of observable clues, the vibrational or energy field will still have changed and can be detected through more subtle perceptions such as intuition or a strong knowing that something is off, or even by the behaviour of other dogs who can smell it.

Observable symptoms may include loss of appetite, fatigue, indigestion/vomiting, abdominal bloating, thirst or excessive urination and panting.

Causes

Since most cases of liver cancer are not primary, the underlying cause will be found in the original affected organ including the intestines. Most cases of cancer in dogs, no matter the location, are caused by imbalanced or inappropriate diet, food toxicity, environmental chemicals, hormone imbalances, bacterial or viral infections, and the sponging of the disease from people in the household.

Natural Health Program

Diet

- Ensure a low-fat diet.
- Avoid canola oil, soya oil, and excessive saturated fats from meat/eggs.
- Discontinue all fat supplements including fish oils and omega oils.
- Rely on natural foods for healthy fats, e.g., vegetables, seeds and fresh fish (if your dog tolerates fish).
- No red meat such as beef, pork, bison, elk or venison.
- No organ meats.
- No wheat or corn gluten.
- No artificial colourings, flavourings or preservatives.
- Emphasize dietary vegetables.
- Some dogs will have to go completely vegetarian for a time to cleanse and detoxify the toxins, chemicals, drug residue, acids and hormones found in meat and poultry. (See Chapter 3)
- Increase dietary fibre.

Nutrients

Vitamin B12 and C are important supplemental nutrients since the liver's capacity to produce them will be compromised.

- **vitamin B12** [*one dose daily*]† - liver detoxification, metabolic function, appetite, and energy
- **vitamin C** [*one dose daily*]† - liver support, antioxidant, promotes a healthy immune system, helps

eliminate toxic heavy metals

- **selenium, organic** [*one dose daily*][†] - liver detoxifier, anti-oxidant; chelates chemicals and toxins out of the body

Herbal & Home Remedies

- **milk thistle seed, tincture** [*one dose daily for 4 to 6 weeks*][†] - liver detoxifier; improves liver function, neutralizes toxins, and blocks allergy reactions
- **dandelion root or leaf** [*one dose daily for 4 to 6 weeks*][†] - liver tonic; stimulates bile flow to encourage the elimination of toxins, improves digestion
- **shiitake** and/or **Maitake mushroom** [*one dose daily indefinitely*][†] - liver support; improves immune function, helps prevent metastasis, relieves digestive ailments, helps eliminate toxic heavy metals

Riva's Remedies

- **Pro-Colon, probiotic** [*one dose daily for 2 months*][†]

- probiotics and prebiotics discourages the growth of unfriendly bacteria and viruses, supports nutrient absorption, promotes optimum digestion, and maintains the intestinal immune system

- **Immune Boost, herbal blend** [*one dose daily*][†] - promotes the healthy function of the liver and immune system; provides nutrition for energy and organ health
- **Detox Dog, herbal blend** [*one dose daily for 4 to 6 weeks*][†] - promotes the detoxification of elimination organs: skin, liver, kidneys and colon. Supports the immune system.
- **Pro-Dygest, herbal blend** [*one dose daily*][†] - intestinal detoxifier; cleanses the intestines of mal-digested debris and acids
- **Gastricol, homeopathic**[*one dose once or twice daily for 14 days, or as needed*][†] - liver toxicity; nausea, vomiting, indigestion, and bloating

[†]See Appendix for recommended dosages and duration for all supplements.

Also available as a Riva's Remedy

Natural Health Programs for Kidney and Bladder Health

The kidneys are very complex organs responsible for filtering and detoxifying the blood of wastes that are produced by old cells, toxins, and many drugs. Waste from the metabolism of food is also filtered. This is accomplished through the work of thousands of microscopic nephrons through which the toxic filtrate passes before forming urine, which is then released into the bladder pouch for storage until urination. Thus the urine excretes waste from drugs, chemicals, some heavy metals, toxins, creatinine (from the breakdown of muscle), and acids including uric acid. The kidneys are also responsible for eliminating all of the waste products from the metabolism of meat protein including urea and ammonia.

Therefore, a toxic liver, drugs, dietary fats, diabetes, and high meat protein diets can all strain the kidneys and increase acid levels. High protein diets produce excess ammonia which is converted by the liver to less toxic urea which is then eliminated by the kidneys and also by the skin. But if the dietary protein is too high and/or the liver is too congested, the excess urea will overload the kidneys, forcing the skin to eliminate more urea than

usual - often resulting in skin problems. Any urea that is not completely eliminated will convert to uric acid which then deposits into the joints and muscles for storage causing joint pain, stiffness and arthritic-like symptoms. The kidneys also regulate levels of electrolytes, the volume of blood and blood pressure. The kidneys also reabsorb water, sugar, and amino acids (from protein) back into the blood for circulation.

Kidney Disease and Toxicity

Symptoms

If the kidneys are under-functioning to the point where they are unable to eliminate toxins, the debris will build up in the blood causing systemic toxicity. Kidney problems may manifest with symptoms such as an increase or decrease in urination, straining to urinate, incontinence, discoloured urine, bloody urine, vomiting and/or fatigue.

Causes

General kidney toxicity will compromise kidney function and predispose the kidneys to infections as well – bacteria, yeast, viruses and/or parasites. Kidney function can also be adversely affected by various medications and/or poisons as well as auto-immune problems whereby the immune system is attacking the kidney tissues. But this is not a problem with the immune system *per se*, it's a problem with kidney toxicity and inflammation first which then triggers an immune reaction. See Chapter 7 for details on auto-immune conditions.

Older dogs are prone to weaker kidneys as their kidneys can become less efficient in concentrating urine. There are, however, many senior dogs that have perfectly normal kidneys as a result of appropriate diets, exercise and low stress. As dogs age, it is important to decrease their overall dietary meat protein levels to compensate for a lower metabolic rate and more sedentary lifestyles.

Chronic kidney disease can occur from any long-term kidney problems but may not manifest symptoms until the condition is more advanced and up to 75 percent of the kidney function has been lost. The kidneys are very good at hiding any damage that affects function because the kidneys can hold unused nephrons (the basic structural unit of the kidney) in reserve until they are needed to replace dead ones. However, eventually the healthy nephrons become depleted, at which point the kidneys cannot restore themselves. It's amazing how both the liver and kidneys have this incredible ability to "march on" despite increasing pressures from nutritional damage and toxicity.

Natural Health Program (for Chronic Toxicity)

Diet

- Decrease all meat proteins and organ meat or eliminate completely for as long as necessary.
- Dogs with chronic kidney disease may have to go on a vegetarian diet indefinitely. (See Chapter 3)
- No red meat such as beef, bison, venison, or elk.
- Ensure a low-fat diet.
- Avoid canola oil, soya oil.
- Ensure that there is clean drinking water available – preferably spring water (not tap water or tap water from inexpensive filters). Dogs with kidney problems lose more water than normal.

Nutrients for Kidney Function

- **potassium citrate** [*one dose daily*]† – regulates acidity (pH), eliminates waste; supports normal urinary flow, supports protein digestion
- **vitamin E** [*one dose daily*]†* – anti-oxidant protecting from free radicals; helps support normal blood pressure and circulation
- **folic acid** [*one dose daily*]† – infections; supports tissue repair, immune function, and energy

Herbal & Home Remedies

- **parsley tea** [*one dose daily*]† – blood tonic, natural diuretic, source of potassium

Riva's Remedies

- **Kidney Care, herbal blend** *one dose daily*]† – kidney support and nutrition; cleanser and detoxifier of acids and waste; promotes normal kidney function
- **Detox Dog, herbal blend** [*one dose daily for 4 to 6 weeks*]† – promotes the detoxification of elimination organs: skin, liver, kidneys and colon; supports the immune system.
- **Pro-Colon, probiotic** [*one dose daily*]† – probiotics and prebiotics supports immunity and normal digestion; balances the urinary ecosystem

†See Appendix for recommended dosages and duration for all supplements.

*Also available as a Riva's Remedy

Kidney and Bladder Infections

Symptoms

Bladder infections (cystitis) are caused by bacterial overgrowths in the lining of the bladder, which in turn cause irritation and inflammation. This will normally cause frequent and uncomfortable urination, and the urine may have a cloudy appearance. Dogs may also be licking the area more than usual.

Kidney infections can be more difficult to detect since the dogs might not show symptoms for several days. Watch for squatting without urinating, blood in the urine, odorous urine, increased thirst and/or urination, poor appetite, fever, lethargy and/or mid-back pain (near the kidneys).

Causes

Urinary infections can be caused or exacerbated by diet, poor nutrition, blood sugar problems, poor immunity, and medications such as steroids. Bladder infections can also be caused by undiagnosed yeast overgrowths treated as bladder infections with antibiotics. The antibiotics work for a short time only to be followed by a repeat of the same symptoms, at which point the antibiotics may be repeated *again*. Some of these dogs are prescribed two or three courses of antibiotics with no lasting relief, indeed such treatments lead to increased levels of yeast production instead which can trigger the same symptoms.

Frequent or chronic infections are normally a result of poor diets, poor immunity, leaky gut, or long-standing infections in the teeth. The holistic model of health does not focus on the "germ theory", rather it suggests that it is the health of the terrain that determine whether pathogens can flourish.

Natural Health Program

Diet
* Decrease all meat proteins and organ meat or eliminate completely for a few days.
* No wheat or corn gluten.
* Eliminate dry kibble in favour of high moisture foods.
* Ensure that there is clean drinking water available – preferably spring water and not tap water, well water, or tap water from inexpensive filters. Urinary infections require a lot of water to flush out the bacteria and their toxins.
* Ensure healthy teeth that are free of bacterial infections since the bacteria can migrate to the kidneys.

Nutrients
* **iodine, liquid** [*one dose daily*]† – important nutrient for the urinary tract and bladder; bacteria, yeast and parasites
* **potassium citrate** [*one dose daily*]† – helps regulate acidity (pH), eliminates waste; promotes normal urinary flow; supports protein digestion
* **vitamin C** [*one dose daily*]†* – infections, supports immunity and healthy kidney function

Herbal & Home Remedies
* **blackberries, raspberries and/or cranberries – fresh or dry but unsweetened** [*crush and add to food – 1 tsp*

to 1 Tbsp depending on the size of your dog] – anti-oxidants and anti-inflammatories; prevents bacteria from adhering to the urinary tract walls and helps increase urine acidity

Riva's Remedies *for Infections*
* **Para+Plus, tincture** [*once daily if required for parasites*]† – bacteria, yeast and urinary support
* **Infection Drops, homeopathic** [*5 to 10 drops twice daily for 3 to 4 days*]† – supports healthy bladder function; for discoloured urine, frequent urging
* **Pro-Colon, probiotic** [*one dose daily for 3 to 4 weeks*]† – probiotics and prebiotics discourages the growth of unfriendly bacteria, balances the urinary ecosystem, and supports the immune response

†See Appendix for recommended dosages and duration for all supplements.
*Also available as a Riva's Remedy

Urinary Crystals and Stones

Symptoms

Crystals and/or stones found in the urinary tract is a condition known as urolithiasis and is one of the most common health problems that affect our dogs. When multiple crystals accumulate, they join to form a stone (urolith). Unbound crystals may cause mineral deposits. There are two main types of crystals: one is composed of magnesium ammonium phosphate (struvite stones) that tend to form in alkaline urine, and the other is calcium oxalate which forms in acidic urine. Both can form in the kidneys or urethra but are more common in the bladder. Stones irritate the lining of the urinary tract or bladder, and if they get large enough, they can partially block the flow of urine which interferes with the elimination of waste creating a toxic condition. Symptoms of urolithiasis include frequent urination with urgency, frequent urination of small amounts, dribbling, straining, bloody urine, loss of appetite, pain, and sometimes vomiting. Not all affected dogs exhibit symptoms.

Cause

The primary cause of urinary stones is a diet of processed dog food and/or a diet high in protein - excess protein is associated with the formation of new crystals and the preservation of existing ones. And even though research tells us that struvite stones form as a result of bacterial infections (bacteria gathers in one place around which a stone develops) bacterial overgrowths are not so much about the bacteria as they are about the health of the terrain which predisposes the body to bacterial overgrowths. As per usual then, frequent or chronic bacterial infections, including urinary infections, are due to poor diet, nutrient deficiencies, poor immunity and/or toxic colons.

Other contributing factors of crystal formation include lack of exercise, infrequent urination as might occur if dogs are not let outside often enough, and/or if they are not getting enough water as is the case with feeding dry kibble which is very low in water (compared to raw food). Reduced frequency in urination as caused by low water intake, for example, results in concentrated urine which leaves behind mineral deposits.

Calcium oxalate stones, aside from diet, are also caused by certain medications such as steroids, some diuretics, and/or antibiotics; antibiotics reduce the numbers of specific strains of friendly bacteria – this is not a good thing since healthy bacteria controls levels of oxalate. When are medical practitioners - animal and human alike - going to stop this incessant over-prescribing of antibiotics? They need more tools in their tool box!

Certain dog breeds are more genetically prone to kidney or bladder stones: Miniature Schnauzers, Shih-Tzu's, Bichon frises, Miniature Poodles, Cocker Spaniels, Yorkshire terriers, Lhasa Apsos and Deerhounds.

Natural Health Program

Most stones can be dissolved within a few weeks on an appropriate diet with well selected supplements. For chronic urinary infections, refer to this chapter's section on kidney and bladder infections. Long-term use of antibiotics in small dosages is not appropriate and will eventually cause more health problems.

Diet

- Decrease meat protein; meat breaks down into urea (i.e. ammonia), which is one of the building blocks of struvite stones.
- No red meat such as beef, bison, elk, or venison. Red meats contain higher levels of arachidonic acid which are inflammatory acids that increase the likelihood of crystals and stone formation.

- No organ meats.
- No wheat or corn gluten.
- Eliminate or reduce dry kibble.
- Ensure plenty of clean, healthy drinking water to encourage the flushing out of bacteria, wastes, minerals and acids.
- Don't use extra salt in the food to make them thirsty. Dogs instinctively know when and how much to drink so long as they like the water.
- Provide spring water rather than tap water from inexpensive filters, distilled water, or reverse osmosis (RO). Distilled water is deficient in calcium and magnesium.
- Some dogs don't like drinking out of metal water bowls.
- Increase dietary fibre from healthy whole grains and vegetables. Fibre binds with acids and toxins in the intestines and can then be eliminated through the stool rather than through the kidneys.
- Continue to feed raw meaty bones. Dietary calcium has no effect on bladder stones.
- Ensure regular exercise.

Nutrients

- **potassium citrate** [*one dose daily*][†] – helps regulate acidity (pH), eliminates waste, promotes normal urinary flow, supports protein digestion

Herbal & Home Remedies

- **lemon juice** [*one dose daily*][†] – helps dissolve crystals and prevent the formation of new ones; helps normalize pH balance
- **horsetail shavings** [*one dose daily*][†] – for urinary incontinence and bladder stones

Riva's Remedies

- **Kidney Care, herbal blend** [*one dose daily*][†] – kidney support and nutrition, cleanser and detoxifier of acids and waste, promotes healthy urination
- **Pro-Colon, probiotic** [*one dose daily for up to 2 months*][†] – probiotics and prebiotics to maintain urinary immunity
- **Detox Dog herbal blend** [*one dose daily*][†] - Promotes the detoxification of the liver, kidneys and colon; supports the immune system

[†]See Appendix for recommended dosages and duration for all supplements.

Incontinence

Symptoms

Dogs with incontinence usually have a weak urethral sphincter which is controlled by muscle contractions. The urethral sphincter is at the base of the bladder and opens into the urethral tube through which the urine is eliminated. This sphincter is responsible for opening when the bladder needs to release and closing when the bladder needs to hold back. Incontinent dogs urinate involuntarily and may urinate in their sleep, dribble, leak, or begin urinating in the house – usually because the pet parent doesn't yet recognize that there is a problem, and the dog needs to go outside more often.

Causes

Physical reasons include bladder stones, bladder infections, diabetes, obesity, loss of elasticity or poor muscle tone due to aging in senior dogs, and low estrogen in spayed females where 5 to 20 percent of spayed females can end up with bladder problems. Puppies should not be spayed before three months of age since this increases the likelihood of an estrogen deficient incontinence. The later you wait the better.

Side effects from medication can also cause increased urination.

Dogs can also suffer poor bladder control due to stiffness, inflammation, or injuries in the lumbar area of the back (previous or past), all of which can affect the nerve supply from the spine to the bladder. All cases of incontinence should have a chiropractic assessment.

Emotional reasons are common too, for a dog who is excited, scared, startled, angered or submissive can have a sudden release of urine. Some dogs urinate to get your attention – when all else has failed – and are desperately trying to communicate to you what is important to them. This can be anything from their own physical health, to your health, to your emotional state, or perhaps a stressful situation that you are caught up in. Realize that if *you* are stressed your dog is stressed, and chronic stress affects all hormones including cortisol and antidiuretic hormones.

And remember, your dog doesn't like it any better than you do – most of them are embarrassed. Incontinent dogs should never be scolded, reprimanded, or have their nose rubbed in it. This is cruel behaviour based on ignorance and lack of understanding.

Natural Health Program

For bladder stones, kidney/bladder infections, and general toxicity, refer to appropriate section for treatment programs.

Diet

- Do *not* restrict dogs with incontinence problems from drinking. This is an unhealthy practice and causes more stress which causes more urination.
- Watch for any food allergies that could be causing inflammation in the urinary tract.
- Overweight dogs need to lose weight. Extra weight pressures the pelvic muscles.
- Is your dog hungry? Ensure that your dog is getting fed often enough since hunger can promote frequent urination.
- Eliminate all foods and treats which contains artificial flavourings, colouring, or preservatives as many of these are urinary or bladder stimulants.

Nutrients

- **vitamin E** [*one dose daily*]†* – promotes healthy circulation, supports muscle function in all dogs and helps balance reproductive hormones in females

Herbal & Home Remedies

- **horsetail shavings** [*one dose daily*]† – urinary incontinence, bladders stones, and infections; strengthens connective tissue and muscle tone
- **licorice root powder** [*one dose daily for one month*]† – natural anti-inflammatory and stress relief; for spayed females can improve estrogen levels
- **pituitary, 200C, homeopathic** [*one dose daily*]† · urinary incontinence which occurs after spaying

Riva's Remedies

- **Bladder Drops, homeopathic** [*one dose twice daily as needed*]† – incontinence, frequent urination, dribbling, stress relief and tension
- **Calm-Aid, homeopathic** [*one dose twice daily as needed*]† – supports calm behaviour in dogs who urinate due to anxiety, stress and nervousness

†See Appendix for recommended dosages and duration for all supplements.

*Also available as a Riva's Remedy

The Detoxification of Phoebe Evans

Phoebe is an elderly Sheltie who was rescued in 2015 by Jackie Evans of Elderdog Canada. Phoebe was thought to be 13 or 14 years old and became Jackie's "furever" dog. Phoebe wasn't feeling very well when Jackie took over; her hind end was weak, her energy was low, she was depressed, her weight was up, and she had weak kidneys. Rather than blame old age, Jackie sought help in restoring Phoebe's health and vigour.

Phoebe

To take the load off the kidneys and to improve liver detoxification, Jackie reduced the meat proteins in Phoebe's diet and added healthy whole grains, vegetables, and soup broths. We then added sea salt and potassium-rich parsley to the diet to balance the electrolytes in her kidneys. Potassium is a gentle kidney cleanser and helps to balance pH levels. Phoebe was also given Pro-Colon probiotics to support digestion, the intestinal immune system and the liver; Vitamin E for circulation; Bone-Up (calcium and vitamin B6) for joint support; and Joint-Clear, an effective herbal blend to promote comfortable muscles and joints and healthy colon function. Within two weeks, Jackie reported that Phoebe's back end was stronger, that she had lost weight, had more energy, and was much happier, with no depression.

A few weeks later after *that*, Jackie reported that Phoebe was trembling a lot and she was worried that the trembling was a sign of the chills or some other ill health. After checking in energetically with Phoebe, I suggested that Phoebe had been trembling with unexpressed emotions. She was trying to express gratitude for her new and caring, loving home. From that time, Jackie reported that Phoebe did not tremble again because Phoebe knew that she had been heard and that Jackie now understood how she was feeling.

Wow.

Bonnie – A Good Old Hound Dog

"Bonnie is now 15-1/2 years old; she is a black and tan coonhound. She started to get stiff on her hind legs in 2014 and had more difficulty getting up on chairs. She also slept a lot. We thought that maybe Christmas 2014 would be her last Christmas with us. I started giving her your Joint Clear herbal blend and she is a lot more mobile now and sometimes even jumps up onto the chair and every so often has a mad couple of minutes like she used to! A lady who first spent Christmas with us last year said how much better she seemed this Christmas over the previous one. I am going to keep her on the Joint Clear herbal blend and she gets the Immune Boost herbal blend every second day. As well, Bonnie had a geriatric blood panel and urinalysis done in July 2017 and the results were all good and within range, which the vet and I put down to the use of your supplements; previous ones done in 2013 and 2014 had shown very high liver enzyme counts.

Also that same July Bonnie had some bacteria and yeast in her ear, the one eye was weepy and she had been licking her rear end quite a bit. The vet gave me some drops for her ear and for her eye and gave me some cream to put on her rear end until she had the results back from the culture to see which antibiotic to put her on for that. When she phoned me with the results and told me to come in and get the antibiotics I mentioned that she seemed good and was no longer licking and the vet asked me to bring her in. She re-checked her and said she was fine and didn't need the antibiotics and mentioned that she didn't think the cream alone would have cleared it up and that whatever I was giving her must have also played a part. I had been giving her your homeopathic Infection Drops for a few days in addition to the Immune Boost and Joint Clear that she is normally on.

She has a good appetite and being she is a hound dog, food is very important to her as is comfort lying on our sofa! Here are some pictures of Bonnie on her chair. It used to be our sofa and Bonnie would lie on the one end of it. Now, however, it has all become hers and she kindly lets us sit where we can!! As my daughter says 'at her age she can do whatever she wants'. Thanks for helping me keep an old hound dog healthy!" —Anita A.

Bonnie

6. Heart, Lungs & Respiratory Health

Circulation & Oxygen

The heart and lungs work together to take in air from the environment, diffuse it to the blood, and then nourish every cell, tissue, and organ with a steady supply of oxygen – without which the body would perish and die. Oxygen is life's most abundant element and the single most important substance in the body. It is required for all chemical reactions, detoxification processes, and immune function. Furthermore, it is necessary for homeostasis, the process by which the body maintains a condition of balance and equilibrium within its internal environment.

The Heart

The heart is located between the lungs, slightly to the left of the breastbone. De-oxygenated blood returns in the veins to the receiving chamber of the right side of the heart (atrium), passes through the tricuspid valve into the right ventricle, which pumps it into the lungs, where it releases carbon dioxide and absorbs oxygen. The oxygenated blood is returned to the receiving chamber of the left side of the heart (atrium) via the pulmonary veins, passing through the mitral valve into the left ventricle. The left ventricle then pumps the blood through the aortic valve into the aorta (the largest artery of the body), which delivers blood via the arteries and capillaries to all the organs, tissues, and cells of the body. Thus, the left side of the heart is a stronger muscle than the right. Blood flow from the heart not only delivers oxygen and nutrients to every cell in the body, but also removes carbon dioxide and waste products produced by those cells. The heart itself must be nourished by a continuing supply of oxygen and nutrients which is transported through the heart's own arteries - called the coronary arteries.

The heart of an eight-kilogram dog weighs approximately 60 grams. Puppies and small dogs have a heart rate between 120 to 160 beats per second while larger dogs are between 60 and 120. The larger the dog, the slower the heart rate.

The canine circulatory system.

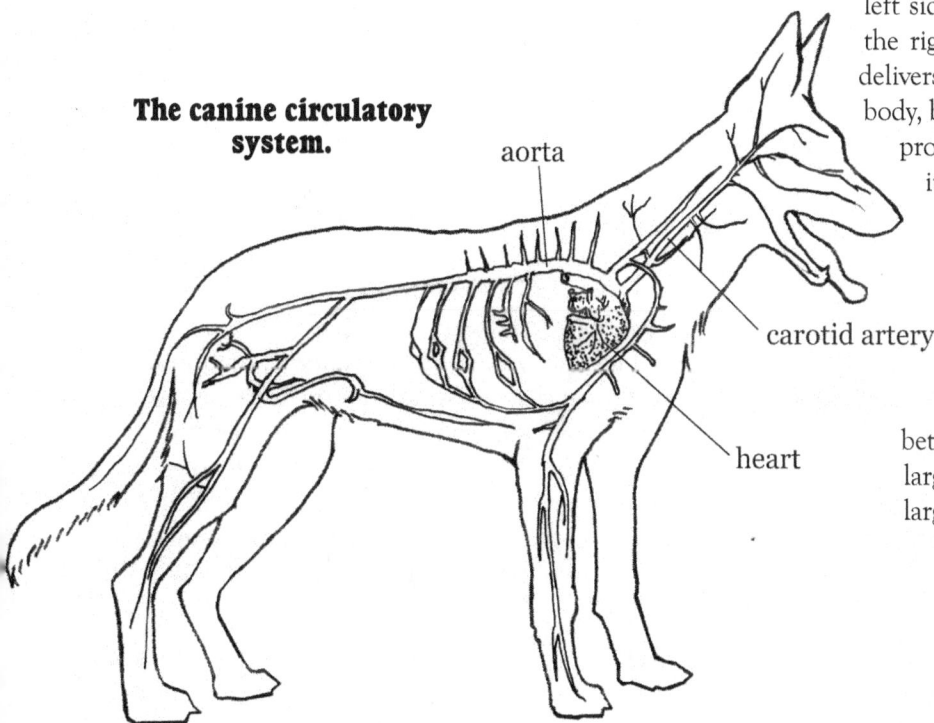

aorta

carotid artery

heart

~~~~~~~~~~~~~~~~~~~~~~~~ 🐾 ~~~~~~~~~~~~~~~~~~~~~~~~

Heart Disease

Symptoms

Congestive heart failure or CHF occurs when the heart's ability to pump blood is decreased and is always the result of pre-existing heart disease. When the heart is unable to pump the blood that it receives, it causes fluid to accumulate due to the increased blood pressure in the heart. Fluids then congest the tissues and accumulate in the chest and lungs, which inhibit the lungs from expanding normally and deprives the blood of oxygen. This can cause coughing, difficulty in breathing, excessive panting, fatigue, changes in appetite and/or exercise intolerance. If fluids accumulate in the right side of the heart, fluid will also accumulate in the abdomen (ascites).

In addition, the compromised blood circulation affects the nutrition and the regular detoxification of all other organs and body systems.

Types of common heart diseases resulting in CHF include: weakened heart valves, a weak and enlarged heart and pulmonary stenosis where the valves are blocked and narrowed.

- Diseased valves make up 75 percent of all heart disease in dogs and affects small breeds over the age of five: Cavalier King Charles spaniel, Dachshund, Miniature poodles, Shih Tzu, Maltese, Chihuahua, Cocker Spaniels, Miniature Schnauzers, and Pomeranians. Congenital mitral valve diseases affect the larger breeds: Bull terrier, Great Dane, German shepherd, Rottweiler, Labrador retriever and Weimaraner.

- Weak and enlarged hearts account for 8 percent of heart disease and affects primarily large breed dogs: Doberman pinscher, Boxer, Scottish deerhound, Irish wolfhound, Great Dane, Saint Bernard, Afghan hound, Golden retriever and Cocker Spaniel.

- Pulmonary stenosis describes valves that are blocked and narrowed which can cause either murmurs, arrhythmias and/or congestive heart failure. Stenosis affects the English bulldog, Mastiff, Scottish terrier, Samoyed, wirehaired fox terrier, miniature schnauzer, West Highland white terrier, Beagle, Chihuahua, cocker spaniel, boxer, Newfoundland and Rottweiler.

And bad breeding has resulted in heart vessels that don't close in some puppies – this results in a 50 percent mortality rate and affects the Cocker Spaniel, English springer spaniel, German shepherd, Maltese Terrier, Poodle, Pomeranian, Collie, Shetland Sheep Dog and Australian cattle dog.

~~~~~~~~~~~~~~~ 🐾 ~~~~~~~~~~~~~~~

Bad breeding has resulted in heart vessels that don't close in some puppies – this results in a 50 percent mortality rate.

~~~~~~~~~~~~~~~~~~~~~~~~~~~~~~~~

Causes

Heart disease is most commonly caused by either weakened heart valves which allow a back-flow of blood into the heart or a weakened left ventricle which lacks the contractile strength to pump the usual outflow of blood. Heart disease can be caused and/or exacerbated by diet, nutrient deficiencies, lack of exercise, stress, and sponging heart problems from their owners. The heart can also be affected by long-term grief or loss as these are the primary emotions stored in the heart. See Chapter 15 for more information on the relationship between emotions and physical health.

A healthy heart relies on a continual supply of nourishment to maintain optimum performance. The heart is also dependent on optimum liver function to remove all toxins and unhealthy fats from the blood – the heart is very sensitive to toxicity and unhealthy and/or rancid fats, which easily degenerate the heart, causing acute symptoms or chronic symptoms of heart disease over time. Therefore, dogs with heart disease need to be extremely selective with dietary fats because the heart uses fat for energy, not sugar. In addition, because the heart is sensitive to toxicity, the general diet and the cleanliness of the intestines is very important in maintaining a healthy heart.

High cholesterol in dogs, as in humans, is not a

disease and does *not* cause heart disease. It can be an indicator of cardiovascular problems but is rarely the cause. Cholesterol is an important hormone produced by the liver and required for cell structure, nerve cells, brain function, bile production, and the digestion and absorption of fats. Dogs should not be automatically put on cholesterol lowering drugs; rather, they should be put on a liver detoxification program and a high fibre/low fat diet with plenty of exercise. High cholesterol levels can also be caused by high blood sugar levels and/or low thyroid function. It's also not unusual for dogs to have high cholesterol levels because the people that they live with do.

A healthy heart is also dependent on healthy oral hygiene. Migrating bacteria from dental infections is a risk factor for heart problems (see Chapter 12 for more information on periodontal disease). Heart damage can also occasionally occur from viruses or parasites.

Natural Health Program

Diet

- Ensure a low-fat diet.
- Avoid canola oil, soya oil, coconut oil, and excessive saturated fats from meat.
- Use caution with long-term fat supplements including fish oils and omega oils.
- Rely on natural foods for healthy fats, e.g., vegetables, seeds, and fresh fish (if your dog tolerates fish).
- No red meat such as beef, pork, bison, elk, or venison.
- No organ meats.
- No wheat or corn gluten.
- No artificial colourings, flavourings or preservatives.
- Emphasize dietary vegetables.
- Dogs with advanced heart disease should go completely vegetarian.
- Increase dietary fibre.
- Overweight dogs need to lose weight.

Nutrients

- **folic acid** [*one dose daily*]† – promotes elasticity and tissue repair, supports bioavailability of nitric oxide which is a vasodilator
- **vitamin B12** [*one dose daily*]†* – aids the metabolism of fats; supports oxygen and energy levels
- **magnesium citrate** [*one dose daily*]†* – maintains heart

muscle function, calms electrical activity; promotes normal blood pressure

- **potassium citrate** [*one dose daily*]† – promotes urination, helps regulate fluid levels, aids waste elimination, heart nutrient
- **vitamin E** [*one dose daily*]†* – nutrition for heart, blood, and circulation

Note: Avoid all nutraceuticals containing glucosamine, chondroitin and MSM – these have been linked to heart irregularities and increased blood pressure.

Herbal & Home Remedies

- **cayenne pepper, powder** [*once daily with food for 30 days*]† – blood circulation, blood pressure, normal heart action and fatty liver

  - Some dogs may develop a burning sensation in the stomach and esophagus; therefore, use for 30 days to start, then discontinue for 7 to 14 days, then resume for another 30 days if needed. Watch for any signs of discomfort at which point it should be discontinued. Note: do not inhale or let your dog inhale the powder, for while it's harmless, it can be very irritating to the eyes and nose

- **hawthorn berry, tincture** [*one dose daily*]† – promotes oxygenation, blood flow and healthy heart function

- **olive oil, light** [*one dose daily*]† – natural anti-inflammatory; provides energy for the heart, promotes the flow of liver bile

Riva's Remedies

- **Vital Force, herbal blend** [*one dose daily*]† – supports endurance, stamina, and immunity; maintains and provides nutrition for heart health

†See Appendix for recommended dosages and duration for all supplements.
*Also available as a Riva's Remedy

Lungs and Bronchial Tubes

The lungs receive de-oxygenated blood from both the pulmonary arteries and bronchial arteries. Upon inspiration, air travels down the main bronchial tube into the bronchi which divides into small branches (bronchioles) inside the lungs. Inside the bronchioles are tiny air sacs called alveoli, which absorb oxygen from inhaled air, re-oxygenating the blood, which is then carried to the left side of the heart through the pulmonary veins. The alveoli also release carbon dioxide, a waste gas from the metabolism of food, which travels back up through the lungs and is exhaled out through the breath and into the air. When the oxygen levels in the blood are too low (hypoxemia) as caused from anemia, for example, a dog may show signs of panting, shortness of breath and/or coughing.

The respiratory system protects its airways from foreign invaders by warming the inhaled air and filtering out irritating particles which are then destroyed by the immune system. Large particles are trapped in the mucus lining of the airways and then carried to the throat for swallowing or coughing.

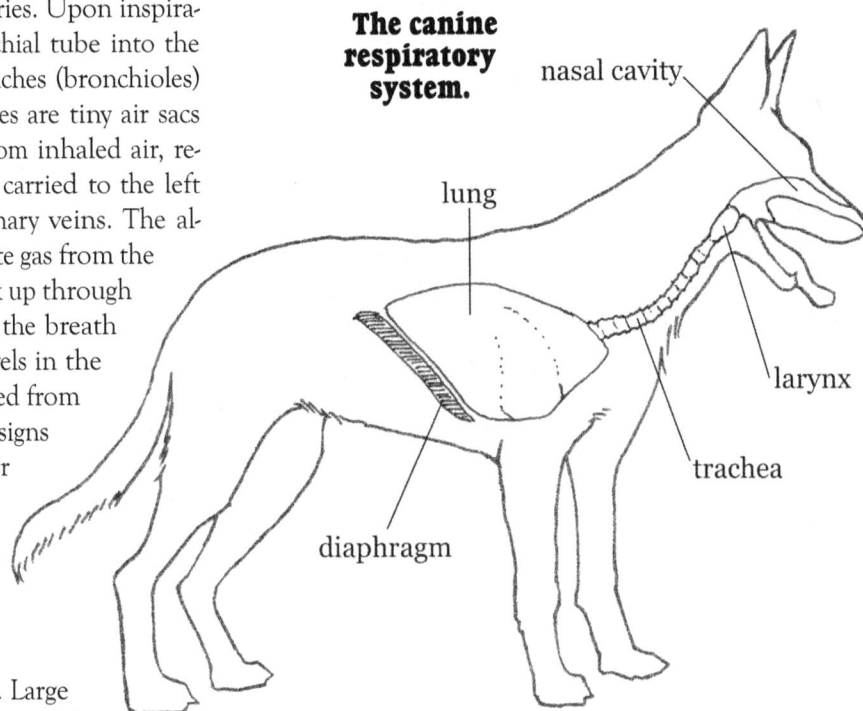

The canine respiratory system.

nasal cavity

lung

larynx

trachea

diaphragm

Natural Health Programs for the Respiratory System

Flus, Colds, Kennel Cough, and Distemper

Symptoms

Problems with the respiratory system including infections and/or allergies will usually manifest with symptoms such as coughing, sneezing, congestion, shortness of breath or laboured breathing, gagging, exercise intolerance and/or nasal or eye discharge. Some dogs will reverse sneeze, where air is pulled rapidly and noisily into (instead of out) the nose which then makes a snorting sound.

Kennel cough (Bordetella), despite the lucrative vaccine campaigns, is nothing more than a flu or cold comparable to what a human commonly experiences and is rarely serious. Affected dogs usually maintain a normal appetite, temperature, and energy levels but develop a dry cough. Unfortunately, dogs who are vaccinated against kennel cough are thought to be contagious for weeks after vaccination.

Canine distemper is a contagious, viral disease of dogs seen worldwide. It also affecting foxes, wolves (of course), and raccoons. Affected dogs usually run a fever and may experience a runny nose, pus-like discharges from the eyes, fatigue, and/or loss of appetite. The infection may be mild or progress to advanced stages where neurological symptoms are possible. It is, therefore, important to support the immune system at the first sign of any viral or bacterial conditions.

Most bacteria and viruses are contracted through the mouth and throat and then enter the lungs through the upper airways and settle in specific areas of the lungs. But bacteria that enter the lungs through the blood are usually more diffuse and settle throughout the entire lung.

Causes

Infections are caused by bacteria, viruses, or other unhealthy pathogens. If the body is toxic or out of balance or if the normal defense mechanisms are not working, then the body is unable to protect itself and the pathogens will flourish and propagate. Continuing toxicity, poor nutrition, and nutrient deficiencies will result in reoccurring infections or they will become chronic. All chronic infections are secondary to other underlying health conditions which have not been resolved: food allergies/intolerances, intestinal parasites, leaky gut, anemia, low thyroid, function, adrenal malfunction as in Cushing's disease, and/or stress.

The holistic model does not subscribe to the conventional "germ theory" which hunts, identifies and then designs a drug to kill the germ. Repeated courses of medications such as antibiotics or steroids will perpetuate toxicity, cause poor digestion, compromise the immune system, and deplete important nutrients - all of which are risk factors for infections. The holistic model focusses on the terrain, the health of which is the *only* factor that determines the ability of the pathogen to flourish and propagate.

Natural Health Program

Diet

- Eliminate wheat, corn gluten, dairy products, soy products, rancid oils and all known food allergies and intolerances (see Chapter 7 for more information).

- Ensure that the dietary meat source is clean and free of pathogens.

- Avoid feeding added or excess oils including canola oil, soya oil, coconut oil, fish and vegetable oils.

- Add more seeds to the diet to provide a natural source of essential fatty acids, for example flax, chia and/or hemp.

Nutrients

- **vitamin A, liquid** [*one dose daily*]† - supports immunity and prevents infections

- **vitamin C** [*one dose daily*]†* - liver support; immunity, infections

- **Iron-Up (iron gluconate)** [*one dose daily*]†* - an iron deficiency may result in chronic infections, low energy and poor immunity

- **Lysine (amino acid)** [*one dose daily*]† - supports immunity in cases of herpes virus which can affect puppies

Herbal & Home Remedies

- **echinacea** [*one dose daily*]† - bacteria and viruses; immune support; not for use with auto-immune conditions

Riva's Remedies

- **Para+Plus, tincture** [one dose daily as needed]† - bacteria, yeast and parasites; liver support

- **Immune Boost, herbal blend** [*one dose daily as needed for immune problems*]† - supports digestion, liver, and immune system with nutrition, cleansing and detoxification

- **Infection Drops, homeopathic** [*one dose twice daily for 3 days*]† - an immune formula for symptoms of skin infections, abscesses, eruptions, and discharges

- **Flu-Ease, homeopathic** [*one dose twice daily for 3 days or as required*]† - symptoms due to colds and flus, e.g., cough, congestion, discharge and fevers

†See Appendix for recommended dosages and duration for all supplements.

*Also available as a Riva's Remedy

Bronchitis (COPD), Asthma and Allergies

Symptoms

Bronchitis, also known as chronic obstructive pulmonary disease or COPD, occurs when the mucous membranes of the bronchial airways are inflamed. Asthma occurs when the upper bronchi spasm, constrict, swell and narrow as a result of inflammation and/or fluid and mucus production. This is usually in reaction to allergens, resulting in wheezing, shortness of breath, difficulty breathing, panting and/or low energy. An overproduction of mucus and/or inflammation is always a defense mechanism where the immune system is trying to protect itself from some kind of irritant – bacteria, viruses, inhalant allergies and/or food allergies.

If the lungs become very inflamed secondary to bacterial and viral infections, it is called pneumonia, which results in an accumulation of immune cells and fluid in the airways and the alveoli. Pneumonia can be either bacterial or viral, with the above-mentioned symptoms in addition to a possible fever, lack of appetite, wheezing and/or rapid breathing.

Causes

Respiratory problems can be caused by bacteria including *Pseudomonas*, *E. coli.* and *Streptococcus* for example, with the most common one being *Bordetella* or Kennel Cough. The most common virus affecting the respiratory system is canine influenza or parainfluenza (a mild form of the flu). Bronchitis is also normally preceded by bacterial and/or viral infections. In persistent respiratory problems, parasites such as roundworms could be a problem, especially in puppies, since the larvae can migrate from the intestines and encyst into the lungs (see Chapter 4 for more information).

Asthma or "allergic bronchitis" is almost always caused by allergic reactions to inhalant allergens (atopy), environmental chemicals, or food allergies. Common inhalant allergens include dust, pollens, trees, mold spores, feathers and hair; dogs can even react to their own hair and the particles in it. Environmental chemicals include household cleaning supplies, air fresheners, deodorizers, candles, perfumes and smoke (wood fire, tobacco or pot). Remember a dog's nose is much closer to the ground than yours.

Dogs can react to inhalant allergens without the symptoms of asthma (i.e. spasms and constriction) and alternatively manifest general symptoms of coughing, sneezing, congestion, reverse sneezing, nasal discharge and so on. (These symptoms can also be caused by food allergies.) In most cases of atopy or inhalant environmental allergies that I have seen in my practice, it is the dog's pet parent who has developed the allergies first, and the dog is sponging sensitivities from them. (See Chapter 17 for information on sponging.)

Food allergies are also a very common cause of asthma though they are often overlooked as a primary cause. Food allergies can cause severe inflammation and reduced respiratory immunity (see Chapter 7 for more information on food allergies and the immune system). Overweight dogs are also more prone to respiratory problems.

Respiratory problems are common in flat-faced dogs because flat-faced dogs have narrowed or partially blocked airways, the nostrils are narrower, the trachea or windpipe is often deformed, they draw in less oxygen and because of a shorter nose they don't cool off as quickly. And because they constantly struggle with less oxygen in their blood they are more prone to heart problems. These dogs include: French bulldogs, English bulldogs, Boston terriers, pugs, Cavalier King Charles spaniels, shih-Tzu's and boxers.

Natural Health Program

Treating the terrain and strengthening the immune system, rather than killing the pathogen, is particularly important in respiratory problems and diseases since a compromised immune system and/or unhealthy airways will predispose a dog to attracting more bacteria and viruses. Aside from diet and inflammatory reactions, one of the most common nutritional conditions affecting the health of the lungs is anemia with low levels of iron, B12, and/or folic acid. However, this is often not likely to show up in the bloodwork since the blood is a poor indicator of nutrient levels in the tissues. Lung tissue has one of the highest oxygen contents of any organ in the body, and therefore, when the iron levels in the lung tissue are low, it affects oxygen levels, immunity, and the ability to resist respiratory diseases and pathogens.

Diet

- No wheat or corn gluten.
- Determine whether there are food allergies/intolerances in the current diet that are respiratory triggers, causing inflammation. Beef and chicken are common allergens.
- No artificial colourings, flavourings, sulphites, or preservatives in the diet which can cause reactions.
- Overweight dogs need to lose weight.

NOTE: Eliminate all chemical cleaning solutions, fragrances, and fresheners from the affected dog's vicinity. It's better for you too! And don't forget the car.

Nutrients (General Nutrients)

- **beta-carotene** [*one dose daily*]† – supports immunity, inhalant allergies; protects mucus membranes
- **vitamin B5** [*one dose daily*]† – adrenal and immune support; helps relax airways
- **vitamin C** [*one dose daily*]†* – adrenal support; immunity, respiratory nutrient, necessary for iron absorption

Nutrients (Anemia)

- **Iron-Up (iron gluconate)** [*once dose daily*]†* – anemia, energy, circulation, immunity
- **vitamin B12** [*one dose daily*]†* – anemia, metabolism, energy
- **folic acid** [*one dose daily*]† – anemia; supports immunity, respiratory function, oxygen levels and energy

NOTE: Discontinue *all* nutraceutical supplements containing sulphur such as glucosamine sulphate, chondroitin sulphate, or MSM. Many dogs are sensitive to sulphur, resulting in shortness of breath, coughing, and low energy.

Herbal & Home Remedies

- **eucalyptus oil** – add a few drops of oil of eucalyptus and thyme to a pot of warm water, cover the pot and your dog's head with a towel and allow her to breathe the vapors; make sure the water is not too hot in case of a spill; vapours break up congestion and help open airways
- **fenugreek tea** [*one dose daily*]† – soothes mucus membranes, dissolves mucus, and helps with allergies, cough, and sore throats
- **lemon juice** [*one dose daily*]† – helps to reduce mucus build-up and congestion in the respiratory tract

Riva's Remedies

- **Allerg-Ease, homeopathic** [one dose daily for 7 days, then as needed]† – sensitivities to dust, molds, pollens, and alder; supports immunity
- **Flu-Ease, homeopathic** [*Treatment: One dose twice daily as needed*]† [*Prevention: before exposure to bacteria/viruses: One dose daily for 3 days; then one dose twice per week*]† – cold and flu symptoms: congestion, colds, coughs and fevers
- **Infection Drops, homeopathic** [*one dose, once or twice daily for 3 to 4 days*]† – for symptoms due to bacteria and viruses
- **Immune Boost, herbal blend** [*one dose daily*]† – promotes immunity and normal respiratory function; liver support
- **Detox Dog, herbal blend** [*one dose daily for 4 to 6 weeks*]† – promotes the detoxification of elimination organs: skin, liver, kidneys and colon; supports the immune system

†See Appendix for recommended dosages and duration for all supplements.
*Also available as a Riva's Remedy

Infections

Symptoms

Infections can affect the ears, skin, intestines, sinuses, nasal passages, respiratory system, urinary system, and the heart. Symptoms may include fevers, discharges, pus, inflammation, swelling, pain, fatigue and tenderness (see the relevant chapters for more details on specific body systems).

Causes

Infections are caused by bacteria, viruses, or other unhealthy pathogens. If the body is toxic or out of balance, or if the normal defense mechanisms are not working, then the body will be unable to protect itself and pathogens will flourish and propagate. Continued toxicity, poor nutrition, and nutrient deficiencies will result in infections re-occurring and/or they will become chronic. All chronic infections are secondary to other underlying unresolved health conditions such as food allergies/intolerances, intestinal parasites, leaky gut, anemia, low thyroid, function, adrenal malfunction as in Cushing's disease, and/or stress. Repeated courses of medications such as antibiotics or steroids will perpetuate toxicity, cause poor digestion, compromise the immune system, and deplete important nutrients – *all* of which are risk factors for infections.

The holistic model does not subscribe to the conventional "germ theory" which hunts for pathogens in order to identify them and then designs a drug to counteract them. The holistic model focusses on the terrain, the health of which is the only factor that determines the ability of the pathogen to flourish and propagate.

~~~~~~~ 🐾 ~~~~~~~

Repeated courses of medications such as antibiotics or steroids will perpetuate toxicity, cause poor digestion, compromise the immune system, and deplete important nutrients – all of which are risk factors for infections.

~~~~~~~~~~~~~~~~~

Natural Health Program

Diet

- Eliminate wheat, corn gluten, dairy products, soy products, rancid oils, and all known food allergies and intolerances (see Chapter 7 for more information).

- Decrease overall meat consumption.

- Avoid feeding added or excess oils including canola oil, soya oil, coconut oil, fish and vegetable oils.

- Add more seeds such as flax, chia, and/or hemp to the diet to provide a natural source of essential fatty acids.

Nutrients

- **vitamin A, liquid** [*one dose daily*]† – supports immunity; nutrient to combat infections and fatigue

- **vitamin C** [*one dose daily*]†* – promotes optimum immunity and healthy liver function

- **Iron-Up (iron gluconate)** [*one dose daily*]†* – supports immunity for symptoms of chronic infections, promotes optimum energy levels

- **lysine** [*one dose daily*]† – immune support for symptoms associated with the herpes virus

Herbal & Home Remedies

- **echinacea** [*one dose daily*]† –bacteria and viruses; immune stimulant – note: not for use with auto-immune conditions

Riva's Remedies

- **Para+Plus, tincture** [*one dose daily as needed*]† – bacteria, yeast and parasites; liver support

- **Immune Boost, herbal blend** [*one dose daily as needed for immune problems*]† – supports digestion, liver, and immune system with nutrition, cleansing, and detoxification

- **Infection Drops, homeopathic** [*one dose twice daily for 3 days*]† – symptoms of skin infections, abscesses, eruptions, and discharges

- **Flu-Ease, homeopathic** [*one dose twice daily for 3 days or as required*]† – symptoms due to colds and flus, e.g., cough, congestion, discharge and fevers

†See Appendix for recommended dosages and duration for all supplements.
*Also available as a Riva's Remedy

Goldie's Heart

Goldie was a five-year-old Golden Labrador who I never did have the pleasure of meeting in person. Goldie had not been well for several months and was suffering from fatigue, poor immunity, allergies and a chronic cough. I was contacted by Goldie's pet parent who lived in another city. Goldie had been to see two veterinarians but there was no definitive diagnosis to explain what was causing Goldie's symptoms. I didn't have a lot to go on and did not get the opportunity to do a complete consultation – distance or otherwise. Nevertheless, after the phone call, it was Goldie's heart that came to mind, and I intuitively felt the presence of tiny worms which were affecting her heart and apparently creating her various troubling symptoms. It could have been heartworm even though Goldie did not live in an area where heartworm was prevalent, although she may have visited a high-risk area. In any case, I instructed Goldie's mom to pick up the herbal tincture for parasites and give one dose to Goldie twice per day. Two or three weeks later the news was good; Goldie was back to her normal self with improved energy, no coughing and a stronger immune system.

Goldie.

7. The Immune System

Defend & Protect

The immune system includes the thymus gland, the spleen, the lymphatic system, and the liver. It is the body's defense against infectious organisms and any other substances that the immune system has identified as foreign invaders: bacteria, viruses, yeast, fungus, toxins, vaccines, chemicals and cancer cells. The immune system is extremely complex and consists of an army of immune cells, proteins, tissues and hormones. Together with the body's detoxification processes, the immune system is responsible for protecting your dog from both the internal and external environment. Chemicals, pathogens, drugs, medications, and toxins are commonly found in all dog food as well as in the grass, dirt, air, and water.

The immune system is critical in protecting from multiple diseases including cancer. Cancer is now the number one disease-related killer in dogs; in fact the current rate of cancer is higher in dogs than it is in humans.

~~~~~~ 🐾 ~~~~~~

Cancer is now the number one disease-related killer in dogs; in fact the current rate of cancer is higher in dogs than it is in humans.

~~~~~~~~~~~~~~~~~~~~~~~~

Natural Health Programs for the Immune System

~~~~~~~~~~~~~ 🐾 ~~~~~~~~~~~~~

General Infections – Bacterial and Viral

Symptoms

Infections can affect the ears, eyes (pink eye), skin, intestines, sinuses, nasal passages, respiratory system, urinary system, and the heart. Symptoms may include fevers, discharges, pus, inflammation, swelling, pain, fatigue, and tenderness. Corneal ulcers can also be a result of bacteria and viruses (as well as food intolerances and vaccine reactions). See the relevant chapters for more details.

Causes

Infections are caused by bacteria, viruses, or other unhealthy pathogens. If the body is toxic or out of balance or the normal defense mechanisms are not working, then the body is unable to protect itself, and the pathogens will flourish and propagate. Continued toxicity, poor nutrition, and nutrient deficiencies will result in recurring or chronic infections. All chronic infections are secondary to other underlying health conditions that have not been resolved: food allergies/intolerances, intestinal parasites, leaky gut, anemia, low thyroid function, adrenal malfunction as in Cushing's disease, and/or stress.

The holistic model does not subscribe to the conventional *germ theory* which identifies specific pathogens in isolation in order to design a drug to kill or counteract them. The holistic model focusses on the *terrain*, the health of which is the only factor that determines the ability of the pathogen to flourish and propagate. In addition, repeated courses of medications such as antibiotics or steroids can cause further infections as these drugs perpetuate toxicity, cause poor digestion, compromise the immune system, destroy the natural intestinal flora, and deplete important nutrients – all of which are risk factors for infections. Millions of antibiotics are prescribed inappropriately every day, and many of them are completely unnecessary. The reckless use of antibiotics has caused, and is continuing to cause, a widespread problem with antibiotic-resistant strains of bacteria. And foolishly, governments allow antibiotics normally used for serious infections to be used for poultry, beef, and other commercial animals without a prescription. Furthermore, consumers continue to request antibiotics from their healthcare practitioners without being properly informed. There are many other approaches when it comes to restoring health. Educate before you medicate.

Natural Health Program

Diet

- Eliminate wheat, corn gluten, dairy products, soy products, rancid oils, and all known food allergies and intolerances (see Chapter 3 for more information).

- Eliminate all red meats such as beef, bison, and venison.

- Avoid feeding added or excess oils including canola oil, soya oil, coconut oil, fish, and vegetable oils.

- Add more seeds to the diet to provide a natural source of essential fatty acids, for example, flax, chia, and/or hemp.

Nutrients

- **vitamin A, liquid** [*one dose daily*]† – improves immunity with symptoms of infections

- **vitamin C** [*one dose daily*]†* – supports optimum immunity and liver function

- **iodine, liquid** [*one dose daily*]† – bacteria, yeast and viruses; has an affinity for the urinary tract

- **lysine** [*one dose daily*]† –indicated for herpes virus

- **Iron-Up (iron gluconate)** [*one dose daily*]†* – symptoms of chronic infections; supports immunity and vitality

Herbal & Home Remedies

- **echinacea** [*one dose daily*]† – viruses and bacteria; supports immunity – note: not for use with auto-immune conditions

Riva's Remedies

- **Para+Plus, tincture** [*one dose daily as needed*]† – bacteria, yeast and parasites; liver support.

- **Immune Boost, herbal blend** [*one dose daily as needed for immune problems*]† – supports digestion, liver, and immune system with nutrition, cleansing, and detoxification

- **Detox Dog** [*one dose daily*]† - Promotes the detoxification of elimination organs - liver, kidneys, skin and colon; supports the immune system

- **Infection Drops, homeopathic** [*one dose twice daily for 3 days*]† – symptoms of skin infections, abscesses, eruptions, and discharges

- **Flu-Ease, homeopathic** [*one dose twice daily for 3 days or as required*]† – symptoms due to colds and flus, e.g. cough, congestion, discharge and fevers

†See Appendix for recommended dosages and duration for all supplements.
*Also available as a Riva's Remedy

Lyme disease

Positive tests for Lyme disease is on the rise, with reports that between 5 to 7 percent of all dogs tested in the U.S. were affected with the *Borrelia burgdorferi* bacteria, which causes Lyme disease. The most heavily affected areas in the U.S. are the Northeastern regions, the Great Lakes region, and California. In Canada, the highest incidence of reported cases occur in southeastern Manitoba, southern Ontario and Quebec, Coastal B.C., and some areas of New Brunswick and Nova Scotia. However, the number of cases seems to be expanding in all geographical areas, particularly those that have warmer, wetter climates.

Infected dogs show antibodies to *Borrelia burgdorferi*, meaning that their immune system is engaged in defending against it. However, it is important to realize that over 95 percent of dogs that test positive will *never* develop symptoms of Lyme disease. This means that while 5 to 7 dogs out of a 100 are affected, only 1 dog out of approximately 300 to 400 will be *afflicted* with Lyme disease. To look at it another way, 19 times out of 20, a dog that tests positive for the *B. burgdorferi* antibody *won't* develop Lyme disease.

This critical statistic suggests that the diagnosis of Lyme disease is often a "red herring" for many dogs (as well as horses and people) who are sick for other reasons. In other words, if your dog isn't feeling well and presents with symptoms consistent with Lyme disease, your canine health practitioner will run a series of blood tests including a test for *B. burgdorferi* antibodies. And if the antibody test comes back positive, it can be assumed that Lyme disease is the cause of the problem. But that assumption is sometimes, perhaps even *often*, erroneous.

~~~~~~~~~ 🐾 ~~~~~~~~~

To look at it another way, 19 times out of 20, a dog that tests positive for the B. burgdorferi antibody *won't* develop Lyme disease.

~~~~~~~~~~~~~~~~~~~

In cases such as this, a misdiagnosed dog is going to endure several courses of antibiotics - complete with side-effects - with minimal results. Furthermore, in these cases, the true and underlying cause of the un-wellness will be missed completely and, therefore, never be addressed. And even if your dog *does* have an active case of Lyme disease and is exhibiting true Lyme symptoms, your dog still requires a comprehensive health program to build up nutrition, strengthen the immune system, and improve the defenses, which is something that antibiotics cannot do.

Like all pathogenic bacterial conditions, the solution lies within the dog's immune system, *not* in exercising a treatment based on the germ theory, which states that microorganisms are the cause of all infectious diseases. As discussed previously the holistic model advocates that bacteria and viruses are the result of a health problem,

not the cause of the health problem. If we continue to focus on the germ, we only invite more of the same in the usually near future.

This is the same issue with people affected with Lyme disease, and while some may have a legitimate problem with Lyme, most others have been convinced that their symptoms and poor health are due to a tick bite rather than diet, nutrition, and lifestyle problems. Lyme has become the new twenty-first century disease, and everybody wants it. This is good for the pharmaceutical companies promoting antibiotic prescriptions and toxic tick control medications, but not so good if you truly want your health back.

Symptoms

True Lyme dogs will generally present with symptoms 3 to 5 months after infection. Pet parents may notice fevers, swollen lymph nodes, arthritic-type symptoms, shifting-leg lameness that lasts for 3 to 4 days, fatigue, depression (reluctance to move and play and loss of appetite). Fevers are common symptoms and can range from mild to severe with serious cases affecting the kidneys.

A female deer tick.

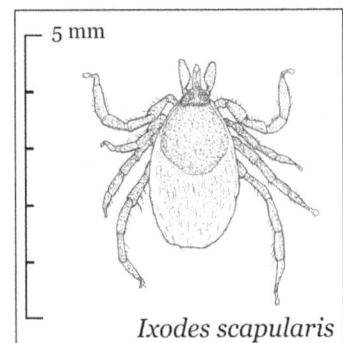

5 mm

Ixodes scapularis

Causes

Lyme disease is caused by three species of spirochete (spiral-shaped) bacteria all belonging to the *Borrelia* genus with *Borrelia burgdorferi* the most common cause in North America. The *B. burgdorferi* is carried by the blacklegged ticks and deer ticks, who pick up the bacteria when they bite infected mice or deer.

Neither dogs nor people are contagious, and cats are rarely affected. However, dogs *can* carry ticks into the living space and/or urban areas. Ticks are incredibly tenacious and can survive harsh outdoor climates and long periods of starvation.

Removing Ticks

To remove an attached tick, it is best to use a pair of fine-tipped tweezers that will allow you to remove the tick without squeezing the body, which may force harmful bacteria into the blood. Grab the tick by the head or mouth parts – not the body – right where they enter the skin. Pull steadily and directly outward, but don't twist which may break the head off. Apply Kava's Healing Oil to the site twice daily to heal the skin and to discourage any bacteria.

Natural Health Program

Diet

- Eliminate wheat, corn gluten, dairy products, soy products, rancid oils, and all known food allergies and intolerances (see Chapter 3).

- Add more seeds to the diet to provide a natural source of essential fatty acids (EFA's), such as flax, chia, and hemp. EFAs are excellent nutrients for all skin conditions.

Nutrients

- **vitamin C** [*one dose daily*]†* – maintains acidity of the skin; parasite resistance, supports immunity and liver function

- **iodine, liquid** [*one dose daily*]† – bacteria, yeast and viruses; immune nutrient

- **Iron-Up (iron gluconate)** [*one dose daily*]†* – optimum immunity, energy and vitality, supports the immune system with chronic or challenging infections

Herbal & Home Remedies

- **yellow dock, tincture** [*one dose daily for 30 days*]† – symptoms due to parasites, promotes healthy blood, skin and immunity

Riva's Remedies

- **Pro-Colon, probiotic** [*one dose daily for 4 to 6 weeks*]† – probiotics and prebiotics for intestinal immunity and colon support

- **Para+Plus, tincture** [*one dose daily for 6 to 8 weeks*]† – bacteria, yeast and parasites; promotes a healthy immune response; liver support

- **Skin-Heal, herbal blend** [*one dose daily*]† – promotes the health of the skin, blood and liver, supports immunity with symptoms of parasites

- **Immune Boost, herbal blend** [*one dose daily*]† – supports the immune response, promotes vitality and energy; nutrition and liver support

- **Detox Dog, herbal blend** [*one dose daily for 4 to 6 weeks*]† – promotes the detoxification of elimination organs: skin, liver, kidneys and colon; supports the immune system

†See Appendix for recommended dosages and duration for all supplements.
*Also available as a Riva's Remedy

Food Allergies and Food Intolerances

Symptoms

The word *allergy* is derived from two Greek words: *allos* (different/strange) and *ergon* (activity). An allergic reaction is an adverse immune response to a food protein (antigen), whereby the offending food invokes the release of antibodies to destroy it or to neutralize its actions. The subsequent discharge of histamines and chemicals causes inflammation that can affect virtually any body system with a variety of symptoms. Food allergies and food intolerances are not the same. True food allergies indicate, not that there is a problem with the food, but rather that there is a problem with the immune system. True allergy reactions are immediate and can occur within minutes (or within two hours) of eating an offensive meal. Reactions commonly result in acute itching, hives, rashes, swellings, breathing problems, diarrhea and/or cramping. As a rule, the faster the reaction, the faster the symptoms disappear.

Food *intolerances*, on the other hand, mean that there is a problem with the food and not necessarily the immune system. It is described as an intolerance because

> Food allergies and food intolerances are not the same; true food allergies indicate that there is something wrong with the immune system while food intolerances mean that there is something wrong with the food.

of the body's inability to digest, absorb, or assimilate these unhealthy foods. Common food intolerances for dogs include, for example, wheat, corn, and soy. Symptoms of food intolerances usually become chronic and can affect the respiratory system, the gastro-intestinal system, the skin, urinary tract, immune system, the eyes (corneal ulcers), the endocrine system (responsible for hormones), the musculoskeletal system and/or nervous system. General symptoms such as fatigue, excessive appetite, blood-sugar abnormalities, and obesity also occur. Chronic infections are also very common, including ear and/or skin infections. If these food problems are not eliminated, lasting health problems will be a certain result. Food intolerances are often hidden, and in contrast to allergies, they mostly cause delayed reactions, beginning several hours later or even the next day. Even after eliminating culprit foods, symptoms can last for up to 72 hours. However, over time, food intolerances, due to mal-digestion, create increasing toxicity, where the process of detoxification can take several weeks.

Both food allergies and intolerances are often responsible for immune problems, skin symptoms, itching, hot spots, infections, recurring ear problems, abscesses, anal itching, and behavioural changes. Insulin deficiency diabetes can also occur as a result of food reactions because they are capable of causing inflammation and damage to the insulin-producing beta cells of the pancreas. This is why dogs on low carbohydrate and grain-free diets can still have problems with blood-sugar imbalances (see Chapter 10 for more information).

Causes

Food allergies provoke an antibody immune response (rather than an attack) because the immune system is compromised. The immune system can be traumatized and damaged not only by food and intestinal toxicity, but also by medications, antibiotics, vaccines and emotional stress – either their own or from their human family.

In addition, immune disorders are exacerbated by anemia, low thyroid, bacterial/viral infections, parasites, and stress – all of which increase the potential for food allergies (see respective chapters for more information). In the case of food intolerances, food is always the primary problem, and unhealthy foods must be eliminated to give the body time to heal.

Many dogs will also have a problem with lectins; these are food proteins which act as toxins that invoke immune responses by causing damage to tissues through antibody attacks. Lectins can bind to membranes on the surface of arteries, intestines, organs, and glands, including the thyroid, pituitary, pancreas, kidneys, liver, brain and adrenals. The subsequent inflammation and cell damage leads to food reactions, hormone imbalances (even if spayed or neutered), auto-immune disorders and degenerative diseases.

Poor digestion and/or leaky gut frequently exacerbate food intolerances and reactions. Because of the resulting intestinal toxicity from eating inappropriate foods, the digestion becomes compromised and the mal-digested food debris, acids, toxins, and pathogens depress the intestinal immune system (see Chapter 4 for more information on "Leaky Gut").

Natural Health Program

There are different methods available for food-allergy testing, including blood, skin, and saliva testing; however, most of them are not completely accurate since food allergies can change from day to day and week to week, so the results of one test can be very different from the next one. And they don't detect the food *intolerances*; most intolerances are hidden and don't cause immediate and acute antibody reactions. These methods of testing also don't offer any explanation for how the animal acquired the sensitivities or reactions in the first place. It's more effective to work with an elimination diet (see below) and/or to conduct a basic kinesiology test using muscle testing (see Appendices for instructions).

The key to overcoming food problems is to heal the immune system by identifying and correcting all the underlying issues, such as allergies, intolerances, diet, nutrient deficiencies, and lifestyle. And remember, one dog's meat is another dog's poison.

Diet

- Eliminate wheat, corn gluten, dairy products, soy products, rancid oils, and all known food allergies and intolerances.

- Food allergies often develop from the foods that are eaten regularly and repetitively. This is because a failing immune system will react to whatever it is exposed to on a regular basis. A common example of this is chicken; millions of dogs eat chicken day in and day out, and thousands (if not millions) of them, are sensitive to it. Therefore, immune-compromised dogs must eliminate all previous staples from their diet until their immune system has cleared it, a process which can take anywhere from 6 to 12 weeks. And even then, affected dogs may continue to react. Always offer your dogs food variety, and change up the dietary staples from time to time.

- Eliminate beef, bison, venison, red meats, and organ meats, for these are common immune triggers which cause inflammation and tissue damage. Frequently this is not because they are an allergen, but because they are high in certain acids. Acidic diets contribute to a higher incidence of allergies as well as inflammatory conditions including muscle and joint pain. Senior dogs, in particular, cannot digest and metabolize red meats as efficiently, which causes problems with toxicity and leaky gut. See Chapter 3 for more information.

- Use caution with fish and sometimes eggs.

- Avoid prescription diets, which often contain wheat, corn, and odd sources of protein such as feathers. They *also* contain hydrolyzed proteins from chicken liver and soy, and *all* hydrolyzed proteins contain MSG (monosodium glutamate).

- Avoid feeding excess oils, including canola oil, soya oil, coconut oil, and vegetable oils. These congest the liver, adversely affecting the immune system and the digestive system.

- No artificial colourings, flavourings, rawhide or preservatives.

- Address a leaky gut (see Chapter 4 "Leaky Gut").

- If the diet your dog is on right now is not working, then change it. Period.

Elimination Diets

If your dog needs more help aside from these guidelines, the next step is a 21-day elimination diet. The best diet programs for healing highly-sensitive dogs with overreactive immune systems are home cooked meals so you can monitor everything that goes in their mouths, including the type of food, the volume of food, and the ratios of meat vs carbohydrates vs fats. It also takes the guesswork as to which foods are most likely to be causing the reactions. Prepare at home and feed twice per day. Quantities should be determined by the size, weight, and health condition of the dog (see Chapter 3 for more extensive information on food groups, individual foods, and details

on specific diets).

Once your dog responds to and improves on a given elimination diet, then it is safe to add more variety, one food at a time, in order to gauge any reactions. Twenty-one days is enough time for the digestion to improve, to repair some of the damage from food intolerances, and for the immune system to strengthen. But it is not long enough to clear the specific food allergies or sensitivities themselves as these normally take several weeks longer as discussed previously.

You can choose from one of the following elimination diets and see how your dog responds. Choose one that is very different from what your dog is eating now, or see the appendix for instructions on kinesiology (muscle testing).

21-day Elimination Diets (Choose One)

1. Paleo

Choose a protein which your dog has not previously been exposed to: lamb, turkey, salmon, or pork. No red meat or organ meats. The meat can be cooked or raw, but it is recommended to offer your dog both options in the beginning to see which one they choose. Don't mix more than one meat protein per meal and combine it with cooked vegetables and/or cooked fruit. You may cook and feed soups, stir-fries, broths, and stews. Bones can be used in cooking liquids, but must be removed before feeding. Raw meaty bones can be fed so long as it is not beef or red meat. You may feed potatoes and/or sweet potatoes once every 4 days. However, some dogs are sensitive to the higher sugar levels in sweet potatoes or yams. No grains of any kind.

2. Egg & Vegetables

Feed only lightly cooked eggs and cooked vegetables. You may cook and feed soups, stir-fries, broths, and stews. No grains, no fruit, no meat protein, and no fish. You may feed potatoes once every 4 days and/or sweet potatoes so long as they are not sugar sensitive. You may also prepare vegetable broths with bones in, but ensure that the bones are removed before feeding. No grains of any kind. The first foods to re-introduce would be extra protein such as poultry, lamb, salmon, or any other staple which they have not been exposed to for several months. Introduce one at a time and very slowly, as in once every 2 or 3 days.

3. Lectin-Free

Eliminate lectins found in dairy products, regular potatoes, tomatoes, nuts, seeds, legumes, and most grains, such as wheat, oats, rye, barley, millet, rice, quinoa and buckwheat. Wild rice and white rice do not contain lectins and are safe to feed. Eggs are high in lectins, but for some reason are not as likely to cause an immune response as often as some of the grains unless the dog is anemic (with low levels of iron, vitamin B12, and/or folic acid).

The meat can be cooked or raw, but it is recommended to offer your dog both options in the beginning to see which one she chooses. Don't mix more than one meat protein per meal and combine with cooked vegetables and/or cooked fruit. You may cook and feed soups, stir-fries, broths, and stews. Bones can be used in cooking liquids but must be removed before feeding. Raw meaty bones can be fed with this program, but keep beef and red meat to a minimum (as in once or twice per week). Include cooked vegetables and fruit.

4. Vegetarian

A vegetarian program is very useful for those dogs who are highly toxic and acidic from poor diets, excess meat, and meat toxicity (as is often the case with cancer). Meat overload is becoming a more common problem because of sedentary lifestyles, the quality and toxicity of available meats, the popularity of grain-free, the emphasis on raw, and the levels and ratio of proteins in kibble. (See Chapter 3). Feed cooked vegetables and/or cooked fruit. You may cook and feed soups, stir-fries, broths, and stews. You may feed potatoes and/or sweet potatoes once every 4 days; however, be aware that some dogs are sensitive to the higher sugar levels in sweet potatoes or yams. Start with easy-to-digest grains, such as cooked oats, barley, bulgur, and white rice, such as jasmine or basmati. The beta-glucans in barley can be quite healing to the intestinal membranes. If tolerated, add small and well-cooked beans, such as lentils, split peas, black beans, adzuki beans, and pinto beans (see Chapter 3 "Vegetarian Diet" for more details and for instructions on cooking legumes).

Elimination Diet Notes:

- Corn fed at home as a vegetable is not a grain and is safe to feed.

- Add a small amount of sea salt to the food daily for all diet programs.

- Be aware that some highly-sensitive dogs will initially improve and then start to react to some of the foods in the new diet program. If this is the case then all staples – whether a grain *or* a meat – should be fed on a rotational basis with one food fed no more than once every 4 days. Food groups least likely to cause a reaction are cooked vegetables and cooked fruit. Make use of well-selected supplements to support the immune system and to help keep food reactions to a minimum.

- Discontinue all previous supplements, especially long-term ones. The supplements recommended here are beneficial for many dogs and are least likely to cause a reaction in immune-compromised dogs.

Nutrients

- **folic acid** [*one dose daily*][†] – supports the immune response; protein digestion; promotes the natural production of probiotics

- **vitamin B12** [*one dose daily*][†*] – colon support, nerve nutrient, liver detoxifier; carbohydrate metabolism

- **iodine, liquid** [*one dose daily*][†] – bacteria and yeast, important nutrient for immunity, skin health, thyroid function, and metabolism

Herbal & Home Remedies

- **milk thistle seed, tincture** [*one dose daily*][†] – liver support, natural detoxifier; neutralizes allergy reactions

- **arnica 30C, homeopathic** [*one dose twice daily as needed*][†] – symptoms due to acute reactions to food allergies, swellings and trauma

- **thymus glandular 200C, homeopathic** [*one dose twice daily for 7 to 10 days*][†] – supports immune system and thymus gland function

Riva's Remedies

- **Pro-Colon, probiotic** [*one dose daily for 3 to 4 weeks*][†] – probiotics and prebiotics for intestinal support, helps balance the digestive ecosystem and maintains a healthy intestinal immune system

- **Pro-Dygest, herbal blend** [*once daily for 3 to 4 weeks*][†] – intestinal cleanser and detoxifier, added fibre; leaky gut

- **Detox Dog, herbal blend** [*one dose daily for 4-6 weeks*]† – promotes the detoxification of elimination organs: skin, liver, kidneys and colon, supports the immune system.

- **Kava's Primrose Oil, specialized nutrient** [*one dose daily*]† – essential fatty acids, nutritional support for immune function, healthy skin and fur

- **Immune Boost, herbal blend** [*one dose daily*]† – liver and immune support for dogs with food intolerances, frequent infections and/or a history of immune problems

- **Skin-Heal, herbal blend** [*one dose daily*]† – blood, liver and skin detoxification; nutrition for healthy skin; hives, rashes, growths, and chronic skin conditions

Vaccines

Use extreme caution in vaccinating the immune-compromised dog due to the likelihood of vaccinosis, i.e., adverse vaccine reactions. Adverse vaccine reactions can be immediate or insidiously delayed by several days, weeks, or months. Reactions are particularly common in sensitive animals with compromised immunity and can be acute or chronic, affecting the liver, the immune system, skin and the nervous system. See Chapter 8 for more information on vaccine reactions.

†See Appendix for recommended dosages and duration for all supplements.
*Also available as a Riva's Remedy

Auto-Immune Conditions

There are several health conditions in dogs that are considered "auto-immune" diseases. Auto-immune diseases describe the process by where certain body systems and their tissues are thought to be attacked by the body's own immune system. This label is beginning to be used as a catch-all in the veterinary community and among dog parents as an explanation for a number of health problems. Unfortunately, they consider auto-immune to be a defect of the immune system with no known cause. Nothing could be further from the truth. Why would an immune system attack itself for no logical reason? The body has a built-in and inherent intelligence that directs its decisions to protect tissues through various defense mechanisms; rarely does the immune system make mistakes. But if the canine practitioner doesn't understand the cause, then a randomly defective immune system must be to blame, and *that* can then be treated with immuno-suppressant drugs, steroids, and/or removal of the spleen. These are facile Band-Aid remedies at best and barbaric at worst.

Every case of auto-immune dysfunction is a result of some type of systemic toxicity.

So let's take a look at what *really* happens. As we have established, the immune system's primary function is to protect the body from foreign invaders, pathogens, and environmental and dietary toxins. When the body cannot remove these substances faster than they enter, the toxins will accumulate in the tissues or organs for storage. Not only do they cause damage there, but the immune system is signalled to their presence and correctly responds by launching an attack; first the antibodies are deployed as markers, and then the white blood cells as killers. This immune reaction will not let up until the foreign invaders have either stopped being ingested, produced, or reproduced. I have guided hundreds of human and canines with so-called auto-immune conditions back to health with diet, detoxification, and exceptional nutrition. Any powerful immune-suppressant drugs and/or steroids were gradually discontinued as the immune system was no longer in overdrive. The immune system will never betray you or your dog.

White and red blood cells.

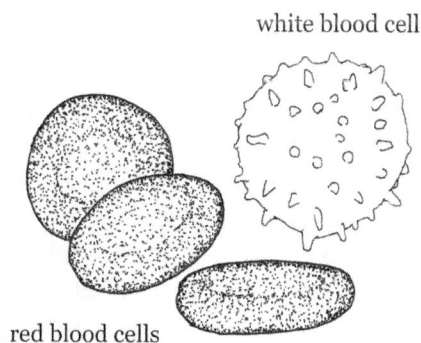

white blood cell

red blood cells

Let's look at some canine conditions commonly diagnosed as auto-immune problems.

• The first is AIHA (Autoimmune Hemolytic Anemia). Anemia is defined as a decrease in the number of red blood cells or the amount of hemoglobin, hemoglobin is how oxygen is carried. Anemia can be caused by blood loss, but is mostly caused by a decrease in the production of new red blood cells due to nutritional deficiencies (see Chapter 12 for more information on anemia). However, hemolytic anemia means that red blood cells are being destroyed faster than usual. This occurs as a result of the cells being marked for destruction by the antibodies in response to parasites, heavy metals, toxins, and/or drugs, such as certain antibiotics, anticonvulsant medication, chemical dewormers, and anticancer medications. Symptoms are gradual and progressive and indicate the body's lack of oxygen: fatigue, lack of appetite, increased heart rate and difficulty breathing. As more cells die, there can be a build-up of bilirubin (a breakdown product of hemoglobin) in the liver causing yellow gums, eyes, and skin. This is commonly known as jaundice.

The clinical signs of AIHA are usually gradual and progressive, but occasionally an apparently healthy pet suddenly collapses in an acute hemolytic crisis. The symptoms are usually related to a lack of oxygen: weakness, lethargy, anorexia, and an increase in the heart rate and respirations. Heart murmurs and pale mucous membranes (gums, eyelids, etc.) may also be present. More severe cases also have a fever. Other canine immune conditions include:

• **Immune-Mediated Thrombocytopenia** or IMT is a condition similar to the hemolytic anemia, but this time it is the destruction of thrombocytes – the clotting cells. Symptoms include excessive bruising, excessive bleeding, and/or bloody urine and bloody stool. Conventional treatment is similar to hemolytic anemia.

• **Pemphigus complex** is a condition that describes a group of four auto-immune skin disorders. Symptoms include blisters, eruptions, and skin ulcers. Lesions are common and can be found in the mouth and the borders of haired skin such as eyelids, lips, nostrils, anus, vulva, groin, and armpits. They can also be found on the face, ears, and foot pads. Depending on the type of disease, lesions can be red and weepy, thick and oozing, or crusty and scaly. Skin infections are common.

• **Discoid lupus** presents as dermatitis on the face in the shape of a butterfly over the nose. Systemic lupus may also present with a butterfly rash as well as fluctuating fevers and stiffness of the muscles and joints.

• **Rheumatoid arthritis** or RA is a common immune disorder whereby the immune system attacks the joint tissues causing varying degrees of destructive inflammation. Rheumatoid arthritis usually affects more than one joint and can shift from one area to another. Joints become swollen, tender, and sore, and the dog may appear stiff or lame.

• **Thyroiditis** affects, as the name suggests, the thyroid gland. The thyroid gland produces important hormones, and when hormone production drops, the condition is called hypothyroidism. This can result in a decrease in the metabolic rate, causing weight gain, hair loss, immune problems, skin problems, dry skin, high cholesterol, constipation and/or depression. However, some dogs may not show any obvious symptoms at all. It is now thought that most hypothyroid cases are auto-immune; however, there are many other reasons for thyroid dysfunction (see Chapter 8).

Causes

Every case of auto-immune dysfunction is a result of some type of systemic toxicity. This toxicity is caused or exacerbated by one or more factors: food intolerances (often hidden), lectins, colon toxicity, leaky gut, excess acidity, pathogenic bacteria, parasites, toxic substances, chemicals, drug residue, vaccines, vaccine contamination, and sometimes heavy metals. However, the most common reasons are vaccinosis, food intolerances, dietary toxicity, and leaky gut. The success rate in resolving auto-immune conditions with therapeutic diet and nutrition is very high.

Natural Health Program

The toxins and poisons in the body will normally deposit themselves into the tissues and/or organs which are already weakened and have the least resistance. This is why auto-immune presents itself in so many different ways. No matter which body system is affected, the body needs to be detoxified and the immune system supported and strengthened – not artificially shut down with powerful steroids, immune-suppressant drugs, and/or serious surgery to remove invaluable immune organs.

The program below addresses generalized auto-immune conditions. See respective chapters for further information and detailed programs to support specific body functions, i.e. anemia, skin, thyroid and musculoskeletal.

Diet

- Eliminate wheat, corn gluten, dairy products, soy products, rancid oils, and all known food allergies and intolerances.

- Use caution with grains, for some dogs need to be grain-free

- Lectins can be a serious consideration in auto-immune conditions (see above section "Food Allergies and Intolerances" for more information).

- Eliminate beef, bison, venison, red meats, and organ meats, for these are common immune triggers which cause inflammation and tissue damage. Frequently this is not because they are an allergen *per se*, but because they are high in certain acids; accumulated acids contribute to a higher incidence of allergies as well as a variety of inflammatory conditions including arthritis and joint pain. In addition, senior dogs cannot digest or metabolize red meats as efficiently. See chapter 3 for more information.

- Use caution with fish and sometimes eggs.

- Use caution with prescription diets which often contain wheat, corn, allergens, hydrolyzed proteins and odd sources of protein such as feathers. It's not necessary to get exotic.

- Avoid feeding excess oils, including canola oil, soya oil, coconut oil, and vegetable oils. These congest the liver adversely affecting the immune system.

- Some dogs will need to go on a vegetarian cleanse (see Chapter 3).

- No artificial colourings, flavourings, rawhide, or preservatives.

- If you need to determine which foods are most toxic for your dogs, including raw meat vs cooked meat or no meat at all, perform regular muscle tests for all foods. See the appendix for instructions on muscle testing (kinesiology). It is recommended to feed only homemade food, at least in the beginning. This way you are very sure of exactly what your dog is eating.

Nutrients

- **folic acid** [*one dose daily*][†] – immune nutrient; tissue repair, promotes the natural production of probiotics

- **vitamin B12** [*one dose daily*][†*] – liver detoxifier; carbohydrate metabolism, colon support, nerve nutrient

- **iodine, liquid** [*one dose daily*][†] – bacteria and yeast; important nutrient for immunity, digestion, skin, thyroid and metabolism

Note: Avoid all nutraceuticals containing glucosamine, chondroitin and/or MSM. See Chapter 14 for more information on the side-effects of these supplements.

Herbal & Home Remedies

- **thymus glandular 200C, homeopathic** [*one dose twice daily for 7 to 10 days*][†] – supports immune system and thymus gland function

- **adrenal glandular 200C, homeopathic** [*one dose twice daily for 14 days*][†] – adrenal support, energy, stress and trauma

Riva's Remedies

- **Pro-Colon, probiotic** [*one dose daily for 3 to 4 weeks*][†] – probiotics and prebiotics for intestinal support, discourages unfriendly bacteria and viruses, maintains absorption of nutrients, leaky gut support; promotes a healthy intestinal immune system

- **Pro-Dygest, herbal blend** [*once daily for 3 to 4 weeks*][†] – intestinal toxicity and cleansing; adds extra fibre, leaky gut support

- **Bone-Up, herbal blend** [*one dose daily*][†] – contains calcium citrate for excess acids; important nutrient for skin, muscles and joints

- **Immune Boost, herbal blend** [*one dose daily*][†] – supports digestion, liver, and immune system with nutrition and and detoxification in dogs with immune problems

- **Detox Dog, herbal blend** [*one dose daily for 4 to 6 weeks*][†] – promotes the detoxification of elimination organs: skin, liver, kidneys and colon; supports the immune system.

- **Kava's Primrose Oil, specialized nutrient** [*one dose daily*][†] – essential fatty acids, nutrition; optimum immunity, skin and joints

- **Skin-Heal, herbal blend** [*one dose daily as needed for* *skin reactions*]† – liver, blood and immune support; nutritional and detox support for skin; hives, rashes, eruptions, and chronic skin conditions

Vaccines

Use extreme caution in vaccinating the immune compromised dog due to the likelihood of vaccinosis, i.e., adverse vaccine reactions. Adverse vaccine reactions can be immediate or insidiously delayed by several days, weeks, or months. Reactions are particularly common in sensitive animals with compromised immunity and can be acute or chronic, affecting a host of tissues including the liver, the immune system, and the nervous system. See Chapter 8 for more details on vaccine reactions.

†See Appendix for recommended dosages and duration for all supplements.

*Also available as a Riva's Remedy

Lymphoma

Cancer is a medical term that refers to cells which grow and multiply abnormally. Whereas normal cells follow a pattern of growth, division, and death, cancer cells grow continuously, outlive normal cells, and then conglomerate into growths which we call tumours. Eventually cells from the tumours break away and migrate to another body part to grow tumours there as well. This process is known as metastasis.

Canine lymphomas are a diverse group of cancers and are among the most common cancers diagnosed in dogs. There are 30 types of lymphomas which represent up to 14 percent of all cancers diagnosed in dogs. They vary greatly in behaviour and in symptoms. Lymphoma affects the lymphocytes (white blood cells) and, therefore, most commonly arises in organs that function as part of the immune system such as the lymph nodes, spleen, and bone marrow. By far the most common type of lymphoma in the dog is multicentric lymphoma, in which the cancer first becomes apparent in lymph nodes. Canine lymphomas are similar to the non-Hodgkin's lymphoma in people.

Symptoms

Symptoms are mostly related to the location of the tumours. Most commonly, growths first become apparent in the lymph nodes where they present as swellings. The enlarged nodes are firm but not tender. From here they can spread to the other immune organs such as the spleen, liver, and bone marrow. Lymphoma can also occur in the gastrointestinal tract causing lack of appetite, indigestion, vomiting, dark diarrhea, and/or weight loss. Tumours in the thymus gland (located in the middle of the chest) can cause shortness of breath and changes in heart sounds as well as a swollen face or front legs. Skin tumours show up as lumps or bumps which look dry, flaky, red, and feel itchy. Skin tumours are sometimes misdiagnosed as infections.

Causes

At the cellular level, cancer is caused by damage to the DNA inside each cell. DNA is found in every cell and is responsible for directing cell behaviour. However, if the DNA becomes damaged and the immune system is unable to repair the damage, the cells can no longer regulate their own division and growth thus they begin to multiply and grow abnormally. Cancer cells use sugar and protein for energy and produce lactate, an acid that converts back to glucose.

Like most cancers, the three main physical causes of DNA damage and subsequent symptoms are in order:

1. Diet and food toxins; obesity

2. Chronic inflammation as caused by pathogens: bacteria, viruses and/or parasites, chronic inflammation releases powerful and destructive free radicals

3. Environmental chemicals, drugs and/or vaccines

All these factors either initiate or encourage abnormal changes in the DNA. They also suppress the immune system; if the immune system is not functioning at an optimum level then cancer cells are easily initiated and are able to proliferate without any controls. However, it is the food factor that has the biggest impact on not only creating the unhealthy and toxic terrain which provides a hospitable environment for infections, inflammation, and mutations, but in determining the strength of the immune system. Unfortunately, the biggest source of toxicity in the dog's diet contributing to cancer is meat!

Various studies for people have shown a strong correlation between cancer and the amount of animal protein, even low-fat animal foods, consumed. Our dogs are no different other than the fact that they eat *much* more meat than we do.

Meat is full of chemicals, additives, antibiotics, medications, hormones, toxic residue of pesticides, heavy metals, diseases, cancer, the animal's body toxins, decay, bacteria and genetically altered substances – many animals raised for meat are eating GMO food. Animal meat is also full of dioxins which are chemicals that are released into the environment. Dioxins are by-products of combustion emitted by waste incinerators, chemical manufacturing plants, and paper and pulp mills. Dioxins are hormone disrupters and are linked to cancer and adverse changes to the immune system. Over 95 percent of dioxin exposure comes in the concentrated form of meat, fish, and dairy products. In addition, animal products, not plants, are responsible for over 80 percent of the herbicides and pesticides that we ingest.

In addition, excess saturated fats from meat and dairy products increase bile acids and steroids, both of which promote the production of unhealthy and anaerobic intestinal bacteria. These unhealthy strains of bacteria can convert bile acids to carcinogenic substances (see Chapter 3 for more information on the toxic effects of meat).

Aside from meat, exposure to petroleum products and benzene are also risk factors.

Natural Health Program

The cancerous body is extremely toxic, thus the most successful approach to restoring health to the body is maximizing nutrition with organic healthy foods to support the process of detoxification and to establish a prime immune system.

Diet

- Feed your dog a home-cooked vegetarian diet with whole grains and lots of healthy vegetables. This is intended to eliminate all meat toxins, rancid and/or unhealthy fats, poor quality grains, additives and preservatives. In addition, a vegetarian diet provides fibre and key nutrients necessary for detoxification and for re-building the immune system. Meat toxicity and its role in cancer cannot be understated (See Chapter 3 for details on feeding vegetarian diet programs).

- No unhealthy or excess oils; oils cause cancer by interfering with oxygen use in the cells and infusing them with toxic material. All cancer cells have depressed oxygen consumption. They also have a concentration of debris which the cell cannot cleanse because it lacks sufficient energy. In addition, large or difficult to digest fat molecules are not absorbed into the bloodstream; instead, these fats are directly delivered to the lymphatic system where they congest and degenerate lymph nodes and organs. This disables the lymph system from protecting the body from cancer cells and other invaders. Therefore, do not feed canola, soya, coconut, vegetable, fish or corn oils. Include a small daily dose of therapeutic oils or seeds, such as flaxseed, chia, and/or hemp seeds, for these contain essential fatty acids which enhance the immune system and decrease inflammation.

- No wheat, dairy products, corn gluten or soy products.

- Absolutely no artificial colourings, flavourings, rawhide, or preservatives.

- Choose all organic food as much as possible.

Nutrients

- **folic acid** [*one dose daily*]† – intestinal immunity, nutrient required for healthy cell replication, cell growth and tissue repair

- **vitamin A, liquid** [*one dose daily*]† – increases the immune response in cancerous conditions, promotes healthy cell growth

- **iodine, liquid** [*one dose daily*]† – bacteria, yeast and viruses; important nutrient for immunity, metabolism, and energy production.

- **selenium, organic** [*one dose daily*]† – anti-oxidant, immune support for cancerous toxicity; liver detoxifier and chemical toxicity

- Notes:

  1. Use caution with calcium and/or iron supplements. If these minerals are in excess, they can exacerbate a cancerous condition. Determine nutritional benefit with a hair tissue mineral analysis and/or a kinesiology session.

  2. Avoid the use of all nutraceuticals including glucosamine, chondroitin and/or MSM. See Chapter 14 for more information on side effects.

Herbal & Home Remedies

- **thymus glandular 200C, homeopathic** [*one dose daily for 7 to 10 days*]† – supports immune system and thymus gland function; allergy reactions

- **Pau D'arco (taheebo)** [*one dose daily*]† – bacteria and yeast; acts on the lymph system as a cleanser, purifier and decongestant; immune support

- **shiitake mushroom** [*one dose daily*]† – supports immune function, anti-tumour activity, helps eliminate toxic heavy metals

Riva's Remedies

- **Pro-Colon, probiotic** [*one dose daily for 3 to 4 weeks*]† – probiotics and prebiotics for intestinal support, discourages unfriendly bacteria and viruses, absorption of nutrients, leaky gut support, maintains a healthy intestinal immune system.

- **Detox Dog, herbal blend** [one dose daily for 4 to 6 weeks]† – promotes the detoxification of elimination organs: skin, liver, kidneys and colon; supports the immune system.

- **Immune Boost, herbal blend** [*one dose daily*]† – supports digestion, liver, and immune system with nutrition and detoxification in dogs with immune problems

- **Happy Pets** or **Happy Pets Senior, herbal blend** [*one dose daily*]† – an all-natural plant and seaweed blend rich in organic minerals, vitamins, and fibre; antioxidant activity. Optimum immunity; skin, hair and nails.

Vaccines

Use extreme caution in vaccinating all dogs, but particularly those who are immune compromised and/or in a toxic condition. Canine vaccines contain heavy metals such as mercury and aluminum compounds as well as other chemical and carcinogenic adjuvants including formaldehyde (see Chapter 8 for more information on vaccines).

†See Appendix for recommended dosages and duration for all supplements.

Jasper's Mystery Illness

Jasper was an eight-month-old, very healthy golden mountain dog who settled into a comfortable sleep one night and then woke up the next morning and could not get up. His mouth and legs were swollen, and he was very sore; he was so sore he could not get up and walk. Jasper's parents first tried a prescription anti-inflammatory, but this only made his symptoms worse, and he started to drool and foam at the mouth. Then he started to develop ulcers throughout his mouth and on his tongue, hot spots began erupting on his legs, his leg hair started falling out, and he started biting himself. He also became depressed and lethargic. They had him admitted to the local veterinary clinic, but his spinal taps and blood tests came back normal. He was then given two different types of antibiotics, after which, he still didn't show any signs of improvement, and in fact, he continued to worsen. His pet parent writes:

"I didn't know what else to do, so I scheduled a distance consultation with Marijke. She told me to bring him home and change his diet. She explained that Jasper was having an auto-immune reaction which was causing all his acute symptoms. She identified that Jasper was reacting to chicken, corn gluten, and wheat – all of which he was eating daily in his kibble.

Jasper.

Healing Dogs Their Way

"In addition, she explained that his now exhausted adrenal glands were impeding his recovery and making it difficult for him to control the inflammation due to the food reactions. As well, his liver and immune system had been recently compromised by both the medications as well as vaccinations. He was started on iron, folic acid, potassium, licorice root, and Pro-Colon probiotics as well as specific homeopathic remedies. Within two weeks, Jasper was back to one hundred percent. I cannot thank Marijke enough for her support and help with saving Jasper." —Tiffany (Victoria, B.C.)

In all immune conditions, the offending foods must be eliminated since all food reactions cause inflammation. True food reactions cannot be overcome with supplements, remedies, or medications. But, after the diet is corrected, well selected vitamins and minerals administered in therapeutic dosages will be highly beneficial as they correct the nutrient deficiencies, support liver function and the immune system, as well as mitigate the adverse effects from vaccinosis. In this case, the iron was required for optimum immunity and circulation, and the folic acid helped with protein digestion, the intestinal immune system, and the nervous system. Licorice root was used short-term to promote healthy adrenal function.

Molly's Miracle Mouth

Diane brought in her ten-year-old black Lab, Molly, one day. Molly had just been diagnosed with oral cancer. She had a growth on the roof of her mouth identified as an aggressive squamous cell carcinoma. The prognosis that Diane was given was pretty grim – Molly's growth would continue to metastasize and invade the surrounding bone and tissue until eventually she would not be able to eat or drink at which point euthanasia would be her only option. Diane knew very little about what natural health would have to offer animals, including Molly, but because her own health had improved with my nutritional programs, she wanted to give it a try for Molly too.

We changed Molly's diet by reducing her overall proteins, adding more vegetables, removing all added oils and increasing her essential fatty acid levels with flax seeds. Diane was instructed to cook a few more home-cooked meals for Molly to improve her overall nutrition. We added some key nutrients including probiotics, vitamin C, beta-carotene and herbal blends to support her immune system and maximize her nutritional intake. If necessary, I was prepared to make Molly's program stricter and change up her supplement program on her next visit. But I only saw Molly once. A year later, Diane came in for her own personal appointment and casually remarked – as if nothing unusual happened – that Molly was doing just fine, and as far as they were concerned, there were no more life-threatening issues. I'm sure the power of positive thought by Diane on the intended outcome was an important factor in Molly's good health too!

Molly.

8. Vaccinosis

Have We Gone Too Far?

Vaccinosis is the term used to describe the symptoms or adverse health reactions that occur after a vaccine has been administered. Vaccinosis can occur immediately within minutes, or can be insidiously delayed by several days, weeks, or months in which case most dog parents never make the connection.

There are three types of vaccines: modified live vaccines or MLV, killed vaccines, and recombinant vaccines. The premise of vaccine therapy is based on the discovery that when a virus is injected into the body, it multiplies and stimulates the immune system's production of antibodies. This is thought to create an immune response that protects the body from the same virus in case of exposure to the disease.

~~~~~~~~ 🐾 ~~~~~~~~

Vaccinosis can occur immediately within minutes, or can be insidiously delayed by several days, weeks, or months in which case most dog parents never make the connection.

~~~~~~~~~~~~~~~~

With MLV vaccines, the causative live organism, i.e., the virus or bacteria, has been weakened or modified so that it is no longer virulent. Modified live vaccines are manufactured by growing a live virus in different cells sourced from other species, such as eggs, chicken embryos, calf serum, or any other cells that reproduce quickly and repeatedly. Once the virus is grown, the specific protein which contains the virus is isolated/harvested from the cells themselves. But unfortunately, food proteins, food particles, and gelatin from the medium it was grown in are extracted along with the viral material

and are, therefore, still present in the vaccine. Long-term consequences of injected food proteins have never been investigated, despite the fact that they could be causing a number of health problems. Risky business indeed. Now the manufacturers must add adjuvants, a substance that increases or exaggerates the immune response. Adjuvants are commonly made from unhealthy GMO vegetable oils such as soybean, corn, or peanut. Not surprisingly these oils are suspected in many immune diseases including cancer. And now the stabilizers and preservatives are added, which often contain mercury and/or aluminum – toxic heavy metals are frequently responsible for brain ailments and neurological conditions. Formaldehyde may also be used; formaldehyde is a gas used in construction materials and is a known carcinogen.

With a killed vaccine, the causative organism has been killed or inactivated so it cannot revert to virulence and cause the same disease that it is supposed to be preventing (although this is a frequent occurrence anyway). Larger quantities of the bacterium or virus are required in the manufacturing process of killed vaccines than in the MLV vaccines. In addition, the process used to kill the virus can include ionizing radiation and/or toxic chemicals such as formaldehyde, ethyleneimine (EDTA), acetylethyleneimine, and propiolactone. Unfortunately, these chemicals cannot be completely eliminated from the final vaccine, thus killed vaccines frequently result in hypersensitivity and immune reactions – both short-term and long-term – and pain and swellings in the injection site. And even though killed vaccines are considered the safest vaccine type because the virus or bacterium is inactivated and killed, adverse reactions, both local and systemic, are *more* common with these supposedly non-infectious vaccines than with the infectious MLVs. Killed vaccines are also known to aggravate auto-immune conditions. Adjuvants, stabilizers, and preservatives are also added to killed vaccines except for Bordetella, Leptospira and Lyme, which do not include adjuvants but do include preservatives.

Recombinant vaccines are based on a new technology whereby genetic material is sourced from a live virus from another species and is then genetically engineered to only use portions of the pathogen. Similar to the process with MLVs, the virus is isolated but then the manufacturers break specific segments off the gene to isolate them. Using various methods, the genes are then inserted back into the virus DNA to produce large quantities of the antigens that the genes are coded for. The antigen is the substance that induces the immune response. The antigens are then harvested, purified and preserved before injecting. Thus, recombinant vaccines do not include the whole virus, but just those segments which are thought to produce the best antibody response. Using segments is thought to lessen the chances of adverse reactions as well as to help prevent the contraction of the same disease that they are being immunized against. In contrast, a virus used in its whole form remains virulent because it has not been totally weakened. It's interesting to note that, historically, the experts have never publically addressed the growing problem of vaccine reactions, but here they are researching new ways to minimize them.

There are several vaccines available for dogs, and the following are currently considered the *core* vaccines: distemper (respiratory and digestive), adenovirus (hepatitis), parvovirus (digestive) and rabies. Others such as Bordetella (kennel cough), canine influenza, leptospirosis (mild flu), and Lyme disease are considered optional, or *lifestyle*, vaccines. This is because the exposure risk of these vaccines is very low in the general dog population. Keep this in mind when you are asked to vaccinate your dog against these low-risk diseases as a prerequisite to attend training classes, group activities or use the services of a boarding kennel.

Distemper, adenovirus, para-influenza (a milder form of the flu), intranasal Bordetella, and parvovirus are all MLV vaccines. Killed vaccines include rabies, leptospirosis, influenza, Lyme and injectable Bordetella.

Symptoms

All vaccines are capable of triggering both immediate and delayed adverse reactions. Reactions are particularly common in sensitive animals with compromised immunity and can result in both acute and chronic health conditions. Reactions frequently affect the liver, the immune system, the adrenal glands, and the nervous system. With a growing body of scientific research, vaccine reactions have now been implicated in allergies, skin conditions, hair loss, immune problems, auto-immune disorders, blood diseases, thyroid conditions, cancer and organ dysfunction.

Many dogs can also display personality changes, behavioural problems such as anxiety and/or aggression (as can follow the rabies vaccine for example), and commonly neurological conditions including epilepsy. Hypertrophic osteodystrophy is a joint condition in large breed puppies associated with the MLV distemper vaccine.

Causes

Vaccinosis, or adverse vaccine reactions, are caused by the injection of foreign pathogenic particles (including live or dead viruses and bacteria), food proteins from other animals, unhealthy oils, toxic chemicals, and/or heavy metals directly into the bloodstream. A number of factors can put dogs at risk including age, size (small breeds are 10 times more likely to have a reaction than large breeds), breed, neutered status, strength of the immune system, health history, past vaccination history, incidence of vaccine reactions, and the number of vaccines administered at one time.

Modified live distemper and adenovirus vaccines – both of which are found in MLV combination vaccines – have been shown to create several days of immune suppression afterward. This immune suppression predisposes dogs to infections and a host of other immune disorders. Aside from weakening the immune system, vaccines can trigger hereditary conditions and/or affect the genetic code itself (see the Epigenetics in Chapter One) which would otherwise remain dormant.

In a study conducted by the Purdue University, many of the vaccinated animals developed auto-immune issues whereby antibodies were produced against their own tissues in the body. Cell structures, collagen, thyroid tissue, heart valves, red blood cells, and their own DNA were all affected.

The Canine Health Concern Vaccine survey in England analyzed the history of over 3,800 dogs after vaccinations were administered which shows what *they* feel is a statistically significant correlation between a vaccine event and the onset of various illnesses in subsequent months. It should be noted that Canine Health Concern did not use a control group and, therefore, was not the most rigorous of studies and is also susceptible to confirmation bias, or in other words a tendency to interpret the results to confirm pre-existing beliefs.

All that being said, you cannot simply dismiss studies like this out of hand – because it is not as though the opposing pro-vaccine side is entirely without vested interest either. In fact, a strong case can be made that the veterinary health industry (and Big Pharma) manages the arguments around vaccination so as to protect their statistics (and their profits). The fact is that vaccines represent a lot of money for the pharmaceutical industry, and wherever big profits exists, a certain level of scrutiny needs to be brought to bear.

For instance, the duration of the veterinary health industry testing only considers the first few *days* after the vaccine has been administered. This means that any health concerns reported by the dog parents beyond those few days is consistently ignored and disregarded. This is frustrating for the dog parents and detrimental to our dogs, but it is of huge economic importance to the drug manufacturers who can then also avoid taking responsibility for all but a few vaccine reactions.

Even within a three-day window, there is disagreement as to the risk of vaccination-related reactions. In another Canine Health Concern study of dogs and cats, it was reported that adverse reactions were diagnosed within three days of vaccine 1 in 10 times (10%). This contradicts the vaccine manufacturers' statistics, where they state that less than 15 adverse reactions in 100,000 (0.015%) occur in vaccinated animals.

It would not be unreasonable to assume that the true figure lies somewhere in between.

Holistic veterinarian Dr. Deva Khalsa states that the parvo virus did not exist prior to the late 1970s, after which, it suddenly appeared simultaneously around the world and killed millions of dogs in North America, Australia, and Europe. According to Dr. Khalsa, the other vaccine stocks used for the annual boosters had been contaminated with a cat virus, which was not *thought* to be capable of infecting dogs. However, the cat virus mutated, which enabled it to jump species producing the canine version of parvo. Of course, those same drug companies were quick to manufacture millions of vaccines against the new canine parvo – you can make of that what you will. Also the contamination of vaccines with a cancer-causing virus is also thought to be the primary cause of vaccine-associated-sarcoma at the injection site.

Do Dogs Need to be Vaccinated?

Viruses frequently affect puppies or younger dogs with an uncertain history, poor healthcare, and/or poor nutrition. But few scientific studies have demonstrated the need for healthy dogs to be vaccinated or for any dogs to be re-vaccinated after the initial vaccines. Annual and repetitive vaccines have simply not been proven to be beneficial. In 1999, Dr. Ronald Schultz, a veterinary immunologist and vaccine researcher at the University of Wisconsin, indicated that all core vaccines except rabies had a duration of immunity of 7 years by challenge and 15 years by serology. Rabies was found to be 3 years by challenge and 7 years by serology. But vaccine immunity could last even longer – perhaps even the lifetime of the dog. In other challenge studies for example, more than 97 percent of the dogs were found to be immune to the diseases beyond the duration of immunity that Dr. Schultz studied. Dr. Jean Dodds, DVM, in her research and experience also indicates that core vaccines last 7 to 9 years and are likely protective for life.

⚬⚬⚬ 🐾 ⚬⚬⚬

Few scientific studies have demonstrated the need for healthy dogs to be vaccinated or for any dogs to be re-vaccinated after the initial vaccines.

(Challenge testing means to inject the dog with the infectious virus and then observe to see whether they develop the disease. This is an undesirable and inhumane method of animal testing, but this is how vaccines are evaluated in most research laboratories. Serology is a measurement of antibody production via a blood test. The presence of any antibodies means that the dog is generating immunity.)

Mainstream veterinary associations are beginning to listen. In 2011, the American Animal Hospital Association (aaha.org and the accrediting body for all companion animal hospitals in Canada and the U.S.) and their Canine Vaccination Task Force updated their vaccination guidelines to announce that distemper, adenovirus, and parvovirus are now recommended at 3 or more year intervals. They have also acknowledged that parvo and distemper vaccine immunity lasts 5 years and that adenovirus lasts 7 years. The World Small Animal Veterinary Association have emphasized the importance of administering vaccines without added adjuvants; they argue against needless vaccinations and support the testing of antibodies before vaccinating.

In other countries, including Sweden and Norway, dogs are never vaccinated beyond their puppy vaccines (and all human vaccines are, as of May 2017, now non-mandatory).

Determining Immunity

The testing of antibodies is known as titer testing and can be used by all veterinarians to determine immunity – a desirable method rather than proceeding with unnecessary vaccine boosters. If your dog shows adequate immunity, there is no need to re-test titers for at least another 3 years. Research has shown that once a dog's titer stabilizes, it remains constant for many years, providing protection against the disease. The question of adequate immunity can be somewhat confusing, however, since a negative titer (i.e. no antibodies) can still mean that antibodies are present in the tissues, not just in the blood. This is a common problem with blood tests in general; they don't test tissue levels. Animals can also acquire immunity by contracting the actual viral disease itself. Dogs who have contracted the disease may have a subtler form of protection and have not been forced into a high antibody count with the more aggressive vaccine therapy.

Titers are very beneficial for puppies. Maternal antibodies will protect puppies up to 16 weeks of age. At 12 weeks, you can have an antibody titer test done, and if the test shows the presence of antibodies, you can re-test again at 5 to 6 months. However, during this time, puppies should be allowed to socialize with other dogs at all times so they can expose themselves to various viruses and bacteria while they are under maternal protection. This is exactly how dogs develop natural immunity, and it is very effective. As well, you can administer specific

Never vaccinate a sick dog.

homeopathic nosodes during this time before re-testing the titers at 5 to 6 months. Use nosodes in a 30C potency and give daily for 3 days, then once per week for 4 weeks.

Vaccine Cautions

If you do decide to vaccinate, don't vaccinate puppies under the age of 16 weeks since this will more than likely knock out the maternal antibodies, or conversely, the maternal antibodies will knock out the artificial vaccines. The solution by the vaccine industry is to administer recombinant or genetically engineered vaccines which are thought to disable the maternal antibodies from neutralizing the vaccines. Is this even logical?

And, if you are vaccinating, use single vaccines rather than combinations, and space them out accordingly. Combination or "lifestyle" vaccines have a poor efficacy rate as well as a high reaction rate and should be used with extreme caution. This is true for all animals.

Never vaccinate a sick dog. Even vaccine manufacturers caution against administering vaccines to sick dogs, including dogs with infections, malnourished dogs, dogs who are immune-compromised, dogs on steroids or other immune-suppressant medications, as well as dogs who are stressed. Unfortunately, these cautions are routinely ignored. Pets with existing health problems are more at risk for adverse reactions resulting in fevers, seizures, auto-immune conditions including allergies, and even anaphylactic shock reactions. As well, vaccines administered to sick dogs are unlikely to develop an adequate immune response anyway, so money is better spent on improving your dog's diet and adding natural immune remedies.

Homeopathic Nosodes

The use of homeopathic nosodes to prevent canine diseases is called homeoprophylaxis. Homeopathic remedies are highly diluted substances prepared from plants, minerals, or animal products and are very safe. Nosodes are remedies which are prepared from the actual disease material – such as the nasal discharge from a dog with a type of influenza for example - and then administered to a dog to initiate a natural immune response. However, homeoprophylaxis is not *true* homeopathy since homeopathic remedies are generally prescribed based on the symptom picture where like treats like. In other words, the symptoms that the substance causes in its crude form can be treated by the same substance in its homeopathic or diluted form. Nevertheless, the Law of Similars is somewhat in place here because like also *prevents* like. Studies of homeoprophylaxis efficacy have been done showing positive results although there are more large scale ones underway at the time of this writing. See the Appendix for references to more information on scientific studies and research done in the field of homeoprophylaxis including epidemic diseases with people.

It's very difficult to confront homeopathy with medical testing and clinical trials since homeopathic remedies, including nosodes, work on the principle of energy fields. The results are determined by the response of the immune system to a specific vibration, i.e. the remedy, which contains a broad sphere of information capable of shifting disease patterns. However, because of the sensitivity of these energy fields, the remedy can be influenced by the dynamics of the study itself, as well as the people involved.

Nevertheless, in 2010, a homeopathic protection plan was put into place for people in an area of Cuba to prevent an outbreak of leptospirosis after the hurricane season. There was a reduction of infection in 85 percent of the people after only two doses, and the outbreak was controlled. This was not the case in other parts of Cuba who did not partake in the homeopathic treatment.

Homeopathic nosodes can be safely used for puppies during the first few months since with this preventative program you will be testing the antibodies anyway to ensure protection. And if they work well, the remedies should play a role in continuing to support healthy levels of antibodies. Similarly, now that we have established the facts on the risks of re-vaccination, there is no harm in using homeopathic nosodes for adult dogs either, especially if faced with a risk of exposure or for those who have suffered vaccine reactions.

The Best Prevention

- There are many animals (and people) who carry viruses without ever manifesting the symptoms. Why? Because the best prevention against all diseases, including viral diseases, is a strong natural immune response as created by a healthy diet, good nutrition, regular exercise, companionship and low stress levels – both for the dog and the pet parents.

- Avoid owning or housing multiple dogs in one location in overcrowded conditions.

- Don't own more than one or two dogs unless absolutely necessary.

- Support spaying and neutering programs to avoid several unwanted puppies born in a barn or a poor home environment.

- Don't buy puppies from a puppy mill, pet store, backyard breeding operations, animal hoarders or other questionable breeding operations.

- Rescue dogs.

- Stop breeding dogs!

Natural Health Program for Vaccinosis

In addition to the information below, be sure to follow the programs under the specific health problems in related chapters, i.e. skin reactions, allergies, epilepsy and so on.

Diet

- Eliminate wheat, corn gluten, dairy products, soy products and/or rancid oils

- Eliminate all known food allergies and intolerances

- Use caution with grains, for some dogs need to be grain-free.

- Eliminate beef, bison, venison, red meats and organ meats, for these are a common cause of inflammation and tissue damage.

- Avoid feeding excess and/or unhealthy oils, including canola oil, soya oil, coconut oil and vegetable oils. These congest the liver and lymph system, both very important immune organs.

- No artificial colourings, flavourings, rawhide or preservatives.

Nutrients

- **vitamin C** [*one dose daily for 4 to 6 weeks*]†* – supports immunity, nutritional support for acute and chronic vaccine reactions; adrenal and liver health

- **selenium, organic** [*one dose daily*]† – promotes the natural detoxification of chemicals, toxins, and heavy metals; liver and muscle support

Herbal & Home Remedies

- **milk thistle seed, tincture** [*one dose daily for 30 days*]† – liver support, natural detoxifier; immune support for acute vaccine reactions and food allergy reactions

- Choose *one* of the following homeopathic remedies to start:

  o **thymus 200C, homeopathic** [*one dose daily for 7 to 10 days*]† – supports immune system and thymus gland function in animals with symptoms of toxic reactions

  o **thuja 200C, homeopathic** [*one dose daily for 7 days*]† – for chronic skin problems and/or growths from vaccinosis, history of vaccine reactions, chronic ear infections and/or fatigue

  o **silicea 200C, homeopathic** [*one dose daily for 3 to 4 days*]† – for ill effects of vaccination; abscesses, pyoderma, oversensitivity or irritability

  o **arsenicum 30C, homeopathic** [*one dose daily for 4 days*]† – acute reactions resulting in anxiety, fear, poor appetite and/or digestive problems

  o **sulphur 30C, homeopathic** [*one dose daily for 4 days*]† – extreme itching, hot spots, digestive issues; general detoxifier

Riva's Remedies

- **Vac-Aid, homeopathic** [*one dose daily for 7 days*]† – acute and chronic vaccine reactions; liver and immune support

- **Joint-Clear, herbal blend** [*one dose daily*]† – adrenal support; swellings, discomfort and acute allergy reactions

- **Immune Boost, herbal blend** [*one dose daily*]† – liver support; nutrition to promote the healthy function of intestines, skin, and immune system

- **Skin-Heal, herbal blend** [*one dose daily*]† – liver, blood and skin; supports immunity and promotes healthy skin

- **Detox Dog, herbal blend** [*one dose daily for 4 to 6 weeks*]† – promotes the detoxification of elimination organs: skin, liver, kidneys and colon; supports the immune system

Nosodes

Homeopathic nosodes can be used to both mitigate the adverse effects of a vaccine injection and to prevent further problems with vaccinosis. This is particularly helpful where vaccines and/or boosters are mandatory, e.g., rabies and/or international travel. Homeopathic nosodes are available for all canine diseases including distemper, parvo, influenza, rabies (Hydrophobinum) and Lyme's.

For prevention of adverse vaccine reactions use the appropriate nosode in a 30C potency and administer once daily for 3 days before vaccinating and then daily for 2 to 3 days after vaccinating. Then give one dose per month for 1 to 3 months thereafter, if needed.

For use after exposure to disease, use the specific homeopathic nosode in a 200C potency and administer once daily for 3 days.

† See Appendix for recommended dosages and duration for all supplements.
* Also available as a Riva's Remedy

Roxy Reacts

Roxy was a one-year-old boxer who was taken into the local clinic for her puppy boosters in a combination vaccine known as DHPP (distemper, adenovirus parainfluenza, and parvovirus). Within 24 hours Roxy began itching and scratching all over her body. Within a few days, rashes were developing and her hair started to fall out. She was also getting episodes of diarrhea which she had never had before. It was obvious that Roxy was suffering immune problems that had never affected her previously and that her immune system had been chemically traumatized.

Roxy was put on a program with specific homeopathic remedies to neutralize her original vaccine reactions. Then Riva's Immune Boost herbal blend was given to cleanse the liver and support the immune system. Vitamin C and organic selenium were added for their beneficial effects on the liver and immune system and to scavenge chemical debris. And Roxy was administered homeopathic silicea 200C daily for 4 days as a specific remedy to address vaccine toxicity.

Roxy.

phase, the

Roxy's diet was also changed because, often during the reaction immune system becomes depressed, which causes many dogs to react to the foods or the food staples that they are eating at the time of the vaccine injections. So Roxy's diet program was changed from primarily chicken to lamb.

Because Roxy's symptoms were an acute reaction, it was obvious that the trigger had been her recent vaccinations. However, the health and immunity of many other dogs are weakened slowly over time after vaccine injections. This makes it more difficult for the pet parent to make a connection identifying vaccine reactions as the culprit. These dogs may end up on a never-ending cycle of medications and/or diet changes without anyone ever suspecting the inoculations.

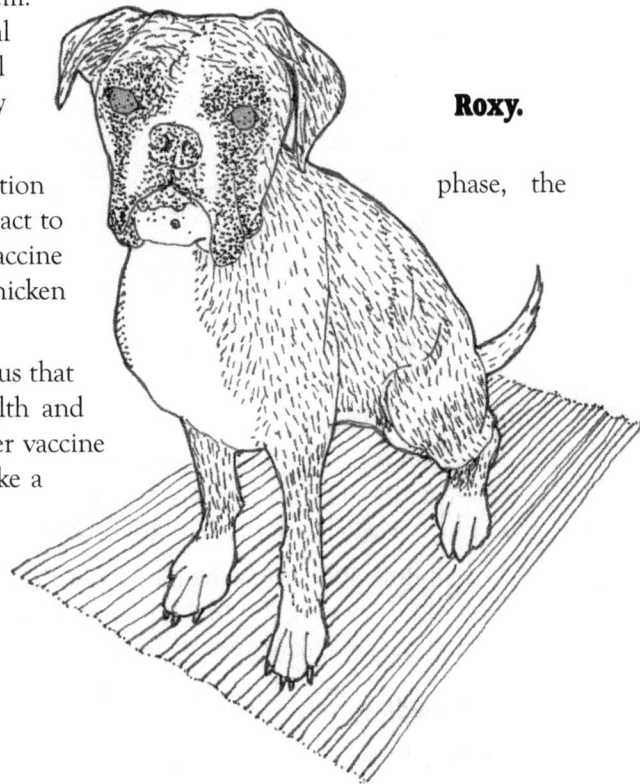

Healing Dogs Their Way

9. Skin, Hair & Nails

Protect & Eliminate

Skin

The skin is the largest organ of the body. Its function is to grow hair, protect the body from the environment, regulate body temperature, and feel sensations. The skin can represent anywhere from 12 to 25 percent of total bodyweight.

Along with the kidneys, liver, lungs and colon, the skin is a major elimination organ, helping to rid the body of toxins accumulated from food, water, digestive metabolism, bacteria, viruses, parasites, dead cells, stress, and environmental toxins, which include heavy metals, chemicals, and pesticides. Both external and internal toxins can affect metabolism, immunity, hormones, brain function, arteries, the heart, as well as the skin.

Hair Coat

Aside from making dogs look beautiful, the hair coat is designed to protect the skin from physical damage and ultraviolet light damage as well as help regulate body temperature. Everything but the nose and paw pads is covered in a hair coat.

Dogs have both long, thick guard hairs and soft downy under-hairs which provide insulation. Each follicle has one guard hair and up to 15 secondary hairs emerging from the same follicle. The type and length of hair varies widely between dog breeds. For example, cold-weather dogs have longer and finer guard hairs to conserve heat since these hairs are better able to trap dead air space. Wolves and large dogs with long, thick hair coats can sleep comfortably in temperatures below minus 40°C. Dogs are also able to absorb warm air through their paw pads which then heat the blood which circulates throughout the entire body for added warmth. Warm-weather dogs have shorter, thicker hairs and fewer secondary hairs, which allow air to move through the coat to facilitate cooling. Warm-weather dogs should never be left outside in cold weather. Hair is also used by many dogs to express emotion as in the raising of hackles in aggression, for example.

Dogs normally shed hair in the early spring and early fall. Hair shedding is determined by the amount of light in a day, which alerts the pituitary and/or the pineal gland to produce hormones to either initiate hair loss or growth. Continuing warm or cold temperatures will also affect hair growth. Abnormal changes in hair growth can indicate hormone problems, especially pituitary or thyroid imbalances, as well as side-effects from medication, nutrient deficiencies, allergies, or environmental issues.

Heat Loss and Detoxification

Although dogs have sweat glands on their feet, they primarily release heat through their mouth. When a dog pants it allows moisture in the mouth and on the tongue to evaporate releasing the internal heat. Panting also evaporates moisture, well as toxins, from the surface of the lungs. The heavier they breathe, the more heat they release, but dogs with shorter noses and flat faces such as a Shi Tzu or a Pug must work harder to release excess body heat since the surface area in the mouth is smaller. But dogs are also able to utilize their blood vessels by dilating the vessels located on their face and ears. This allows the blood to flow closer to the surface of the skin and release heat to the exterior. This mechanism is mostly available with over-heating due to exercise. The dilation of blood vessels also serves to eliminate toxins because it increases blood and lymphatic circulation. This increase in circulation enables the other elimination organs to detoxify more efficiently as well. And so, even though the kidneys, liver, and lungs normally eliminate much more waste than the skin, when these organs become congested or overloaded, the skin must compensate and eliminate more toxins than usual. Therefore, skin conditions such as rashes, dermatitis, hives, eruptions, growths and so on are mostly a sign of increased systemic toxicity with a challenged immune system.

Heat Stroke

In the summer fur can act as a barrier to the outside heat, but in a continuously hot environment the temperatures inside the hair coat build up and cannot escape or dissipate through the fur. In this way dogs can become overheated on hot days or in hot cars or any other warm environment. On a hot day, especially if they are active, they can overheat which is a condition known as hyperthermia and can lead to heat stroke if they don't cool off. Symptoms of heat stroke are rapid panting, a bright red tongue/gums, weakness, dizziness, confusion, and sometimes vomiting. If your dog has overheated immediately bring her to a cool place, gently spray the fur with cool (not cold) water, and provide drinking water. If a dog has a hot face, dilated pupils and/or confusion give one or two doses of homeopathic belladonna 30C.

Natural Health Programs for Skin, Hair & Nails

~~~~~~~~~~~~~~~~ 🐾 ~~~~~~~~~~~~~~~~

Skin Allergies, Rashes, Seborrhea, Itching, Hot Spots, and Hives

Skin problems in dogs are completely rampant and have become an unnecessary epidemic in the dog population affecting almost all breeds. Thousands of dogs are sadly being euthanized because their dog parents cannot find a solution beyond medications and the plastic cones. These skin condition symptoms are completely preventable and treatable with a solid health program that modifies the diet, corrects the nutritional deficiencies and strengthens the immune system. Let's learn how.

Symptoms

There are a variety of skin symptoms observed on a dog with unhealthy skin, including redness, heat, inflammation, round scaly patches, bald patches, black skin, hives, itchiness, hot spots, rashes, eruptions, scabs, pus, abscesses, infections, swellings, bumps and foul odors. Any of these problems can cause dogs to scratch, itch, lick, chew certain areas or rub against the floor and furniture. Areas with intense itching or heat are known as hot spots. Skin symptoms can also affect ears and paws.

- Skin problems have become epidemic with almost all breeds but some breeds are more prone to skin problems including Cocker Spaniels, German Shepherds, Bulldogs and Golden Retrievers.

Causes

There are various health problems that cause skin symptoms, and many times these problems are present all at once.

1. Almost all skin conditions are accompanied by food and diet problems, particularly food allergies/intolerances as a well as a faulty immune system. Culprit foods can provoke an antibody immune response as well as chronic inflammatory reactions anywhere in the body including the skin. Follow the guidelines in Chapter 7 for correcting food problems and strengthening the immune system.

2. Inappropriate feeding programs including excess meat or grains, wheat, corn gluten, fats or oils also eventually cause a leaky gut. Leaky gut is a major

contributor to skin problems because of the acids, food toxins, pathogens and debris which first damage the intestinal membranes of the large colon, leak through, and then migrate to various body systems and organs. Because the skin is a major elimination organ, it is very often seen there first. Leaky gut also exacerbates food intolerances. Poor diets also compromise the intestinal immune system. See Chapter 4 for specific programs to address leaky gut including intestinal immunity and strengthening digestion.

3. The immune system can also be damaged and adversely affected by medications, antibiotics, vaccinosis (symptoms from over-vaccinating) and emotional stress – either their own or from their human family.

4. Untreated intestinal parasites produce a variety of waste products and toxins, depress the immune system, and if present, frequently cause skin conditions.

5. Use extreme caution in vaccinating the immune-compromised dog due to the likelihood of vaccinosis (see Chapter 8). Adverse vaccine reactions can be immediate or insidiously delayed by several days, weeks, or months. Reactions are particularly common in sensitive animals with compromised immunity and can be acute or chronic. Reactions frequently affect the liver, the nervous system, the immune system, and the skin.

6. Inhalant or environmental allergies do not normally cause skin problems although the same underlying immune problems that cause the environmental allergies (diet, nutrient deficiencies, and poor immunity) are often also the ones causing the skin problems.

Natural Health Program

Diet

- Eliminate wheat, corn gluten, dairy products, soy products, rancid oils and all known food allergies and intolerances (see Chapter 7).

- Food allergies often develop from the foods that are eaten regularly and repetitively. This is because a failing immune system will react to whatever it is exposed to. A common example of this is chicken – millions of dogs eat chicken day in and day out and thousands, if not millions, of them, react to it. Therefore, immune-compromised dogs must eliminate all previous staples from their diet until their immune

system has cleared it, this can take anywhere from 6 to 12 weeks. Always offer your dogs some dietary variety and change up the dietary staples from time to time.

- Eliminate beef, bison, venison, red meats and organ meats, for these create toxicity because they are high in certain acids. These acids result in inflammation and tissue damage. Accumulated acids also affect the intestinal immune system and contribute to a higher incidence of allergies, which can affect all body systems including the skin. In addition, senior dogs cannot digest or metabolize red meats as efficiently as younger dogs.

- Many dogs, especially senior dogs and very toxic dogs, must go on a vegetarian cleanse. Then once the symptoms have improved, small amounts of meat protein can be carefully and slowly re-introduced. (See Chapter 3).

- Avoid prescription diets which often contain wheat, corn gluten, unhealthy oils, and odd sources of protein such as hydrolyzed soy protein isolate, hydrolyzed chicken liver, and even feathers.

- Avoid feeding added or excess oils including canola oil, soya oil, coconut oil, fish and vegetable oils. While a small amount of essential fatty acids are necessary, excess oils will congest the liver, kidneys, and the lymph system, pressuring the skin to eliminate the overload. This often results in a variety of skin symptoms.

- Add more seeds, such as flax, chia, and hemp, to the diet to provide a natural source of essential fatty acids.

- Treat for leaky gut as per Chapter 4.

Nutrients

- **vitamin A, liquid** [*one dose daily*][†] – dry flaky skin, skin allergies, skin infections; immune nutrient

- **zinc citrate or picolinate** [*one dose daily for 30 days only*][†] – a skin nutrient that helps heal wounds, scaling and crusting of food pads and supports the immune response. Important nutrient for skin, hair and nails; maintains stress resistance

- **vitamin E** [*one dose daily*][†*] – anti-oxidant used for skin health, circulation, wound healing and dry skin

- **iodine, liquid** [*one dose daily*][†] – bacteria and yeast; abscesses, supports immune response

- Iron-Up (iron gluconate) [*one dose daily*][†*] – iron deficiency symptoms include chronic infections, allergies and immune conditions; circulation and anemia

Herbal & Home Remedies

- **milk thistle seed, tincture** [*one dose daily*][†] – liver support; promotes bile flow and detoxification, acute allergy reactions

- **coconut oil, olive oil,** or **calendula ointment** [*apply to affected area twice daily*] – use separately or make a blend; nutrition and comfort for the skin; scar tissue

- **zinc ointment** [*apply to affected area twice daily*] – dry, scaly and crusted skin; rashes

  Riva's Remedies

- **Kava's Primrose Oil, herbal blend** [*one dose daily for 30 days*][†] – provides essential fatty acids and nutrition for optimum immunity; promotes healthy skin and hair coat

- **Skin-Heal, herbal blend** [*one dose daily as needed*][†] – supports the healthy function of the liver, blood and skin in dogs with hives, rashes, growths, and chronic skin conditions

- **Detox Dog, herbal blend** [*one dose daily for 4 to 6 weeks*] – promotes the detoxification of skin, liver, kidneys and colon; supports the immune system

- **Happy Pets** or **Happy Pets Senior, herbal blend** [*one dose daily*][†] – provides a plant-based source of over 60 trace minerals, vitamins, fibre and anti-oxidants; superior nutrition for hair coat, hair growth, skin and nails.

- **Immune Boost, herbal blend** [*one dose daily as needed for immune problems*][†] – supports colon, liver and the immune system with nutrition, cleansing, and detoxification

- **Infection Drops, homeopathic** [*one dose twice daily for 3 days*][†] – for symptoms of skin infections, e.g. abscesses, eruptions, discharges

- **Kava's Healing Oil** [*spray onto affected area externally twice daily*] – soothes hot spots, rashes, itching, wounds and abscesses

[†] See Appendix for recommended dosages and duration for all supplements.

[*] Also available as a Riva's Remedy

Infections – Acute & Chronic

Symptoms

Bacterial infections of the skin (pyoderma) may appear as bumps, lesions, pustules, open sores, oozing sores, red and irritated rashes, loss of hair, and abscesses. If dogs constantly lick the irritation, it may cause more skin damage which promotes more bacteria. Fungal or yeast infections are usually found in the folds of skin such as ears, paws, and/or armpits. Yeast infections can itch, burn, smell rancid, and result in a variety of skin eruptions.

If a dog is suffering from an ear infection they may scratch their ears, shake their heads, and/or move their heads from side to side. Ears infected with bacteria may also discharge yellow or green fluid which can be foul smelling, and ears infected with yeast can discharge a brown, waxy substance which smells yeasty. Some dogs may have problems with jumping or running if their balance is affected.

Causes

Most infections are caused by bacteria and/or fungus that enter through damaged skin or intestinal membranes (i.e. leaky gut), which then cause further damage to the skin. Common bacteria affecting the skin and ears include *Streptococcus*, *Staphylococcus*, *E. coli*, *Proteus* and *Pseudomonas*. Yeast infections are frequently caused by *Malassezia dermatitis*. If the normal defense mechanisms of the skin and/or the immune system is not able to protect itself from these pathogens, the infections will become chronic. All chronic infections are a secondary problem to underlying health conditions which have not been resolved, such as food allergies/intolerances, intestinal parasites, leaky gut, nutrient deficiencies such as iron, low thyroid function, adrenal malfunction as in Cushing's disease, and/or stress. Fungal or yeast infections also frequently occur after antibiotic use as well as steroids, which depress the immune system. Irritations and inflammation of the ears is also frequently seen in dogs with multiple food reactions.

Natural Health Program

Diet

- Eliminate wheat, corn gluten, dairy products, soy products, rancid oils, and all known food allergies and intolerances (see Chapter 7 for more information).

- Eliminate beef, bison, venison, red meats, and organ meats, for these create toxicity because they are high in certain acids. These acids result in inflammation and tissue damage; accumulated acids also affect the intestinal immune system and contribute to a higher incidence of allergies, which can affect all body systems including the skin. In addition, senior dogs cannot digest or metabolize red meats as efficiently as younger dogs.

- Avoid feeding added or excess oils, including canola oil, soya oil, coconut oil, fish, and vegetable oils.

- Add more seeds, such as flax, chia, and/or hemp, to the diet to provide a natural source of essential fatty acids.

Nutrients

- **vitamin A, liquid** [*one dose daily*][†] – skin infections, dry flaky skin, allergies, fatigue; supports immunity

- **zinc citrate or picolinate** [*one dose daily for 30 days only*][†] – nutrition for wound healing, immunity and stress resistance; beneficial for skin, hair and nails; scaling and crusting of foot pads

- **iodine, liquid** [*one dose daily*][†] – bacteria and yeast; supports immune response

- **Iron-Up (iron gluconate)** – [*one dose daily*][†*] – nutrition for the immune system with chronic infections; circulation, energy and anemia

- **vitamin E** [*one dose daily*][†*] – promotes circulation for healthy skin and wound healing

Herbal & Home Remedies

- **apple cider vinegar** [*dilute 1 part vinegar to 3 to 4 parts water and apply to affected areas twice daily*]

Riva's Remedies

- **Para+Plus, tincture** [*one dose daily as needed*][†] – bacteria, yeast and parasites; promotes healthy liver function

- **Skin-Heal, herbal blend** [*one dose daily*][†] – colon, liver and skin health; supports immunity for all skin conditions

- **Detox Dog, herbal blend** [*one dose daily for 4 to 6 weeks*] – promotes the detoxification of skin, liver, kidneys and colon, supports the immune system

- **Happy Pets** or **Happy Pets Senior, herbal blend** [*one dose daily*][†] – provides a plant-based source of over 60 trace minerals, vitamins, fibre and anti-oxidants; superior nutrition for hair coat, hair growth, skin, and nails

- **Immune Boost, herbal blend** [*one dose daily as needed for immune problems*][†] – supports digestion, liver, and immune system with nutrition, cleansing, and detoxification

- **Infection Drops, homeopathic** [*one dose twice daily for 3 days*][†] – supports healthy skin with symptoms of infections, e.g. abscesses, eruptions, discharges

- **Kava's Healing Oil, herbal blend** [*spray externally onto affected area twice daily*][†] – soothes hot spots, rashes, itching, wounds, cuts, and abscesses

[†] See Appendix for recommended dosages and duration for all supplements.
[*] Also available as a Riva's Remedy

Nail Problems

The toenails or claws grow out of the end of each toe. Claws are necessary for traction, climbing, and digging. They are normally very strong, but they can be injured and affected by poor nutrition or nutritional deficiencies.

Symptoms

Toenails can become soft, brittle, thickened, discoloured, ingrown, inflamed or infected with bacteria and/or fungus. They may appear red and/or swollen. Dogs with sore or tender claws may lick the affected paws, have trouble walking, hold one paw up, track bloody paw prints, or groan when sleeping.

Causes

Ingrown toenails can happen with any nail, including the dew-claws, which are the high nails on the inside of the leg. Any claws that don't make contact with the ground or have normal wear can become ingrown.

Bacterial and fungal infections are almost always secondary to an underlying cause (barring injuries) including food reactions, especially when more than one claw is affected. They can occur in the nail or the nailbed. See "Chronic Infections" above for more information and health programs. Infected paws may look swollen, feel tender, bleed, or ooze discharges.

Toenails which are deformed, brittle, soft, or discoloured are normally caused by dietary problems and/or nutrient deficiencies.

Natural Health Program

All toenails should be trimmed regularly to prevent trauma, splitting, fracturing, injured skin, and/or to remove infected or diseased portions. Loose, sloughing, damaged, and/or injured nails may need to be removed by a veterinarian.

Diet

- Eliminate wheat, corn gluten, dairy products, soy products, rancid oils, and all known food allergies and intolerances as described in Chapter 7.
- Add more seeds, such as flax, chia, and hemp, to the diet to provide a natural source of essential fatty acids.

Nutrients

- **selenium, organic** [one dose daily]† - deficiency can cause dry, brittle nails; supports the immune response, liver and muscle strength
- **biotin** [one dose daily]† - helps thicken and strengthen weak nails

Herbal & Home Remedies

- **horsetail shavings** [one dose daily for 30 days]† - rich in silica for nail strength and growth; skin and bone nutrient
- **thuja 200C, homeopathic** [one dose daily for 7 days]† - for brittle, soft, or distorted nails and eruptions between the toes
- **silicea 200C, homeopathic** [one dose daily for 3 days]† - for ingrown toenails, fragile or brittle nails; flexures between toes and cracked paws; nail fungus

Riva's Remedies

- **Kava's Primrose Oil, herbal blend** [one dose daily for 30 days]† - essential fatty acids for skin health, hair coat and immune function
- **Para+Plus, tincture** [one dose daily as needed]† - bacteria, yeast and parasites; liver support

- **Happy Pets** or **Happy Pets Senior, herbal blend** [one dose daily]† - plant-based blend containing over 60 trace minerals, vitamins, and anti-oxidants; superior nutrition for nails, skin, and coat
- **Infection Drops, homeopathic** [one dose twice daily as needed for 3 days]† -supports the immune response with discharge/pus, and abscesses
- **Kava's Healing Oil, herbal blend** [spray externally on affected nails twice daily] soothes hot spots, rashes, itching, wounds and abscesses

† See Appendix for recommended dosages and duration for all supplements.

Hair Loss – Alopecia

Any changes to the hair coat with loss of hair – partial or complete – is technically defined as alopecia although we often think of alopecia as large bald areas where large amounts of hair were lost. As we know, shedding is a normal process in most dog breeds where dead hair falls out to make room for the new hair growing in. Excessive shedding can occur when the seasons change, for example, or when a dog is unhealthy, but normal shedding does not typically result in bald patches or loss of large quantities of hair as seen in alopecia.

Symptoms

Hair loss is visible as a single small bald patch, multiple small bald patches; sometimes there is complete body-hair loss. Dogs with bald areas can also be more prone to bacterial and fungal infections of the skin.

Causes

The causes of alopecia can be divided into two main categories: inflammatory and non-inflammatory. Inflammatory skin problems leading to hair loss are usually easy to detect as they are most commonly caused by food allergies, a variety of medication side-effects, immune deficiency, flea bites, lice, mange and/or bacteria. Once you have determined the cause of the inflammation, refer to the respective sections in this book. If the hair loss is part of a chronic skin condition, refer to the section above on skin health.

Non-inflammatory types of alopecia can be more

challenging to address since there are often no definitive or clinical signs of an underlying cause. However, most non-inflammatory types of alopecia are commonly caused or exacerbated by:

a) Specific nutrient deficiencies which affect the health of the follicles including the hair growth rate.

b) Higher than normal requirements for certain nutrients, which are required for optimum skin health and for growing a full hair coat.

c) Hormonal imbalances that affect the adrenal, thyroid, and/or pituitary function, causing low hormone production. Hair follicles have a high metabolic rate, and are thus particularly sensitive to concentrations of thyroid hormones. They are therefore profoundly influenced by a deficiency or excess of thyroid gland derived hormones. (See Chapter 10 for more information about thyroid function).

Hair loss can sometimes be seen with some female dogs during pregnancy and/or lactation, which indicates reproductive hormonal imbalances which put extra demands on the thyroid and pituitary; hair loss in pregnancy-related alopecia will eventually grow back.

d) Stress can be a significant factor in alopecia because it depletes specific nutrients and depresses the endocrine glands, particularly the adrenal glands (see Chapter 15 for more information).

Natural Health Program

Diet

- Eliminate wheat, corn gluten, dairy products, soy products, rancid oils, and all known food allergies and intolerances (see Chapter 7 for more information).

- Avoid feeding added or excess oils, including canola oil, soya oil, coconut oil, fish, and vegetable oils. While a small amount of essential fatty acids are necessary, excess oils will congest the liver, kidneys, and the lymph system, pressuring the skin to expel these oils, often resulting in a variety of skin abnormalities including hair loss.

- Add more seeds, such as flax, chia, and hemp, to the diet to provide a natural source of essential fatty acids.

Nutrients

- **vitamin A, liquid** [*one dose daily*]† - nutrition for hair that pulls out easily, thick foot pads, dry flaky skin, skin infections and fatigue

- **zinc citrate or picolinate** [*one dose daily for 30 days*]† - skin and hair nutrient for dogs with crusty skin, hair loss, and alopecia; stress and hormone nutrient; adrenal support

- **biotin** [*one dose daily*]† - promotes hair growth, aids food metabolism

- **vitamin B6** [*one dose daily*]†* - nutrition for hair growth, hormone balance, the nervous system and healthy skin

- **iodine, liquid** [*one dose daily*]† -bacteria and yeast; supports the immune response and the healthy function of thyroid and adrenal hormones

Herbal & Home Remedies

- **licorice root powder** [*one dose daily for 30 days*]† - adrenal support and immunity; supports hormone production during lactation or post-pregnancy - NOTE: not for use during pregnancy

- **coconut oil** [*massage into bald areas daily*] - nutrition for healthy skin

- mix **essential oil of rosemary** with a small amount of **light olive oil** [*massage daily into bald areas*]

Riva's Remedies

- **Kava's Primrose Oil, specialized nutrient** [*one dose daily for 30 days*]† - essential fatty acids and nutrition for optimum immune response and skin health; supports hormone function

- **Happy Pets** or **Happy Pets Senior, herbal blend** [*one dose daily*]† - provides a plant-based source of over 60 trace minerals, vitamins, fibre, and anti-oxidants; excellent nutrition for hair coat, hair growth, skin, and nails

- **Hormone Boost, herbal blend** [*one dose daily as needed for any kind of hormonal imbalances*]† - supports all endocrine glands and their hormone function: adrenal, pituitary, thyroid, testes and ovaries

NOTE: Dogs with insufficient hair coats do not have as much protection from the elements as dogs with full hair coats do. Until their hair grows back your dog may need to wear a coat or sweater during cold months and will need extra protection during the summer to prevent sunburn or heat stroke.

† See Appendix for recommended dosages and duration for all supplements.
˙Also available as a Riva's Remedy

Excessive Licking

Symptoms

Dogs may lick one spot on their body over and over again, which can sometimes cause a skin injury known as acral licking dermatitis. Other dogs become obsessed with licking people or other animals.

Causes

Licking can be caused by any kind of skin ailment as discussed above: allergies, itching, bacteria or fungal infections, sores, rashes and/or abscesses. Licking can also be initiated by pain, injuries, or inflammation anywhere in the body. Licking can also be a way for your dog to tell you that they have digestive problems such as heartburn, bloating, and/or pain. However, the most common physical cause of licking is soreness and inflammation caused by food allergies and/or excess dietary meat protein especially in senior dogs. Licking or chewing the paws is a very common telltale of food problems.

Emotional problems also cause licking: boredom, anxiety, stress, excitement, worry and/or depression can all manifest in this way. Remember, if you are not listening or communicating with your dog on a deeper level, she must get your attention in other ways. At no time should excessive licking be considered a neurosis without known cause; dogs can be highly emotional or determined to get the attention that they need to communicate their feelings and/or their opinions about themselves and their human family. Their thoughts may surprise you.

See Chapters 15 and 17 for understanding canine emotions and learning about animal communication.

~~~~~~~ 🐾 ~~~~~~~

Licking or chewing the paws is a very
common telltale of food problems
such as food allergies and/or excess
dietary meat protein.

~~~~~~~~~~~~~~~~

Natural Health Program

See the respective sections in this book for dealing with the specific problems underlying the lick behaviour - whether physical or emotional. Broaden your abilities to communicate with your pet on all levels.

Fleas, Lice, Mange and Ringworm

Many dogs are plagued with parasites, resulting in a variety of skin symptoms. However, it is very important to realize that parasites are attracted to those animals that have a compromised immune system and/or damaged skin, which is not always apparent. For example, immune compromised dogs are the ones most likely to suffer allergic reactions to flea bites; flea allergy dermatitis, caused by a sensitivity to flea saliva, is a very common skin condition of dogs.

Symptoms

Fleas survive by biting into the skin and feeding on the blood of their host which causes the dogs to itch and scratch. At the same time, the flea's saliva comes into contact with the blood, which is what causes the allergy reactions in sensitive dogs. Dogs with flea allergies will react with red and inflamed skin, intense scratching, biting at the tail, poor immunity and sometimes hair loss.

Lice either suck blood or chew skin and spend their entire 21-day life cycle on the dog. They do not survive in the external environment, as do fleas, thus infestations occur from contact with another infested pet. Lice lay eggs (nits) on the shafts of the hair that are easier to see than the adult lice. The most common symptoms are itching and dry, scruffy hair.

Mange in dogs is caused by different types of mites which embed themselves into the skin and hair follicles and lay eggs there. There are two different types of mites:

a) Sarcoptic mange - also known as scabies - is highly contagious and can affect all animals as well as humans; it is also known as scabies. They cause intense itching, hair loss, red and irritated skin, blisters, and can form a crust on the skin that can sometimes become infected. They are most common on the face, legs, elbow, and ears before spreading to the entire body.

b) Demodectic mange are mites that are natural inhabitants of dogs and are not transmitted to humans. Healthy dogs can live in harmony with these mites; but in dogs that are immune-compromised, such as some puppies, senior dogs and/or dogs with pre-existing health conditions, demodectic mange can become a more serious problem. If this is the case, then affected dogs may present this type of mange with hair loss, bald spots, and sores with secondary bacterial infections in severe cases.

Ringworm is more uncommon and is a fungus which usually occurs in the fall and winter. It causes a small round lesion and the skin in the middle looks scaly. It *can* be itchy, but not always. They mostly occur on the head but can sometimes affect the legs, feet, or tail. It is often confused with demodectic mange.

Causes

As discussed, animals with a compromised immune system and/or damaged skin are far more likely to suffer problematic parasites from all sources than healthy animals with a strong immune system. But no matter how healthy your dog is, an infested environment inside the house that is not treated will make it very difficult to keep the dog parasite-free.

Adult fleas live on the dog, but they only live for 4 days if they lose their host. Once the female flea feeds on blood, she will breed and lay eggs which then drop off the host and into the surrounding environment. All the eggs and larvae live and then hatch out in a few days on the bedding, carpeting and/or outdoors preferring warm, humid and/or shaded areas outside. The typical lifecycle from egg to adult can be anywhere from 1 to 8 months depending on the temperature and/or the amount of food available. The flea population consists of 50 percent eggs, 35 percent larvae, 10 percent pupae – all of which live in the environment - and 5 percent adults all of which live on the dogs. Dogs living in warmer climates have more of a problem with fleas than those living in colder climates. Once the temperature falls below freezing for several days in a row, adult fleas outside will die but the larvae will not. And of course, freezing temperatures have no effect on indoor fleas and/or their larvae.

Mites (causing mange) separated from their host in a typical home at room temperatures can live for up to a week. The female mite dies after laying her eggs on the dog, with the lifecycle from egg to larvae to adult taking 2 to 3 weeks.

The incidence of ringworm infections in dogs with skin problems is very small with younger dogs mostly at risk. Ringworm can also be a problem for dogs on steroid medication. Ringworm is a fungus that can be transmitted by direct contact with an infected animal, or contact with an item that is contaminated with the spores. Spores can survive for 1 to 2 *years* in the environment, thus a dog can contract ringworm from just about anywhere that has been frequented by other dogs and/or cats.

Natural Health Program

For fleas and mange, all the bedding must be cleaned and/or washed daily. The surrounding area should be vacuumed twice daily until there are no longer signs of any parasites on the dog. Then apply a few drops of essential oils on the bedding and flooring to discourage the lifecycle. Oils of peppermint, cedarwood, orange, and/or pennyroyal are effective; however, for stronger oils, or more sensitive dogs (or if there are cats in the house), dilute the oils and only apply a very small amount. Diluted essential oils can also be used directly on dog to prevent fleas from jumping on board, but use with caution, for a dog's sense of smell is many times more acute than yours.

Diet

- Eliminate wheat, corn gluten, dairy products, soy products, rancid oils, and all known food allergies and intolerances (see Chapter 7).

- Add more seeds, such as flax, chia, and/or hemp, to the diet to provide a natural source of essential fatty acids. EFAs are excellent nutrients for all skin conditions.

Nutrients

- **vitamin C** [*one dose daily*]†* –promotes parasite resistance, supports the immune response and healthy liver function

- **vitamin A, liquid** [*one dose daily*]† – skin nutrient; dry flaky skin, promotes skin repair, supports the immune system

- **iodine, liquid** [*one dose daily*]† – bacteria and yeast; maintains the immune response

- **Iron-Up (iron gluconate)** [*one dose daily*]†* – undiagnosed low iron levels is a common condition for many dogs, especially those who are infested with parasites that feed on blood. The lower the iron, the lower the immunity, the more parasites, the more iron loss and so the cycle continues. Blood tests cannot be consistently relied upon for assessing nutrient levels. See Chapter 14 for more information on blood testing.

Herbal & Home Remedies

- **yellow dock, tincture** [*one dose daily for 30 days*]† – bacteria and skin parasites; promotes healthy blood and skin

- **milk thistle seed, tincture** [*one dose daily*]† – flea allergy reactions, liver detoxifier

- **coconut oil** [*apply to the hair on affected areas twice daily*] – coconut oil is thick, which makes it very difficult for lice to attach themselves to the hair shaft; it also makes it difficult for fleas and mites to move freely in the hair coat once attached; soothes and support skin health

Riva's Remedies

- **Skin-Heal, herbal blend** [*one dose daily*]† – promotes healthy skin in dogs with chronic skin conditions; parasite resistance, excellent for all skin and parasite conditions

- **Immune Boost, herbal blend** [*one dose daily*]† – promotes healthy immune function in dogs with frequent illnesses, predisposition to infections, and chronic skin conditions

- **Detox Dog, herbal blend** [one dose daily for 4-6 weeks] – promotes the detoxification of skin, liver, kidneys and colon, supports the immune system

- **Happy Pets** or **Happy Pets Senior, herbal blends** [*one dose daily*]† – provides a plant-based source of over 60 trace minerals, vitamins, fibre, and anti-oxidants for healthy skin; excellent nutrition for hair coat, hair growth, skin, and nails

- **Kava's Healing Oil, herbal blend** [*apply twice daily to all affected areas*]† – symptoms of skin parasites - bald patches, hot spots, ringworm, scabs, crusts, sores and inflamed areas

†See Appendix for recommended dosages and duration for all supplements.

Growths – Benign and Malignant

Dogs can present with a variety of different lumps and bumps, especially as they get older. Warts, sebaceous cysts, sebaceous adenomas, and lipomas are common growths which can be unsightly but are rarely harmful. In a small percentage of cases, growths are found to be malignant and diagnosed as skin cancer.

Symptoms

Warts or papillomas can appear on the eyelids, face, feet and footpads, or in the mouth. They normally appear on puppies, older dogs, or immune-compromised dogs. Warts are firm, fleshy, and cauliflower like, with a rough surface or like little mushrooms with a smooth surface.

Sebaceous cysts are very common and are found on sebaceous glands above the hair follicles that have become blocked and enlarged. They can develop on the head, neck, body, and upper legs. They can range from a few millimetres to 3 to 4 centimetres. They are round, smooth, and firm and may have a blue tint to them. Any discharges may be grayish white or brown, which consist of a greasy paste of oil, bacteria, and skin cells. All sebaceous cysts are benign and non-painful.

Sebaceous adenoma is a benign tumor that normally occurs later in the dog's life. Sebaceous adenoma growths also result from sebaceous glands and are mostly found on the eyelids or legs. They are often mistaken for warts; however, adenomas are oily if squeezed, whereas warts are dry and solid. Sebaceous adenomas can appear as single or multiple tumors which are less than 2 centimetres wide with or without hair growth.

Lipomas are fatty tumours containing adipose tissue (i.e. body fat) but are always benign, never malignant. Like cysts and adenomas, lipomas also occur in the middle-age and older dogs. They grow very slowly over months or years and, depending on the size of the dog, they can range from 2 to 20 centimetres.

Skin cancer can include melanomas, mast-cell tumours, and squamous cell. Melanomas can appear on the skin, eyelids, nails, and mouth. Mast cell tumours originate from the bone marrow and are part of the immune system; they can be either benign or malignant. They are usually found anywhere in the connective tissue and release histamines into the body, which can result in itching, digestive problems, and/or allergy type reactions.

Squamous cell cancer is more uncommon, but is normally found in older dogs. Squamous cell cancer occurs when the upper layers of the skin are mutated causing uncontrolled growth. They have a cauliflower appearance that bleed easily. They are single tumours and slow growing. They may appear on the body, legs, toes, anus, lips, or nose. For all cancers, watch for growths which change colour, scaly/crusty lesions, tumours that bleed easily, suspicious lumps, and/or an area which the dog is continually licking or scratching.

Causes

As a rule, all lumps, bumps, growths, and tumours are a result of dietary excesses, unhealthy foods (including certain fats and oils), systemic toxicity, a compromised immune system, and/or poor liver function. All skin problems are created by internal conditions, not external ones. It is thought that cysts of all kinds, abscesses, adenomas, and lipomas are "collection vessels" for toxins and/or unhealthy materials which could otherwise damage other body tissues and/or the immune system.

Warts are caused by the papilloma virus and will frequently disappear on their own unless the dog's immune system has been weakened by medications such as corticosteroids, certain diseases, or vaccinosis; multiple warts are often an indication that the dog has been over-vaccinated. Papilloma viruses are contagious between dogs (but not cats or people) if they come into contact with a break in the skin or through the mucous membranes in the mouth. Viruses, like bacteria, thrive in hosts who provide a hospitable terrain.

Sebaceous cysts are caused by obstructed hair follicles. Sebaceous glands produce sebum to protect and nourish the skin and hair coat. Sebum is emptied into the hair follicles, but if abnormal amounts of sebum are produced – or if the consistency of the sebum changes and becomes thicker or greasier than normal – the hair follicles will become plugged. Because sebum is comprised of fatty acids and fat metabolites, excess production or a thicker consistency can be due to unhealthy or excess dietary fats and/or poor fat metabolism. In addition, hair follicles have a very high metabolic rate so anything that slows down the metabolism (thyroid health, adrenal function, poor diet, weight gain and/or lack of exercise) can be a contributing factor.

Sebaceous adenomas are benign and non-viral and, like cysts, may be caused and/or exacerbated by unhealthy sebum or by the abnormal production of sebum.

Lipomas are seen more often in older dogs, overweight dogs, and particularly overweight female dogs. Overweight, sedentary dogs and insulin-resistant dogs have unbalanced levels of various hormones, including insulin and cortisol, both of which affect fat metabolism. Review the diet to identify unhealthy fats, grains, or just excess food. See Chapters 3 and 10 for dietary information for overweight dogs.

All skin problems are created by
internal conditions, not external ones.

Skin cancer, like all cancers, are caused by systemic toxicity, chemical toxicity, dietary problems and a weak immune system which causes cells to grow and multiply abnormally. Whereas normal cells follow a pattern of growth, division, and death, when the skin cells become cancerous, they grow continuously, outlive normal cells, and then conglomerate into growths which we call tumours. Eventually cells from the tumours break away and migrate to another body part to grow tumours there as well. This process is known as metastasis. A toxic colon, poor intestinal immunity, and a toxic liver are major contributing factors to poor skin health and abnormal cell growth – in the skin and elsewhere. Dogs are thirty-five times more at risk for developing skin cancer than humans.

Natural Health Program

The appropriate nutritional health program often prevents further growth and/or helps decrease their size or even eliminate them completely. However, if the growth is not responding surgery should be considered if: (1) a growth is affecting mobility, (2) the dog is irritated by it, (3) it is affecting eyesight, (4) it is bleeding regularly, or (5) it is in an area where it is constantly rubbed or irritated.

Diet

- Eliminate wheat, corn gluten, dairy products, soy products, rancid oils, and all known food allergies and intolerances (see Chapter 7).
- Review the diet for excess dietary fats and oils as

well as unhealthy oils. This includes canola oil, soya oil, coconut oil, and fish and vegetable oils. While a small amount of essential fatty acids is necessary for good health excess, rancid, or unhealthy oils will congest the lymph system as well as sebaceous glands and their production of sebum. Use caution with fat/oil supplements, including fish oil.

- Add more seeds, such as flax, chia, and/or hemp, to the diet to provide a natural source of essential fatty acids.

- Always include lots of healthy vegetables – cooked or raw.

- Overweight dogs need to lose weight and exercise regularly. See Chapter 10.

- Senior dogs should reduce or temporarily eliminate meat protein.

- If your dog has been diagnosed with skin cancer refer to Chapter 7 and follow the dietary guidelines there for cancer.

Nutrients

- **vitamin A, liquid** [*one dose daily*]† – promotes healthy skin growth and sebum production, nutrition to prevent skin infections; supports a healthy immune system

- **vitamin E** [*one dose daily*]†* – anti-oxidant for circulation, blood flow and wound healing

- **folic acid** [*one dose daily*]† – supports immune response; nutrition for skin health, tissue repair, health cell replication and cell growth

- **selenium, organic** [*one dose daily*]† – anti-oxidant for liver and immune support. Promotes the detoxification of chemical toxicity; supports healthy sugar metabolism

Herbal & Home Remedies

- **milk thistle seed, tincture** [*one dose daily for 30 days*]† – supports detoxification and allergy reactions

- **thuja 200C, homeopathic** [*one dose daily for 4 days*]† – warts and growths on face, paws and toes; warts that appear after vaccinations

- **silicea 200C, homeopathic** [*one dose daily for 3 days*]† – growths, cysts, warts, abscesses; unhealthy, easily infected skin

- **calc sulph 200C, homeopathic** [*one dose daily for 3 days*]† – pus and drainage, yellow scabs, abscesses, cystic tumours; promotes healthy fat metabolism

- **castor oil and baking soda** [*mix both together to make a paste and apply to warts twice daily until warts dissolved*] – note: cover with a bandage or wrap if possible so the paste doesn't come off right away

Riva's Remedies

- **Kava's Primrose Oil, specialized nutrient** [*one dose daily for 30 days*]† – essential fatty acids and nutrition for a healthy immune response and skin health

- **Skin-Heal, herbal blend** [*one dose daily*]† – promotes healthy blood and skin in dogs with growths and tumours; cleanser and detoxifier

- **Detox Dog, herbal blend** [*one dose daily for 4 to 6 weeks*] – promotes the detoxification of elimination organs: skin, liver, kidneys and colon; supports the immune system

- **Immune Boost, herbal blend** [*one dose daily*]† – supports immune function. skin and liver with nutrition and cleansing

- **Kava's Healing Oil, herbal blend** [*apply externally to wounds, open sores and/or any skin irritations*] † Soothes abscesses, open sores and/or growths

† See Appendix for recommended dosages and duration for all supplements.
* Also available as a Riva's Remedy

Mr. Reese Helps His Hairless Skin

Mr. Reese is a toy Xoloitzcuintli (Mexican hairless) dog who was suffering from itching, hives, scaly patches, and dry skin every spring and summer. These issues were very noticeable, of course, on a hairless dog. Mr. Reese's pet parent, Crystal, had already tried many other therapies.

Mr. Reese's case of unhealthy skin was a little more unique, not because he was hairless, but because his skin reactions were accompanied and appeared exacerbated by environmental allergies in the spring. These allergies caused him congestion, sneezing, and discharges from his eyes and nose. And while inhalant or spring allergies do not normally cause skin problems directly, they do compromise the overall immune system, potentially creating more immune problems.

Mr. Reese.

Mr. Reese's complete health program discontinued pork and all red meats, including beef, venison, elk, and bison. Red meats are high in arachidonic acids and other acids and can cause liver and kidney toxicity. By reducing the toxicity in these important elimination organs, the skin, also a major elimination organ, would not be required to eliminate excess toxins and acids. Mr. Reese enjoyed "cooler" meats like duck, turkey, lamb, rabbit, and fish. Then we also added the Riva's Immune Boost and Skin-Heal Herbal Blends to support the immune function and to further detoxify his system. This was in addition to vitamin B6, vitamin E, selenium, and folic acid, all given in therapeutic dosages to support the skin and immune function. In addition, his health program included the homeopathic Allerg-Ease to neutralize any dust, mold, or pollen allergies –which would stress the immune system. Not long after Crystal reported:

"This was the first summer since I've owned Reese (five years) that he didn't have a horrible spring/summer due to horrendous allergies - hives, peeling and flaking skin, inflammation, sore, itchy, sensitive to the touch, redness, watery eyes…. I am so happy I could almost cry and it is all thanks to Marijke's assessment and Riva's Remedies. He was in quite a bad flare up when we started so Marijke originally recommended quite a few supplements and vitamins to get him through. By the end of that summer he was just on Riva's Skin Heal and Kava's Primrose Oil. We didn't need anything at the end of fall and into winter. The following summer he had a minor flare up a little later than his allergies usually tend to start so he started a few of the vitamins again with Riva's Skin Heal. He stayed on this for the summer and fall. This spring, summer and fall his symptoms again started later than usual in the season and it was very minor AND he's not had a single red, itchy, flaky flare!!! I put him back on his Riva's Skin Heal as soon as I noticed his skin change and within the week his symptoms cleared up and did not return. Finally!!! He had a great summer and he was so much more at ease, his eyes were bright, his skin is soft and not itchy or sensitive, he had a beautiful tan, his was in such a great mood. All he needed this season was Riva's Skin Heal. I also have my Chinese Crested on the minimal dose of Skin Heal which has done wonders for her blackheads and minor acne. I LOVE Riva's Remedies and have recommended them to many people with dogs, cats and horses. I am so pleased with Marijke's assessment, follow up help and the products. I really appreciate her care and dedication to the animals and their humans. Thank you again, Marijke." —Crystal McC.

Beautiful Bailey

"Hi. My beautiful Malamute Bailey is twelve years old and living a bright and energetic life. But she wasn't always so healthy. She was actually very sick most of her life due to her dog food. I tried all kinds of kibble, and while many of these foods have a good reputation, they sure didn't sit well with Bailey!

"Bailey had several skin lesions, and she was lethargic, inflamed, and her joints and muscles were always very sore. I decided to take further action. With your guidance, we started cooking all her food at home and then put her on a supplement program including the Para+Plus Tincture, Immune Boost Herbal Blend, Pro-Colon probiotics, and Iron-Up. She bounced back in under six months! She has lost 35 lbs, her fur is shiny, and her eyes are nice and bright. She doesn't limp anymore and takes *me* for walks now, instead of lagging behind. Thank you SO much. I now have a very healthy senior Malamute." — Karla

Bailey.

Healing Dogs Their Way

10. The Endocrine System

Hormone Production & Regulation

The primary endocrine glands include the pancreas, pineal, hypothalamus, pituitary, thyroid, thymus, adrenals, ovaries and testes – all of them function to secrete hormones directly into the bloodstream. Hormones are extremely powerful chemicals that make it possible for all the body systems to communicate with one another in order to affect the activity of another part of the body (target site). Thus, hormones serve as messengers that control and coordinate activities throughout the body; they regulate muscle activity, alter metabolism, control growth and development, balance energy, help with immunity, and direct reproductive processes. Together with the nervous system, the endocrine system coordinates the functions of all body systems.

In the conventional veterinary health model, the emphasis is on the dysfunction of the organ itself; in the holistic health model the emphasis is on the underlying condition – mostly nutritional - which prompts the imbalances in the organs and/or the tissue receptors in the first place. The endocrine system, with its various organs, work together in beautiful harmony, sending messages to one another, communicating excesses and deficiencies, and working hard together to regulate the entire body. For example, problems with the adrenal glands can trigger the pituitary to increase cortisol levels, sluggish ovarian function will cause the adrenal glands to produce more estrogen, and high insulin levels will increase adrenal cortisol production, and so on.

The canine endocrine system.

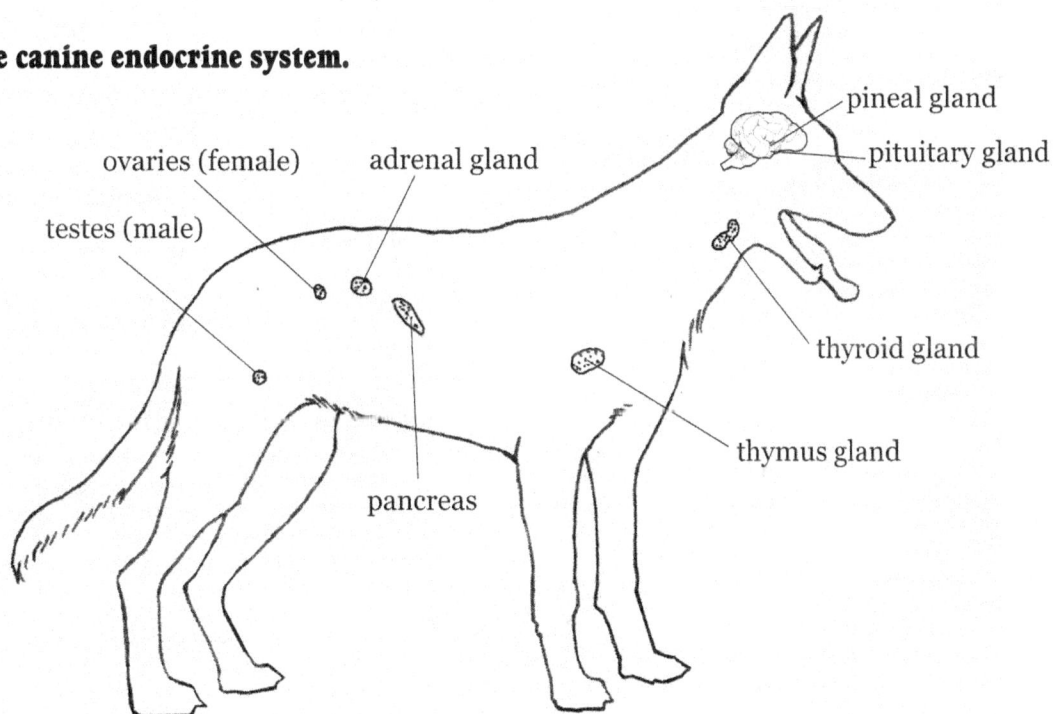

Natural Health Programs for Pancreas/Insulin Function

~~~~~~~~~~~~~~~~~~~~ ❧ ~~~~~~~~~~~~~~~~~~~~

Insulin Resistance, Obesity & Diabetes

Insulin resistance, obesity and diabetes are all types of metabolic problems. All of them are associated with diet and weight gain however diabetes in dogs has two forms: insulin resistance diabetes or IR and insulin deficiency diabetes or ID. Insulin resistance diabetes is caused by the condition of insulin resistance as initiated by poor diets and/or lack of exercise; whereas insulin deficiency diabetes is caused by inflammation of or damage to the beta cells in the pancreas disabling them from producing insulin. However, ID is also often a result of dietary imbalances and intolerances as well.

Symptoms

Insulin resistance and insulin resistance diabetes is most noticeable in middle age or older dogs who show weight gain, fatigue, increased or ravenous appetite, increased thirst, and an increase in urination as the body tries to eliminate the extra sugars. Overweight dogs are much more likely to experience joint pain and arthritis (fat cells are inflammatory), respiratory problems, fatigue, depression, fatty liver, depressed immunity, and cancer. Insulin deficiency diabetes causes a decrease in appetite, weight loss as caused by the breakdown of body fat, and a "chemical" smell on the breath. Over time, diabetes can create cataracts, hardening of the arteries, kidney problems, and neurological problems including peripheral neuropathy, which your dog can't tell you about and your veterinarian can't find. Dogs with peripheral neuropathy will feel numbness, tingling, pins and needles, and possibly loss of sensation in their paws. Peripheral neuropathy can be present in any case of poor sugar metabolism, not just diabetes. Diabetes is also the primary cause of cataracts in dogs.

Causes

Any kinds of sugars, including refined carbohydrates such as corn, wheat, or white rice, have a very high absorption rate, meaning that the sugars enter from the small intestine into the bloodstream very rapidly. This rate of absorption is known as the Glycemic Index. The faster the sugars enter the bloodstream the faster the insulin must be produced and secreted by the pancreas to lower the sugar in the blood. It does so by attaching to and prompting the receptors in the muscles and liver to open like a gateway through which the sugars can be transported and then used for immediate energy or converted into and stored as glycogen, a type of starch. Then when the simple sugars are required again for energy or to raise the blood sugar, the glycogen in the liver is signalled to convert back into sugars. A dog who is overweight is most likely to be "insulin resistant" which means that the receptors have become resistant to opening even though the insulin is signalling them to do so. Since the sugars have nowhere to go, they are now forced into storage as fat. However, if the condition is not corrected, the fat stores will either become full and/or the demands of insulin production will overwhelm the pancreas to the point where it is no longer able to produce adequate amounts of insulin. Either way, the sugars are trapped in the blood, and blood sugars continue to rise; a permanent condition of high blood sugar is a metabolic condition known as diabetes. Both diabetes and insulin resistance is exacerbated by a lack of exercise and a lack of dietary fibre.

Many overweight dogs improve considerably when put on a grain-free diet combined with an appropriate exercise program. However, some dogs don't respond to a higher-protein/lower-grain diet. Usually this means that the metabolism is stuck at a certain set point as can occur with insulin deficiency diabetes, or if a meat-protein diet is too high in calories, or if they have become intolerant to certain types of meat. ID (insulin deficiency diabetes) can be caused by either food intolerances and/or autoimmune reactions also caused by food. A combination of food reactions and nutrient deficiencies can be very destructive to all organs including the pancreas. See Chapter 7 for specific details on these type of immune reactions and the various inflammations which can interfere with any physiological functions of the body including insulin production.

Metabolic conditions can also be caused and/or exacerbated by thyroid imbalances, which in turn, are frequently caused by insulin, cortisol, and pituitary imbalances.

Stress is a significant cause of ID; the shock of a stress reaction causes a major upset to the delicate balance between insulin, glucagon, cortisol, adrenaline, and canine growth hormone. Most of these hormones do not recover without nutritional help. Remember, unless you are very astute, dogs cannot express to you just how stressful an event really was for them or how it has affected them physiologically. But just like people the canine physical body and its electrical field will store a permanent record of any stressful reaction, acute or chronic, past or present.

Spaying and neutering can also affect weight regulation because of the sudden drop in hormone levels. See relevant section below.

> Stress is a significant cause of diabetes; the shock of a stress reaction can cause a major upset to the delicate balance between insulin, glucagon, cortisol, adrenaline, and canine growth hormone.

Natural Health Program

Diet

- Overweight dogs need to lose weight and exercise regularly.

- Eliminate all sugars, sugar treats, wheat, corn gluten, dairy products, soy products, and/or rancid oils.

- Identify and eliminate all known food allergies and intolerances (see Chapter 7).

- Review the diet for excess dietary fats and oils as well as unhealthy oils, including canola oil, soya oil, coconut oil, fish, and vegetable oils. While a small amount of essential fatty acids are necessary for good health, excess oils produce excess cortisol, the stress hormone. Also use caution with fat/oil supplements including fish oil.

- Add more seeds, such as flax, chia, and hemp, to the diet to provide a natural source of fibre and essential fatty acids.

- Increase dietary fibre; fibre slows down the Glycemic Index, i.e., the rate of sugar absorption into the blood. Whole cooked grains such as brown rice

or barley, seeds, and all vegetables are an excellent source of fibre as well as extra nutrition.

- A grain-free diet with healthy meats is strongly indicated if the dog has been eating grains as staples, particularly wheat, corn gluten, or other poor quality grains.

- If the dog is *already* on a grain-free diet, add healthy whole grains and more fibre which slows down sugar absorption.

- Portion control feeders can be useful for weight regulation; however, if a dog is voracious and still always hungry this means that the blood sugar and/or insulin levels are still erratic and/or the food is not suitable nor satisfying.

Nutrients

- **vitamin B6** [*one dose daily*]†* – promotes healthy sugar metabolism and blood sugar levels; supports hormone production

- **zinc citrate or picolinate** [*one dose daily for 30 days, repeat if necessary*]† – supports sugar metabolism, promotes healthy immunity; stress nutrient

- **selenium, organic** [*one dose daily*]† – maintains carbohydrate metabolism, liver support, and muscle strength

- **vitamin B12** [*one dose daily*]†* – maintains carbohydrate metabolism; promotes healthy liver function and a healthy nervous system; supports energy levels

NOTE: Discontinue all glucosamine and chondroitin products. These nutraceuticals are concentrated sugars which block the beta cells of the pancreas from producing adequate levels of insulin. Glucosamine is therefore contraindicated in all cases of insulin resistance, weight gain, and/or diabetes.

Herbal & Home Remedies

- **dandelion root, tincture or leaf** [*one dose daily for 30 days or as needed*]† – supports urinary eliminations; kidney cleanser, liver detoxification, promotes healthy immunity and digestion

Riva's Remedies

- **Blood Sugar Formula, homeopathic** [*one dose daily for 2 to 3 weeks*]† – supports blood sugar levels and insulin production

- **Vital Force, herbal blend** [one dose daily] [†] – helps maintain normal blood sugar levels and healthy adrenal function; nutrition for hormone production; rich in fibre, minerals, and vitamins

- **Kidney Care, herbal blend** [one dose daily][†] – promotes the elimination of urinary toxins and sugars; kidney and liver support

[†] See Appendix for recommended dosages and duration for all supplements.
[*] Also available as a Riva's Remedy

Natural Health Programs for Adrenal Function

Cushing's Disease

Cushing's disease or Hyperadrenocorticism is becoming too common in dogs, especially over the age of six, a testament to stressful lifestyles and inappropriate diets. Diseases don't just happen to dogs; they are created by the domestic environment. In sharp contrast to the medical view, the true and underlying cause of Cushing's disease is caused by metabolic problems, and is the end result of insulin resistance, weight gain, and/or diabetes. This information is not available to veterinary students nor practitioners, who are, therefore, limited to using destructive drugs with poor results.

Symptoms

Cushing's disease can be very difficult to diagnose, and there is no single test to confirm the condition. In addition, because Cushing's affects the function of all the other endocrine organs, signs and symptoms can vary. Most commonly, dogs will experience hair loss on the body (no itching), pot bellies caused by fat accumulation in the abdomen, an increase in hunger, increased drinking with urination, and poor immunity. Poor immunity can result in a susceptibility to bacterial, viral and yeast infections (e.g. bladder or ears), or infections which may or may not be evident and are, therefore, left undiagnosed. More advanced cases will present with fatigue, weakness, panting, and an enlarged liver and/or adrenal glands.

Diseases don't just happen to dogs; they are created by the domestic environment.

Causes

From a purely physiological perspective, Cushing's disease is caused by the over-production of cortisol by the adrenal glands. In Cushing's this is normally caused by an over-active pituitary gland that is producing excessive adrenocorticotropic ACTH hormone, which in turn, stimulates the adrenal glands to produce more cortisol. This is known as pituitary-dependent Cushing's. On occasion, a dog will be found to have a tumour on the adrenal gland which also results in high cortisol levels – this condition is known as adrenal-dependent Cushing's. Cushing's can also be caused by high doses of steroid medication.

However, the real issue with Cushing's is not primarily a pituitary gland dysfunction, nor an adrenal gland dysfunction, but rather, a cascade of unbalanced hormones as caused by insulin resistance, weight gain, and both forms of diabetes as described above. The continuing high insulin production by the pancreas leads to an over-production of cortisol by the adrenals – cortisol is produced as a response to stress and plays a role in carbohydrate metabolism. If the situation continues, it will eventually engage the pituitary into a defense mechanism as it attempts to regulate or lower the excess cortisol production. Remember how the pituitary is the master gland whose primary duty is to help balance all its co-workers. In any case, the underlying cause of these growths and tumours is the prolonged stimulation of the adrenal and pituitary glands, which eventually become exhausted.

Stress is another major cause of hormonal imbalances including diabetes; stress causes chronic production of cortisol, erratic insulin levels, higher than normal production of adrenaline, and pituitary and thyroid dysfunction. I have worked with many dogs who appeared healthy to their owners but whose nervous systems went into shock following a previous stressful episode. Many times, these dogs were thrown into a hormonal condition which didn't recover until the stress was addressed.

And furthermore, the onset of Cushing's disease is not sudden; it's a slow development of hormonal changes initiated by dietary problems, sugar imbalances, and/or stress. High insulin levels result in elevated cortisol levels, high cortisol levels result in high insulin levels; high insulin and cortisol levels together result in a higher production of pituitary ACTH, which then causes higher output of cortisol – and so the feedback cycle continues. High insulin and cortisol levels also interfere with thyroid hormones, which is another complication for dogs.

Natural Health Program

The allopathic medication treatment for pituitary-dependent Cushing's disease is extremely toxic, carries serious side effects, and does not address the underlying cause. These drugs act as a type of chemotherapy, which erode the cortisol-producing cells of the adrenal cortex. This destruction of organs and their precious hormones results in weakness, lack of coordination, loss of appetite, vomiting, diarrhea, fatigue and depression. This is what I call crowbar medicine at its worst. And if too much adrenal tissue is killed off, the dog must then be given steroid medication, an excess of which causes Cushing's. Okay, now I'm confused, how about you?

As we can now understand, the only effective treatment in the holistic health model of canine Cushing's is through dietary changes, supplements, and stress relief.

Diet – as per Insulin Resistance and Diabetes

- Overweight dogs need to lose weight and be exercised regularly.

- Eliminate all sugars, sugar treats, wheat, corn gluten, dairy products, soy products, and/or rancid oils.

- Review the diet for excess dietary fats and oils as well as unhealthy oils. This includes canola oil, soya oil, coconut oil, fish and vegetable oils. While small amounts of essential fatty acids are necessary for good health, excess or unhealthy oils produce excess cortisol, which causes insulin reactions. See Chapter 3 for more information.

- Add more seeds, such as flax, chia and hemp, to the diet to provide a natural source of fibre and essential fatty acids.

- Increase dietary fibre to slow down the Glycemic Index, i.e., sugar absorption into the blood. Whole cooked grains (if tolerated), seeds, and all vegetables are an excellent source of fibre.

- A grain-free diet is strongly indicated if the dog has been eating grains as staples, particularly wheat, corn gluten, or other poor quality grains.

- If the dog is *already* on a grain-free diet, add healthy whole grains, which will increase the fibre and slow down sugar absorption.

Nutrients

- **vitamin B6** [*one dose daily*][†] – supports sugar metabolism and insulin production, promotes healthy pituitary and adrenal function

- **zinc citrate or picolinate** [*one dose daily for 30 days, repeat if necessary*][†] – supports sugar metabolism, blood sugar levels, adrenal function and hormone production. Stress nutrient.

NOTE: Discontinue all glucosamine and chondroitin products. These nutraceuticals are concentrated sugars which block the beta cells of the pancreas from producing adequate levels of insulin. Glucosamine is, therefore, contraindicated in all cases of insulin resistance, weight gain, diabetes or metabolic disorders.

Herbal & Home Remedies

- **adrenal glandular 200C, homeopathic** [one dose daily for 7 days][†] – promotes the healthy function of adrenal glands as well as hormone balance

- **pituitary glandular or ACTH 200C, homeopathic** [one dose daily for 7 days][†] – pituitary support and hormone balance

- **chaste berry** [one dose daily][†] – pituitary and adrenal support

Riva's Remedies

- **Hormone Boost, herbal blend** [one dose daily][†] – promotes the healthy function and balance of all endocrine glands (adrenals, pituitary and thyroid);

natural adaptogen, supports a healthy stress response

- **Vital Force, herbal blend** [one dose daily][†] - hormone balance and vitality, supports healthy blood sugar levels; nutrition for the nervous system; adds fibre, minerals and nutrition
- **Blood Sugar Formula, homeopathic** [one dose daily for 2 to 3 weeks][†] - maintains healthy blood sugar levels; supports weight loss and normalizes appetite

NOTE: Reduce stress! If necessary and possible remove the dog from an unhealthy emotional environment (see Chapter 15 for healing trauma and managing stress levels).

[†] See Appendix for recommended dosages and duration for all supplements.

[*] Also available as a Riva's Remedy

Addison's Disease & Adrenal Burn-Out

Addison's disease is just the opposite of Cushing's disease but less common. Addison's or hypoadrenocorticism is a condition of low cortisol production (whereas Cushing's is *high* cortisol). In both conditions, the pituitary will increase its production of ACTH in an effort to either decrease (Cushing's) or increase (Addison's) the amount of cortisol produced by the adrenal glands.

Symptoms

Young to middle-aged female dogs at an average age of 4 are most prone to Addison's. Signs and symptoms are highly variable or vague and may appear severe and suddenly or intermittently or gradually. Common symptoms include weakness, depression, vomiting, diarrhea, poor appetite, high potassium, low sodium levels, low blood sugar, joint pain, general inflammation, and an inability to cope with stress, meaning that any stressful situations can increase symptoms. These symptoms can also indicate adrenal burn-out - mostly undiagnosed - rather than a full-blown case of Addison's, which can be considered a severe form of adrenal burn-out and is therefore a clinical condition.

Causes

The inability by the adrenal glands to produce cortisol means that the adrenal cortex is overworked from stress or hormonal imbalances, or that is has been too damaged or inflamed to produce healthy hormones. Alternatively, the pituitary may not be producing enough ACTH to signal the adrenal glands to produce cortisol.

If the female hormones estrogen and/or progesterone levels are low, as is the case after spaying a female, the adrenal glands must then take over with the task of producing enough of these hormones to support the basic functions that rely on reproductive hormones: brain function, mood, weight control, metabolism, skin health, quality of hair coat, and bone and joint health. That's a significant responsibility for the adrenal glands, which are not designed to carry out these functions long-term or throughout a lifetime for that matter. Therefore, for any female dogs who start out with sluggish adrenal function - and/or if they have a high requirement for both reproductive hormones and/or cortisol - the adrenal glands are sure to burn out before long.

Low adrenal function can also be caused by damage and/or inflammation to the adrenal glands as is often caused by auto-immune reactions, mostly triggered by food intolerances and/or allergies (see Chapter 7).

Addison's or adrenal burn-out can follow a traumatic event which has shocked the nervous system. Physical and emotional symptoms can persist for a long time after the stress event has passed. In addition, many puppies can be born with weak adrenal function if their parents were poorly nourished, abused or neglected.

Poor cortisol production can also be a side effect of steroid medication, which causes the adrenals to shut down its natural production to compensate; when the steroids are discontinued, the adrenals cannot manufacture and/or release cortisol quick enough to match the normal levels. For this reason, steroid medication must always be discontinued gradually rather than suddenly to allow time for the adrenal glands to resume the production of cortisol.

Natural Health Program

Diet

- Eliminate all sugars, sugar treats, wheat, corn gluten, dairy products, soy products, and rancid oils.

- Eliminate pork and all red meats, such as beef, bison, venison, and elk. Red meats commonly contribute to reproductive hormone imbalance.

- Add more seeds, such as flax, chia, and hemp, to the diet to provide a natural source of essential fatty acids to support adrenal function.

- Increase fibre and vegetables to ensure maximum nutrition.

Nutrients

- **vitamin B5** [*one dose daily for 30 days, repeat if necessary*][†] – adrenal support, hormone balance, nerve nutrient, fatigue and stress

- **zinc citrate or picolinate** [*one dose daily for 30 days, repeat if necessary*][†] – adrenal nutrient, nerve nutrient; supports hormone production and carbohydrate metabolism

- **vitamin C** [*one dose daily for 30 days, repeat if necessary*][†*] – adrenal support, stress nutrient, immunity and infections

Herbal & Home Remedies

- **adrenal glandular 200C, homeopathic** [*one dose daily for 10 days*][†] – supports adrenal gland function and normal cortisol production

- **pituitary glandular or ACTH 200C, homeopathic** [*one dose daily for 10 days*][†] –pituitary support and hormone balance

- **licorice root powder** [*one dose daily for 30 days or longer if demonstrating benefit*][†] – steroid and phytoestrogen properties; adrenal support, energy and hormone balance

Riva's Remedies

- **Hormone Boost, herbal blend** [*one dose daily*][†] – support for all endocrine glands (adrenals, pituitary and thyroid); natural Adaptogen and stress relief

- **Vital Force, herbal blend** [*one dose daily*][†] – hormone support, vitality, and stamina; adds fibre, minerals, and nutrition important for healthy adrenal function

- **Kava's Primrose Oil, specialized nutrient** [*one dose daily*][†] – essential fatty acids for adrenal support and hormone balance

NOTE: Reduce stress! If necessary and possible remove the dog from an unhealthy emotional environment (see Chapter 15 for healing trauma and managing stress levels).

[†] See Appendix for recommended dosages and duration for all supplements.
[*] Also available as a Riva's Remedy

Natural Health Programs for Thyroid Function

Hypothyroidism (low thyroid)

Hypothyroidism is a common problem in middle-aged dogs and some spayed females, but it is also one of the most over-diagnosed conditions in dogs. (Hyperactive active thyroid glands in dogs are rare and are usually associated with cancer, although some holistic veterinarians report over-active thyroid activity in dogs that eat too much head meat containing thyroid gland tissue.)

Many other health problems and illnesses can mimic hypothyroidism and can often result in low thyroid hormone tests. This is known as *euthyroid sick syndrome*, a complicated label, which simply means that another underlying health condition is responsible for the changes in thyroid hormone production. But the practitioner mistakenly assumes, from the blood tests, that it is a primary problem at which point the dog is prescribed thyroid medication. Thyroid conditions are actually very difficult to diagnose since a deficiency of thyroid hormone affects the function of all organ systems, and therefore clinical signs are diffuse, variable, and nonspecific resulting in over-diagnosis and very often inappropriate medication.

Symptoms

Because the thyroid is the primary organ for regulating cellular metabolism, it has a major influence over bodyweight (usually gain), blood sugar levels (insulin resistance and diabetes), cholesterol levels (elevated) and energy levels. Thus, a low thyroid will normally present with fatigue, weak muscles, weight gain or obesity, dull hair coat, cold intolerance, slow heart rate, toxic liver, puffy face, and poor immunity. Its effect on the immune system is why a poorly functioning thyroid can be a contributing factor to allergies, dry skin and various other skin conditions, digestive problems, heartburn, constipation, hormone imbalances, infertility, miscarriages, incontinence, repeated infections, poor wound healing, and/or other immune conditions. Many times, it causes depression, anxiety, irritability, mental dullness, and/or behavioural problems, such as fear and aggression, for thyroid hormones affect the brain as well.

A low thyroid also commonly results in hair loss, thinning of the hair coat, or excessive shedding. Hair follicles have a high metabolic rate and are thus particularly sensitive to concentrations of thyroid-gland derived hormones. And because thyroid hormones have a global influence on the cellular metabolism of proteins, carbohydrates, lipids, and minerals, the cells of the hair matrix, due to their high degree of metabolic activity, are profoundly influenced by the deficiency or excess of thyroid derived hormones.

Mild anemia (low oxygen levels due to low iron, vitamin B12 and/or folic acid) can also accompany low thyroid function. However, it is likely that these nutrients were low to begin with and, therefore, affecting thyroid function through inadequate nutrition.

Causes

A true case of hypothyroidism is seen as inflammation, damage, or shrinkage of the thyroid gland that, of course, prevents it from producing and secreting the necessary hormones. Damaged thyroid cells can become infiltrated with adipose (fat cells), but this is more than likely a defence mechanism after the damage has been sustained rather than a direct cause of any thyroid problem.

~~~~~~ 🐾 ~~~~~~

It is far more likely that your dog's thyroid issue is a *euthyroid* issue, which means that another underlying health problem is affecting thyroid hormone levels and that the thyroid gland itself is healthy.

~~~~~~~~~~~~~~~~

The concept that true hypothyroidism is an auto-immune condition, i.e. auto-immune thyroiditis, whereby the immune cells of the body are attacking the thyroid tissue is gaining popularity as the primary cause of thyroid problems. However, as discussed in Chapter 7, all auto-immune conditions are caused by systemic toxicity and the immune system's reaction to defend the body from toxins, acids, chemicals, proteins, foreign material, and mal-digested food. Normally the immune system does not attack body organs and/or tissues unless it is has a very good reason for doing so.

However, it is far more likely that your dog's thyroid issue is a *euthyroid* issue, which also explains why canine thyroid problems are so predominate. Euthyroid issues are described as underlying health problems which adversely affect thyroid hormone production but which does not cause any significant damage to the thyroid organ itself. Thus, once these issues are identified and corrected, the thyroid hormones will usually recover. This improvement can be tracked on accurate blood tests as well as hair analysis. There are a variety of different situations that can affect thyroid function:

a) Blood-sugar conditions such as insulin resistance, diabetes, obesity, and Cushing's disease all suppress thyroid function and hormone production. See related sections.

b) Food intolerances potentially causing thyroid inflammation include wheat, corn gluten, and soy. The isoflavones in soy interferes with the production of both thyroid hormones, T4, and T3. GMO corn may also be a factor.

c) Heavy metals such as mercury and arsenic often accumulate in thyroid tissue. Mercury is found in most fish that are higher up in the food chain and is caused by ocean pollution from industrial mercury emissions. Arsenic can be found in chicken and in rice, both of which are frequently a mainstay in many lower-quality dog foods. A hair tissue mineral analysis can identify the presence of toxic heavy metals.

d) Medications: Dozens of drugs and their side-effects affect thyroid function as well as hormone test results. These include steroids, sulphur drugs, anti-convulsant medications, antidepressants, and non-steroidal anti-inflammatories, which are all known to suppress thyroid hormone production. As well, all drugs deplete certain nutrients. Avoid giving your dog thyroid hormone to mask a side-effect from other medications.

e) A healthy thyroid requires very specific nutrients for optimum function. Therefore, deficiencies of vitamin B6, folic acid, selenium, iodine, and/or zinc are commonly seen with thyroid problems.

f) Stress affects nearly every system in the body; however, the endocrine system including the thyroid gland is very sensitive to the cascade of hormones changes which occur during both acute and chronic stress (see Chapter 15 for more information on managing stress).

g) And finally, it is reported that some dogs with thyroid issues may have a history of leash pulling, shock collars, tug-of-wars, and/or other neck injuries which have adversely affected thyroid function. If this is the case have your dog assessed by an animal chiropractor.

Natural Health Program

Conventional treatment of hypothyroidism involves an oral replacement hormone for the rest of the dog's life. But in the holistic model, we seek to identify and correct the real and underlying problems as mentioned above to avoid blaming the thyroid as the primary problem and the subsequent and often unnecessary medications.

Diet

- Eliminate all sugars, wheat, corn gluten, dairy products, and soy products.

- Overweight dogs need to lose weight and exercise regularly according to their energy levels, especially in the beginning.

- Change the protein staple especially if it has been chicken and/or your dog has been on the same meat protein for several months or years.

- Address insulin resistance, diabetes, and/or Cushing's disease with diet and nutrition as outlined above. All of these conditions affect thyroid function.

- A grain-free diet is indicated if the dog has been eating grains as staples, particularly wheat, corn gluten, soy, or other poor quality grains.

- If the dog is *already* on a grain-free diet, add healthy whole grains and decrease the meat protein; meat can also contribute high levels of toxicity to sensitive organs.

Nutrients

- **iodine, liquid** [*one dose daily as needed*]† – thyroid nutrient; supports immunity and metabolism

- **vitamin B6** [*one dose daily*]†* – blood sugar nutrient; supports pituitary, adrenal, and thyroid function

- **folic acid** [one dose daily]† – thyroid support, immune nutrient, promotes healthy cell growth and tissue repair

- **zinc citrate or picolinate** [*one dose daily for 30 days, repeat if necessary*]† – maintains sugar metabolism and blood sugar levels; promotes healthy thyroid hormone metabolism; nerve nutrient

- **selenium, organic** [*one dose daily*]† – thyroid nutrient; immunity, liver and chemical detoxification

Herbal & Home Remedies

- **thyroid glandular 200C, homeopathic** [*one dose daily for 7 days*]† – supports thyroid function and hormone balance

- **pituitary TSH 200C, homeopathic** [one dose daily for 7 days]† – supports pituitary hormone balance

Riva's Remedies

- **Hormone Boost, herbal blend** [one dose daily]† – supports the healthy function of all endocrine glands (adrenals, pituitary and thyroid); Adaptogen and stress

- **Vital Force, herbal blend** [one dose daily]† – maintains vitality, hormone balance and blood sugar levels; adds fibre, minerals, and nutrition important for the metabolism and nervous system

- **Kava's Primrose Oil, specialized nutrient** [*one dose daily*]† – essential fatty acids for thyroid support and hormone balance

† See Appendix for recommended dosages and duration for all supplements.

* Also available as a Riva's Remedy

Natural Health Programs for Reproductive Hormone Function

~~~~~~~~~~~~~~~ 🐾 ~~~~~~~~~~~~~~~

Ovarian and Testicle Hormones

Estrogen and progesterone are produced by the ovaries and testosterone is produced by the testicles. And since most dogs are spayed or neutered, hormone imbalances are more common than we currently know, and they can contribute to many health problems. As discussed previously, if reproductive hormones are low, as is the case with *all* spayed females and *all* neutered males, the adrenal glands must then compensate by producing enough of these hormones to support the important body systems that need reproductive hormones to function. And since this is a responsibility that the adrenal glands cannot easily fulfill, reproductive hormone imbalances are frequent as are adrenal dysfunction disorders. Why are hormone imbalances not diagnosed more often? Because most of these types of hormone imbalances are sub-clinical, meaning that they cannot be detected with blood tests. In addition, there are varying levels of estrogen, progesterone, testosterone and other hormones circulating in the blood which may be high, low, or practically non-existent when the "cut" is made.

Spaying

Spaying of females involves the removal of the entire reproductive tract (i.e. both the uterus and the ovaries) while the dog is under general anesthesia. The traditional age for spaying is 6 to 9 months although some veterinarians are condoning the procedure for puppies as young as 8 weeks and the Veterinary Associations themselves strongly recommend spaying before the age of 5 months; all despite the fact that dogs do not mature sexually until between 6 and 12 months of age. Unspayed females will cycle or "heat" twice per year with each cycle lasting 2 to 3 weeks. There are both benefits and drawbacks to spaying female dogs.

Benefits:

- It avoids unwanted puppies, helps control the pet over-population, and prevents abuse through neglect.
- It limits the spread of rampant genetic diseases and disorders if a dog is unable to pass them on to offspring.
- Spaying your dog will reduce or eliminate her drive to roam during her heats in search of a male. This results in lost dogs and increases their risk of injury. Unspayed females need to be closely watched during heat cycles.
- It must be very difficult and frustrating for dogs to control themselves without a mate during powerful hormone surges. We can, therefore, understand the increase in guarding behaviours, irritability, and aggression.
- Females in heat tend to urinate more often to attract male dogs with the scent of their urine. They can also discharge bloody fluids.
- Not breeding an intact female can be very frustrating for her; if she has a strong maternal instinct, she may go into a false pregnancy showing signs of fatigue, weight gain, mammary enlargement, milk production, guarding, and nesting behaviours.
- Many unspayed dogs suffer unnecessarily because the majority are never allowed to breed. Not only does this go against their natural instincts, but they are often confined, isolated and over-controlled.

Drawbacks:

- Sexual maturation is imperative for bone, brain, and organ development.
- Permanently high production of luteinizing hormone by the pituitary gland as the pituitary responds to the sudden drop in hormones results in an overworked pituitary gland. The pituitary gland is a major player in Cushing's disease.
- Spayed dogs are more likely to have hypothyroid problems; sudden changes in reproductive hormones shock the thyroid as well as the pituitary.
- Many people report that their dogs gain weight after spaying; this is caused by the body seeking to produce

more estrogen through fat tissue and appears to be a risk factor for those puppies spayed before 5 months of age. If your dog is not losing weight on a suitable diet with adequate exercise, then your dog may need help with hormone balance and will benefit from supplements and dietary changes.

- Many dogs spayed before 5 months of age have a significantly higher risk of hip dysplasia and back leg ligament tear. Hormones play a critical role in the closure of bone growth plates

- Dogs spayed before 5 months of age have a significantly higher risk of all cancers including lymphoma as well as mast cell cancers which occur on the skin. Hormones play a critical role in immune system function

- Some spayed females have a higher risk of hermangiosarcoma, an aggressive cancer of the lining of the blood vessels.

- Some studies report that unspayed female dogs who are already aggressive may become more aggressive after spaying. This is caused by a decrease in production of progesterone and oxytocin and an increase of adrenal hormones. Females should not be spayed until two months after their heat cycle at which time the progesterone levels are more likely to be higher and more consistent. Progesterone is an important hormone for feelings of calm and peace.

- Females spayed at 6 months or younger have a higher risk of developing separation anxiety, noise phobias (including thunderstorms), timidity, excitability and hyperactivity. Hormones are very important for mental development.

- Spayed females have an increased risk of developing urinary tract infections.

- Between 5 and 10 percent of female canines suffer long-term incontinence problems after surgery. This is caused by the sudden drop in estrogen levels since estrogen is required for muscle tone and bladder sphincter control. The risk is higher in overweight females and in those who are less than 3 months of age when spayed. Conventional treatment uses medications such as hormone replacement therapy, beta-blockers, and/or antidepressants – all of which come with their own (sometimes serious) side-effects.

- There are more post-operative complications for overweight adults.

- Spaying may not solve undesirable behaviours and unwanted habits, particularly in older dogs. It's not always a quick fix. Behaviour is determined by many other factors including overall health, personality, history, and the health and dynamics within the human family.

Neutering

Neutering males involves removing both testicles along with testicular blood vessels and spermatic ducts. The traditional age for spaying is 6 to 9 months although some veterinarians are condoning the procedure for puppies as young as 8 weeks and the Veterinary Associations strongly recommend spaying before the age of 5 months even though dogs do not mature sexually until between 6 and 12 months of age. And even though surgery in older dogs can be more challenging with the increase in the size of the scrotum and testicles, many holistic practitioners are recommending to wait until the dog is 15 to 16 months of age. Each case is unique, however; and the safety of the dog and its handlers are the first priority. There are both benefits and drawbacks to neutering male dogs.

Benefits:

- It avoids unwanted puppies, helps control the pet over-population and prevents abuse through neglect.

- It limits the spread of rampant genetic diseases and breed disorders if a dog is unable to pass them on to offspring.

- Neutering a male dog will reduce or eliminate the hormonal drive to find a female. The unneutered domestic dog is far more likely to engage in fighting and territorial behaviour, and is more at risk for injury and getting lost.

- It must be very difficult and frustrating for dogs to control themselves without a mate during powerful hormone surges. We can, therefore, understand the increase in guarding behaviours, irritability, and aggression.

- Most intact male dogs suffer unnecessarily because the majority are never allowed to breed. Not only does this go against their natural instincts, but they are often confined, isolated and over-controlled. These are not happy dogs.

Drawbacks:

- Sexual maturation is imperative for bone, brain, and organ development.

- Permanently high production of luteinizing hormone by the pituitary gland as the pituitary responds to the sudden drop in hormones. This results in an over-worked pituitary gland. The pituitary gland is a major player in Cushing's disease.

- Many people report that their dogs gain weight after neutering. This is caused by the body seeking to produce more testosterone through fat tissue and appears to be a risk factor for those puppies neutered before 5 months of age. If your dog is not losing weight on a suitable diet with adequate exercise, then your dog may need help with hormone balance and will benefit from supplements and dietary changes.

- Dogs neutered before 5 months of age have a significantly higher risk of joint disorders including hip dysplasia and back leg ligament tear. Hormones play a critical role in the closure of bone growth plates.

- Dogs neutered before 5 months of age have a significantly higher risk of all cancers including lymphoma as well as mast cell cancers which occur on the skin. Hormones play a critical role in immune system function.

- Males neutered at 6 months or younger have a higher risk of developing separation anxiety, noise phobias (including thunderstorms), timidity, excitability and hyperactivity. Hormones are very important for mental development.

- There are more post-operative complications for overweight adults.

- Many dog owners hope that neutering will benefit undesirable behaviour: roaming, aggression, fighting, dominance and/or leg cocking, but it's not always a quick fix. Behaviour is determined by many other factors including overall health, personality, history, and the health and dynamics within the human family.

Notes & Considerations:
Male and Female Dogs

a) Keeping dogs intact - whether male or female - should only be considered by highly responsible and knowledgeable individuals who are committed to preserving the health of all dogs as well as population control. Most pet owners do not have the knowledge, the skills, the environment, and/or the time required to manage intact dogs. Backyard breeding and puppy mills are to be avoided at all costs. These dogs are not given the care that is required nor is any attention paid to what kind of dogs are being bred and the many resulting undesirable characteristics including serious and debilitating diseases.

b) Many people from all walks of life have a variety of irrational and unfounded reasons on why they should breed their dog, including (1) *my dog is cute/pretty/ adorable,* (2) *my dog is different from other dogs,* (3) *there is no dog as good as mine,* (4) *having more dogs would be fun* (5) *dog breeds might become extinct* and most reprehensibly (5) *puppies could bring us some quick and easy money.* The truth is when it comes to dogs, supply already outstrips demand, and every time you breed your dog, the same number of dogs or more are euthanized somewhere else in the world.

c) It is obvious that the later we spay and neuter the better chance our pets have at a healthy life. Each situation is very different, however; and there will always be exceptions - dogs in shelters or homeless dogs for example.

d) Even though spayed and neutered animals have a higher incidence of certain health conditions as described above, this does not mean that these problems cannot be successfully managed. To the contrary, there are very few physical conditions which do not respond to the appropriate program including diet, nutrition, and natural medicines.

e) If your only concern is preventing breeding, try to find a veterinarian who performs a spaying procedure without removing the ovaries (tubal ligation or removal of the uterus, but not the ovaries) or testes (vasectomy). This way the dog can still produce the many hormones that are essential for well-being. However, be aware that the hormonal behaviours will still be present as your dog will still act and feel intact. Some dogs have more hormonal behaviours than others.

f) Interestingly enough, in many parts of Europe, the removal of ovaries and testes are considered unethical, cruel, and painful. These dog owners may request surgery if they have a good medical and/or social reason, but each dog owner is responsible for his/her own dog's behaviour. We have a long way to go, but think about how our dogs would benefit in North America if we all took responsibility for controlled breeding, homeless dogs, and the humane and healthy care of our beautiful companions who have innocently found themselves in the strange and foreign world of humans.

Symptoms

Estrogen and progesterone imbalances will very often present as mood, mental health, or behavioural problems, including irritability, anger, aggression, depression, sadness, fear, anxiety, withdrawal, lack of focus, and/or poor social skills. Hormone problems can also affect metabolism, resulting in weight gain or loss as well as thyroid and pituitary imbalances. Hormone levels are also important for a healthy immune system, hair coat quality, and the health and density of bones and joints.

Testosterone level imbalances are also seen with behavioural problems, causing irritability, aggression, and increased or excessive libido. Low testosterone levels in neutered males can result in weight gain, fatigue, depression and/or poor mental focus, lack of muscle strength, joint pain and metabolic problems.

NOTE: Dogs used for breeding purposes will not be discussed here, for I sincerely wish to support the thousands of great dogs of all ages who are *already* alive and in need of caring and good quality forever homes. Tens of thousands of healthy dogs and cats are humanely put to death each year because there aren't enough homes available for them. In addition, as a result of indiscriminate breeding by *all* types of breeders the number of genetic diseases is appalling. It's time for us to start taking responsibility. See Chapter 16 for more information on the health of our dogs and breeding.

Causes

Spaying and neutering are the most common cause of health problems due to estrogen, progesterone, and testosterone deficiencies and/or imbalances.

Natural Health Program

Even though most of our dogs have been "cut" we are still able to help them produce, balance, and stabilize their hormones with adrenal support through specific nutrients and remedies.

Diet

- Eliminate all sugars, wheat, corn, dairy products, and soy products.
- Don't let your dogs become insulin resistant by allowing them to gain weight. Insulin resistance stresses all endocrine glands, including the adrenals, thyroid and pituitary.

Nutrients

- **iodine, liquid** [*one dose daily as needed*]† – supports all endocrine glands including adrenal glands
- **vitamin B6** [*one dose daily*]†* – maintains hormone balance, mental wellness and a healthy nervous system
- **vitamin B5** [*one dose daily*]† – adrenal support and hormone balance
- **magnesium citrate** [*one dose daily*]†* – promotes calmness and relaxation in anxious, irritable and moody dogs

Herbal & Home Remedies

- **adrenal 200C, homeopathic** [*one dose daily for 7 days*]† – supports healthy adrenal function, stress and fatigue
- **pituitary 200C, homeopathic** [*one dose daily for 7 days*]† – promotes healthy pituitary function and hormone balance; incontinence after spaying
- **testes 200C, homeopathic** [*one dose daily for 4 to 7 days*]† – promotes calm and hormone balance in male dogs who are irritable, aggressive and/or have excessive libido (neutered or unneutered)

Riva's Remedies

- **Hormone Boost, herbal blend** [*one dose daily*]† – supports hormone balance in spayed females (adrenals, thyroid and pituitary)
- **Vital Force, herbal blend** [*one dose daily*]† – nutritional support for neutered males with low testosterone activity and poor hormone function; promotes healthy hormones, immunity and vitality
- **Kava's Primrose Oil, specialized nutrient** [*one dose daily for 30 days or as needed*]† – essential fatty acids for reproductive hormone balance; adrenal support

†See Appendix for recommended dosages and duration for all supplements.

iv. Senior Dogs and Changing Hormone Levels

Hormones That Decrease

- **growth hormone** or hGH – causing muscle weakness and wasting (pituitary)
- **thyroxine** – causes a drop in metabolic rate (thyroid)
- **cortisol** – lowers immune and stress responses (adrenals)
- **insulin** – results in higher blood sugar levels (pancreas)
- **estrogen** – increases hormonal imbalances and infertility (ovaries)
- **testosterone** – causes lower sperm counts and lowered libido (testes)

Hormones That Increase

- **follicle stimulating hormone** or FSH – increases to stimulate the ovaries (pituitary)
- **luteinizing hormone** or LH – increases to stimulate the ovaries (pituitary)
- **thyroid stimulating hormone** or TSH – increases to stimulate the thyroid (pituitary)

Hormones That Remain Unchanged

- **adrenocorticotropic hormone** or ACTH – except for dogs with Cushing's syndrome in which case it increases (adrenals)
- **adrenaline** – produced for fight or flight and, therefore, important for survival (adrenals)

Testing Hormones Levels

Blood Tests

All endocrine hormones are secreted in periodic bursts, making it difficult to attain blood tests which measure accurate hormone levels. These erratic hormone levels mean that hormone blood levels at any given moment do not truly indicate what the normal levels are over the course of a day. Thus, these rapid fluctuations make it difficult for medical blood tests to accurately assess actual hormone levels for all endocrine glands.

The Barnes method of thyroid testing can be useful for dogs and can be done at home. Take the rectal body temperature at the same time every morning for 4 consecutive days. Normal temperature should be between 37.8 and 39.2°C (100 and 102.5°F). If the temperature consistently falls lower than 37.3°C, then the thyroid can be considered functioning below normal. Because a dog's body temperature is a little higher than a human's body temperature, which is between 36.4 and 37.5°C (97.6 and 99.6°F) you may think that your dog has a fever when, in fact, the temperature is normal. Note that body temperatures can increase abnormally as an immune defense mechanism in the presence of infection or inflammation.

Hair Analysis

Hair tissue mineral analysis can be very useful for assessing the function of endocrine glands and their hormone production. Levels and ratios of tissue minerals relate to the activity of specific organs and glands. An analysis can therefore reveal how well the thyroid, pituitary and adrenal glands are functioning. Blood sugar levels and sensitivities are also detected. See the Appendices for more information on the benefits of Hair Tissue Mineral Analysis.

Abby – Aggression or PMS?

Abby was a three-year-old pit bull when her trainer brought her in. Abby was brought to this professional dog trainer because Abby was starting to show signs of aggression with both people and other dogs, e.g., growling and baring her teeth. She was feeling very distrustful. Abby's pet parents were hoping to resolve the issue before her behaviour escalated into something more serious and she would become another statistic along with thousands of other aggressive dogs. Through observation and energy testing it was determined that Abby had a hormone imbalance with low estrogen and progesterone levels affecting her brain chemistry, her moods, and her tolerance to stress. Abby didn't feel very well in a lot of ways. In fact, this was a case of canine PMS (premenstrual syndrome) even though she was spayed. Can you imagine feeling irritable, depressed, angry and anxious due to hormone imbalances but being unable to tell anyone, much less seek out a solution? Abby's frustrations – in that she was feeling both unheard and misunderstood – were completely reasonable.

Abby.

Abby's program consisted of the elimination of beef and all other red meat to reduce the levels of artificial hormones. She was given the Riva's Hormone Boost Herbal Blend and Kava's Evening Primrose Oil to balance her hormones and to support her adrenal glands – these are the glands which try to produce adequate hormones in the case of low or no production by the ovaries. Homeopathic Nux Vomica was used for extreme irritability, frustrations, distrust, aversion to others, aggression and anger.

Within days, Abby's trainer reported that her demeanor was completely changed and that she was happier, more cooperative, and less irritable and was learning to trust people again. No doubt, there are thousands of other dogs out there just like her whose fate is the unthinkable.

11. Muscles & Connective Tissue
Movement & Mobility

Natural Health Programs for Muscles and Connective Tissue Health

Muscle problems and conditions involving the connective tissue can sometimes be difficult to identify and distinguish from joint and/or bone problems. However, they are often evident from stiffness, soreness, lameness, and sensitivity to touch, heat, and/or other signs of pain and discomfort.

Muscle Tension, Cramps, and Spasms

Symptoms

Muscle tension is a hardness or tightness of the muscles which can be temporary or chronic. A dog with muscle tension may appear stiff, walk awkwardly, and/or have poor mobility. Chronic muscle tension often results in knots in the muscles which causes further discomfort and can further limit the range of motion.

A spasm or cramp is an involuntary contraction of a muscle similar to the muscle cramps or spasms that a human would experience. Spasms are usually short-lived but can be very painful, during which time, the dog is unable to move.

Causes

If muscles, during exertion, require more energy than the body can produce, or if the muscles are deficient in oxygen, they are forced to go into anaerobic glycolysis, a process which produces lactic acid. When lactic acid (or other dietary acids for that matter) is accumulated faster than it can be metabolized, it becomes the primary cause of muscle fatigue, pain, and stiffness, both acute and chronic. When muscles of endurance dogs or other physically fit dogs fatigue, however; it is the result of glycogen depletion (no fuel) rather than a build-up of excess lactic acid. Lactic acid build-up is most common in dogs with poor conditioning, slow metabolism, poor cardiovascular fitness, lack of exercise, and toxicity due to waste products. Diets high in wheat, corn gluten, refined carbohydrates, and/or excess meat can produce enough acid and waste toxins to cause a variety of muscle problems.

Muscle tension can, therefore, be caused by stress, high protein diets, nutrient deficiencies, lack of exercise, poor conditioning, and/or injuries. A muscle that remains constricted and is under a lot of pressure will result in a knot.

Spasms or cramps are caused by nutrient deficiencies, high protein diets, seizures, and/or injuries. Muscles can also frequently spasm during the recovery of an injury such as broken bones. In this case, the muscle will over-react to movement as a defense mechanism to hold the structure in place while it is healing.

Natural Health Program

Diet

- No red meat – beef, bison, venison or pork
- Reduce or eliminate all meat, especially in senior dogs; high protein diets can cause muscles to become overly-acidic, resulting in chronic pain and/or inflammation.

Nutrients
- **magnesium citrate** [*one dose daily*][†*] – promotes relaxation of muscles spasms and tension. Neutralizes acids

- **vitamin E** [*one dose daily*]†* – anti-oxidant; supports muscle circulation and function
- **selenium, organic** [*one dose daily*]† – anti-oxidant, supports muscle strength, chemical detoxifier, liver support
- **calcium citrate** [one dose daily]† – nutrition for the contraction and relaxation of muscles; if administering both calcium and magnesium, give several hours apart since they compete for intestinal absorption

Herbal & Home Remedies

- **arnica 30C, homeopathic** [*one dose twice daily as needed*]† – for muscle tension, soreness, stiffness and swellings
- apply a hot water bottle or heating pad to the affected muscle externally
- arrange a chiropractic assessment

Riva's Remedies

- **Injur-Ease, homeopathic** [*one dose twice daily as needed*]† – support for muscle and joint injuries and trauma
- **Calm & Cool, herbal blend** [*one dose daily*]† – promotes relaxation in nervous dogs with muscle tension; anxiety and stress relief
- **Bone-Up, specialized nutrient** [one dose daily]† – supports the function of muscles, joints and connective tissue, promotes optimum nutrition
- **Arnica Rub, homeopathic** [*massage externally into the affected area twice daily as needed*]† – joint and muscle rub, soothes sore muscles.

† See Appendix for recommended dosages and duration for all supplements.
* Also available as a Riva's Remedy

Strains, Sprains, and Stiffness

Strains and sprains affect the connective tissue that is found throughout the body and binds together the structures. It supports other tissues and organs and includes various kinds of fibrous tissue, fat, bone, cartilage, tendons, and ligaments. Tendons attach muscles to bone, and ligaments attach bone to bone. Tendons and ligaments have poor blood supply, and therefore, any injuries to these tissues can take more time to heal.

Collagen is the main component of connective tissue; it is also found in skin, hair, nails, smooth muscle tissues, blood vessels, bones, the intestinal tract, heart, kidneys and bladder. Collagen is the most abundant protein in mammals, making up 25 to 35 percent of all proteins. Collagen gives strength by acting as the "cement" that holds the tissues together. As dogs age, the production of collagen slows down and the tendons and ligaments become less elastic, stiffer, weaker, and more prone to injury (the same is true of humans).

Strains injure the tendons while sprains injure the ligaments. Strains are mostly like to occur when a dog slips, slides, falls, or jumps. Strains are most common in the hips and thighs.

Sprains are most likely when a dog has fallen or landed hard, which can cause ligament injuries to the wrists and knees including the cruciate ligaments in the knee. Strains and sprains can also occur from repetitive activities such as an agility dog or a sled dog.

Symptoms

Limping, poor mobility, stiffness, heat, swelling, yelping, fatigue, unusual postures, unwilling to exercise and/or change in appetite.

Cruciate ligament (CCL) injuries are very common and result in tears, lameness and swelling.

Senior dogs can present with a weak and "sagging" hind-end, *not* as a result of sprains or strains, but as a result of the gradual weakening of connective tissue and muscle. Hind end weakness is exacerbated by diet and/or nutrient deficiencies.

Causes

Injuries can occur due to accident, over-activity and/or repetitive actions. Injuries can be perpetuated and prevented from healing by diet, nutrient deficiencies, stress and/or lack of exercise. Breeds prone to ligament injuries include: Labrador retrievers, Newfoundlands, German shepherds, Rottweilers, and Golden retrievers. In addition, studies show that 5 percent of males neutered before 12 months and 8 percent of females developed CCL injuries later in life.

Natural Health Program

Diet

- Reduce or eliminate red meat until the injury has healed. High protein diets can cause muscles to become overly-acidic, resulting in chronic pain and/or inflammation which delays the healing process.

- Overweight dogs are at a higher risk and should be put on a diet and exercise program.

Nutrients

- **vitamin C** [*one dose daily*]†* – nutrition for collagen production; trauma, stress and immunity

- **MSM (methylsulfonylmethane)** [*one dose daily for 30 days only*]† – sulphur is an important nutrient in the formation of all connective tissues including cartilage, tendons, and ligaments. Well indicated for muscle injuries but use short-term.

- **calcium citrate** [*one dose daily*]† – support for muscles, tendons, ligaments, and bone

- **vitamin B6** [*one dose daily*]†* – nutritional support for muscles and ligament injuries

Herbal & Home Remedies

- **arnica 30C, homeopathic** [*one dose twice daily as needed*]† – muscle tension, soreness, stiffness and bruising

- **causticum 30C, homeopathic** [*one dose daily for 4 days*]† – hind-end weakness, lower back pain and stiffness, good remedy for senior dogs

- **rhus-tox 30C, homeopathic** [*one dose twice daily as needed*]† – tendon strains, stiffness, and lower back soreness

- Apply a hot water bottle or heating pad to the affected muscle externally

- Gently massage the injured area daily of appropriate or schedule a canine massage therapist

- Ensure regular exercise suitable to the comfort level; injuries of all kinds need movement

Riva's Remedies

- **Injur-Ease Homeopathic Formula** [*one dose twice daily for 7 days*]† – support for strains, sprains, fractures, stiffness and soreness due to injuries and trauma

- **Bone-Up, specialized nutrient** [*one dose daily*]† – supports the healthy function of connective tissue, bone, and cartilage; mobility and flexibility; hind-end weakness

- **Joint-Clear herbal blend** [*one dose daily*]† – promotes ease of movement and comfort for soreness and stiffness; supports flexibility and adrenal function

- **Arnica Rub** [massage externally into the affected area twice daily as needed]† – muscle rub; soothes sore muscles and joints

† See Appendix for recommended dosages and duration for all supplements.

Polymyositis

Polymyositis is a term that refers to chronic inflammation, in the muscles of adult dogs, which can affect the entire body.

Symptoms

Symptoms may include muscle tenderness, pain, muscle weakness, and/or the wasting of muscles. Affected dogs may also lose weight and feel tired, depressed, and weak. Symptoms can be sudden-onset or appear gradually.

Causes

Common causes include diet, toxicity, nutrient deficiencies, and suppression of strong emotions. Chronic conditions of inflammation are often caused by systemic toxicity from diet, leaky gut, parasites, and/or infections. Muscle wasting can also occur as a result of Cushing's disease as well – refer to Chapter 10.

Natural Health Program

Diet

- Eliminate wheat, corn gluten, dairy products, soy products, rancid oils, and all known food allergies and intolerances.

- Use caution with grains; some dogs need to be grain-free.

- Lectins can be a serious consideration in chronic inflammatory conditions (see Chapter 7).

- Eliminate beef, bison, venison, elk, red meats and organ meats, for these commonly cause inflammation and tissue damage. Frequently this is not because they are an allergen, but because they are high in certain acids; accumulated acids contribute to a variety of inflammatory conditions including arthritis and joint pain. In addition, senior dogs cannot digest heavy meats as efficiently.

- Use caution with fish and chicken

- Eliminate vegetable oils

- Some dogs, especially senior dogs, will need a vegetarian cleanse (see Chapter 3).

- No artificial colourings, flavourings, rawhide or preservatives.

- Treat for leaky gut (see Chapter 4).

- Overweight dogs must lose weight.

- Ensure regular exercise suitable to the comfort level; movement is necessary to both detoxify and nourish the muscles.

Nutrients

- **MSM (methylsulfonylmethane)** [*one dose daily for 30 days only*][†] – sulphur is an important nutrient in the maintenance of all connective tissues including cartilage, tendons, and ligaments; well indicated for acute muscle injuries but use short-term

- **calcium citrate** [*one dose daily*][†] – support for muscles, promotes flexibility

  Herbal & Home Remedies

- **arnica 30C, homeopathic** [*one dose twice daily as needed*][†] – soothes muscle soreness, tenderness, bruises and swellings

Riva's Remedies

- **Injur-Ease, homeopathic** [*one dose twice daily for 7 days*][†] – support for muscle injuries and swellings due to injuries or trauma

- **Bone-Up, specialized nutrient (calcium citrate and Vitamin B6)** [*one dose daily*][†] – nutrition for connective tissue, bone, and cartilage; promotes flexibility and mobility

- **Joint-Clear herbal blend** [*one dose daily*] [†] – promotes ease of movement, flexibility and comfort for soreness and stiffness

- **Detox Dog** [*one dose daily*] [†] – Promotes the detoxification of liver, muscles, kidneys and colon; supports the immune system

- **Arnica Rub** [massage externally into the affected area twice daily as needed][†] – muscle rub, soothes sore muscles

Lifestyle

- Explore your dog's emotional imbalances whereby she may be "holding" emotions which she feels are either not safe to express or which are being expressed but are not being properly acknowledged (by you). These emotions may be a reaction to the dog's own emotional situation or a situation within her human family, which she has taken on.

- Emotions such as frustration, anger, and irritability are commonly stored in the muscles.

[†] See Appendix for recommended dosages and duration for all supplements.

Emotions such as frustration, anger, and irritability are commonly stored in the muscles.

Myasthenia Gravis

Symptoms

Dogs experience general muscle weakness, especially after exercise. The weakness may affect all four legs or just the back legs. They can walk with a short stride and a stiff gait and may experience muscle tremors. Weak muscles may also affect the throat, resulting in problems with eating, drooling, swallowing, barking, and breathing.

Causes

Muscle movement is initiated by an impulse to a corresponding nerve which sends an electrical current into the muscle to initiate contraction or shortening. The nerve cell does so by releasing a chemical, known as a neurotransmitter, into the junction between the nerve and the muscle. The neurotransmitter that stimulates muscles is acetylcholine which attaches to a receptor on the muscle which then allows the electrical current to flow into the muscle cell to activate it.

In myasthenia gravis it is thought that this transmission process is faulty. In some uncommon cases the condition is congenital, but most cases occur later on in life. These acquired cases are thought to be an auto-immune process whereby the antibodies within the immune system are attacking healthy acetylcholine receptors. See Chapter 7 for a complete discussion of auto-immune conditions and why the current theory of how a healthy immune system attacks healthy tissue is, in fact, incorrect.

Natural Health Program

Diet

- Eliminate wheat, corn gluten, dairy products, soy products, rancid oils, and all known food allergies and intolerances.

- Use caution with grains; some dogs need to be grain-free.

- Eliminate beef, bison, venison, red meats and organ meats, for these are a common immune trigger which cause inflammation and tissue damage. Frequently this is not because they are an allergen, but because they are high in certain acids; accumulated acids contribute to a variety of inflammatory conditions, which can affect the nerves, muscles and immune system. In addition, senior dogs cannot digest heavy meats as efficiently.

- Identify all food allergens and/or intolerances including chicken and meat protein.

- Some dogs, especially senior dogs, will need to go vegetarian (see Chapter 2).

- Increase foods rich in essential fatty acids, such as salmon, flaxseeds, hemp hearts.

- No artificial colourings, flavourings, rawhide, or preservatives.

- Overweight dogs must lose weight.

- Ensure regular exercise suitable to the comfort level.

Nutrients

- **folic acid** [*one dose daily*][†] - promotes healthy cell growth, maintains a healthy nervous system and immune system, nutrition for protein metabolism

- **vitamin B12** [*one dose daily*][†*] - supports muscle function and nerves; maintains energy and supports mental well-being in dogs with depression

- **creatine monohydrate** [*one dose daily for 4 to 6 weeks*][†] - muscle fuel and energy; increases muscle mass and fibre size

Herbal & Home Remedies

- **thymus glandular 200C, homeopathic** [*one dose twice daily for 7 to 10 days*][†] - supports immune system and healthy thymus gland function

Riva's Remedies

- **Bone-Up, specialized nutrient (calcium citrate and vitamin B6)** [*one dose daily*][†] -nutritional support for muscle and nerve function; promotes mobility and flexibility

- **Immune Boost, herbal blend** [*one dose daily*][†] - supports a healthy immune system with nutrition; maintains healthy liver function

- **Pro-Colon, probiotic** [*one dose daily for 3 to 4 weeks*][†] - friendly bacteria, discourages the growth of unfriendly bacteria and viruses, improves absorption of nutrients, aids the intestinal immune system

- **Detox Dog** [*one dose daily*][†] - Promotes the detoxification of liver, muscles, kidneys and colon; supports the immune system

Lifestyle

- Avoid vaccines of all types (see Chapter 8).

[†] See Appendix for recommended dosages and duration for all supplements.

Senior Chai Feels Young Again

"Chai is doing much better. And I am hoping she stays this way. I think it has been three weeks now since I started her on the Riva's Bone-Up and Iron-Up at the age of 12. The first noticeable change was her coat... much, much softer. Her energy level increased right away also. The last three weeks, I've only been taking her on small twenty to thirty minute walks and usually to the beach so it's easier on her joints on the sand. Yesterday we went for an hour on a forested trail by a lake. She acted like she was five years old again (maybe younger). I put her on her leash a couple of times because she wouldn't stop running and jumping over stuff, and I didn't want her to hurt her legs. She was really tired and stiff last night (although I am pretty sure she fakes the limping a lot, especially when James gets home from work or she isn't getting what she wants). She got up this morning and there doesn't appear to be any stiffness or limping. And, as you recommended, I bought her new ceramic food and water bowls. She seems to like them much better. She is also eating much better because she thinks the Iron-Up and Bone-Up are treats in her food. Lol. So far so good! She is 14-1/2 years old now." – Jessica D.

Anderson and Chai.

Kava's Hind-End Weakness

"Coming up close to his 12th year, my own hound, Kava, started to slip and lose his balance on the laminate flooring in the health clinic. He would make his away across the throw rugs and then very often didn't seem to have the strength to get across the more slippery footing of the laminate. Rather than accepting this as age-related hind-end weakness and adding more carpets, I wanted to address the underlying cause. Thus, I eliminated all the red meat from his diet and put him on Vitamin B6 for muscle strength; B6 also supports the transfer of proteins into the connective tissue. Within just a few days, the clinic staff was very surprised how easily he was able to walk across the flooring again. Then one day, the receptionist reported that he had been slipping and falling on the floor again that day. I didn't make the connection right away until I remembered that he had been given some cooked hamburger at a party the night before. The proof is in the pudding, or the meat I should say!" – Marijke

Me and my sweet hound, Kava.

12. Bones and Teeth

Strength & Structure

Bones

Bone is a specialized form of connective tissue – dogs have approximately 320 bones in their entire body no matter what breed or what size they are although a long tail has more bones than a short one. Dogs have more bones than both horses (205) and humans (206).

Bones are a living, growing tissue, and during a lifetime, bone is constantly being renewed. Old bone is removed, and new bone is laid down in a process of bone remodeling that strengthens bone, increases density, and allows for the repair of micro-fractures. Before new bone can form, cells called osteoclasts dissolve some tissue on the bone's surface creating a small cavity (re-sorption). Then cells called osteoblasts fill the cavities with collagen. Collagen combines with mineral deposits, including calcium and phosphorus as well as trace minerals of zinc, silica, boron, sulphur, manganese, and vanadium. Bone stores these minerals and releases them back into the blood as required. Once bones reach storage capacity, excess minerals are released back into the blood.

And although bone relies on minerals for optimum strength, there is no need to overdo it. An overabundance of mineral supplements can cause imbalances and adverse symptoms; interestingly enough, symptoms of mineral excess often present the same symptoms as a deficiency. This is true for vitamins as well.

When a dog's skeleton is healthy, bone formation and bone re-sorption occur at equal rates. However, when the rate of re-sorption exceeds the rate of formation, bone density and quality of bone decreases, and the bone becomes very porous and weakens. Common bone disorders include osteoporosis (porous bones), osteopenia (low bone minerals), osteoarthritis (degeneration of bone cartilage) and osteomyelitis (infection).

Bone is also an important part of the immune system. The bone marrow is the soft connective tissue that is highly vascular. The red bone marrow is part of the lymphatic system and produces billions of new red blood cells, platelets, and white blood cells every day. Thus the bone marrow helps protect from immune disorders, cancer, and infections. The yellow bone marrow stores fat and, as dogs age, the red marrow is increasingly replaced by yellow marrow.

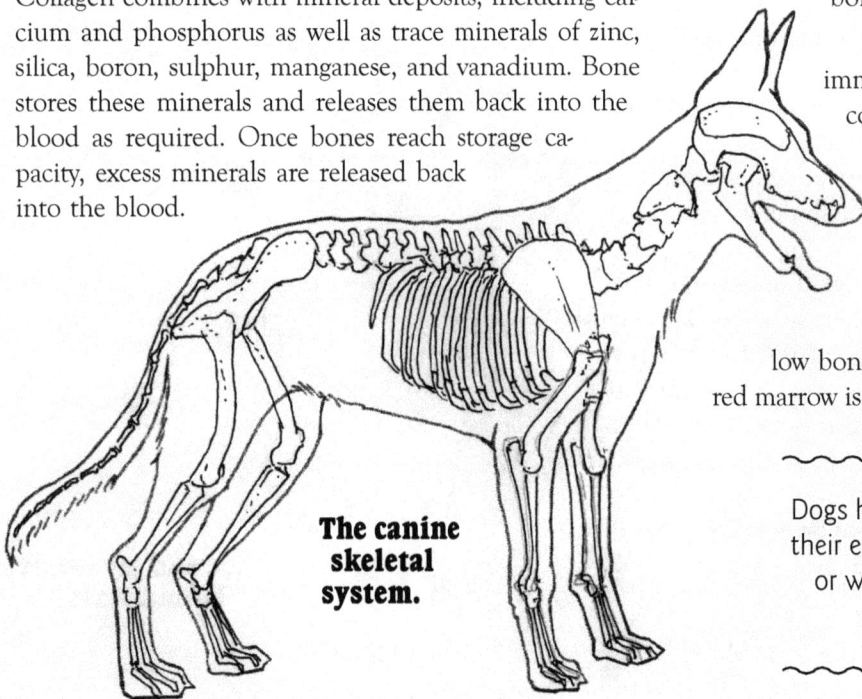

The canine skeletal system.

Dogs have approximately 320 bones in their entire body no matter what breed or what size. Horses have 205 and humans have 206.

Bone Fractures

Symptoms

Lameness, pain, swelling, whimpering, poor mobility, poor appetite, irritability, and/or fatigue.

Causes

Broken bones are usually caused by accidents, falling, or fighting. Fractures can be mistaken for sprains, so it is important to receive a definite diagnosis.

Natural Health Program

Nutrition and natural remedies can help to accelerate healing and prevent complications.

Diet

- No sugars of any kind including fruit.
- No wheat, corn gluten or dairy products.
- Emphasize calcium-rich green vegetables, such as kale, broccoli, spinach
- Choose light proteins, such as poultry, fish, and eggs – as opposed to beef and other red meats.
- Overweight dogs need to lose weight, for excess weight will delay healing and cause an increase in discomfort.

Nutrients

- **calcium citrate** [*one dose daily*]† – supports bone, joint and connective tissue strength

Herbal & Home Remedies

- **symphytum 200C, homeopathic** [*one dose daily for 4 days*]† – the "bone knitter", supports the recovery of injuries and fractures
- Ensure that your dog has a soft pillow to lie on that cushions the painful area.
- Keep stress levels to a minimum.

Riva's Remedies

- **Injur-Ease, homeopathic** [*one dose twice daily for 7 days*]† – homeopathic support for injuries of all kinds with pain, swelling and discomfort
- **Bone-Up, specialized nutrient** [*one dose daily*]† – nutritional support for the recovery of cartilage, joints, and soft tissue; promotes strong bones
- **Arnica Rub** [*massage lightly onto the affected area externally two to three times daily*]† – joint and muscle rub; soothes injuries

NOTE: Avoid the long-term use of non-steroidal anti-inflammatories (NSAIDS) since these medications delay the healing of all injuries. NSAIDS may also cause problems with digestion and intestinal health.

†See Appendix for recommended dosages and duration for all supplements.

Osteoarthritis

Osteoarthritis is also known as degenerative joint disease. It is the most common form of arthritis and the leading cause of pain in all dogs. It happens when the top layer of cartilage between two bone ends deteriorates from wear and tear. Cartilage is the tissue that covers the ends of the bones in all joints. Healthy cartilage functions to cushion the bones and helps the bones glide over each other and absorb the shock of any movement. If the cartilage wears away completely, the bones will rub together resulting in pain and swelling and eventually loss of motion. The continuing inflammation causes further destruction. Bone spurs are created by accumulating calcium deposits on the edges of the joints. Calcium deposits are a defense mechanism to protect the weakened joints, not a cause. If bits of bones or cartilage break off, they can float inside the joint space, which can cause more discomfort.

Symptoms

Stiffness, trouble walking, difficulty in rising from sitting or standing, weakness, swollen joints and reluctance to exercise, although often the dog's flexibility will improve with movement. If the symptoms persist, there may be loss of muscle mass and increased weakness from lack of movement.

Causes

Unfortunately, conventional thinking considers osteoarthritis a disease that is a consequence of aging and has no cure. Neither pain relieving medications nor nutraceuticals have offered solid solutions.

The primary cause of the degeneration of cartilage is the destructive effects of high acid levels, as caused by diet and metabolic waste products, in combination with mineral deficiencies. These acids will increase the re-sorption process and impede the remodeling process, causing damage to bones and joints as well as dental tissue. The only reason that we see more osteoarthritis in older dogs is because the acids have had more years to do their destructive work. However, younger dogs can suffer acidic conditions as well. The deposits of excess acids can be resolved through diet, exercise, and the appropriate nutritional supplements.

Excess acid also affect the integrity of important minerals. Calcium and phosphorus form a mineral complex known as hydroxyapatite which gives teeth and bones a tremendous amount of strength. However, when hydroxyapatite is combined with water and acids, it forms crystals of hydroxyapatite instead. These crystals then deposit themselves in and around the joints causing inflammation and pain which eventually leads to arthritis and other degenerative bone diseases.

～～～～ 🐾 ～～～～

Conventional thinking considers osteoarthritis a disease that is a consequence of aging and has no cure. Neither pain relieving medications nor nutraceuticals have offered solid solutions.

～～～～～～～～～

Other factors that negatively affect the remodeling process are lack of exercise, obesity, nutrient deficiencies, and injuries.

Hip Dysplasia can develop from a poorly fitting "ball and socket" which eventually causes wear and tear on the cartilage resulting in the same process as osteoarthritis. For this reason, the health program for hip dysplasia here is the same as osteoarthritis. The physical condition of the "ball and socket" in hip dysplasia does not entirely determine the severity of the pain and inflammation, however, since it is only one factor. More importantly, it is the osteoarthritic wear and tear caused by the usual physiological factors which is responsible for most arthritic symptoms.

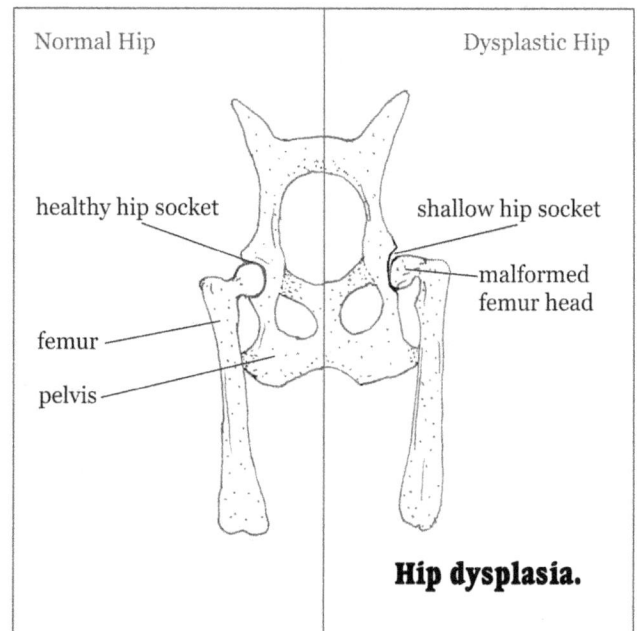

Normal Hip — Dysplastic Hip

healthy hip socket — shallow hip socket — malformed femur head — femur — pelvis

Hip dysplasia.

Hip Dysplasia is a common consequence of certain large breeds due to the heavy muscling from genetics. These breeds include German shepherds, Rottweilers, Great Danes, St. Bernards, Bulldogs, mastiffs, Newfoundlands, American Staffordshire terriers, Labrador retrievers, Old English sheepdogs, Alaskan Malamutes and Samoyeds.

Osteoarthritis also frequently occurs from sloping backs and lower hindquarters particularly in German Shepherds whose stance is now completely abnormal but still sought after in the show ring!

• Long dogs suffer from frequent back problems: dachshund, beagle, basset hounds, corgis, bulldogs, French bulldogs, Cavalier King Charles spaniels and shih-Tzu. And dachshunds, bulldogs and basset hounds have more joint and cartilage problems. Breeding dogs that are abnormally large and fast-growing also puts them at risk for bone and joint problems: Great Danes, Newfoundlands, St. Bernards, mastiffs, wolfhounds and Leonbergers.

Dogs neutered before 5 months of age have a significantly higher risk of joint disorders, including hip dysplasia and back leg ligament tear; hormones play a critical role in the closure of bone growth plates. See Chapter 10.

Natural Health Program

Diet

- No red meats of any kind. Red meats, such as beef, bison, venison, and elk, are high in arachidonic acids, which when accumulated, contribute to a variety of inflammatory conditions, including osteoarthritis and joint pain. In addition, senior dogs cannot digest nor metabolize heavy meats as efficiently therefore creating more toxins.

- No sugars of any kind and no fruit.

- Overweight dogs must lose weight.

Nutrients

- **vitamin B6** [one dose daily]†* - supports protein metabolism in joint capsules; promotes weight loss and normal sugar metabolism.

- **calcium citrate** [one dose daily]† - supports bone, joints and connective tissue

  NOTE: glucosamine products are *not* recommended since they are contraindicated for dogs who are overweight or who are insulin resistant. It is estimated that over 50 percent of all dogs are overweight - many of them senior dogs with arthritis. Glucosamine is a concentrated sugar which can exacerbate diabetes, weight and increase the heart rate. See Chapter 14 for more information.

Herbal & Home Remedies

- **calcium carbonate 200C, homeopathic** [one dose daily for 5 days]† - recommended for dogs who suffer from cold, damp weather; good for bone spurs, joint pain and stiffness. Promotes the healthy metabolism of calcium

- **ruta 200C, homeopathic** [one dose daily for 7 days]† - excellent remedy for bone injuries, bone spurs and bone bruises; trauma to cartilage; sore joints from overuse; has an affinity for the ankles.

- **rhus tox 200C, homeopathic** [one dose daily for 7 days]† - stiffness, limping; better with continued movement. Supports connective tissue and lower back health

- Ensure that your dog has a warm, dry place to sleep; damp and cold aggravates osteoarthritic joints

- Provide a comfortable sleeping pillow that will cushion the joints from a hard surface

- Apply a hot water bottle or heating pad to the affected joint

- Arrange a chiropractic assessment

- Ensure regular exercise; all musculoskeletal conditions benefit from movement (except for severe injuries)

Riva's Remedies

- **Injur-Ease, homeopathic** [one dose twice daily for 7 days]† - supports the recovery of all injuries and trauma - acute and chronic

- **Bone-Up, specialized nutrient** [one dose daily]† - nutritional support for cartilage, joints and connective tissue; promotes pH balance in acidic conditions

- **Joint-Clear, herbal blend** [one dose daily as needed]† - supports adrenal function; provides comfort for bone and joints; promotes flexibility and mobility

- **Arnica Rub** [massage onto the affected area externally two to three times daily]† - joint and muscle rub; soothes sore joints

  NOTE: Avoid the long-term use of non-steroidal anti-inflammatories (NSAIDS) since these delay the healing of cartilage and bone. NSAIDS may also cause digestive and intestinal problems. Do not neuter male dogs before the age of 5 months.

† See Appendix for recommended dosages and duration for all supplements.
* Also available as a Riva's Remedy

Osteomyelitis

Osteomyelitis refers to infections of the bone frequently caused by bacteria such as *Streptococcus*, *Staphylococcus*, and *E. Coli* and less frequently by fungi. Acute infections are usually treated with antibiotics; however, bone infections can become chronic especially in cases of poor immunity.

Symptoms

Dogs may become lame, show signs of pain and discomfort, become depressed, stop eating, run a fever, and/or become lethargic. The infection site may also result in swelling or abscessing.

Causes

Bone infections can occur from bites, puncture wounds, trauma, fractures, penetration from foreign objects, or as a result of some type of bone surgery. In the holistic model, all overgrowths of infectious bacteria that do not respond to antibiotics continue to proliferate because of a hospitable terrain that favours bacteria. Toxicity, a weakened immune system, and/or poor nutrition including nutrient deficiencies such as iron are all risk factors.

Natural Health Program

Diet

- No sugars of any kind including fruit.
- No wheat, corn gluten, or dairy products.
- Overweight dogs need to lose weight; insulin resistance is associated with poor immunity.

Nutrients

- **vitamin C** [one high dose daily for 14 days]†* – nutritional support for infections; supports collagen production and healthy liver function
- **vitamin A, liquid** [one dose daily]† – supports immunity, important nutrient for chronic infections
- **zinc citrate or picolinate** [one dose daily for 30 days, with food]† – nutrient for the immune system and wound healing, promotes Vitamin A activity
- **Iron-Up (iron gluconate)** [one dose daily for 4-6 weeks]† – supports the immune response, oxygenation, general circulation and delivery of nutrients; anemia

NOTE: If vitamin C causes a loose stool, simply reduce the dosage to "bowel tolerance" levels, i.e. this is the lowest dose that does not cause diarrhea.

Herbal & Home Remedies

- **silicea 200C, homeopathic** [one dose daily for 4 days]† – bone remedy; supports healthy bones afflicted by abscesses and infections, promotes the expulsion of foreign objects
- **calcium fluoride 200C, homeopathic** [one dose daily for 4 days]† – indicated for infections, enlargements and swellings

Riva's Remedies

- **Infection Drops, homeopathic** [one dose twice daily for 3 to 4 days]† – promotes a healthy immune system in dogs with symptoms of infections: pus, discharge, foreign materials and abscesses
- **Bone-Up, specialized nutrient** [one dose daily]† – supports cartilage, joints and soft tissue; supports pH balance in acidic conditions

† See Appendix for recommended dosages and duration for all supplements.
* Also available as a Riva's Remedy

Hypertrophic Osteodystrophy and Panosteitis

Symptoms

Hypertrophic Osteodystrophy or HOD is a bone disease that occurs in fast-growing large puppies; symptoms usually appear in the first year. HOD happens when there is a decrease in circulation to the ends of the bone nearest the joints in both legs; other bones can be sometimes affected as well, such as feet, ribs, jaw, and shoulders. Poor circulation means poor nutrient delivery to the bones, which then results in a decrease of bone growth, inflammation, and possible tissue death if not corrected. HOD causes swelling, heat, lameness, difficulty standing, poor weight bearing, and shaking.

Panosteitis describes inflammation of the surface (periosteum) of the long bones of the legs in young and fast-growing large dogs, particularly German Shepherds. It is sometimes referred to as growing pains. It may shift from one area to another and tends to have a sudden onset without an injury or trauma. It usually resolves after the first two years.

Causes

Fast-growing bones can be particularly sensitive to mineral deficiencies and the acids in high meat protein diets which then interfere with normal bone growth. As we learned in Chapter 3, beef, bison, and all other red meats are high in arachidonic and lactic acids, which if allowed to accumulate in the joints, muscles, and connective tissue, will interfere with normal bone development. High acid conditions affect bone density and strength because the bones are forced to give up calcium - which is alkaline - to buffer the acidic blood conditions. As well, long-term inflammation increases cortisol levels, cortisol is an adrenal hormone that is catabolic, meaning that it promotes tissue damage and break down.

In certain breeds, particularly Weimaraners, HOD has been associated with the modified live distemper vaccine since the HOD symptoms can present immediately after the vaccine.

Interestingly enough, I have seen similar conditions in young show horses that were recommended to be euthanized because their lameness issues due to developmental problems during growth could not be resolved. These equine bone conditions were caused by high protein (alfalfa) and high sugar diets (grain) combined with calcium deficiencies. These youngsters were fully recovered with diet changes and mineral supplements.

Natural Health Program

Diet

- No red meats of any kind. Beef, bison, venison, elk, and the like are high in arachidonic acids, and accumulated acids contribute to a variety of inflammatory conditions including HOD.

- No sugars of any kind and no fruit.

- Reduce overall dietary meat protein in favour of fish and/or eggs with poultry meat twice per week until the dogs are symptom free.

- Ensure plenty of nutrient rich vegetables.

Nutrients

- **calcium citrate** [*one dose daily*]† - supports bone, joint and connective tissue; symptoms of growing pains.

Herbal & Home Remedies

- **calcium fluoride 200C, homeopathic** [*one dose daily for 4 days*]† - supports healthy bones with growths and enlargements, supports calcium metabolism

- **ruta 200C, homeopathic** [*one dose daily for 7 days*]† - indicated for injuries to the periosteum (bone covering)

- **silicea 200C, homeopathic** [*one dose daily for 4 days*]† - supports healthy bones with growth abnormalities and abscesses; adverse vaccine reactions

- ensure that your dog has a warm, dry place to sleep; damp and cold aggravates bone pain and discomfort

- provide a comfortable sleeping pillow that will cushion the bones from a hard surface

- apply a hot water bottle or heating pad to the affected bones

- arrange a chiropractic assessment

- ensure regular exercise; all musculoskeletal conditions benefit from movement

Riva's Remedies

- **Injur-Ease, homeopathic** [*one dose twice daily for 7 days*]† - supports the recovery of bone problems due to injuries and trauma

- **Bone-Up, specialized nutrient** [*one dose daily*]† - nutritional support for cartilage, joints and connective tissue; supports pH balance in acidic conditions

- **Joint-Clear, herbal blend** [*one dose daily as needed*]† - supports adrenal function and maintains comfort for bones and joints; promotes flexibility and mobility

- **Happy Pets** or **Happy Pets Senior, herbal blend** [*one dose daily*]† - a plant-based blend of herbs and seaweeds which provides over 60 trace minerals, vitamins, fibre and anti-oxidants for bone health and general immunity

- **Arnica Rub** [*massage onto the affected area externally two to three times daily*]† - joint and muscle rub; soothes sores joints and tissues

  NOTE: Avoid the long-term use of non-steroidal anti-inflammatories (NSAIDS) since these delay the healing of injuries. NSAIDS may also cause problems with digestion and intestinal health.

† See Appendix for recommended dosages and duration for all supplements.

Bone Cancer

Cancer is a medical term that refers to cells which grow and multiply abnormally. Whereas normal cells follow a pattern of growth, division, and death, cancer cells grow continuously, outlive normal cells, and then conglomerate into growths which we call tumours. Cells from the primary tumours break away and migrate to another body part to grow tumours there as well. This process is known as metastasis. Because the red bone marrow plays a very important role in overall immunity, it is a target for the aberrant behaviour of cancer cells.

The most common tumour found in bone is an osteosarcoma, which is responsible for over 95 percent of bone cancers. Bone cancer mostly affects middle-aged to senior dogs and most commonly affects the leg bones. These tumors can be primary, which is to say occurring directly in the bone, or secondary meaning that it has spread from another part of the bone or another organ. Dogs are eight times more likely to develop bone cancer than humans.

Symptoms

Affected dogs will show lameness and swelling at the primary site and, in most cases, the dogs will experience dull, aching pain although pain tolerance varies widely between dogs. Before diagnosis, the bone may also be susceptible to injuries and/or fractures. The dog may also show signs of general un-wellness: irritability, aggression, loss of appetite, fatigue, and restlessness.

Dogs which are genetically prone to bone cancer are primarily large-boned breeds. The Saint Bernard, Newfoundland, Great Dane and Great Pyrenees are at highest risk with Irish Setters, Golden Retrievers, Labrador Retrievers and Boxers also affected.

Causes

At the cellular level, cancer is caused by damage to the DNA inside each cell. DNA is found in every cell and is responsible for directing the cells' behaviour. However, if the DNA becomes damaged and the immune system is unable to repair the damage, the cells can no longer regulate their own division and growth thus they begin to multiply and grow abnormally.

Like most cancers, the three main causes of DNA damage and subsequent symptoms are in order:

1. Diet and food toxicity.

2. Chronic inflammation as caused by pathogens: bacteria, viruses and/or parasites. Chronic inflammation releases powerful and destructive free radicals.

3. Environmental chemicals, drugs and/or vaccines.

All these factors either initiate or encourage abnormal changes in the DNA. They also suppress the immune system; if the immune system is not functioning at an optimum level, then cancer cells are easily initiated and are able to proliferate without any controls. However, it is the food factor that has the biggest impact on not only creating the unhealthy and toxic terrain which provides a hospitable environment for infections, inflammation, and mutations, but in determining the strength of the immune system. Unfortunately, the biggest source of toxicity in a dog's diet is meat.

Various studies for people have shown a strong correlation between cancer and the amount of animal protein, even low-fat animal foods, consumed. Our dogs are little different than us in this regard other than the fact that they eat, relatively speaking, much more meat than we do.

Meat is full of chemicals, additives, antibiotics, medications, hormones, toxic residue of pesticides, heavy metals, diseases, cancer, the animal's body toxins, decay, bacteria and genetically altered substances – many animals are eating GMO food. Animal meat is also full of dioxins, which are by-products of combustion emitted by waste incinerators, chemical manufacturing plants, and paper and pulp mills. Dioxins are hormone disrupters and are linked to cancer and adverse changes to the immune system. Over 95 percent of dioxin exposure comes in the concentrated form of meat, fish, and dairy products, not plants. And animal products are responsible for over 80 percent of the herbicides and pesticides that we ingest. See Chapter 3 for more information on the toxic effects of meat.

In addition, excess saturated fats from meat and dairy products is stored in the bone marrow, interfering with both the production of red blood cells and the white immune cells. Saturated fats also increase bile acids and

> ❧
> Various studies for people have shown a strong correlation between cancer and the amount of animal protein, even low-fat animal foods, consumed. Our dogs are little different than us in this regard other than the fact that they eat, relatively speaking, much more meat than we do.

steroids, both of which promote the reproduction of unhealthy and anaerobic intestinal bacteria. These unhealthy strains of bacteria are able to convert bile acids to carcinogenic substances.

Aside from meat, exposure to petroleum products and benzene are also risk factors.

Bone tumours normally occur spontaneously; a dog's risk of developing a bone tumor after a fracture, fracture repair, or total hip replacement is very uncommon.

Natural Health Program

The gold standard in conventional healthcare is limb amputation, with or without chemotherapy. The gold standard in natural healthcare is nutrition.

Diet

- Feed your dog a home-cooked vegetarian cleanse intended to eliminate all meat toxins, rancid and/or unhealthy fats, dairy products, poor quality grains, additives and preservatives. In addition, a vegetarian diet provides fibre and key nutrients necessary for detoxification and for re-building the immune system. See Chapter 3 for details on feeding vegetarian diet programs.

- No unhealthy or excess oils; oils cause cancer by interfering with oxygen use in the cells and infusing them with toxic material. All cancer cells have depressed oxygen consumption. They also have a concentration of debris which the cell cannot cleanse because it lacks sufficient energy. In addition, large or difficult to digest fat molecules are not absorbed into the bloodstream; instead, these fats are directly delivered to the lymphatic system, including the bone marrow, where they congest and degenerate lymph nodes and organs. This disables the lymph system from protecting the body from cancer cells and other invaders. Therefore, do not feed canola, soya, coconut, vegetable, or corn oils. Include a small daily dose of oils or seeds, such as flaxseed, chia and/or hemp seeds - these contain enough essential fatty acids to enhance the immune system and decrease inflammation.

- No wheat, dairy products, and/or soy products.

- Absolutely no artificial colourings, flavourings, rawhide, or preservatives.

- Choose all organic foods wherever possible.

Nutrients

- **folic acid** [*one dose daily*]† - important nutrient for immunity; nutrition for healthy cell replication and cell growth

- **iodine, liquid** [*one dose daily*]† - bacteria and yeast; important nutrient for immunity, metabolism, and energy production

- **vitamin A, liquid** [*one dose daily*]† - supports the immune response in dogs with cancer; promotes healthy cell growth

- **vitamin C** [*one high dose daily for 30 days*]†* - supports the immune response and liver function in dogs with cancer; essential for bone and cartilage formation (collagen)

- **selenium, organic** [*one dose daily*]† - anti-oxidant, supports the immune system in dogs with cancer, natural detoxifier of chemicals and heavy metals; liver support

- **zinc citrate or picolinate** [*one dose daily with food for 30 days only*]† - nutrition for healthy bones, hair and nails; nutrition for the immune system and healthy cell growth and reproduction, nutrient for sugar metabolism
  NOTES: (1) Use caution with calcium and/or iron supplements. If these minerals are in excess they can exacerbate a bone condition and prevent re-modeling. Avoid supplementing in cases of bone cancer unless determined to be of benefit by a hair tissue analysis or a kinesiology test. (2) If vitamin C causes a loose stool, simply reduce the dosage to "bowel tolerance" levels, i.e. the lowest dose that does not cause diarrhea.

Herbal & Home Remedies

- **thymus glandular 200C, homeopathic** [*one dose daily for 7 to 10 days*]† - supports the immune system and thymus gland function; allergy reactions

- **silicea 200C, homeopathic** [*one dose daily for 4 days*]† - indicated for healthy bone, skin, hair and nails; supports normal growth and bone density; ill effects from vaccines

- **calcium carbonate 200C, homeopathic** [one dose daily for 4 days]† - supports bone growth and remodeling; supports healthy bones with tumours and cysts - note: use 2 to 3 weeks after homeopathic silicea; don't use these two remedies together

- **Pau D'arco (taheebo)** [*one dose daily*]† - bacteria, yeast and fungus; support for a healthy lymph system; natural cleanser and detoxifier

- **reishi mushroom** [*one dose daily*]† – known as an anti-aging herb; supports the immune system and healthy cell growth
- **shiitake** [*one dose daily*]† - promotes strong immunity and healthy liver function; promotes the elimination of toxic heavy metals such as lead which damages bone marrow and is a known carcinogen

Riva's Remedies

- **Pro-Colon, probiotic** [*one dose daily for 3 to 4 weeks*]† – probiotics and prebiotics for intestinal support; discourages the growth of unfriendly bacteria and viruses, promotes nutrient absorption; supports the recovery of leaky gut and the intestinal immune system
- **Detox Dog, herbal blend** [*one dose daily for 4 to 6 weeks*]† – promotes the detoxification of elimination organs: skin, liver, kidneys and colon. Supports the immune system
- **Immune Boost, herbal blend** [*one dose daily*]† – supports digestion, liver, and the immune system with nutrition and detoxification in dogs with immune problems

- **Joint-Clear, herbal blend** [*one dose daily*]† – promotes mobility and flexibility; supports adrenal function; maintains comfort in soreness and stiffness
- **Happy Pets** or **Happy Pets Senior, herbal blend** [*one dose daily*]† – a plant-based blend of herbs and seaweeds which provides over 60 trace minerals, vitamins, fibre and anti-oxidants for bone health and general immunity; contains natural silica to support bone health

Vaccines

- Use extreme caution in vaccinating all dogs, but particularly those who are immune compromised and/or in a toxic condition. Canine vaccines contain heavy metals such as mercury and aluminum compounds as well as other chemical and carcinogenic adjuvants including formaldehyde (see Chapter 8 for more information).

† See Appendix for recommended dosages and duration for all supplements.
* Also available as a Riva's Remedy

Teeth

Dogs, not surprisingly, have a lot of teeth. The 28 puppy teeth are replaced, within 6 months, with 42 permanent teeth. There are four different types of teeth: incisors for cutting and scooping up food and objects, canines for holding prey and tearing, premolars for holding and breaking food into small pieces, and molars for grinding food into small pieces.

Tooth enamel is the hardest and most highly mineralized substance in the body and covers the entire tooth above the gum line. Enamel is composed of calcium phosphate arranged in a crystal structure called hydroxyapatite; the high mineral content of enamel gives it incredible strength and hardness, but can also make it brittle. Inside the centre of the tooth, including the root, is the pulp which contains the connective tissue, nerves, and blood vessels that nourish the tooth. The rest of the tooth, between the enamel and the pulp, is composed of dentin, which is softer than enamel but as hard as bone. It can detect touch, heat, and cold.

Most dogs do not have problems with dental cavities –unless they have been given a lot of sweet treats, of course. However, the biggest concern for dogs is the accumulation of plaque and tartar on the teeth.

Natural Health Programs for Dental Health

Periodontal Disease

Periodontal disease begins when excess bacteria in the mouth forms a sticky substance called plaque in and around the teeth – just like in people. If it is not removed, it will eventually combine with food particles and minerals from saliva and calcify to form a rough, hard deposit which is called tartar. Tartar promotes further plaque formation and provides an environment that promotes even higher levels of bacteria. Tartar not only forms on the teeth, but also above and below the gum line, where bacterial toxins and acids can cause further irritation and damage. Tartar inflames the gums (gingivitis) and can cause damage to the gum tissues that support the tooth, and if the tooth loses its supporting tissues, the tooth will fall out. Loss of bone and tissue around the teeth is known as periodontitis. Gingivitis can also cause infections and abscessing.

It's interesting to note that, in people, these bacterial acids demineralize and damage the tooth enamel leading to cavities. However, since cavities in dogs are rare, the tooth enamel is not as susceptible to damage as the gum tissue is.

Symptoms

Bacteria from rotten food or tissue or mouth infections will cause bad breath that may smell sour or acrid. Dogs may also have red, inflamed, or even sometimes *bleeding* gums. Dogs may have trouble chewing, chew on one side of their mouth, refuse crunchy foods, gulp their food, or produce more saliva. Increased salivation or pawing/rubbing their face can indicate oral pain. Teeth may be loose or falling out. Abscesses will sometimes form lumps that can be felt from the outside. Abscesses can also reach up into the sinuses, resulting in nasal discharge and/or sneezing.

Chronic tooth infections may cause fatigue and will compromise the immune system predisposing them to other infections or immune conditions. Oral bacteria, commonly *Streptococcus*, can also migrate to the liver, kidneys, and heart; in fact, periodontal disease is a risk factor for heart problems. Migrating bacteria can also produce sticky materials in the arteries, which eventually thickens the walls or contributes to blood clotting.

Causes

There is much debate out there over the role of diet in preventing tartar build-up. But many pets develop dental tartar no matter what kind of diets they are on, whether raw, cooked, or kibble. And some dogs *never* develop tartar. This is not to say that canine diets high in sugars and/or refined carbohydrates are acceptable, but it does appear that certain dogs appear to be more predisposed to tartar deposits. Risk factors include:

- Dogs with a poor or misaligned bite which prevents them from effectively removing debris from their teeth
- Dogs that have chronically poor health and/or immune problems, conditions that give them less defense over pathogenic bacteria and their toxins
- Dogs with intestinal toxicity including low levels of probiotics
- Dogs that are overweight, insulin resistant or diabetic, all of which affect the immune system
- Dogs that are naturally acidic as evident by tartar build-up, joint soreness, allergies and/or skin problems, for example
- Dogs with low levels of exercise
- Dogs with a dry mouth and/or low saliva production
- Senior dogs, due to slower metabolism and detoxification

Natural Prevention and Health Program

Diet

- Eliminate all sugars and refined carbohydrates.
- Eliminate wheat and corn gluten.
- Do not feed rancid or rotten meats or other rotten foods of any kind.
- Provide fresh food as often as possible.
- Include foods with roughage that are high in trace minerals such as wheat germ, bulgur, cooked oats,

lentils, dark leafy greens, cauliflower, and/or peas. These foods are also high in molybdenum, a deficiency of which is associated with tooth and gum decay.

- Provide clean drinking water, preferably spring water, and make sure that they like the water dish. Many dogs don't like tap water, and they don't like certain water dishes.

- Allow your dog to chew on bones once or twice per week. Bone chewing stimulates the gums, helps to scrape dental plaque and the connective tissue in the bone helps to naturally "floss" the teeth (see Chapter 3 for choosing appropriate bones).

Nutrients

- **iodine, liquid** [*one dose daily for 14 days two-three times per year*]† – bacteria and yeast; important nutrient for immunity and metabolism

- **coenzyme Q10** [*one dose daily for two 30-day cycles (with 30 days in between); repeat the cycles if needed*]† – antioxidant; prevents tissue damage and gum bleeding, increases cellular energy, promotes healthy gums in dogs with gingivitis

Herbal & Home Remedies

- **grapefruit seed extract** [*one dose daily as needed*]† – immune support for dogs with yeast and bacteria

- **baking soda** [*add a little to the toothpaste regularly to help neutralize the acids in the mouth*]

Riva's Remedies

- **Pro-Colon, probiotic** [*one dose daily for 3 to 4 weeks*]† – probiotics and prebiotics for intestinal support, discourages the growth of unfriendly bacteria, supports nutrient absorption

- **Bone-Up, specialized nutrient** [*one dose daily*]† – supports healthy teeth and gums; promotes pH balance in acidic conditions

- **Infection Drops, homeopathic** [*one dose twice daily for 3 to 4 days*]† – homeopathic support for teeth with infections, abscesses, and swelling

- **Injur-Ease, homeopathic** [*one dose twice daily as needed*]† – promotes comfort in dogs with teething problems and/or dental trauma or surgery

† See Appendix for recommended dosages and duration for all supplements.

Teething Puppies

With so many teeth being replaced, it is no wonder that puppies have the same teething problems and discomfort as our human babies.

Symptoms

Adult teeth start to come in at approximately 3 months and finish around 8 months, during which time, puppies may want to increase their chewing behaviour to alleviate teething pains.

Causes

Inflammation of the gums as the new teeth are erupting.

Natural Health Program

Provide appropriate chew toys such as teething rings and pacifiers so your puppy doesn't eat shoes, socks, clothes, and furniture.

Diet

- Provide safe bones for chewing on; bone chewing strengthens the teeth and gums through stimulation and through providing extra calcium. See Chapter 3 for more information on dog bones.

Nutrients

- **magnesium citrate** [*one dose daily as needed*]†* – soothes and comforts teething pains,

Herbal & Home Remedies

- Combine the following homeopathic tissue salts in a 6X potency and give 2 to 3 times per day as needed: **calcium fluoride**, **calcium phosphate**, **magnesium phosphate** and **silicea**. They may be available commercially as one combination. Indicated for teething pains.

Riva's Remedies

- **Injur-Ease, homeopathic** [*one dose twice daily as needed*]† – promotes comfort in dogs with teething problems and/or dental trauma or surgery

- **Bone-Up, specialized nutrient** [*one dose daily*]† – supports healthy bones, teeth and gums in growing puppies; promotes pH balance in acidic conditions

† See Appendix for recommended dosages and duration for all supplements.
* Also available as a Riva's Remedy

Twiggy and Fozzy – The St. Bernards

"Twiggy was five years old when she was diagnosed with bone cancer, and it was very swift and aggressive. In the beginning of May 2016, we took her to the vet for a slight limp and a bump on her leg. It was then that the vet suspected cancer after seeing the x-rays. After two bone biopsies, we still had no proper diagnosis. She then had a CT scan, and we finally had confirmation. The tumour on her leg was getting larger and more painful for her by the minute as we continued to wait for answers from all the testing. When we finally had an answer, we opted to have her leg amputated right away. By this time, her appetite had decreased severely, and she was not herself. This was June 2016. After surgery, she had regained her appetite; however, she ate in an almost panicked fashion, like she couldn't get enough. Once we felt she was stable enough, we booked an appointment to see you in July 2016. After seeing you and getting her on the new diet and supplements, her appetite normalized and the lipomas that she had since she was about a year and a half old completely dissolved. Her spirit came back. Physically, she surprised everyone as she could run and still hop up on the couch. She had a couple of follow-up visits with the vet who was astonished to see how well Twiggy was. Her fur was good, her energy was high, and her weight remained steady. She continued on this path through to November when my husband took both dogs out on a Sunday for a walk down by the river. He said she was having the time of her life running around. Starting the next few days after that, it was as if a switch had been flicked, and she deteriorated very quickly. Her fur became coarse, and she rapidly lost weight despite eating. She was staying on her bed and was standing very little. This took place in less than a two-week period, and then she moved on. It may sound crazy, but it almost seems to me that, with winter coming, and after the play day out running by the river, Twiggy was okay with moving on – the change was just so sudden. Her tail never did stop wagging, though; she was always happy. I am positive, had we not brought her to you, we would not have had those happy and healthy months with her.

Twiggy and Fozzy.

As for our big six-year-old Fozzy bear, we had taken him to the vet, for what the vet suspected was ligament damage from running. We decided not to have x-rays done or any further diagnostics done with the vet, as we did not wish to put any stress on Fozzy. When we brought him to you, his limp was quite pronounced, and we couldn't even take him for a short walk without him being very stiff and sore for days. During our visit with you, you had also said that you suspected that the ligament damage was not the only thing bothering him. You suspected that his hips were stiff from his diet of too much elk and bison and that this was what precipitated the ligament injury. We switched to feeding him fish instead and added the suggested supplements. There is now a visible difference in his whole demeanour. Just watching him walk, his limp is minimal even though he can occasionally have a bad day. I agree that his hips must have been bothering him. He just seems so much freer in his movements. He now trots along in the back yard – he never was a speed demon! He also handles going up the stairs with less of an effort, and the odd time he will get playful and do some jumping around. Not bad for 190 pounds! He also seems happier in general. Individually the changes may be small, but when all the changes are added up he is definitely feeling much better. Thank you!" —Heidi.

Twiggy's initial health program included a low protein diet with an emphasis on salmon, fish, and cooked eggs. He was allowed all vegetables and all grains except for wheat and corn. For supplements and remedies, we included the Pro-Colon probiotics and Pro-Dygest Herbal Blend for colon cleansing, detoxification, and immunity as well as the Happy Pets Herbal Blend for plant-based natural nutrition. In addition, we added Shiitake mushroom for the liver, immune system and bone health as well as vitamin B5 (pantothenic acid) for adrenal support and homeopathic phosphorus for the phantom pain and neuralgia, which I intuitively sensed was present after the amputation.

Fozzy's new diet also eliminated all the meat – these large breeds can be very prone to the negative effects of high acids from excess meat which inflame their bones, joints, and muscles. We used the Bone-Up (calcium and vitamin B6) to support the strength and function of the hip joints, Joint-Clear Herbal Blend to promote joint health and adrenal strength and bromelain as a digestive enzyme and natural anti-inflammatory. Fozzy was also taken off his previous glucosamine supplement due to side-effects and because it did not appear to have helped the joint pain.

13. The Brain & Nervous System

The Canine Computer

The canine brain is an amazing and fascinating organ that acts as a control centre to receive, interpret and direct sensory information throughout the body. It receives multiple messages through five physical senses: sight; smell; hearing; touch and taste. The forebrain (frontal lobe) is responsible for receiving and processing this information to think and perceive. The midbrain conducts auditory and visual responses, while the hindbrain allows your dog to maintain balance, equilibrium and coordination, as well as controlling the autonomic functions of breathing, heart rate and digestion. The brain is protected by thick skull bones and cerebrospinal fluid as well as the blood-brain barrier which is an intricate system of small blood vessels that block the entry of many substances found in the bloodstream: drugs, toxins, chemicals and pathogens such as bacteria and viruses.

The absolute weight of the canine brain varies according to size and breed; however, it generally weighs up to 0.5 percent of the dog's bodyweight. Thus, a 40-kilogram dog will have a brain that weighs up to 200 grams. However, a brain of any size has a very high metabolic requirement and receives a tremendous amount of blood flow to deliver oxygen and nutrition. In addition, the brain is "washed" several times per day by the cerebrospinal fluid or CSF, which is produced by the brain and surrounds the brain and spinal cord. This fluid acts as a protective cushion, circulates nutrients and chemicals, and cleanses the brain of waste products and toxins.

The brain signals the body into actions and behaviours (such as catching a ball) by sending messages down the spinal cord and into the smaller nerves which stem from the spinal cord. These messages or communications are accomplished

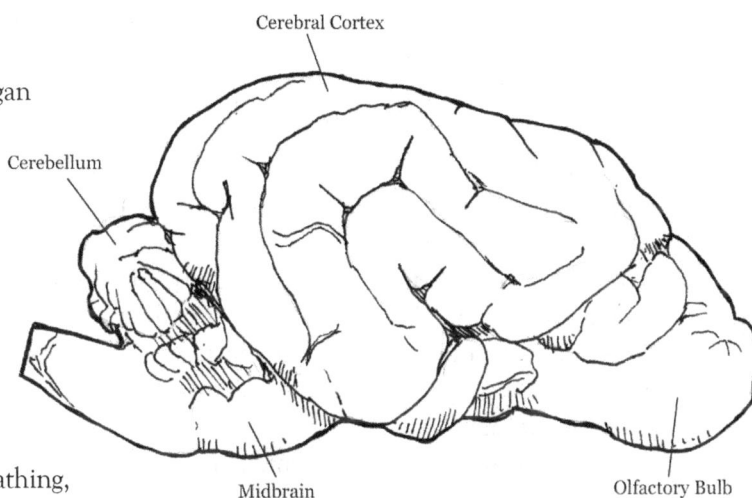

The canine brain.

through a complex electrical system made up of neurons (nerve cells) and the chemical transmitters that fire them to carry the signals from neuron to neuron. Neurotransmitters are so powerful they are measured in nanograms or picograms, which are respectively one billionth or trillionth of a gram.

The tiniest discrepancy in quantity can have a profound impact on a dog's behaviour. That's why brain function, mood, and behaviour can so easily be altered by drugs, hormones, lifestyle, diet, stress levels, attitude, and even electrical and light stimulation. And nutrient deficiencies commonly affect the brain and behaviour: vitamin B12, folic acid, potassium, magnesium, iron, copper, and zinc are examples of very important brain nutrients. The brain and CNS (central nervous system) are also very sensitive to the effects of food intolerances, food allergies, and food toxins, all of which frequently result in inflammation, irritation, and malfunction of the neurons and the neurotransmitters. Food, therefore, is a common factor in behavioural problems and can affect memory, focus, learning abilities, motor control, behavioural abnormalities, and moods. It is the same process for our human children too.

The Importance of Brain Fats

For some reason, we often neglect to realize that the brain and the nervous system are very specialized organs that require nourishment from food and specific nutrients just as any other organ does. About two-thirds of the brain is composed of fats, and the myelin sheath, which is the protective sheath that covers the neurons, is 70 percent fat. These brain fats require healthy essential fatty acids such as omega-3s and omega-6s to maintain their integrity and to allow oxygen, blood sugar, and nutrients to enter the brain. Essential means that the body cannot synthesize these fats and must, therefore, have them provided in the diet. Fatty acids are commonly found in hemp, chia, and flaxseeds. Docosahexaenoic acid or DHA is also an omega-3 fatty acid and is found in cold-water fatty fish, such as salmon. It is available in fish oil supplements, along with EPA (eicosapentaenoic acid); however, it is better to provide essential fatty acids through the diet rather than concentrated oils, especially long-term. Vegetarian sources of DHA are available in seaweed.

The structure of the fatty membranes in the brain are sensitive and can be compromised by stress, nutrient deficiencies, infections, hormone imbalances, poor diets and the damages of trans-fatty acids. Trans-fatty acids are produced when cheap, poor quality oils are hydrogenated through high heat and pressure with hydrogen gas. Trans-fatty acids are implicated in a number of diseases, including cancer, diabetes, obesity, liver diseases, and degenerative disease. What we are not commonly aware of, however, is that these bad fats invade brain cell membranes, including the myelin, where they displace healthy fats, harden the membranes, disrupt communication, and affect how the neurons fire. Avoid anything hydrogenated, although not many dog food bag labels, if any, will admit that the oils – such as canola and soy – have been hydrogenated.

Wolf Brain vs. Dog Brain

Over the course of evolution, wolves that interacted regularly with humans became smaller, and so did their brains. Today the brain of a large dog is approximately the same size as a four-month-old wolf. Presumably the canine brain became smaller because it no longer needed the faculties necessary to strategize hunts when meals were already provided. A large brain is not required to eat out of a dog dish. The cunning and strategic behaviour of a wolf to run down their prey requires a very different kind of brain activity than what is required of the domestic dog. The domestic dog, instead, must spend much of the time in the emotional centre of the brain, trying to figure out how and where she fits into her new world. The strange and crazy ways of the human pack must seem completely erratic and emotionally illogical, all of which is completely foreign to dogs.

~~~~~~~ ❧ ~~~~~~~

Today the brain of a large dog is approximately the same size as a four-month-old wolf.

~~~~~~~~~~~~~~~~

Smart Dogs

According to dog training experts, some dog breeds are smarter than others, but clearly this does not have anything to do with brain size given that Papillons and German shepherds both made the smart list. These measurements of canine intelligence are based on trainability and how easy they are to teach. And while this might be a determination of how well they follow orders, there are hundreds of other dog breeds, mixed breeds, as well as individual dogs out there who are extremely intelligent but may not follow orders well. Personality traits such as independence, superiority, arrogance, distrust of authority, attention deficit disorders, distractibility, hyper-excitability, emotional disturbances, and health problems are all significant factors, which can either interfere with or cause reason to resist human command.

And then there is the whole matter of *emotional* intelligence, wisdom, common-sense, and intuition – all of which make a dog extremely intelligent by other parameters. Many dogs are stunningly astute, perceptive, and intuitive - although this is often not apparent to the pet parent or expert merely because the dogs may not demonstrate its intelligence with common overt behaviours. Dogs are also known for their kindness, compassion, and their ability to "connect" on an emotional level.

Admittedly, trainability and intelligence is a factor in the merits of service dogs, but in fairness to *all* dogs, most of us common pet people need to leave behind the traditional model of intelligent trainability. We don't want to miss out on the vast knowledge and wisdom that dogs have about everything else. And we need to fully appreciate how profound our dogs really are - no matter the breed - and explore the untapped potential of the value that they can bring to the human family. You may think you know your dog, but most of us do not receive our dog's deeper communications or feelings. In addition, dogs have a vast spiritual consciousness that has not even begun to be understood by the masses. Like other animal species, dogs are here to teach, guide, and improve our lives on a much broader scale... if only we could learn to tune in. See Chapter 17 to learn more about the human-canine relationship.

〰〰〰 ❖ 〰〰〰

Like other animal species, dogs are here to teach, guide, and improve our lives on a much broader scale ...is only we could learn to tune in.

〰〰〰〰〰〰

Natural Health Programs for Brain and Nervous System Health

〰〰〰 ❖ 〰〰〰

Epilepsy

Epilepsy refers to a condition wherein a dog repeatedly suffers seizures or convulsions. It is the most common neurological condition in dogs. Physiologically, seizures are caused by an electrical storm in the brain where the brain is overstimulated by excitatory neurotransmitters causing uncontrolled muscle activity. Most of these seizures are considered by the veterinary community to be idiopathic, which is to say they don't know why or how it is happening. There can be two types of seizures which affect dogs. The first is a generalized or *grand mal* seizure, which is an electrical imbalance that affects the whole brain. The second is what's known as a focal seizure, which only affects one small area of the brain.

Some dogs will have regular seizures which follow a schedule or a pattern (e.g. full moon, every two weeks, a weather change), while other dogs seem to have random episodes or may be triggered by stress and/or excitement.

Symptoms

Most seizures in dogs occur when the pet is relaxed or sleeping, although seizures can also be associated with stimulation to the nervous system such as exercise, anxiety, excitement, or other stressors. Seizures usually appear within the first 2 or 3 years of a dog's life although many senior dogs will develop seizures for the first time in their lives - usually due to food reactions.

A typical grand mal seizure can present with stiffening of the muscles, loss of consciousness, drooling, dilated pupils, and loss of control of the bowels or bladder. In severe seizures, the dog may scream and yelp. The episode is usually (though not always) quite brief and can be followed up by a chomping of the jaws, jerking, or paddling by the legs - after which the dog may lie still or he may get right back up again as if nothing had happened. Most dogs will be disoriented afterward which can have them pacing, walking, or running aimlessly, circling and/or bumping into objects. Rarely are epileptic seizures fatal.

A seizure that originates from one focal area of the brain, will affect the movement of the area that the affected part of the brain controls. Most commonly one side of the face is affected with twitching and blinking.

Some dogs (but not all) will signal an impending seizure with abnormal behaviour such as anxiety, seeking out the owner, hiding, or withdrawing. And sometimes this phase of the behaviour will be apparent for several weeks or months without actually developing into a full-blown seizure. If this appears abnormal, then this is a good time to initiate a preventative program.

The symptoms of petit mal seizures, also known as absence seizures, can be mild enough to be missed by the pet parent as an abnormal event altogether. Symptoms may include "zoning out", staring blankly, blinking, twitching, repeated head shaking, trembling, difficulty standing or odd body postures. Again, this is a good time to implement a program to support a healthy nervous system.

Some breeds are prone to seizures because their skulls are too small for their large brains. This frequently happens with small dogs bred to look like dolls: Brussels griffon, Cavalier King Charles Spaniels, Chihuahuas and their crosses.

Other dog breeds prone to general seizures/epilepsy include small breeds such as beagles, dachshunds, cocker spaniels, poodles, miniature schnauzers and fox terriers; as well as larger breeds such as Siberian huskies, Irish setters, Labrador retrievers and St. Bernards.

Causes

There are a variety of different underlying causes of brain dysfunction that lead to seizures. In addition, the underlying problems vary from dog to dog, making it very difficult to standardize the causes as well as the treatments. Here is a list of the most common imbalances that can cause excitatory influences on nerve cells leading to seizures of the brain:

- **Infections**. Infections of the brain (encephalitis) or chronic systemic infections can affect brain function (see Chapter 7 for addressing infections naturally).

- **Circulation**. If the brain doesn't get an adequate supply of oxygen and/or nutrients for its high demands, then the excitability of the cells may increase or decrease. Therefore, heart problems can also be a factor (see Chapter 6 for more information on heart disease).

- **Chiropractic issues of the neck**. It is reported that dogs who are frequently tied and/or have sustained excessive pressure on their collars are prone to subluxations of the vertebra in the neck. This constricts the nerve supply to the brain, which can affect brain function. Have your dog assessed by an animal chiropractor.

- **Blood sugar imbalances such as hypoglycemia (low blood sugar) and diabetes (high blood sugar)**. Sugar is the only fuel that the brain uses for energy, and it requires a continuous supply of glucose delivered to the neurons for the conduction of neurotransmitters. Therefore, any highs or lows in the delivery of sugar to the brain affects its function. Stress has a major impact on blood sugar levels as well as the efficiency of the delivery of glucose to the brain.

- **Parasites produce a number of toxins including ammonia**. Ammonia can cross the blood-brain barrier and interfere with the transport of potassium into the brain glial cells. The potassium then accumulates around the nerve cells, causing them to absorb excessive amounts of potassium and chloride. Thus, elevated concentrations of ammonia in the brain can cause poor memory, short attention span, ataxia, mood changes, encephalitis, and seizures.

- **Food allergies and intolerances** can cause inflammatory reactions to any organ or tissues including the brain. Reactions can range from mild to extreme (see Chapter 7 for more information).

- **Liver toxicity or liver failure**. The liver is the primary organ responsible for detoxifying all toxins, chemicals, preservatives, food toxins, sugars, and drugs. If the liver becomes congested or diseased, any organ in the body that is susceptible will be adversely affected by the increasing levels of toxicity (see Chapter 5 for liver cleansing programs).

- **High-meat-protein diets** especially in senior dogs can congest the liver and kidneys, affect the heart, and produce excess levels of ammonia.

- **Fevers from teething or viral infections** can cause seizures.

- **Toxic heavy metals and chemicals**. Toxic levels of copper, lead, arsenic, mercury, manganese, hydrocarbons, organophosphates, and others have a major impact on brain function. The brain needs minimal exposure to toxins and chemicals and a tremendous amount of quality nutrition to maintain optimum function. A hair tissue mineral analysis can determine levels of toxic metals that could be affecting the brain.

- **Veterinary medications**. Many medications can cause seizures as side-effects. Non-steroidal drugs, antihistamines, antidepressants, and diabetic medications are all known to have caused seizures.

- **Flea and tick prevention treatments** use chemicals

and neurotoxins that have a direct impact on the brain and are known to cause seizures. Keep your dog away from chemicals (and your human family too).

- **Vaccinosis.** The adverse effects of vaccines are strongly associated with the onset of epilepsy in dogs as well as humans. Sadly, seizures relating to this widespread and frequently unnecessary practice is blamed on genetics instead. In fact, medical scientists in one television documentary admitted, after extensive testing, that a recent vaccination was responsible for causing severe epileptic episodes in a 13-year-old girl. But the family was told that it was inevitable because of her genetic predisposition. Really? What a convenient way of completely absolving themselves of responsibility. See Chapter 1 for the true story on genetics and epigenetics. Vaccines contain chemicals, preservatives, and heavy metals, and can damage the liver, the immune system, and the nervous system (see Chapter 8 for full details on vaccine risks as well as health programs for vaccinosis).

- **Stress** is a common cause of changes to the brain chemistry. If severe enough, it can easily trigger seizures, especially if combined with other risk factors. The events, traumas, and dynamics of the human household family is a major contributor to a dog's stress levels. Many times, I see the family dog's nervous system completely overwhelmed with the crises affecting the people in his life. Relationship problems, mood swings, addiction to drugs and/or alcohol, anger issues, financial stress, and worry become part of the dog's life and his health. Take a moment to recognize how sensitive a dog really is (see Chapter 17 for more information on the human-canine relationship).

Natural Health Program

Refer to all the notes in the "Causes" section above and see the relevant sections in this book.

Diet

- Eliminate wheat, corn gluten, dairy products, soy products, rancid oils, and all known food allergies and intolerances.

- Eliminate refined carbohydrates and reduce all carbohydrates, especially if the dog has been on a high-carbohydrate diet.

- Food allergies often develop from the foods that are eaten regularly and repetitively. This is because a failing immune system will react to whatever it is exposed to on a regular basis. A common example of this is chicken; millions of dogs eat chicken day in and day out and thousands, if not millions of them, are sensitive to it. In addition, chicken contains arsenic due to the content of this heavy toxic metal in commercial chicken food.

- Eliminate beef, bison, venison, red meats and organ meats, for these are a common immune trigger which cause inflammation and tissue damage. Frequently this is not because they are allergens themselves, but because they are high in certain acids. Acidic diets contribute to a higher incidence of allergies as well as inflammatory conditions, which also affect the nervous system.

- For senior dogs with late-onset seizures and/or anxiety, eliminate all high-protein foods and meat except for fish and eggs (if tolerated). Eliminate all high-protein kibbles and cook home-made meals. Meat protein should be decreased for any dog that is protein sensitive and/or has been on a high-protein diet for many years.

- Avoid feeding excess oils including canola oil, soya oil, coconut oil and vegetable oils. Avoid all hydrogenated oils. Excess oils congest the liver adversely, affecting the immune system, digestive system and nervous system.

- Ensure dietary essential fatty acids by providing hemp seeds, chia seeds, flaxseeds, evening primrose oil and/or salmon.

- Avoid all artificial colourings, flavourings, rawhide, or preservatives.

- Choose all organic foods where possible.

NOTE: A ketogenic diet is sometimes recommended on the basis that ketone bodies are generated by the liver and will partly replace glucose as fuel for the brain. This helps to stabilize sugar levels in the brain and supplies the brain with consistent amounts of brain food or fuel. A ketogenic diet contains no carbohydrates, moderate fat, and high protein similar to what many of our dogs are already doing. However, while this diet may be effective for some dogs, especially those dogs with metabolic/blood sugar imbalances, use extreme caution since high protein diets and toxic meat can also trigger epilepsy as well as other health conditions in some dogs, especially senior dogs.

Nutrients

- **magnesium citrate** [*one dose daily*]†* – promotes relaxation in dogs with nervousness, tremors, spasms or hyperactivity; nerve nutrient

- **manganese** [*one dose daily*]† – important nutrient for synthesis of neurotransmitters, cellular energy, and detoxification

- **vitamin E** [*one dose daily*]†* – blood circulation, promotes oxygenation and delivery of nutrients to the brain

- **zinc citrate or picolinate** [one dose daily with food for 30 days]† – nerve and brain nutrient; essential for the function of neurotransmitters, reduces high copper levels, promotes emotional balance

- **vitamin B12** [*one dose daily*]†* – nerve and brain nutrient; metabolism of carbohydrates, liver detoxifier

Herbal & Home Remedies

- **passion flower** [*one dose daily*]† – promotes relaxation in dogs with spasms, tremors, hyperactivity, twitching, trembling, nervousness and seizures

- **skullcap** [*one dose daily*]† – supports the nervous system in dogs with nervous irritations, twitching, tremors, nervous exhaustion and restlessness; combines well with passion flower and lemon balm

- **belladonna 1M, homeopathic** [*one dose daily for 4 days; thereafter as needed*]† – indicated for dogs with convulsions, head pain, hallucinations, twitching; seizures of sudden onset

- **nux vomica 200C, homeopathic** [*one dose daily for 7 days; thereafter as needed*]† – indicated for dogs with cerebral accidents, twitching, tics, tremors and muscle spasms; supports a healthy nervous system after ill effects of medications and/or chemical toxicity

Riva's Remedies

- **Calm & Cool, herbal blend** [*one dose daily*]† – promotes relaxation in dogs with nervous tension, muscle tension, restlessness, irritability and hyperactivity

- **Calm-Aid, homeopathic** [*one dose 2 to 3 times daily as needed*]† – homeopathic support for promoting calm in dogs with nervousness, fear of noise, and phobias

- **Happy Pets** or **Happy Pets Senior, herbal blend** [one dose daily]† – a plant-based blend of herbs and seaweeds which provides over 60 trace minerals, vitamins, fibre and anti-oxidants to support the nervous system, liver and immune system

- **Kava's Primrose Oil, herbal blend** [*one dose daily*]† – provides essential fatty acids for nutritional support

NOTES: During any epileptic episode: (1) Stay calm and speak in a soft, quiet voice. (2) Reduce stimulation by turning off all music, sound and lights. (3) Sit with your dog on the floor and stroke your dog quietly with your hands if safe to do so. (4) Perform any kind of hands-on-healing including energy work, reiki, colour therapy, crystals, and so on.

† See Appendix for recommended dosages and duration for all supplements.
* Also available as a Riva's Remedy

Degenerative Myelopathy

Symptoms

Dogs diagnosed with this condition are mostly senior dogs. DM causes them to lose strength, muscle, and coordination in their hind end. This can result in wobbling, dragging their hind feet and sometimes "knuckling" over. They appear weak and uncoordinated. Symptoms usually start in one hind leg and then the other. In advanced cases, the dog is unable to walk. Dogs with DM do not appear to be in any discomfort other than the changes in mobility.

Causes

In DM, the myelin sheath that protects the spinal neurons begins to disintegrate, which exposes the underlying nerve fibers and disrupts the communication pathways between the brain and the spinal cord. This myelin coating around the spinal cord is crucial for healthy brain-body communication. When myelin degenerates, so does the ability of the brain to send commands to the limbs, and for sensory information to travel from the limbs to the brain. Nevertheless, the condition of DM is very difficult to diagnose and a true diagnosis is only possible upon autopsy.

According to current research, the spinal cord in dogs with DM do not appear to be inflamed, thus the cause is now thought to be an infection of some kind. However, studies do show that the lesions found on the spinal cord are similar to those found in certain vitamin deficiencies. It is also likely that pet parents who suspect that their dog has been afflicted with this condition have been told that it is an auto-immune condition, meaning that the immune system is randomly attacking a healthy spinal cord (see Chapter 7 for more information on why this explanation is inaccurate).

Senior dogs who begin to have problems with degeneration of their spinal cord have the same issues going on as causes the degeneration of any tissues: toxins, food intolerances, meat toxicity, nutrient deficiencies, heavy metal toxicity, and poor circulation can all contribute to these seemingly random health conditions.

Natural Health Program

Diet

- No red meats of any kind - beef, bison, venison, elk, etc.
- No poultry - chicken, turkey, duck or fowl.
- No dairy products.
- No wheat or corn gluten.
- Feed fish or eggs for a protein source.
- Emphasize vegetables, whole grains, and high fibre.
- Increase foods rich in essential fatty acids: salmon, flax seeds, chia seeds, hemp hearts.
- Overweight dogs must lose weight.

Nutrients

- **folic acid** [*one dose daily*]† - supports the immune response, promotes cell growth and tissue repair; spinal nutrient

- **vitamin B12** [*one dose daily*]†* - supports liver detoxification, energy and the nervous system

- **potassium citrate** [*one dose daily*]† - nerve nutrient; balances pH in acidic conditions; aids waste elimination

Herbal & Home Remedies

- **flaxseed oil** [*one dose daily in 30-day cycles with 30 days in between*]†

- apply a hot water bottle or heating pad to the affected areas to improve circulation

- arrange a chiropractic assessment

- ensure regular and targeted exercises to improve strength, mobility, and balance; exercise also helps to detoxify affected tissues

Riva's Remedies

- **Injur-Ease, homeopathic** [*one dose twice daily for 7 days*]† - homeopathic support for dogs with joint and nerve injuries or trauma

- **Bone-Up, specialized nutrient** [one dose daily]† - maintains the health of cartilage, joints, nerves and connective tissue; promotes a healthy acid-alkaline balance

- **Joint-Clear, herbal blend** [one dose daily as needed]† - supports adrenal gland function and provides nutrition for bones, joints, and nerves; maintains flexibility and mobility for senior dogs

- **Happy Pets** or **Happy Pets Senior, herbal blend** [one dose daily]† - a plant-based blend of herbs and seaweeds which provides over 60 trace minerals, vitamins, fibre, and anti-oxidants to support the nervous system, liver and immune system

† See Appendix for recommended dosages and duration for all supplements.
* Also available as a Riva's Remedy

Rabies

Rabies is a viral disease that affects mammals and causes fatal inflammation of the brain. In North America the natural reservoir species for the virus include raccoons, skunks, foxes, and bats (especially bats). These are the species that dogs are most likely to contract the virus from.

According to the WHO (World Health Organization) rabies is currently responsible for tens of thousands of human deaths worldwide every year, and approximately 99 percent of those death are transmitted from dogs. In humans, rabies that goes untreated until such time as it becomes neurologically symptomatic is fatal - prior to 2004 it was 100 percent fatal, but new protocols have whittled that down to 92 percent (by contrast the average strain of Ebola virus is about 50 percent fatal).

Now as dire as that sounds, the reality in North America and most of Europe is that cases of rabies are very rare indeed; the overwhelming majority of reported deaths occur in Africa and India. In North America, there are between 80 to 100 cases of rabies reported in dogs each year (out of 96 million!) and one or two human deaths. Vaccine proponents will, of course, point to this disparity as unequivocal proof of the iron-clad efficacy of vaccination. And it is hard not to concede that widespread rabies vaccination programs in North America and Europe have played a part without being deliberately obtuse. As the buffer species between humans and wild reservoir species, vaccinated dogs form a logical natural firewall.

That being said, while North American rabies rates were once much higher than they are today, they were never at levels seen currently in Africa or India. Same virus, different results. Furthermore, the rabies rates in North America had dropped almost to current levels before the widespread canine vaccination against the virus. So how do you explain that?

The larger truth is that even without vaccination, healthy dogs are only 10 to 15 percent likely to contract rabies through direct exposure. What you see in regions with high rabies transmission rates are vast populations of malnourished, often feral, (and immune-compromised) dogs – and in many cases malnourished, immune-compromised humans.

I am not suggesting that you not vaccinate your dog against rabies if your dog has a high risk of exposure to one or more of the natural reservoir species in the wild. Certainly, I would be the last to argue that dogs in North America are uniformly healthy. What I am suggesting is that the best defense against any sort of infection including viruses is a robust healthy immune system. A healthy dog has less to fear than an unhealthy one and not just from rabies.

Bats are common reservoir species for rabies.

~~~~~~~~~~ 🐾 ~~~~~~~~~~

While North American rabies rates were once much higher than they are today, they were never at levels seen currently in Africa or India. Same virus, different results.

~~~~~~~~~~

Symptoms

The rabies virus affects the hippocampus in the brain which is then unable to mediate or regulate powerful emotions. So the aggressive urges of the hypothalamus will override any emotional controls which normally prevent outbursts and the dog (or person) is free to express primal behaviours at its deepest level with no restraints or controls. Thus the rabid dog snarls, bites, fights and rages. It's a frightening example of what lies deep inside the reptilian brains of all species.

Thus the virus attacks the nervous system and inflames the brain causing excitability, aggression, frothing at the mouth, and random biting at themselves or others. Symptoms can take from 3 to 8 weeks to appear, but the symptoms progress quickly once they appear. "Furious" rabies is characterized by anxiety and psychological disturbances such as confusion, agitation, rage, dis-orientation, hallucinations, hyper-responsive to stimulation and fear of water. "Dumb" rabies causes depression, drooling, drooping head or jaw, choking sounds and paralysis which usually starts in the hind end and progresses forward. Most animals will constantly lick the site of the bite.

In both types of rabies death occurs from paralysis of the respiratory system which results in breathing failure. Both types of rabies are incurable after the onset of neurological symptoms.

Causes

Dogs are infected mostly by rabid raccoons, skunks, foxes and sometimes bats through the transfer of saliva by biting: the rabies virus is shed at high levels in saliva. Recent research from the University of Calgary found that bats are not as disease ridden as the stigma suggests; rather than the previous estimate of 10 percent, the numbers are closer to less than 1 percent. But normally it is only the unhealthy bats that come into contact with people and with dogs.

But where did the rabies virus come from? Rabies is one of the most well-known viral diseases and also has an ancient history. Records date back to 2300 BC in the old Babylon and reached both China and Europe by the fifth century. The first recognized case in North America was 1768 in Boston. And why would a virus filled with such rage and aggression even exist? It is my view that viruses matter to life and directly exchange genetic information between living organisms. They are important messengers within the web of life itself, and it is very likely that the information that they contain is both informed and regularly altered by the behaviours of other species of life, including plants, animals, and people. And since anger and aggression have been rampant and destructive energies on this planet since the beginning of life, we must seriously consider whether these viruses have been manufactured by powerful emotional energy fields. As could be the case with all global viruses. Either way, it's time that we get our emotions under control.

Veterinary Treatment

If you fear your dog has been exposed to the virus, take them immediately to a veterinarian. If the creature that exposed your dog is available (usually if your dog has killed it) it too can *carefully* be brought to the veterinarian to be tested. Your dog may be given a rabies shot, and your right to decline may vary depending on where you live. You may be asked to quarantine your dog (perhaps for months) at home and watch for symptoms.

NOTE: The rabies virus in only transmissible from animals who are symptomatic (i.e. showing signs of the disease) or in rare cases animals about to become symptomatic.

The following natural health program can be used for quarantined dogs, dogs with adverse reactions to a rabies vaccine or dogs with suspected rabies who cannot get immediate emergency health care. It can also be added to a conventional treatment program for dogs who are not responding well. The goal is to help ensure that your dog doesn't develop the disease after exposure.

Natural Health Program

Nutrients

- **magnesium citrate** [one dose daily]†* – promotes relaxation in dogs with nervousness, fears, spasms and muscle tension

Herbal & Home Remedies

- **skullcap** [*one dose twice daily*]† – promotes a healthy nervous system; indicated for dogs with nervous irritations, spasmodic afflictions, anxiety, twitching and/or confusion

- **lyssin 200C, homeopathic** [*one dose daily for 4 days*]† – indicated for dogs with raging, irritable and biting behaviours; convulsions, hypersensitive to stimulation and phobias; adverse effects of rabies vaccine

- **belladonna 1M, homeopathic** [*one dose daily for 4 days*]† – dogs who suffer from hallucinations, convulsions, dilated pupils; fear of other dogs; delusions of bats

† See Appendix for recommended dosages and duration for all supplements.
* Also available as a Riva's Remedy

Boomer's Midnight Seizure

Boomer arrived on my porch late one night in the arms of a neighbor. Boomer was a three-year-old English pointer/Husky x who had been training earlier that day for his job as a sled dog. But on this day, Boomer collapsed shortly after his training session and lost consciousness. But by the time he arrived here, it was clear to see that he was in the middle of a grand mal seizure and along with stiff muscles, jerking and paddling, his terrifying screams and yelps could be heard from afar. His concerned owner held on tight and tried to keep Boomer calm, but it was obvious that Boomer's distress was going to last longer than a few minutes. I ran to my home remedies cabinet to see what I had available as I did not have time to go to my clinic. It's not easy, nor advisable, to administer anything orally to a dog that's in the middle of an epileptic episode. But herbal tinctures and especially homeopathic remedies are a safer choice since they dissolve immediately in the mouth.

I chose an herbal nerve tincture containing passion flower, skullcap and lemon balm – herbs that can address muscle spasms, seizures, and extreme nervous tension. Boomer became a little more relaxed, but was still yelping and jerking. We waited a few minutes, and then I chose homeopathic belladonna in a 1M potency followed by repeated doses of the Riva's homeopathic Calm-Aid (containing aconitum, arsenicum, chamomila, ignatia, passiflora and phosphorus). Thankfully, within a few passing minutes we were all relieved to see that Boomer's muscles became more relaxed and his blood-curdling shrieks settled right down into a whimper. The whole ordeal lasted at least 20 minutes (hard to know since the episode was extremely intense) and by the time he went home, he was subdued and only expressing quiet whimpers. Boomer slept all night and the next morning and showed no more signs of his distressful event the night before. Due to circumstance, I never saw Boomer again to identify the underlying causes(s) nor put together a prevention program in case of future problems.

Boomer.

Healing Dogs Their Way

14. Nutritional Therapy

Vitamins & Minerals to Promote Health

Nutrient Deficiencies

A nutrient deficiency is the lack, or in some cases absence, of certain amino acids, vitamins, minerals, and/or essential fatty acids required for normal growth, development, and physiological and chemical reactions which affect all body systems. Nutrient deficiencies are common but often undetected.

For many years, pet owners and their health practitioners were educated to believe that a bag of commercial pet food would provide all the nutrition that their pets would ever need to stay healthy. However, with the current epidemic of well-kept but diseased dogs everywhere, most of us have since learned that there is no possible way that any diet, particularly a processed diet, will provide the appropriate levels of vitamins, minerals or any other essential nutrients that are required to sustain the numerous body functions and processes that dogs need to support life, maintain health, prevent disease, and optimize wellness. Unfortunately, many humans too are still trusting in their processed and inorganic diets to provide everything they need.

A nutrient-deficiency disease is when an illness or disease occurs as an actual result of one or more nutrient deficiencies and presents with clinical symptoms. Therefore, when the specific deficiencies are replenished or corrected, the symptoms disappear and the disease is so-called cured. Nutrient-deficiency diseases can manifest from incomplete or inappropriate diets; poor digestion, absorption, and assimilation of nutrients from food; faulty metabolism, toxicity, illness, abuse or neglect, over-training, unhappy households and/or periods of high nutritional demands. All these situations can deplete nutrients, and if left depleted, they will eventually lead to more health problems, which lead to more deficiencies, which lead to more health problems...and so it continues. Therefore, nutritional supplementation is an invaluable therapy in all health conditions and diseases. (See chart on next page.)

In addition, all medications, without exception, deplete certain nutrients which then adversely affect the health problems which the medications are prescribed for. But these very common deficiencies, despite their significance in health care, are mostly over-looked and rarely addressed. Why is this? And why are veterinarians so complacent about it?

Aside from physical health symptoms, many dogs can also show certain signs or behaviours which may be indicative of one or more nutritional deficiencies. Watch for excessive licking, eating feces, dirt, wood, or rocks; excessive hunger or begging (also a sign that the diet is not satisfactory), and premature aging.

~~~~~~~ 🐾 ~~~~~~~

For many years, pet owners and their health practitioners were educated to believe that a bag of commercial pet food would provide all the nutrition that their pets would ever need to stay healthy.

~~~~~~~~~~~~~~~~

Drug Name	Nutrients Depleted	Health Risks
Antibiotics	probiotics, biotin, folic acid, all B-vitamins	poor digestion, decreased nutrient absorption, diarrhea, poor immunity, increased stress, skin disorders
NSAIDs (non-steroidal anti-inflammatory drugs)	vitamin C, potassium, folic acid, selenium, magnesium, iron, zinc, calcium	infections, slow wound healing, bone density, heart symptoms, fatigue, anemia, arthritis
Corticosteroids	vitamin C, potassium, zinc, all B-vitamins, calcium, magnesium	depressed immunity, osteoporosis, increased appetite, weight gain, bruising, insomnia, diabetes, eye symptoms
Antacids & ulcer medications	vitamin B12, iron, folic acid, zinc, calcium	osteoporosis, heart disease, fatigue, anemia, poor immunity, infections, leaky gut
Diabetic medications	B-vitamins, folic acid, magnesium, vitamin C	low blood sugar, skin problems, heart symptoms, weight gain, poor immunity, increased stress, kidney function
Cholesterol-lowering drugs	coenzyme Q10	low energy, poor immunity, increased risk of heart disease, liver function
Antidepressants	B-vitamins, folic acid, zinc, calcium, magnesium, selenium, coenzyme Q10	fatigue, immune suppression; disorders of the skin, eyes and nerves; heart symptoms, liver function

Testing Methods to Identify Nutrient Deficiencies and/or Individual Requirements

Blood Tests

Most conventional animal health practitioners rely on blood tests for information on nutritional status, believing that these tests are accurate in determining whether their dogs need vitamin or mineral supplementation. Unfortunately, blood tests are not accurate indicators for evaluating nutritional deficiencies and/or individual requirements – for your dog, or for you. Here's why.

- Nutrient levels in the blood fluctuate from day to day and hour to hour.
- Nutrient levels in the blood do not reflect nutrient levels in the tissues and organs, which are often deficient when the blood is not.
- Nutritional physiology takes place at the cellular level, not in the blood.
- Many nutrients have different storage sites within the body. No blood test can accurately determine how much calcium is in the muscles or bones, for example. Blood tests will also not detect any minerals that have precipitated out into soft tissue.
- The blood is the last vehicle to change its chemical content, especially in times of deficiency. For example, the lungs can be starved for oxygen caused by low iron levels in the lung tissue long before the blood will become depleted enough to show a deficiency on a blood test. Therefore, undetected tissue deficiencies of iron can go on for weeks, months, or even a lifetime.

Blood tests are not accurate indicators for evaluating nutritional deficiencies and/or individual requirements.

- Blood levels of nutrients and minerals are kept within very narrow limits by the body and are slow to change.

- Certain vitamin and mineral levels may test as adequate without being bioavailable to certain tissues due to other deficiencies and/or the health condition of the dog.

- Every individual dog, no matter the breed, has a unique biochemistry – nutrient levels that are adequate for one dog can be woefully inadequate for another. Nutrient demands are affected by exercise, stress, disease, lifestyle, inadequate diet, medications, health history, age and breed.

~~~~~~~ 🐾 ~~~~~~~

A hair mineral analysis can detect nutritional imbalances and problems, where often conventional blood testing cannot.

~~~~~~~~~~~~~~~~~~~

Hair Tissue Mineral Analysis

A hair analysis is a scientific test which accurately measures the mineral content of the hair using atomic absorption methods. A hair analysis can detect nutritional imbalances and problems, where often conventional blood testing cannot. Nutritional physiology takes place at the cellular level, not in the blood. And, because blood levels of nutrients and minerals are kept within very narrow limits by the body blood levels are not a true reflection of the nutrient status within the tissues, organs and glands which are all too often depleted before the blood is. In contrast, tissue mineral analysis provides information about cellular activity within the tissues and the metabolism of nutrients throughout the body. Therefore, mineral content of the hair reflects the mineral content of the body's tissues.

Hair mineral analyses are also very accurate in determining the levels of toxic heavy metals – a problem which is becoming all too common in an ever-increasing toxic world. Toxic metals such as mercury, aluminum, arsenic and/or lead can have a profound and destructive impact on many health conditions. Routine blood tests cannot detect chronic heavy-metal poisoning.

A mineral hair analysis can also reveal a variety of different nutritional and health problems as well as the status of many organs and glands, including the liver and kidneys; and thyroid, pituitary, and adrenal glands. It can detect adrenal dysfunction, digestive disturbances, thyroid and pituitary dysfunction, blood sugar imbalances, anemia, and inflammation.

See the Appendix for more information and/or to arrange a test.

Kinesiology

Kinesiology is a type of muscle testing or energy testing used to evaluate health status and to ascertain specific health, diet, and nutrition requirements. It can be used for both people and for animals. For testing a dog, it involves "surrogate testing" whereby the dog's response to a particular food or nutrient is measured by applying pressure to the arm muscles of another person (the surrogate) while the substance is held close to the dog's body. The arm will become stronger, weaker, or remain neutral when certain foods, nutrients or other supplements are tested. I prefer to refer to it is as energy testing, rather than muscle testing, since the muscle itself is simply used as an instrument to assess strength.

Energy testing is made possible by the understanding that anatomical body parts and systems including connective tissue, blood, the nervous system, the immune system, and all body organs are surrounded by an electromagnetic field. This field is a fundamental force of nature. It is a physical field that is produced by electrically charged particles and is a combination of an electric field and a magnetic field. The interaction between these two fields is mediated by units of light or photons. The photons and the fields themselves respond to and are altered by variables such as food, nutrition, emotions, and thoughts. And this electrical response is instantaneous.

When testing specific supplements, kinesiology works by checking the resonance of a substance, remedy, vitamin, or food against the resonance of the body's electrical field. Remember that all substances also have a unique vibration. When the two electrical fields between the animal and the substance is harmonic – meaning that the dog will benefit from its use – the arm will feel stronger, sometimes much stronger, and will have more resistance. When the substance is disharmonic or dissonant, the arm will feel weaker. A weak muscle response is very common when testing a food allergy for example. When the resonance is neutral, the muscle strength won't change either way. Done correctly, this is a very accurate method of determining what is, and what is not, of benefit. See the Appendix for more information.

Therapeutic Nutrition

Therapeutic nutrition means that when vitamins, minerals, amino acids, essential fatty acids, probiotics, and phytonutrients are supplemented well above the recommended daily dose, they have a significant impact on health by altering the course and the outcome of the disease. All nutrients nourish the body and provide the elements for it to prevent and heal its own diseases and imbalances. Therapeutic nutrition is not based on identifiable or overt signs of deficiencies, nor does it focus on the so-called balanced diet or minimum daily requirements, since these guidelines are clearly not adequate. Rather, it operates on the premise that all nutrients must be present at optimum levels in order for all physiological processes – including the immune system – to function properly. Therapeutic nutrition is also able to address deficiencies that are sub-clinical and impossible to detect on a blood test, much less to the untrained eye.

Rarely, is there a health condition that does not benefit from – or even derive a cure from – applied therapeutic nutrition. I consider it a primary therapy for all health conditions, and it belongs smack-dab in the middle of mainstream healthcare.

Because nutritional deficiencies and individual requirements are difficult to diagnose with conventional medical tests, and because nutritional therapy is poorly understood by most healthcare practitioners, clinical nutrition of any kind is not considered as a primary therapy by the mainstream. Most animal health practitioners have little to no knowledge about the relationship between nutrition and disease. It just wasn't in their training – and this despite the fact that clinical nutrition is a strong science. This lack of training is unfortunate because nutrient deficiencies are very common, and the benefits of therapeutic dosages have a major impact on health and wellness, as well as disease prevention and treatment.

For example, some of the most common (yet seldom identified) deficiencies affecting our dogs include calcium (muscle strength, joints, arthritis, anxiety); magnesium (nerves, heart, muscles); potassium (protein digestion and elimination of acids and toxicity); iron (anemia, energy, circulation, immunity and allergies); vitamin B12

~~~~~~~~ ❧ ~~~~~~~~

Therapeutic nutrition operates on the premise that all nutrients must be present at optimum levels in order for all physiological processes – including the immune system – to function properly.

~~~~~~~~~~~~~~~~~

(anemia, energy, appetite, and nerve nutrient); and folic acid (protein digestion, parasite resistance, nerve nutrient, and tissue repair). When any deficiency is replenished, it has a significant influence over the health of your pet. They feel better, digest better, eat better, build better resistance to disease, become more flexible and mobile, and experience improved quality of life. After working with animals and people for so many years I have seen hundreds of success cases that may have seemed like miracles to the parents, but were simply the results of improved diet and nutrition.

And while it is true that food and a wholesome diet provide the best sources of nutrition, there are too many times in today's world where either the dogs and/or the diet have become so unbalanced that effective and therapeutic dosages cannot be provided by food alone. At least in the beginning. But food *is* required to optimize the absorption and assimilation of all nutrients.

Important Nutrients for Dogs

(See Appendix for Suggested Dosages & Guidelines to Feeding Supplements)

Vitamin A or Beta-Carotene

Beta-carotene is the precursor to retinol, which is the active form of vitamin A. In most cases beta-carotene is converted into vitamin A in the body. Both forms are metabolized inside the cells to support important biological functions. Use these important nutrients for a compromised immune system, frequent infections, eye problems, skin lesions, and dry skin. Both forms are beneficial for promoting healthy skin cell growth. Beta-Carotene is more specific for inhalant allergies, cancer, intestinal ulcers, irritations, and any time that the mucous membranes need support. Vitamin A is best used for infections, vision problems, cataracts, night blindness, and fatigue.

Healthy Food Sources for Vitamin A: fish liver oils, eggs

Healthy Food Sources for Beta-Carotene: yellow and orange vegetables, such as carrots, yams, sweet potatoes, and squash

Vitamin C (ascorbic acid)

While it is true that dogs manufacture their own vitamin C, they often don't produce enough to keep up with the nutritional demands for this important vitamin – especially when they are sick. The demands for vitamin C increase during periods of stress, infections, cancer, wounds, liver distress, and dental problems with both teeth and gums. Vitamin C also improves iron absorption. Always use as ascorbic acid, rather than buffered forms such as calcium ascorbate. If your dog finds ascorbic acid too acidic or if it creates a loose stool then either use a smaller dose or feed Vitamin C-rich foods.

Healthy Food Sources: All leafy greens, cabbage, cauliflower, currants, broccoli, sprouts and parsley.

Vitamin E

Vitamin E benefits all skin conditions, wound healing, circulatory problems, muscle weakness, cramps, and heart conditions. It also supports cognitive function of the brain. Use from natural source, such as d-alpha tocopherol and *not* dl-alpha tocopherol, which is synthetic and a by-product of the petroleum industry.

Healthy Food Sources: Dark green leafy vegetables, wheat germ, nuts, eggs, legumes, brown rice and wild rice.

Vitamin B5 (pantothenic acid)

Vitamin B5 is important for the metabolism of all foods. It maintains a healthy nervous system by helping to produce the neurotransmitters in the brain and by supporting adrenal function. Use for all stress conditions, nervous disorders, neurological problems, and adrenal burn-out. Use daily for 30-day cycles and only repeat if beneficial.

Healthy Food Sources: Eggs, potatoes, fish, legumes, vegetables.

Vitamin B6 (pyridoxine)

Vitamin B6 supports the production of neurotransmitters and healthy brain function. It can benefit dogs with depression, mental irritability and/or aggression. It is a major nutrient for thyroid and pituitary function. Vitamin B6 provides joint support as it allows for the transport of protein in and out of the joint capsules. It is a beneficial nutrient for sore joints, hormonal problems, blood sugar abnormalities and obesity. It combines well with calcium for joint and muscle support.

Healthy Food Sources: Eggs, salmon, spinach, carrots, peas, sunflower seeds, wheat germ, brown rice, bananas, legumes.

Vitamin B12 (cyanocobalamin)

Vitamin B12 is a very common nutrient deficiency in dogs. It is a significant nutrient for the nervous system, brain function, energy levels, liver detoxification, and colon support. It also contributes to conditions of anemia. It should be used in dogs with physical nerve damage, neurological conditions, epilepsy, depression, anxiety, anemia, liver conditions, and loss of appetite and/or diarrhea. It also maintains energy levels.

Healthy Food Sources: Egg yolks, salmon, sardines, herring, beef. Organ meats are also high in vitamin B12 but should be avoided for senior dogs and/or arthritic dogs. Feed moderate amounts once or twice weekly to younger dogs if they like it.

Folic Acid (folacin)

An extremely important nutrient for multiple body functions, but it is mostly overlooked and rarely supplemented for dogs. Folic acid is required for cell replication, cell growth, and all tissue repair for the intestines, blood vessels, and organs. It maintains a healthy nervous system, supports the immune system, and provides nutritional support for mental wellness. Folic acid promotes the natural production of probiotics and aids protein digestion. It provides support for the colon, stomach function and also helps to prevent parasites. Use to promote the healthy digestion of meats protein and maintain stomach health in dogs with ulcers. Folic acid is an important nutrient for hormone balance, slow growth in puppies, depression, fatigue, anxiety and anemia.

Healthy Food Sources: Dark leafy greens, sprouts, sunflower seeds, asparagus and broccoli. Folic acid is also found in organ meats but should be avoided for senior dogs and/or arthritic dogs. Feed moderate amounts once or twice weekly to younger dogs if they like it.

Coenzyme Q10

Coenzyme Q10 is a vitamin manufactured and mostly stored in the dog's liver and heart. It is a key nutrient in energy production and as an anti-oxidant. The liver requires adequate levels of coenzyme Q10, for it helps to neutralize environmental toxins and free radicals.

Recommended for periodontal disease and dental problems, heart disease, liver conditions, and muscle weakness. Use in 30 day cycles with 2 to 4 weeks in between each cycle. This will prevent excess anti-oxidant activity resulting in lower energy levels.

Healthy Food Sources: Broccoli, dark leafy greens, nuts and fish.

What About Vitamin D?

Vitamin D (cholecalciferol) is known as the sunshine vitamin because we absorb Vitamin D when we are exposed to the sun. However, this is the inactive form of Vitamin D and it must therefore be transported to the liver and kidneys for conversion into calcitriol, the active form of Vitamin D which promotes the absorption of minerals, especially calcium. Calcitriol also promotes the growth and reconstruction of bone. While clinical deficiency symptoms of Vitamin D cannot be disputed – rickets, osteoporosis, muscle spasms, cardiovascular conditions and some bone-related health problems – the continuing media attention on vitamin D is suspect.

Vitamin D is a fat-soluble vitamin meaning that the body does not easily eliminate excessive amounts and therefore a build-up of Vitamin D levels is entirely possible. While acute symptoms of taking too much vitamin D would include poor appetite, nausea, vomiting, low energy, frequent urination and kidney problems there is also evidence that long-term excessive use will damage the liver as well as the arteries, including the coronary arteries. In fact, many years ago when I was researching the fortification of milk with Vitamin D I spoke with a Nutrition Professor at a B.C. University whose research indicated that excess Vitamin D would eventually damage the cardiovascular system including the coronary arteries. And a more recent study conducted by the University of Aberdeen in England revealed that Vitamin D did not provide substantial support in preventing the onset of heart attacks or cancer! Hmm...

So why are the news reports so persistent about its benefits but not advising caution in any way? And why haven't so many other beneficial and safer nutrients not received the same media attention? I don't know about you, but whenever a new miracle drug or vitamin hits the airwaves claiming to be a panacea that treats everything I am suspicious of the agenda. We have seen this many times before – glucosamine, turmeric and coconut oil for example. And now vitamin D. I call it slick marketing to dupe people into thinking that there is a magic remedy out there to ward off all disease. We should know better. In the meantime, make sure that your dog gets lots of time outside to soak up those sun rays.

Minerals

Calcium

Calcium is an extremely important mineral for the formation of and the maintenance of strong bones, teeth, and nerves. Calcium is a relaxant and is also required to regulate the contraction and relaxation of muscles. It aids digestion, blood clotting, and the immune system. Calcium is also important for buffering excess acids due to high protein diets. Use in all cases of joint and muscle pain, bone ailments, dental problems, meat toxicity and restlessness. Use as a citrate to ensure maximum absorption and assimilation.

Healthy Food Sources: Bones, dark green leafy vegetables, canned salmon and sardines, broccoli and kale.

Magnesium

Magnesium helps relax muscles and nerves and relieves spasms. It promotes healthy sugar metabolism in cases of insulin resistance and is also an important heart nutrient. It is an important nutrient for dogs with cramps, anxiety, nervousness, heart conditions and muscle tension. Use as a citrate to ensure maximum absorption and assimilation.

Healthy Food Sources: Green leafy vegetables, brown rice, peas, whole grains, nuts and seeds.

Potassium

Potassium is an important nutrient for the nerves, for the heart, and for the muscles where it is necessary for muscle contraction. Potassium helps to balance pH levels and to eliminate excess acids from the body as well as digestive wastes. It is also important for the stomach and protein digestion. Use as a citrate to ensure maximum absorption and assimilation.

Healthy Food Sources: Vegetables, dried fruit, legumes, whole grains, bananas, sunflower seeds.

Iron

Iron is commonly deficient either with or without anemia (a deficiency of red blood cells and/or hemoglobin). Iron is required for the production of red blood cells and is, therefore, necessary for carrying oxygen to the cells, producing energy, and maintaining circulation. Iron is also necessary for a healthy immune system and cognitive function. Low iron levels can cause fatigue, weakness, poor concentration, immune conditions, chronic infections, liver toxicity, a predisposition to allergies, digestive problems, loss of appetite, and increased gas and bloating. It can also increase susceptibility to parasites.

Blood tests frequently don't detect low iron levels, and as a result, the incidence of low iron is much more common than high or toxic levels of iron. Nevertheless, anemia is one of the most common nutrient deficiencies in dogs, and most times it is left untreated. Even if the tests show positive for anemia and/or iron deficiencies, many health practitioners tend to look for a cause of red blood cell loss rather than address the fact that the diet and/or absorption and assimilation of minerals is faulty. As well, low iron levels *without* anemia is also very common. And many times, vitamin B12 and folic acid need to be added to the program to address anemia. Always use a citrate or a gluconate form of iron, never a sulphate. Iron also needs available vitamin C and copper present for absorption.

Healthy Food Sources: Beef, liver, dark leafy green vegetables, whole grains, legumes. Don't use beef, bison, venison or organ meats as an iron source for senior dogs and/or arthritic dogs.

Iodine

Iodine is critical for the immune system and is a natural antibiotic (particularly for urinary infections), antifungal and antiviral. It helps to regulate metabolism, energy, and growth, and is very important for the immune system. Iodine is necessary for the function of all the endocrine glands, especially the thyroid. Iodine deficiencies can result in fatigue, depression, hormonal imbalances, weight gain, and thyroid conditions, although an iodine deficiency does not *always* result in thyroid problems. Use iodine in liquid form for yeast infections, urinary infections, intestinal bacteria, sluggish metabolism, fatigue, allergies due to a low thyroid, and hormonal cancers.

Healthy Food Sources: Sea salt, Himalayan crystal salt, kelp, Irish moss, dulse, baked potatoes, eggs, fish, bananas.

Selenium

Selenium is an extremely important nutrient for the immune system. It is an effective anti-oxidant which protects all cells from chemical damage by converting free radicals into harmless substances. Selenium is also very important for muscle function and carbohydrate metabolism and is a significant thyroid nutrient. Deficiency symptoms include weak muscles, fatigue, hair loss, and brittle nails. Use for cancer, muscle weakness, liver detoxification, immune dysfunction, and any kind of toxic chemical exposure. Always use selenium in organic form, rather than inorganic since organic selenium has no known toxicity and is effective in smaller doses. Organic selenium can be identified as selenium yeast or selenomethionine. Selenium, in the inorganic form is labelled as selenite. Give one dose daily for 30 days and only repeat if beneficial.

Healthy Food Sources: Meat, nuts, oats, brown rice, fish.

Nutraceuticals... Use with Caution

Nutraceuticals such as MSM, chondroitin, and glucosamine have been so widely marketed for arthritis that they are now being used for every ache, pain, and joint discomfort imaginable – and even symptoms that are completely unrelated. There are thousands of different arthritis products available for dogs (as well as people). Nutraceuticals are even routinely added to the dog food. Such is the power of marketing. But panaceas don't exist – even though we are often sold on the promise that they do – and can even cause other health problems.

Glucosamine and Chondroitin

Glucosamine with or without chondroitin is used by many as a treatment for inflammation and osteoarthritis because it is sometimes capable of regenerating bone cartilage. However, symptoms similar to the MSM reactions are also common with the use of GLS (glucosamine sulphate) or chondroitin sulphate since the sulphate molecule on GLS can create the same adverse immune reactions. Because of these sulphur sensitivities, glucosamine is also available in non-sulphur forms such as glucosamine hydrochloride.

But there are other problems with glucosamine. Glucosamine is a unique type of sugar concentrated into a capsule. Glucosamine therefore inhibits the pancreas from producing insulin, and low insulin levels raise blood-sugar levels. It also stresses the liver because the liver must metabolize all sugars. It is likely that glucosamine can *initiate* obesity and insulin resistance, rather than just perpetuate these conditions. Glucosamine is, therefore, contraindicated in several health conditions and should not be used in dogs (or people) with weight gain, obesity, insulin resistance, diabetes, blood sugar imbalances, metabolic problems, and/or Cushing's syndrome. As well, glucosamine has been implicated in causing an increase of blood pressure and can cause changes in heart rhythm in sensitive animals (and people). Some of these symptoms are more detectable with people, but of course, your dog cannot *tell* you that they feel shaky inside or that their heart doesn't feel right.

MSM (methylsulfonylmethane)

MSM is a form of sulphur which can be valuable for arthritis, joint pain, and swellings. It can be particularly beneficial for acute muscle injuries and some forms of arthritis as it strengthens connective tissue and helps to increase the permeability of the joint and muscle membranes, allowing the release of excess fluid. This can result in a relief of swelling as well as drainage of inflammatory toxins. However, many animals are sensitive or intolerant to sulphur compounds, which can then result in fatigue, shortness of breath, congestion, immune issues, and/or skin problems. In addition, the long-term use of MSM depletes calcium levels. All these symptoms can occur shortly after taking the supplement or appear more slowly over time. No matter how you or your pet responds, dose on the side of caution and limit the use of MSM to thirty days unless obvious benefit is demonstrated without side effects beyond that time.

Considering that millions of dogs are taking MSM and/or glucosamine products over long periods of time, we know that there are thousands of cases of fatigue, shortness of breath, poor performance, immunity issues, heart symptoms, and metabolic problems occurring as side effects. But to date – even though millions of people and their dogs are using these products – there is little awareness of the problems that are occurring with these purportedly *safe* supplements. Rather, the symptoms are blamed on other issues, and your dog may even be wrongly medicated.

Despite the very effective mass marketing of nutraceuticals, they should not be considered a panacea for every joint ailment. There are no panaceas; if it sounds too good to be true, it probably is. Always seek the underlying cause of all ailments, be it diet, lack of exercise, and/or nutritional deficiencies. Diet, especially excess meat protein, is a major cause of joint pain and/or arthritis. And never use *any* supplements long-term unless they have demonstrated obvious benefits.

Toxic Heavy Metals

Toxic heavy metals can contribute to a variety of diseases and/or a complex set of unhealthy symptoms which are difficult to diagnose. Heavy metals are normally accumulated over long periods of time, but they are mostly disregarded as a serious factor in canine healthcare, or any healthcare for that matter. However, with the availability of increasing research and information on these minerals, our dogs can now benefit from a full and comprehensive health-care program which includes detoxification programs to help eliminate any destructive heavy metals. Toxic heavy metals can be detected on a hair tissue mineral analysis. Here are the most common toxic heavy metals found to be elevated in canine hair tests.

Aluminum

Aluminum blocks the action potential of nerve cells and inhibits important enzymes as well as neurotransmitters in the brain. For this reason, most symptoms of aluminum toxicity affect the nervous system: poor memory, lack of coordination, confusion, disorientation, paralytic muscle conditions, and behavioural changes. Aluminum can also reduce intestinal activity resulting in excess gas, indigestion, heartburn, poor appetite, and even a distaste for all meat. Aluminum can intoxicate the liver and kidneys. It can also cause low blood sugar levels (hypoglycemia).

Because aluminum impairs calcium metabolism it can result in dental cavities, joint pain, softening of the bone and weak, aching muscles. Aluminum can also impair thyroid or pituitary function.

Aluminum can be ingested through municipal water, any food product prepared with water, baking powder, regular salt (contains aluminum silicate as a drying agent), and bleached flour. Vaccines are a common source of aluminum as it is used as an additive. Puppies can be born with elevated aluminum that is passed through the placenta.

Antagonistic Nutrients: vitamin C, zinc, calcium, magnesium, selenium

Arsenic

Small amounts of arsenic may be necessary for some body functions such as growth and blood formation. However, arsenic is an enzyme inhibitor and interferes with the uptake of folic acid. Symptoms of chronic arsenic toxicity include abdominal pain, bloating, diarrhea, vomiting, lack of appetite, skin rashes, kidney and liver dysfunction, excess thirst, lack of balance and weakness. Acute symptoms may mimic food poisoning after which the dog doesn't seem to recover. Regular exposure to even small amounts of arsenic can increase the risk of bladder, lung, and skin cancer as well as heart problems and diabetes.

Inorganic arsenic can be acquired from pesticides, table salt, eating paint, rat poison, fungicides, and wood preservatives such as creosote. It is also found in commercial chicken feed, and studies show that it is therefore present in the meat. This is a major concern for the millions of dogs (and people) who eat chicken every day. Another problem for dogs (and people) is the arsenic levels in rice. Rice is found in soil and water and tends to absorb arsenic more readily than many other plants. Brown rice has the highest levels with white rice and basmati rice the lowest. Moderate amounts of various home-cooked rice are not likely to create health issues. However, the millions of dogs that eat rice every day – especially with chicken – are at risk for accumulating enough arsenic in the tissues to cause health problems.

Antagonistic Nutrients: iodine, selenium and folic acid.

Copper

Normally copper is an important nutrient for many body functions. It is necessary for iron absorption, circulation, the nervous system, brain function, hormone production, energy production, strong connective tissue, bone health and the immune system. However, if a dog becomes chronically stressed and the adrenal gland function decreases, it affects the efficiency of the liver to metabolize copper. If the stress levels don't ameliorate and the liver is toxic, the copper levels will accumulate in various body tissues and very quickly cause toxicity symptoms. Low levels of zinc and/or toxic levels of mercury can also be associated with high copper. Copper toxicity may cause behavioural problems, anxiety, phobias, depression, fatigue, joint pain, arthritis, poor dental health, blood sugar imbalances, and exhausted adrenal glands.

Copper sources include shellfish, organ meats, nuts, seeds, soy products, yeast, bone meal, vegetable oil, copper water pipes.

Antagonistic Nutrients: zinc, sulphur, manganese, molybdenum, vitamin C

Lead

Lead toxicity can adversely affect a number of body functions by interfering with hemoglobin and destroying red blood cells (anemia), displacing calcium in the bones, affecting brain neurotransmitters, inhibiting energy production, inactivating thyroid hormones, raising acid levels, and decreasing the bioavailability of zinc, manganese, copper, and iron. These actions can result in fatigue, hyperactivity, behaviour problems, depression, epilepsy, neurological symptoms, lack of concentration, anemia, kidney problems, digestive issues, constipation, joint pain, and immune conditions.

Lead exposure for dogs can occur through second hand cigarette smoke exposure, lead-based paint, lead water pipes, pesticide residues, sardines, anchovies, industrial waste, and contaminated water. Within thirty days of exposure, most lead is removed from the blood and stored in body tissues. Dogs with anemia or low iron levels will absorb more lead and dogs with a faster metabolic rate will accumulate lead faster because of the loss of calcium. However, heavy exposure to lead is not necessary for toxic symptoms to develop, especially if the nutrition is compromised.

Antagonistic Nutrients: calcium, magnesium, iron, selenium, modified citrus pectin.

Mercury

Mercury is highly toxic and becomes concentrated in the kidneys, brain, and central nervous system as well as the adrenal, thyroid, and pituitary glands. It impairs energy production in all cells and degenerates nerve fibres which can result in numbness, leg pain, visual disturbances, weakness, falling, neurological symptoms, and tremors. It can also cause skin rashes, headaches, depression, fatigue, and behavioural disturbances. Elevated mercury has a marked effect on the immune system.

The most common sources of mercury for the family dog are vaccines where it is used as a common preservative (see Chapter 8 for more information on vaccines). It is also found in fish such as tuna, swordfish, mackerel, pike and many farm-raised fish, so use caution with all-fish diets. Seeds, grains, and vegetables treated with mercury-containing fungicides also contain high mercury levels.

Antagonistic Nutrients: selenium, zinc, vitamin C, modified citrus pectin.

Thomas – From Alive to Lively

Thomas was a thirteen-year-old Rottweiler cross who was really slowing down and seemed very tired most of the time. He was unable to walk without panting and could only exercise at a normal walking pace. He was tired and depressed. Rather than blame old age, Thomas's owner, Eva, booked a long-distance consultation to assess his overall health. I was able to identify that Thomas was having a problem with parasites, he was anemic (anemia can be caused by parasites) and he had a sluggish pituitary. We started him on Para+Plus Tincture, vitamin B12 and Iron-Up as well as homeopathic remedies for his pituitary. We also changed his diet and eliminated all red meat and fish. And hemp hearts were added to his food every day for essential nutrition and energy.

Thomas at thirteen.

"Since the first day he went on Marijke's program, he started improving, steadily gaining energy and participating in life more and more every day. He became livelier and was able to run some distances; he even showed some of his goofy personality of earlier years. I am so happy about having taken the step to work with Marijke – it has given my old dog a new lease on life." —Eva Goertz

Thomas lived to be seventeen years old, and he looked younger at seventeen than he did at thirteen. Dogs don't need to get old!

Thomas at seventeen.

15. Emotions, Stress & Behaviour

Health & Lifestyle

Emotional Dogs

All dogs, no matter what age or breed, are naturally emotional and demonstrate many different emotions on a regular basis. Anxiety, fear, anger, aggression, jealousy, rivalry, impatience, irritability, frustration, protective behaviours, sadness, grief, depression, guilt, rejection, love, joy and all other emotions that humans experience are part of their lives too.

Most pet parents are tapped into the fun, companionship, and love that dogs provide but often miss the deeper elements of how the dog experiences its world. Until a pet parent learns to recognize the deeply emotional nature of dogs – and all other animals for that matter – the human-canine relationship will lack the profound and meaningful connection that our dogs are not only capable of gifting us with but are anxiously waiting for.

Thankfully, the twenty-first century shift appears to be motivating us to deepen our emotional relationships with all sentient beings including dogs, allowing us to observe and experience them on a much more profound level. This is turning out to be a huge benefit to people and dogs alike as our dogs are showing us what 'heart' and unconditional love really means. This would not be possible if we were not already accepting the deeper nature of our furry companions. I don't know about you, but I skipped the flesh and blood part a long time ago; this enabled me to understand, guide and help restore thousands of clients' dogs whose ailments were based in emotional problems. As a heart-based medical intuitive, I inwardly smile every time I read the brainchild of an academic animal psychologist who is working to prove, through clinical research, that animals feel emotions. And while proof may be required for some, I trust that you nor your animals need to be clinically studied to prove that we all have a heart and soul! But being emotional is not always easy as we know, and our loving, feeling, emotional fur babies are subject to the same stress conditions that we are with the same expressions. Negative emotions, such as fear, anxiety, or aggression, to name but a few, can create both physical and emotional health problems of all kinds resulting in uncomfortable situations for both our dogs and our households.

Stress

A stressor is an event that causes a physiological reaction known as stress. Both acute and chronic stressors are responsible for certain health conditions and contribute to almost all others. Just like people, some dogs don't get stressed at all and are able to roll with the flow, while other dogs get stressed very easily. Sensitive dogs can react to new babies, relocating or changing homes, neutering, teething, and weather changes. Ill health can also cause stress; vaccines, skin problems, immune issues, allergies, medications and/or surgeries are very traumatic for many dogs. Lifestyle stressors include confinement, isolation, neglect, puppy mills, bad breeding and abuse. Poor handling methods are also a problem for dogs as they are often punished for unwanted behaviour, rather than rewarded for desired behaviour. Improve your canine communications by telling and showing dogs what it is you would like them *to* do, instead of telling them what *not* to do. To learn more, enroll in a dog training class which uses a positive reward-based technique (less stress), rather than a dominance alpha based technique (more stress).

Another major stressor for dogs is, well, *humans*. Dogs must carry the energetic and emotional energies of their human family, a task that I'm sure no dog is ever fully prepared for. They are wolves, remember? I can assure you that there is *nothing* more stressful than living in a human household, observing and absorbing all the dynamics between these two-legged alien beings with very little hair and even fewer hunting and communication skills. Every dog, without exception, observes, absorbs, and processes every single one of your events, experiences, emotions, and relationship conflicts. Your dog could share with you a lot of helpful advice and wisdom – if only you would listen (see Chapter 16 for more information on animal communication).

~~~~~~~ 🐾 ~~~~~~~

Another major stressor for dogs is, well, humans. Dogs must carry the energetic and emotional energies of their human family, a task that I'm sure no dog is ever fully prepared for.

~~~~~~~

The brain's response to stress is the production of endorphins, feel-good chemicals produced in various parts of the brain and spinal cord in response to stress, fear, and pain. Endorphins are thought to be stronger than heroin and act to control emotions (including fear), calm the nervous system, block pain, and elevate mood from sadness and depression.

But nevertheless, stress of all kinds immediately depresses the immune system; rarely is there a health condition that is not exacerbated and/or caused by stress.

The physical response to prolonged stress occurs in three stages:

1. The alarm reaction is the so-called *fight or flight* response. It is initiated by the hypothalamus in the brain, which signals the adrenal glands to produce the stress hormones adrenaline and cortisol. Huge amounts of sugar, blood, and oxygen are delivered by increased circulation to the organs in danger; the brain becomes more alert, the muscles strengthen, and the heart pumps harder. Digestion is negatively affected as are the kidneys. If acute stress is not relieved, it will progress into the next phase – resistance.

2. The resistance reaction is a longer-term reaction whereby the pituitary and thyroid glands now begin to produce more hormones in an effort to support and regulate the over-active adrenal glands.

3. The exhaustion stage occurs when the resistance stage cannot be sustained, and the adrenals literally burn-out. Adrenal burn-out is very common with animals that have endured long periods of physical and/or emotional stress. These dogs cannot handle any kind of pressure or stimulation; they experience more depression and anxiety, and suffer more immune-related health problems. Without support, exhausted adrenal glands will usually persist even if the stressor has been removed.

Physical Ailments That Affect Emotions

Emotional imbalances are not always due to temperament, genetics, or household dynamics - unusual or undesirable behaviours in dogs are commonly blamed on breed, lack of training, handling, puppyhood, old age, and/or previous owners. While it's true that these factors can influence certain behaviours, stress and physical health are also major contributors. But we often don't make the connection between poor physical health and emotions. This is unfortunate because emotions very often determine behaviour. Sadness may cause dogs to be antisocial, grief can cause low energy or depression, resentment or fear may cause aggressive reactions, and worry or anxiety could cause an unwillingness to play or affect their appetite.

While all illnesses affect mood and energy levels, here are four common physical conditions that affect emotions and behaviour but are, nevertheless, frequently overlooked.

Anemia

This condition is one of the most common nutrient deficiencies in dogs, and too often goes undiagnosed and thus untreated. Blood tests are unreliable since they cannot test tissue levels, and even if the tests do show positive for anemia and/or iron deficiencies, many animal health practitioners look for an elusive cause of red blood cell loss rather than address dietary deficiencies and/or nutrient absorption problems with supplements. Anemia can also be caused by vitamin B12 and/or folic acid deficiencies, two very important brain and nerve nutrients (see Chapter 14). Common behavioural symptoms of anemia include fatigue, depression, lack of motivation, anxiety and an unwillingness to participate in play and exercise.

Hormone Imbalances

Hormone imbalances are rarely identified since imbalances are usually sub-clinical and are only suspected in the presence of obvious clinical diseases such as Cushing's disease or thyroid disorders. Reproductive hormones such as testosterone, estrogens, and progesterone all stimulate neurotransmitter activity in the brain and, therefore, have a direct effect on emotions and behaviour. For example, if a male dog has a high level of serum testosterone, or a mental sensitivity to testosterone, their behaviour will reflect this with aggression, irritability, biting, and/or taking offense easily. Similarly, females with low or high levels of estrogen or progesterone will exhibit symptoms of human PMS with the same patterns of irritability, aggression, and general un-wellness. Imbalances can occur in either male and female dogs whether they are spayed or neutered or not (see Chapter 10). And unless you are an experienced animal communicator, your dogs will have a hard time telling you that they feel "hormonal" or that their irritability is due to fluctuating testosterone or estrogen levels.

Blood Sugar Abnormalities & Hunger

Blood sugar problems include hypoglycemia, insulin resistance, and diabetes. Even borderline blood sugar conditions can create constant fluctuations of sugar levels and insulin production, resulting in hunger pangs, irritability, anger, and frustration. In addition, blood sugar problems, including Cushing's disease, are frequently stress induced, meaning that the symptom picture could be twofold. Blood tests cannot be relied upon here either to accurately detect sub-clinical problems affecting sugar and insulin levels. In addition, many dogs are not nutritionally satisfied with their food, fed too infrequently, not fed enough and/or fed too much of the wrong food, all of which could result in low blood sugar, hunger, anxiety, fatigue, irritability and depression.

Food Sensitivities

Food allergies and intolerances are frequent causes of behavioural problems and abnormal emotions since food reactions affect the adrenal glands, brain, and nervous system. As well, unhealthy diets result in toxic conditions that encourage unfriendly bacteria, yeast overgrowths, toxins, leaky gut, metabolic by-products, and inflammatory substances. All this can impact emotions and behaviour; toxins in the brain create chemical imbalances resulting in anxiety, depression, brain fog, obsessions, and attention deficit.

Natural Health Programs for Emotional Health

Aggressive and/or Reactive Dogs

Symptoms

Aggressive behaviour - biting, snapping, growling, baring teeth and/or sometimes attacking people or other animals.

Causes

Aggression is almost always a cover-up for fear. It can be fear of physical or emotional harm to the dog or its loved one, fear of hunger, and/or fear of territory take-over (which is really about food or mating).

Unfortunately, most of the canine aggression that we see has been caused by humans. Wolves, for example, are shy and introverted with very soft energy. They also tend to be more *flighty* (as opposed to fighty) and, of course, more fearful of humans. Dogs have evolved to be more social and outgoing, but they have also become more aggressive over time and are responsible for hundreds of thousands of bites and/or attacks every year, some of them fatal. Wolves, on the other hand, have never once been documented with an attack on a human except by a wolf in captivity or ones that have been foolishly released. Granted, there are more dogs than wolves living with humans, but this does not account for the changes in behaviour. What *does* account for aggressive behaviour in dogs is breeding, lifestyle, and handling. And of course, the personality of the dog owner. Angry, irritable owner; angry, irritable dog.

~~~~~~~~ ❧ ~~~~~~~~

Unfortunately, most of the canine aggression that we see has been caused by humans. Wolves, by contrast, are shy and introverted with very soft energy.

~~~~~~~~~~~~~~~~

Historically, certain breeds were popularized and bred by humans for their aggressive characteristics, and those characteristics were then perpetuated by how the dogs were conditioned and handled. Then as dogs continued to be domesticated, many of them were confined, isolated, underfed, and maltreated, all of which resulted in highly stressed dogs, some of whom reacted with offensive behaviour – especially if it was already in their breeding. Why did humans seek to create aggressive dogs? Because humans too were afraid. They were afraid of theft, personal attacks, starvation, territorial boundaries, personal boundaries, low self-esteem, and a shortage of females. Like human, like dog.

Aggression can also be caused by health problems, lack of exercise, lack of socialization, unnecessary confinement, food, pain, a damaged nervous system, nervous disorders, high anxiety, vaccinosis, medications, history of abuse, and extreme hypersensitivity to noise, touch, or even odors.

Natural Health Program

Diet

- Conventional experts insist that high levels of dietary meat, raw meat, and/or bones have no impact or influence over increasing aggressive behaviour in dogs. However, from an energetic standpoint, aggressive dogs can be stimulated by anything that awakens their primitive DNA codes and signals them to fight for their food and/or for their territory to protect their food (or their pack). Thus, the scent of blood and the action of tearing into a chunk of meat is more likely to be a behavioural catalyst than lapping up a bowl of vegetable soup. Furthermore, parents of vegetarian dogs, report that the temperament of their dogs change as they slowly lose their taste for flesh and blood and, therefore, their desire to hunt and kill, making them friendlier and gentler companions with all animals, large or small. It could, therefore, be beneficial to eliminate or reduce meat, organ meats, and bones for problem reactive dogs, particularly red meats such as beef, bison, venison, or elk. And while putting a dog on a vegetarian diet may go against everything you believe in, know that if what you are doing now isn't working, some kind of change is in order. One step ahead is better than no steps at all. You could save a dog's life.

- Identify any food triggers that could cause foul moods.

- Add essential fatty acids, such as hemp seeds, chia seeds, flaxseeds and/or salmon oil to the diet to support brain health.

- Ensure that the dog is getting enough to eat or is feeling satisfied with the meals; hunger and/or dissatisfaction may create irritability, anger, and aggression.

Nutrients

- **magnesium citrate** [*one dose daily*]†* – promotes relaxation in dogs with nervous tension, irritability and aggression

- **folic acid** [*one dose daily*]† – nutrient for nerves and stress, promotes mental wellness

- **vitamin B12** [*one dose daily*]†* – important nutrient for dogs with nervousness, irritability, fatigue and stress; promotes mental wellness and energy

- Have a hair tissue mineral analysis conducted to test for toxic heavy metals; toxic levels of lead, aluminum, cadmium, manganese, and copper are associated with violence and/or aggression

Herbal & Home Remedies

- **belladonna 200C, homeopathic** [*one dose daily for 4 days, then as needed*]† – sudden and explosive anger, epilepsy; desire to bite, strike and pull; fear of other dogs

- **chamomila 200C, homeopathic** [*one dose daily for 7 days, then as needed*]† – angry dogs; biting, fear biting, hypersensitivity to pain and touch, nervous irritability, and hostility

- **staphysagria 1M, homeopathic** [*one dose daily for 5 days*][†] – dogs with a history of physical abuse, emotional suppression, abandonment and unreleased anger; can rage in later stages

- **stramonium 200C, homeopathic** [*one dose daily for 4 days*][†] – promotes emotional balance in dogs who are aggressive as a result of nervous disorders such as epilepsy, hyperactivity or fevers; dogs who fear death, water, the dark, and being alone

- **poison oak flower essence** [*2 to 4 drops, twice daily (morning and bedtime)*][††] – dogs prone to fight, rather than flight; for dogs with fear of intimate contact or bonding, dogs who are protective of personal boundaries, dogs with fear of being violated, hostile dogs

- **vine flower essence** [*2 to 4 drops, twice daily (morning and bedtime)*][††] – dogs who like to domineer and dictate, are intolerant and/or selfish dogs

- **willow flower essence** [*2 to 4 drops, twice daily (morning and bedtime)*][††] – dogs who are resentful, angry, bitter and irritable; dogs who hold grudges or carry a victim mentality

Riva's Remedies

- **Calm & Cool, herbal blend** [*one dose once or twice daily*][†] – promotes recovery in dogs with a hyperactive nervous system and/or adrenal stress

- **Calm-Aid, homeopathic** [*one dose two - three times daily*][†] - helps calm nervous behaviour and promotes relaxation

[†]See Appendix for recommended dosages and duration for all supplements.
[††]See Appendix for more information on flower essences for dogs.
[*]Also available as a Riva's Remedy

Lifestyle Notes

- Ensure regular exercise.

- Keep confinement and isolation to an absolute minimum.

- Work on socialization with dogs and people.

- Hire a competent dog trainer experienced with reactive dogs.

- Work on your own anger management and/or tendencies to irritability and aggression.

- Never punish a dog for being aggressive or reactive; remember, aggression is a fear-based behaviour, and violence begets violence. Anyone who thinks that punishing a reactive dog is an effective tool has a poor understanding of the dog's mental and emotional underpinnings (or their own for that matter).

Anxiety, Fear, and Adrenal Burn-Out

Symptoms

Dogs can be afraid of a lot of things: being alone (separation anxiety), loud noises, fireworks, doorbells, thunder, wind, heights, grooming, veterinary appointments, kids, men, strangers, fighting, yelling, other dogs, and riding in cars. Anxiety symptoms can include cowering, hiding, trembling, barking, biting, growling, running away, excitement, urinating, excessive licking, hyper-vigilance, and/or hyperactivity. Some dogs will even leap into bed with you, especially during a thunderstorm or fireworks. And some dogs have a free-floating anxiety causing them to be afraid of everything, which results in a state of chronic anxiety. This is often due to adrenal burn-out and they are less able to cope with even minor stressors. If fear escalates to extreme symptoms, with panic and anxiety attacks, the fear is known as a phobia.

Chronic or acute anxiety can also lead to OCD (obsessive compulsive disorder) behaviours. OCD dogs engage in repetitive behaviours when stressed, such as licking, circling, and tail chasing, or chewing. Many dogs with OCD also have burned out adrenal glands (see Chapter 10 for adrenal health programs).

Causes

There are many causes which underlie fear and anxiety. It may require astute observation, experience, and even intuitive communications to exactly identify what is causing a specific animal to be afraid.

- **insecurity** is often caused by early weaning, premature separation from mother, and lack of early socialization including deprivation of play with other puppies
- **lack of confidence**
- **abandonment issues**
- **confusion**
- **boredom**

- lack of exercise
- **housebound dogs** – dogs need regular outings to familiarize themselves with the world and with new things
- **lack of training**, for mental activity and learning builds confidence
- **lack of purpose** – give your dogs a job to do
- **trauma or abuse** from the past
- **adrenal burn-out** which makes it very hard to cope with stress, no matter how small
- **diet** is especially problematic with senior dogs who suddenly demonstrate symptoms of newfound anxiety; in most cases this is due to reactions to their food which they can no longer metabolize efficiently (either commercial kibble or high protein levels)
- **poor immunity** (see Chapter 7)
- **blood sugar imbalances** and **Cushing's disease** (see Chapter 10)
- **neurological conditions** (see Chapter 13)
- **medications**, especially if the anxiety appeared shortly after starting them
- **unpredictable behaviours in the household**
- **separation anxiety** when people leave
- **sponging behaviours** from nervous, anxious, and unconfident human parents (see Chapter 16)

Natural Health Program

Diet

- Identify any food triggers that lead to nervous behaviour. Food allergies and/or intolerances commonly cause nervousness and anxiety. Change the food or cook at home as a trial.

- For senior dogs, eliminate all commercial food and meat except for fish and eggs. Make home-cooked meals. Senior dogs are prone to anxiety caused from poor metabolism of protein and/or commercial food.

- Avoid wheat and corn gluten.

- Add essential fatty acids by way of hemp seeds, chia seeds, flaxseeds, evening primrose oil and/or hemp oil to the diet to support nerve health.

- Ensure that the dog is getting enough to eat; hunger and/or dissatisfaction cause blood sugar fluctuations and adrenaline surges with trembling, anxiety, and fear.

Nutrients

- **magnesium citrate** [*one dose daily*]†* – promotes relaxation in nervous dogs and dogs with nervous tension and irritability
- **folic acid** [*one dose daily*]† – vitamin support for nerves and stress, promotes mental wellness
- **vitamin B12** [*one dose daily*]†* – nutrient for dogs with nervous tension, anxiety and low energy; promotes mental wellness
- **potassium citrate** [*one dose daily*]† – supports adrenal function and helps maintain pH levels reducing acidity

Herbal & Home Remedies

- **arsenicum 30C, homeopathic** [*one dose (2 or 3 pellets) twice daily for 7 days*]† – dogs who experience anxiety and panic attacks with trembling and restlessness, fears going outside; insecure dogs, fears being alone

- **chamomila 200C, homeopathic** [*one dose (2 or 3 pellets) daily for 7 days, then as needed*]† – dogs with anxiety, worry, nervous irritability, hypersensitivity to pain and touch; dogs who fear bite

- **natrum muriaticum 30C, homeopathic** [*one dose (2 or 3 pellets) once or twice daily for 4 days*]† – dogs with the following fears: the dark, strangers, burglars, people at the door, heights and wind storms; claustrophobia and sensitivity to noise

- **phosphorus 30C, homeopathic** [*one dose (2 or 3 pellets) daily for 4 days, then as needed*]† – dogs who suffer anxiety when left alone or who are easily startled, for fear of the dark or loud noises, especially thunderstorms or fireworks; fears water and earthquakes; for dogs who may sometimes appear "spaced out", phosphorus dogs are enthusiastic and love company

- **evening primrose flower essence** [*2 to 4 drops, twice daily (morning and bedtime)*]†† –dogs with feelings of rejection and abandonment; history of neglect or abuse

- **lavender flower essence** [*2 to 4 drops, twice daily (morning and bedtime)*]†† – promotes calming in dogs or are easily overwhelmed or overstimulated; high-strung with spiritual sensitivity

- **bleeding heart flower essence** [*2 to 4 drops, twice daily (morning and bedtime)*]†† – separation anxiety when people or dog friends leave or die; grief and loss

- pink yarrow flower essence [*2 to 4 drops, twice daily (morning and bedtime)*] †† – dogs who pick up emotional and psychic negativity from other animals or people resulting in nervous or emotional overwhelm

Riva's Remedies

- **Calm & Cool, herbal blend** [*one dose daily*]† – promotes recovery in dogs with a hyperactive nervous system, extreme fear and/or adrenal stress

- **Calm-Aid, homeopathic formula** [*Acute: One dose every 2 hours. Chronic: One dose twice daily or use as needed*]† – promotes calming in dogs who dislike car rides, loud noises, grooming, visitors and/or medical appointments; separation anxiety and/or general nervousness

†See Appendix for recommended dosages and duration for all supplements.
††See Appendix for more information on flower essences for dogs.
*Also available as a Riva's Remedy

Lifestyle Notes

- Ensure regular exercise, and get your dog out of the house more often.

- Keep confinement to an absolute minimum and avoid boredom.

- Work on socialization with other dogs and people.

- Get them out of their heads by taking them outside and giving them a job to do such as pick up a slipper, get the newspaper, visit a sick neighbour, keep another dog company... dogs need a purpose just like we do.

- Practice regular bodywork, such as reiki, acupuncture, massage and energy healing.

- Play soft, soothing music.

- Diffuse essential oils such as lavender, ylang-ylang, orange or bergamot

- Work on your own fears and anxieties and work towards peace and harmony in the household.

Depression

Symptoms

Dogs who are feeling depressed will sleep more, eat less, feel tired and lethargic, appear bored, lose their motivation to play or go for walks, become clingy or detached, and may lose or gain weight.

Causes

Boredom, lack of purpose, lack of exercise, grief from the loss of a friend (be it human or animal) unhealed trauma, abandonment, abuse, adrenal burn-out, a dog attack or a physical injury. Senior dogs often feel depressed because they can no longer fulfill their duties as an active companion or guard dog. Poor diet, nutrient deficiencies, diabetes, Cushing's disease, immune disorders, and anemia are also common causes of depression. Some dogs will also get depressed if they don't like their food – not surprising. And many, many dogs are depressed because their pet parents are depressed.

Natural Health Program

Diet

- Make a diet change, especially if the dog has been eating the same food or protein staple for a very long time. Food allergies and/or intolerances can impact mood. Try a home-cooked diet as a trial.

- Eliminate all wheat and corn gluten products, both common culprits in depression and fatigue.

- Add essential fatty acids to the diet to support brain health: hemp seeds, chia seeds, flaxseed, evening primrose oil, hemp oil or cooked fish

Nutrients

- **folic acid** [*one dose daily*]† – supports nerves, brain function and promotes wellness in dogs with depression, fatigue, and stress

- **vitamin B12** [*one dose daily*]†* – promotes mental wellness in dogs with fatigue, depression and nervousness; nutrition for anemia and metabolism

Herbal & Home Remedies

- **ignatia 200C, homeopathic** [*one dose daily for 7 days, then as needed*]† – depression after grief, dogs who are easily hurt or offended, frequent sighing, fear of rejection

- **natrum muriaticum 30C, homeopathic** [*one dose once or twice daily for 4 days*][†] – silent grief and depression from sadness, nat mur dogs prefer to be alone and dislike sympathy, can be irritable

- **gorse flower essence** [*2 to 4 drops, twice daily (morning and bedtime)*][††] – feelings of hopelessness with an expectation of suffering, pessimism

- **gentian flower essence** [*2 to 4 drops, twice daily (morning and bedtime)*][††] – discouragement after a setback, such as a trauma, injury, or disappointment; helps regain confidence

- **bleeding heart flower essence** [*2 to 4 drops, twice daily (morning and bedtime)*][††] – separation distress or loss of a loved one

- **evening primrose flower essence** [*2 to 4 drops, twice daily (morning and bedtime)*][††] –feelings of rejection and abandonment; history of abuse; good remedy for rescue dogs

Riva's Remedies

- **Calm & Cool, herbal blend** [*one dose daily*][†] – promotes recovery in dogs with adrenal burn-out

- **Calm-Aid, homeopathic formula** [*One dose twice daily or use as needed*][†] – promotes calming in dogs who suffer anxiety with depression

- **Iron-Up (iron gluconate)** [*one dose daily*][†*] – anemic dogs with fatigue, depression, compromised brain function, and poor circulation

Lucy Grieves

Lucy was a springer spaniel/border collie whose best friend was a cocker spaniel named Doogie. Lucy and Doogie lived together for many years until Doogie suffered kidney problems and died at age eleven. After Doogie died, Lucy's pet parent noticed that Lucy became depressed and tired and did not seem to be enjoying her usual activities. She just lay in her basket and moped. A week later, Lucy still was not feeling any better, so her parent dropped into our homeopathic clinic to see if there was anything that we could offer. She was sent home with Bleeding Heart flower Essence and homeopathic Ignatia 30C. Lucy's response was quick. Within 48 hours, she was back to her old self and out hunting for pocket gophers in the field and enjoying her agility classes.

- **Vital Force, herbal blend** [*one dose daily*][†] - promotes vitality, stamina and mental wellness; physical and nervous fatigue

[†]See Appendix for recommended dosages and duration for all supplements.
[††]See Appendix for more information on flower essences for dogs.
[*]Also available as a Riva's Remedy

Lifestyle Notes

- Ensure regular exercise; a healthy brain and nervous system needs movement.

- Keep your dogs busy both mentally and physically.

- Keep confinement to an absolute minimum and avoid boredom.

- Give your dog a purpose, such as helping with chores, picking up the mail, bringing your slippers, greeting visitors and so on.

- Spend quality time with your dogs through walking, swimming, playing, hiking, agility or other canine activities organized for dogs.

- Work on healing your own depression. This is very important for many of you. Like dog, like owner – and your dogs *want* you to feel good too.

Lucy.

Rudy's Release

One woman named Lauren had a very sensitive, loyal ten-year-old golden cocker spaniel named Rudy. Lauren and her husband had recently moved and were getting settled into a new town and new jobs. Shortly after moving, Rudy began to have episodes of diarrhea with no apparent cause or reason, and Rudy was physically healthy in all other ways. Lauren tried a variety of different diet changes and supplements to calm Rudy's digestion and to bulk up his stool with more fibre. But diet changes didn't help and Lauren's husband was verbally punishing Rudy for having accidents in the house, which worsened the problem and frustrated Lauren. But Lauren was noticing that she was becoming increasingly frustrated with her marriage of many years for other reasons as well. And instead of expressing or communicating her needs, she suppressed all her feelings *including* anger. Lauren was focussed on her own emotional problems, of course, and had no idea that Rudy, who was very bonded to her, was becoming increasingly upset and anxious with the interactions between his pet parents. The relationship stress was building up for Rudy too, and he was becoming increasingly nervous and internalizing *his* feelings as well. Many of the emotions relating to disruptive relationships are contained in the second chakra, and so, not surprisingly, the diarrhea was his release. In time, Lauren began to recognize that she needed to make changes both within herself and within her relationship. Around the same time Rudy's diarrhea began to quiet down, but it wasn't until many months later, when she and her husband no longer lived together, that she made the connection to the timing of Rudy's diarrhea and her own personal catharsis.

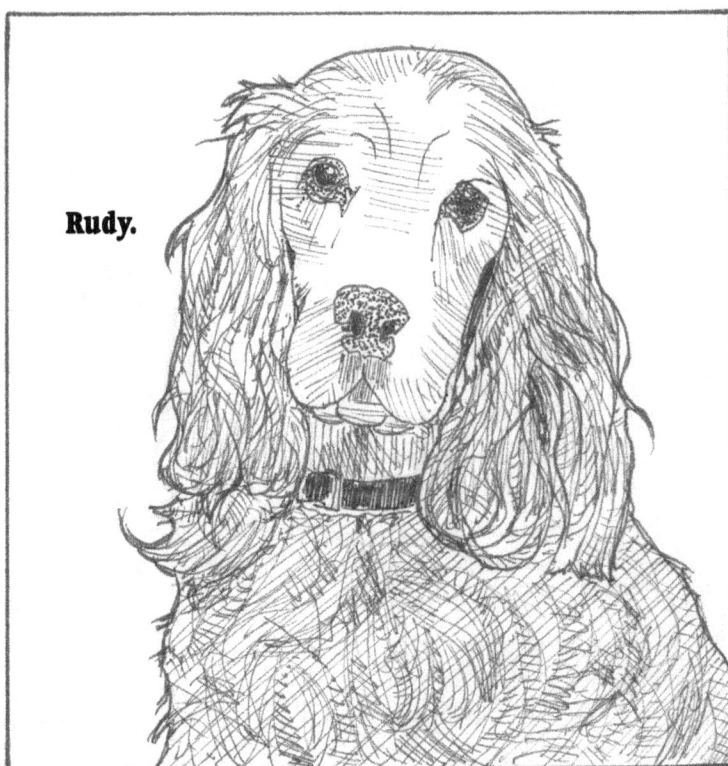

Rudy.

Healing Dogs Their Way

16. The Breeding Game
Stop the Madness

The Domestication of Dogs

Remains of wolf bones have been found in caves and other locations dated back to as early as 400,000 years ago. The ancient ancestry of dogs was once thought to be a prehistoric Eurasian gray wolf that lived in Europe or Asia anywhere between 9,000 to 34,000 years ago. However, with modern genetic research techniques, scientists have determined that both dogs and wolves share a common ancestor, rather than a direct lineage, so it is possible that the ancestral wolf is much older. The earliest finding of a truly domesticated dog was uncovered in a grave in Germany that dates back 14,000 years ago.

Modern dogs (*Canis lupus familiaris*) share 98.9% of their DNA with the gray wolf (*Canis lupus*) with whom they share a common ancestor. This is approximately the same genetic correlation as humans and chimpanzees, who too share common ancestry though not as direct.

Most specific dog breeds have roots that only go back about 200 years, however; since cross-breeding didn't accelerate until the nineteenth century. Some experts believe that the first fully distinct breed was the saluki, also called the Arabian greyhound, whose name translates to "noble". (I owned a saluki cross at one time; he was highly intuitive and high strung, he could outrun rabbits, keep up to fast-moving cars, climb ladders, and jump 6 foot smooth fences.) It didn't take long for humans to develop the nearly 400 different breeds found today. This evolution of breeds has been primarily based on human need and preferences for dogs that could hunt, shepherd, guard (bark), work, and provide companionship; thousands of years ago, the Romans even owned lapdogs.

Anthropologist Rob Losey, in his research, found dogs in the Siberian Arctic that were buried alongside their humans in cemeteries from 5,000 to 8,000 years old. Some of these dogs were wearing decorative collars or had special objects placed near them. He found that there were more dog burials in prehistory than there were of horses or cats. Not only were these dogs important partners to their humans, but they were possibly thought of as higher spiritual beings. And chemical analysis of the bones also showed that ancient dogs in Siberia were fed the same diet as humans. But sadly, humans have also used dogs for food, as they have done periodically throughout history including today's world.

―――――― 🐾 ――――――

> Not only were these dogs important partners to their humans, but they were possibly thought of as higher spiritual beings.

―――――――――――

And recent findings have discovered engravings carved into a sandstone cliff in Saudi Arabia which depicts dogs with lines running from their necks to a man's waist. These are thought to be leashes tethered to a hunter armed with a bow and arrow, suggesting that humans mastered the art of training dogs many thousands of years earlier than previously thought. This dog art is thought to be at least 8,000 to 9,000 years old making them the earliest depictions of domestic dogs.

It's possible that, in the beginning, humans hunted the wolf for their furs and meat. However, it is likely that the wolves also became scavengers on human refuse around their settlements. From here it is theorized that

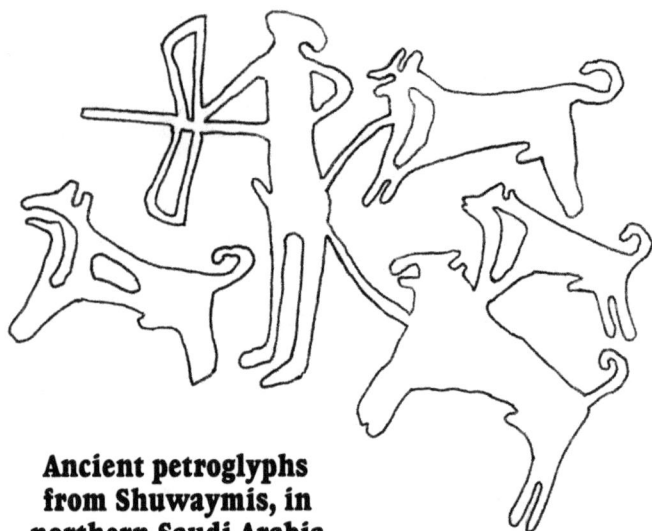

Ancient petroglyphs from Shuwaymis, in northern Saudi Arabia

wolf puppies – or even young, sociable, adults – could be captured, tamed and trained as companions, workmates, guards, sled dogs, or for tracking during hunts. The wolf had many useable skills and talents. And perhaps only wolves of a calmer, more submissive nature would have been suitable for taming and training, leaving the stronger-minded, aggressive and/or skittish animals out of the domestic evolutionary chain. And so the selective breeding of dogs began. And while some of the other wolf descendants died out, the dog herself grew into a distinct subspecies significantly affected by the presence, interactions, behaviours, and emotions of humans – both consciously and unconsciously. We fed them, bred them, and then spread them from continent to continent. It's true, we invented the dog. How exciting is that? And we did it through artificial selection, perhaps *not* so exciting. Read on...

Do wolves make good pets?

The short answer is no. *Canis lupus familiaris* diverged and developed thousands of years ago, and their shared history with humans has forged a profound bond between our species. No other subspecies of wolf shares that bond. As a result, wolves do not make good pets. And this is not to suggest that dogs are somehow intrinsically *better* than wolves; no animal is better or worse than any other animal. But if you are talking about suitability – to an environment or circumstance – some animals are *unquestionably* more suitable. Dogs make good pets because they have developed alongside humans for thousands of

generations. Wolves don't make good pets because they haven't. It's as simple as that.

Even wolf-dog hybrids are a challenge depending on what percentage of wolf genes they carry. Many people have acquired a wolf or wolf hybrid based on their fantasies only to find out that the training is beyond their capabilities or that the animal has no interest in pleasing its human owner, or that it has become a threat to other dogs and children. Even highly socialized wolves will never bond to humans like dogs do – given the chance they will choose to bond with other dogs first. Unlike my mixed breed two-year-old rescue who, despite repeated attempts by local and hopeful coyotes to lure her into the bush and pair up, she continues to choose me as her partner.

And unfortunately, when the human wolf owners are unable to cope, the wolf is either passed off onto another bad home, sentenced to a life in a cage or on a chain, or released into the wild in the middle of the night where it is sure to die of starvation or be shot because of its familiarity with people. And while some of you may know some success stories, they are outnumbered by the problem stories.

Either way, it doesn't benefit the wolf. The role of the domestic dog is very different from the role of the wolf. A dog is here to interact and work with humans in a social human environment; the purpose of the wolf is to act as an ambassador for the Earth, which it cannot do tied up in your back yard. Let wolves live as wolves as they have been doing since time immemorial.

～～～ 🐾 ～～～

Even highly socialized wolves will never bond to humans like dogs do – given the chance they will choose to bond with other dogs first.

～～～～～～～～

Healing Dogs Their Way

Breeding: License to Breed or License to Kill?

There are 400 dog breeds in existence today, and the American Kennel Club recognizes 187 of them although only a few of these are the most popular. Given the close genetic relationship to wolves, this diversity is nothing short of amazing. Long hair, short hair, no hair, tall, short, fluffy, small, large, giant, long faces, squished in faces, short legs, long legs, fat, skinny, big ears, no ears, bushy tails and screw tails...and anything else that you can imagine. And in recent years, designer breeding has become a new trend. In fact, it's currently fashionable to breed dogs to look like other animals or dolls all for the idle amusement of human consumer culture. After all, "cute" sells. And of course, what breeding can't accomplish outright can sometimes be accomplished with the knife. Off with those tails, crop back those ears. There... *so* much cuter.

It's barbaric.

While diversity of appearance may capture your heart (and fill up Instagram), the whole matter of breeding dogs is often disturbing and grotesque. Here's how selective breeding practices have hurt the entire dog species - likely including the dog sitting at your feet right now.

Breeding for Pedigree

The continuous search to create the perfect canine drives an incessant and ambitious need to keep breeding pedigree, i.e. pure bloodlines of the highest quality. We can understand how our own ancestors selectively bred the first few dogs to assist them with a challenging lifestyle focused on mere survival. Success at hunting, tracking, herding, searching and guarding would often decide the difference between life and death. But in today's world, physical survival is not usually dependent on a dog. Rather, most breeding is intended to change the appearance of the dogs to conform to kennel club standards for showing purposes - standards which are mostly based on the whims of human opinion.

Will dogs ever be perfect enough? Apparently not. Kennel club standards are not interested in emotional health, temperament, or behaviours; they are interested in physical appearance. In fact, one official commented that consumers should look for the breed standard so they know what their new dog will look like. Really? But even the breed standard is no longer perfect enough anymore. Dogs are continually bred to so-called perfection and if that isn't perfect enough they can be subjected to plastic surgery! Dogs are having their ears perked up, their noses fixed, their faces lifted and are receiving testicular implants to help neutered dogs regain their masculinity! In 2011, dog parents spent over $62 million dollars in plastic surgery for their dogs.

But even more serious are the health problems that we have propagated. Statistics are obviously difficult to calculate but one American veterinarian went on record to say that nine out of every ten purebred dogs in her office had at least one genetic disease. No health standards for breeding exists, and the insatiable quest for the perfect "pedigree" has seriously affected the health and lifestyle of millions of dogs. These suffering and disabled animals cannot be helped, even with plastic surgery.

❧

No health standards for breeding exists, and the insatiable quest for the perfect "pedigree" has seriously affected the health and lifestyle of millions of dogs.

Here are some of the most common diseases and health disorders that we human "caretakers" have propagated through careless, inconsiderate, and indiscriminate breeding.

- Many dog breeds are prone to heart conditions, many of them fatal. The most common heart problems in dogs are diseased valves and makes up 75 percent of all heart disease in dogs. It affects small breeds over the age of five: Cavalier King Charles spaniel, dachshund, miniature poodles, Shih Tzu, Maltese, Chihuahua, cocker spaniels, miniature schnauzers, and Pomeranians. Congenital mitral valve diseases affect the larger breeds: bull terrier, Great Dane, German shepherd, Rottweiler, Labrador retriever and Weimaraner.

- A weak, dilated heart accounts for 8 percent of heart disease and affects primarily large breed dogs: Doberman pinscher, boxer, Scottish deerhound, Irish wolfhound, Great Dane, Saint Bernard, Afghan hound, golden retriever and cocker spaniel.

- Pulmonary stenosis describes valves that are blocked and narrowed which can cause either murmurs, arrhythmias and/or congestive heart failure. Stenosis affects the English bulldog, mastiff, Scottish terrier, Samoyed, wirehaired fox terrier, miniature schnauzer, West Highland white terrier, beagle, Chihuahua, cocker spaniel, boxer, Newfoundland and Rottweiler.

- Some heart vessels don't close in puppies just after birth – this results in a 50 percent mortality rate. Known as patent ductus arteriosus it affects the cocker spaniel, English springer spaniel, German shepherd, Maltese terrier, poodle, Pomeranian, collie, Shetland sheepdog and Australian cattle dog.

- Breeding dogs that are abnormally large and fast-growing puts them at risk for bone and joint problems, hip dysplasia, bloating, thyroid problems, heart problems and cancer. Extra-large breed dogs also tend to have a shorter life span. Think Great Danes, Newfoundlands, and St. Bernards, mastiffs, wolfhounds and Leonbergers.

- Large breeds are frequently affected by hip and elbow dysplasia and cruciate ligament problems: German shepherds, Rottweilers, Great Danes, St. Bernards, bulldogs, mastiffs, Newfoundlands, American Staffordshire terriers, Labrador retrievers, Old English sheepdogs, Alaskan Malamutes and Samoyeds.

- Some breeds have more joint and cartilage problems than others: dachshunds, bulldogs and basset hounds, are genetically predisposed to these problems.

- Osteoarthritis frequently occurs from sloping backs and lower hindquarters particularly in German shepherds whose stance is now completely abnormal but still sought after in the show ring.

- Long dogs suffer from frequent back problems: dachshund, beagle, basset hounds, corgis, bulldogs, French bulldogs, Cavalier King Charles spaniels and Shih Tzu.

- Breeding small and frail toy breeds or "teacup" puppies results in mothers who die in childbirth, liver shunts, blood sugar problems, heart problems, soft spots on the skull, seizures, respiratory problems, digestive problems, blindness, seizures, limb deformities and broken bones to name but a few. Cute, huh?

- Many dogs have eye problems including cherry eye, cataracts, glaucoma and corneal ulcers. Some eye conditions can lead to partial or total blindness. English springer spaniels, Siberian huskies, miniature poodles, collies, Boston terriers and German shepherds.

- Flat faces result in severe breathing disorders, dental problems, heart problems, and an inability to regulate temperature in hot weather: French bulldogs, English bulldogs, Boston terriers, pugs, Cavalier King Charles spaniels, Shih Tzus and boxers.

- Dogs with excessively loose skin forming folds on their face or body are more likely to suffer from painful skin conditions and/or sore eyes: Neapolitan mastiffs, bloodhounds, shar-peis, boxers and French bulldogs.

- Some breeds are prone to seizures because their skulls are too small for their large brains. This frequently happens with small dogs bred to look like dolls: Brussels griffon, Cavalier King Charles spaniels, Chihuahuas and their crosses.

- Other dog breeds prone to general seizures/epilepsy include small breeds such as beagles, dachshunds, cocker spaniels, poodles, miniature schnauzers and fox terriers; as well as larger breeds such as Siberian huskies, Irish setters, Labrador retrievers and St. Bernards.

- Some breeds are unable to mate or give birth without Caesarians. English bulldogs and French bulldogs have heads that are too big for the birth canals. How natural is that?

- Some breeds have continuing problems with bladder or kidney stones: miniature schnauzers. Shih Tzus, bichon frises, miniature poodles, cocker spaniels, Yorkshire terriers, Lhasa Apsos and deerhounds.

- Some large breeds have a life expectancy as low as 6 years: mastiffs, Great Danes, Bernese mountain dogs and Irish wolfhounds.

- Many dogs have very strong impulses to herd, hunt, chase, and fight often whereby they end up at rescue facilities – or worse – because they are too difficult to manage for the uninformed buyer in an average suburban home.

- And then there are the many dogs bred that produce offspring who are reactive, irritable, fear-biters, human aggressive, dog aggressive, anxious, high-strung and/or fearful. And no, our dogs are not expected to be perfect, but at least let's give them a good running start.

In summary, here are the top ten dogs who are reported to have the most health issues. I hesitated to include this list at all since these congenitally sick dogs are suffering through enough troubles without us adding a further "stigma" to their breed. But without knowledge of their predicaments we cannot begin to take action to stop the insanity of breeding dogs which knowingly cause them a lifetime of suffering. The most common reasons why people turn pets over to shelters or humane societies are because of problematic behaviours, aggressive behaviours, the dogs grew larger than expected, or the dog's health problems were more than the pet parent could handle.

1. Cocker spaniels - epilepsy, heart disease, liver disease, eye diseases, knee problems, hip dysplasia, skin problems, ear infections, kidney stones, allergies and immune problems.

2. German shepherds - hip dysplasia, cruciate ligament problems, osteoarthritis, anal fistulas, esophageal weakness, degenerative myelopathy, exocrine pancreatic deficiency, panosteitis, pancreatitis, cancer, skin problems, cataracts and epilepsy.

3. Bulldogs - this breed is considered the most extreme example of genetic manipulation in the dog-breeding world. They suffer respiratory problems, elbow dysplasia, internalized tail, heart problems, cherry eye, skin problems, allergies, poor digestion, gas and over-heating.

4. Golden retrievers - hip/elbow dysplasia, lymphoma, hemangiosarcoma, allergies, skin conditions, heart problems, and cataracts.

5. St. Bernards - bone cancer, eye problems and heart disorders.

6. Basset hounds - joint problems, elbow dysplasia, immune conditions, eye problems and blood disorders.

7. Labrador retrievers - cancer, hip dysplasia, cruciate ligaments, exercise-induced collapse, muscular dystrophy and obesity.

8. Rottweilers - epilepsy, bone diseases, hip dysplasia, heart problems, cruciate ligaments and cancer.

9. Newfoundlands - heart issues, hip and elbow dysplasia.

10. Miniature poodles - eye problems such as cataracts and glaucoma, epilepsy and bone degeneration

Over half of all dogs are purebreds, and many of them come from mass breeders. Unfortunately, many buyers believe that they are buying a sophisticated and refined dog of the highest quality who is in the best of health. A registration certificate does not guarantee *any* of these standards. And unfortunately, mixed breed dogs now suffer relatively high rates of genetic disease as well because of their discernible purebred parentage. And despite the claims to the contrary breeding dogs with known health problems is not, in any way, improving the breed nor the lives of the pet parents. Breeding dogs with known health problems should be outlawed. Period.

If you love dogs stop buying dogs with known health problems. Or, better yet, rescue one of the nearly 2,000 shelter dogs - purebreds and mixed breeds - that are euthanized every day. And do not, do not purchase dogs from "back-yard" breeders, animal hoarders, pet stores, or puppy mills thinking that you are rescuing a dog from a bad situation. Put them out of business! Someone has to speak for the dogs - will it be you?

And if you are a breeder reading this take a step back and do the right thing.

In-Breeding

Dog breeding is the practice of mating two dogs based either on a specific valued breed characteristic expressed by both dogs and their combined adherence to a set of breed characteristic or aesthetics. This is how breeds are developed and maintained.

Some people have strong emotional attachments to specific breeds. Some merely have their own subjective associations with certain breeds. Some people want a certain breed of dog for what they perceive that breed will say about them - a "brand" as it were. Some people want a specific breed based on what they've heard or read about that breed's behavioral characteristic. And yet other people - many people - want a specific breed of dog based on nothing more than their looks. In other words, many people don't just want a dog, they want a certain breed of dog.

But that is human nature; where choice is available, we want to choose. Unfortunately, that demand for choice comes at a price.

The more valued a particular breed characteristic is or the more rigorous the standards of overall breed conformity are, the smaller the pool of dogs will be considered "viable" as breeders. This naturally leads to what is known as in-breeding, which is to say the breeding of closely related dogs, such as brother/sister or mother/son. It is estimated, for instance, that all of Britain's 10,000 pugs are descended from 50 individuals.

The problem with splashing around in a gene pool that is artificially shallow is that it's not only the desirous characteristics that are amplified. Genetic predispositions to a host of health issues also become amplified and intrinsic to the breed. Robust health and well-rounded behavioural characteristics require the contribution of a deep pool of genetic diversity.

In-bred dogs have more immune problems and therefore contract more illnesses including infections, colds, viruses and digestive ailments. This is particularly relevant since more and more dogs are being diagnosed with immune-mediated type health conditions. In-bred dogs are also predisposed to joint conditions, inflammations, and arthritis-type conditions. They also have more behavioural problems, are less easy to control, and are frequently more aggressive because they bite, chase, and play rough.

In-breeding is an intolerable practice which cannot be continued to be ignored. It's time that we show respect and take responsibility for the massive amount of suffering that we inflict on our dogs in the name of whim and fashion. Manipulating and exploiting dogs as commodities for economic gain and entertainment value should be outlawed along with breeding health problems. Period. Our dogs deserve so much more.

Can we reverse the damage? Short of stopping the practice altogether, it's highly unlikely. The restrictive gene pools pose a huge challenge for any breeders who might try and tentatively reintroduce healthier traits back into the population (i.e. reverse breeding) while maintaining the breed. The best thing we can do as consumers is to stop buying faulty purebreds animals. We need to start accepting dogs – all dogs – just as other dogs do, as beautiful individuals deserving of love, respect and good health.

~~~~~ 🐾 ~~~~~

Manipulating and exploiting dogs as commodities for economic gain and entertainment value should be outlawed along with breeding health problems.

~~~~~

Extinction

When wild animals go extinct, it's often due to circumstance as in loss of natural habitat, food or chemical pollution. But a domestic dog's natural habitat is the world of humans. Historically, people have bred dogs to perform a job or a function without any aesthetic guidelines. But eventually the need for our dogs to perform utilitarian work – pulling sleds, catching rats, baiting bulls, herding boars, and hunting foxes, for example – vanished with the times and their professional roles disappeared. So bring in the Victorian age where the British now wanted to breed dogs that would symbolize their social status and reflect their perceived nobility. Not very different from owning a Ferrari except that you can't breed cars. Dogs of this era became ornamental, and the market exploded as did the breeding operations based on trends and human fashion. Unfortunately, or maybe not, many breeds went extinct simply because the fashionable interest was no longer there. Others were integrated into new breeds, and yet others were wiped out by diseases caused by the in-breeding.

Fast-track breeding is completely against the laws of nature. A breed is not the same as a species or even subspecies. Species develop naturally through evolution, and subspecies diverge based on those same evolutionary forces to adapt to various environmental niches and circumstances. This happens slowly and naturally over hundreds or thousands of generations, and health and viability are intrinsic to that process. Differentiation from wolf to dog took thousands of years, perhaps tens of thousands of years. Modern breed differentiation, on the other hand, is simply a parlour trick of man.

So, over time, there was a human need for pedigree and organizations were formed to determine exactly what these different breeds should look like. They were now expected to look and behave a certain way and conform to certain standards. Breed clubs ensured that these "purebred" standards of height, weight and colour were adhered to. However, despite the more than 400 international recognized living dog breeds that exist today, one analysis determined that only 10 breeds are actually considered popular and comprise over half of the AKC registrations. And the 50 least popular breeds only comprise less than 1.2 percent of registered dogs.

Dogs don't see breed. Anyone who has ever watched dogs at a dog park knows that. A dog will intrinsically recognize another dog as simply a fellow dog. The truth is that if you took a population of a dozen different pure-bred dogs and simply allowed them to breed without human interference, in only a couple of generations you would be hard pressed to point out distinct breed characteristics at all.

In fact, when you look at feral populations of dogs around the globe, you notice they all look uncannily similar. The so-called pariah dog is a good approximation of what *Canis lupus familiaris* looks like without human interference. Not just dogs before human interference either, but dogs after human interference actually comes to an end.

And yes, people have strong emotional ties to certain breeds, especially the breeders. But this emotional investment can blind them to the bigger picture, namely that a dog is a dog first and a breed second. And despite our attachments it's time now to take responsibility and actually allow breeds that suffer multiple health problems to become extinct – after all these dogs were never adapted to the "wild" anyway, but were adapted to a completely foreign human culture. And let's take a tight control over breed populations and breed health instead of pedigree!

"Dogs just want to be dogs."

The Homeless

There are millions of homeless dogs in North America and only a small percentage – 3.5 million make it to an animal shelter. And of those 670,000 dogs are euthanized every year. That's such a painful statistic it's hard to even think about it – but we must.

And still, 70,000 dogs are born every day. And that's just in North America. Many people from all walks of life have a variety of irrational and unfounded reasons on why they should breed their dog, including (1) *my dog is cute/pretty/adorable,* (2) *my dog is different from other dogs,* (3) *there is no dog that looks or behaves as good as mine,* (4) *having more dogs would be fun* (5) *I like the breed* (6) *I like puppies* (7) *dog breeds might become extinct* and most reprehensibly (8) *puppies could bring us some quick and easy money.*

The truth is when it comes to dogs, supply already outstrips demand.

But perhaps not surprisingly so-called professional breeders are responsible for over 70 percent of those birth dogs – many of whom are doomed to poor health by way of genes. Whether or not you purchase a dog from a breeder who you consider to be reputable or from one who breeds for money or from a horrid puppy mill it does not change these disturbing numbers.

Every time you breed or buy a dog, rather than rescue, another dog somewhere dies. Only 20 percent of dog buyers rescue, which means that millions of people spend thousands of dollars to support breeders. However people want to rationalize breeding (and there are plenty of rationalizations out there), the idea of producing more dogs while hundreds of thousands of dogs are waiting to die in over-crowded shelters is beyond belief. Are we really this shallow? We have created a huge problem here, and no one appears to be taking responsibility. But if we don't show some compassion and get a handle on this, who will?

Shelters everywhere are staffed by amazing volunteers who are continually strapped for enough space and money to help more dogs. The hundreds of thousands of dollars currently spent on buying dogs could easily be used to help the shelters and the millions of homeless dogs. If you are hung up on the idea of a specific breed, you should know that almost any type of breed, including purebreds, are available at your local shelter. With a little patience, you can find the perfect dog for you and your family while contributing to creating a kinder, safer, world for *all* dogs. Every dog deserves a loving home. So let's put an end to this gross over-population of suffering pets and provide homes for dogs who really need them.

We could end pet homelessness within one generation if we just took action today.

—~~~~~— 🐾 —~~~~~—

There are 670,000 dogs euthanized every year. We could end pet homelessness within one generation if we just took action today.

—~~~~~————~~~~~—

Every dog deserves a loving home.

17. Animal Communication

The Inter-Species Bond

Owning Dogs

So why do we own dogs? Clearly, aside from utilitarian purposes, there is a strong impulse to bond with one another and an ancient compulsion to share our lives and our homes with animals. And there is no question that dogs are devoted to their human partners. And that people are in love with their dogs because of this devotion and because dogs love us unconditionally – just what people everywhere need. In what often appears to be a hostile, unloving, and unforgiving world, a dog provides us with a steadfast, reliable, and unwavering friendship. No matter who you are, what you've done, or what you look like, your dog will always love you just the way you are. Dogs are now used in senior homes, hospitals, prisons and various other therapies. We have much to learn from our dogs, do we not?

It all starts with the eyes. A pituitary hormone called oxytocin is released when we look into each other's eyes, no matter the species. This is the same hormone that is produced during sex, pregnancy, and mother-child bonding. In fact, a study done in Japan showed that higher levels of oxytocin were produced during a gaze between a human and a dog than during petting or talking to your dog. When we look into a dog's eyes, a mutual recognition is apparent which reflects thousands of years of evolutionary bonding. This loving bond has become a part of both of our chemistries and is the foundation from where all other communications derive.

Talking: Human to Dog

Humans think that they are quite good at communicating to their dogs. Consciously or sub-consciously people employ body language, eye contact, hand signals, physical contact, food, voice commands, tone of voice, and daily routine to communicate their intentions. Dogs have been shown to have superior social-communicative abilities with a great awareness of even subtle cues from humans. Dogs can read pointing fingers, eye movement, and facial expressions including glancing and gazing.

Examples of more direct communication can include a threatening posture or stance, making eye contact to amplify aggression, stroking the animal with your hand, kissing your pooch, rewarding behaviour with a food treat or yelling "no!" Indirect communication can be accomplished by such behaviours as packing your suitcase or arriving home at the same time every day. Dogs too may use some of these practices to communicate with people (many of them would pack their suitcase if they could), but also to communicate with other dogs, although admittedly dogs do more licking than people do.

Talking: Dog to Human

Canine communication methods may not be more sophisticated, but they are certainly more dynamic than the methods people rely on to communicate - methods that dogs undoubtedly find boring and mundane. Nevertheless, most of them respond to this foreign language and do as they are told. Most dogs are very social and have a wonderful set of dramatic body language techniques to augment their dog-to-dog and dog-to-human communication. A play bow can signal *let's play!* It can also indicate a sort of apology - *whoops, I got out of hand but I'll be gentler now*. Rearing on the hind legs is a sign of affection, usually done during playtime. Play bites are just that – little nips that avoid sensitive areas on their play mate. They also have a myriad of facial expressions which help us humans (and no doubt other dogs) to read their mood. Confused dogs wrinkle their foreheads, happy dogs wag their tails, very happy dogs smile by pulling their lips back (this is mostly shown to people as opposed to other dogs), nervous or stressed dogs frequently yawn and alert dogs perk up their ears...

Dogs can even urinate as a communication tool. Consider the behaviour of marking territory when unsure of their claim to a place, peeing when afraid, or peeing in your shoe when they are angry with you or need attention.

Vocal cues such as howling, whining, groaning, growling, and barking are types of communication used by many dogs. Howling can be heard at times when a dog is extremely distressed, but also many dogs are compelled to howl when they hear high-pitched sounds such as sirens or musical horns – *this* type of howling is more a form of expression than it is a type of communication.

Dogs whine when they are afraid or want something they can't have (the latter like many humans I know). Whining is usually a higher pitched tone sure to get attention. Whimpering is softer than whining and can be an indicator that the dog is in pain – or sometimes highly excited. Groaning is also a sign of discomfort or pain, for instance, as an older dog may groan every time she lays down because her joints hurt. A golden cocker spaniel I once had was groaning in his sleep every night because I had not noticed that one of his toe nails was too long and irritating his skin. Another dog I owned was groaning in his sleep for several weeks until I finally realized that he was eating too much for supper every night and was feeling bloated and uncomfortable for the first few hours of his sleep. Most dogs just eat whatever you give them.

Growling is your dog's way of telling you, or anyone else who cares to listen, that they are feeling scared or threatened. As your dog's guardian, it is your responsibility to assess the dog's response to a situation and determine if it is justified or not. A *stay away from my food* growl is different from a *here comes a stranger* growl, which is different from an *I'm playing rough right now* growl. A dog who growls to threaten in a non-threatening situation needs to be understood and helped at a much deeper level – either physically or emotionally, or both. Unfortunately, these dogs are usually labelled as aggressive or

reactive and are often handled by people with minimal training or understanding, which results in an unpleasant life or an undesirable outcome for the dog.

Barking of course, is a very specialized kind of language – at least between dogs. Barking may be a result of domestication because, unlike dogs, wolves rarely bark. In fact, barking only comprises about three percent of a wolf vocalizations. Obviously, for security purposes, we would prefer loud, persistent barking. Thus, early humans would favour such a dog in their selective breeding practices, and thus the barking genes would perpetuate. Or perhaps integrating dogs into the lives of humans was such a stressful transition it warranted the evolution of a new language to cope with their strange new world. Either way, most humans do not seem to understand barking, and as a result, spend much of their pet parent lives yelling at barking dogs to stop.

When the doorbell rings, for example, dogs run and bark all the way to the door, with the pet parent in hot pursuit yelling at them the whole way to stop barking. This at-the-door chaos signals the dog that the alert has now become a "code 9" alarm and that they should step up the action, leading to even further chaos. What your dog really needs you to do, from the onset, is to stay calm and pet him to assure him that he has done a very good job in alerting you to the doorbell, and that you will now take care of the situation. Then reward him handsomely for backing off.

Dogs like to talk; no doubt about it. They bark for all kinds of different reasons: alert, alarm, loneliness, boredom, fear, distress, fun and/or excitement, or to just irritate the neighbours (especially if they know that the neighbours irritate you). And depending on why they are barking, barks vary in timing, pitch, and amplitude. The bark of a distressed dog who might be scared or alone is high-pitched and repetitive. The alert bark is sharper and more intense, especially if it becomes an alarm bark. Fear barking is lower in tone but usually faster. For most dogs, barking is not a sign of aggression, but rather an alarm signal. That's why domestic dogs bark more than wild canines do; they consider it their duty to warn people that they can smell, hear, or see something out of the ordinary.

Rio's Body Talk

I had a nice little golden cocker spaniel named Rio at one time. He was kind and loyal and very, very sensitive. When I trained the horses - either on the ground or in the saddle - in a large outdoor arena, Rio liked to sit right smack-dab in the middle of the action. Amazingly, he never feared for his safety either and refused to move off his front row seat no matter how many hooves thundered close by him. I think he took a special interest in all of this because he had attended so many horse shows in the past and he knew what to look for when judging a horse and rider. In fact, he really did! It turned out that Rio had a better feel than I did at the time, and the minute he saw the least bit of stress or tension in one of the horses' eyes, facial expressions, tail or body movement he would immediately stand up and start to fidget. He could also sense when I was getting uptight or the least bit frustrated when things were not going as I thought they should be. (It turns out that it was the horses who knew how things should be, but that is a whole other story.) In any event, I learned to trust little Rio, and if I wanted to know what the emotional atmosphere was or how the horses were receiving my tricks and tools, I only had to look at Rio's body communication to guide my behaviour. And I *did* learn to listen to Rio; his wisdom played a big role in fine-tuning my interactions with all animals, and people too.

Talking: Dog to Dog

Research indicates that people can distinguish between the different types of barking. Well, dogs can too. However, people are not as adept at identifying individual dogs by the sound of their bark as dogs are. Dogs can easily tell who specifically is doing the barking and they use barking mostly for long-distance communication. Face to face communication is more likely accomplished with direct cues: body movements, pawing, facial expressions, odor, whining, and growling are the primary types of direct communication.

Dogs also use urinary scent to communicate - scenting is used to mark territory and let other dogs know where the boundaries are. Wolves display the same behaviour, particularly during breeding season.

Dogs use special scents called pheromones to communicate their emotions with one another. Pheromones are highly specialized types of chemicals that can identify the sex and age of the dog, emotions, what type of food they are eating, and can even relay information about their health, including whether a female is in estrus, is pregnant and/or lactating. Anger, fear, insecurity, confidence, and jealousy are just some of the emotions that can be detected through smell. Many of the pheromones are dissolved in a dog's urine, and sniffing where another dog has urinated gives out a great deal of information about that dog. The height of the marking is also important as it tells other dogs about dominance as determined by the size of the dog.

Humans produce pheromones as well, and while we don't have a strong enough sense of smell to detect the emotions of one another through scenting, our smell does relay all the same information that dogs pick up from other dogs. Diet, health, disease, emotions, hormone levels and who you have been physically interacting with. Dogs can even detect what kind of disease you have based on your breath - they can smell lung cancer, breast cancer, bladder cancer, colon cancer, Parkinson's, diabetes, and low blood sugar. And as studies continue, it is likely that it will be discovered that they can detect a whole lot more about people, and that perhaps our dogs know us better than we know ourselves.

Go easy on the fragrances - a dog's sense of smell is up to 40 times more sensitive than a human. Hounds for example, have 200 million scent receptors while humans have 5 million. Some of our odors must completely overpower them - keep this in mind before you apply strong perfumes, deodorants, scented products, artificial room deodorizers, or other strong fragrances. It's healthier for you too!

Dogs can even detect what kind of disease you have based on your breath.

Don't Be Rude

Dogs are highly sensitive beings, no matter how physically small or big they might be. And they are inherently more sensitive, intuitive, and dare I say, more spiritual than humans (as discussed below). Approach dogs with discretion not arrogance. Don't walk straight up to a dog, don't assume they want a belly slap, and don't make hard eye contact. Dogs don't do this with one another and neither should we. Humans are held in different esteem than dogs and most of us tower several feet above them. Try crawling around the floor on your hands and knees for a couple of days in a group of people to get an idea of what it is like down there at eye level. You could end up growling.

In the people world, making eye contact with someone you don't know can be seen as a sign of honesty, warmth, or courage. Not so in the dog world. Direct eye contact with a strange dog is confrontational and impolite to say the least.

Try hard not to yell at your dogs. Your dog's hearing is acute compared to yours. She can hear twice the range of frequency and can make out sounds at four times the distance. In other words, there is no need to yell. Besides, yelling at a dog to stop barking is almost always counterproductive and does nothing to calm their temperament. Yelling is rude, and is an indication that you are not effectively communicating with your dog at that moment (and perhaps not many other moments either). You should stop yelling at your kids too, especially if you have a dog in the house.

All this raises the question of how to best communicate with our dogs.

Intuitive Communications: Listening

Listening to Ourselves

Intuitive communications, also known as animal or inter-species communication is a type of communication beyond the five senses of vision, hearing, smell, taste, and touch. It involves a quieting or meditative state of the mind from where you can tune into your higher levels of faculties and perception. This opens a place of deeper knowing and empathy. Empathy is the ability to "feel" the emotions, thoughts, pains, and physical sensations that another sentient being is experiencing. Empathy is a gift that is natural to everyone and is known to nurture compassion and benevolence.

The more empathetic we are, the more telepathic we are. In other words, the more we open our hearts, the more telepathic we become. Telepathy is the ability to receive feelings and information outside of our five senses. All of us have the gifts of empathy and telepathy – it's a natural part of being alive, but many of us were shut down years ago or conditioned to believe that the material world is the only world. And because so many of us are busy and these areas of perception are not normally utilized in our day-to-day routine, we continue to rely on more superficial levels of communication with *all* species. What a shame.

Information that is gleaned from a dog intuitively can be received in different ways:

1. **Clairsentience** means to have a "clear feeling" or a clear knowing that enables us to know that a dog is feeling happy, depressed, or jealous, for example, without the typical body language. Emotions are the easiest to identify because the vibrational field around emotions is one of the strongest. Inspirations and insights are also common with clairsentience and people often experience a gut feeling or instinct about a person or animal. Most people use this form of intuition all the time without being consciously aware of it. It's why we apply for certain jobs, avoid a particular situation or change our travel plans. It is why we are sometimes compelled to call a friend in need before they call us. Or to think of someone just before they call us. Clairsentients also frequently feel the physical sensations of another person or pet in their own bodies. They may "feel" their headaches,

joint pain, tingling, or anxiety for example. Many energy healers make use of these clairsentient skills to identify a health problem, or to track emotional traumas and past events hidden in the physical body. The clairsentient is highly empathetic and very aware of the energy fields, patterns, and vibrations around others.

2. **Clairvoyance** or sixth sense means "to see clearly" and often results in a visual impression or image of a particular situation. The medical intuitive may see intestinal parasites, a broken heart or an inflamed liver. The gifted chiropractor might see a spur on a vertebra, and the neurologist might see a growth on the brain. The visual image of this sixth sense is generated by the third eye in the middle of the forehead, and not the eyes. Clairvoyant visuals can be very colourful.

3. **Clairaudience** means "to hear clearly" with the ability to perceive sounds or words that are not physically spoken and not audible to the normal ear. You may hear a word spoken when you are drifting off to sleep at night. Or perhaps you may hear music. After a coyote snatched my beloved fifteen-year-old cat, I was distraught for a long while. But I could often hear her singing, no doubt trying to sooth me. Before she passed, she was aware that I wanted to sing more often, and so she understood that singing represented joy to me.

Listening to Our Dogs

We are quick to take our dogs to obedience school to teach them how to understand us, how to listen to us, and how to ensure that they fit nicely into our human worlds with minimal disruption. But we are not so quick to attend an animal communication class to learn what it is our dogs need *us* to know.

When we quietly attune ourselves to a place of emotional and spiritual connection, specific information may be received: feelings, emotions, thoughts, words, images, sensations, sounds, or just a strong knowing are all common communications. The exchange of information is possible because all events – whether they are physical, emotional, mental or spiritual – are created and shaped by an electromagnetic field. This field is a fundamental force of nature that binds us all together as one energetic unit. Communicating with animals/nature is not

magical. It is possible because of the energy network that exists between all living things everywhere in the universe.

The world of intuitive communications is a direct two-way channel of information. Dogs, like all animals, are absolute masters at feeling, making them profoundly aware of everything, everybody, and every vibration around them. They don't need any training like we do – they are already tuned in. They are deeply connected and have an incredible knowing on all things emotional and spiritual. What they know would shock you. They live in a permanently expanded state of consciousness (we should be so lucky) which gives them wisdom, important opinions, and mastery over spiritual practices including unconditional love. It's this ability to love with a genuine innocence that hurts us so much when we see them abused.

Listening to Each Other

Interspecies communication is a beautiful and useful skill. It helps us heal ourselves and all of our pets. To heal our animals is to truly heal ourselves. Contrary to what you might think, communicating with a dog on a psychic level is entirely natural; it broadens our awareness to the true nature of the dog's heart and soul. Learning to listen on a psycho-spiritual level has a number of benefits:

- It can help us discover the past traumas and memories that are affecting their current lives.
- It can help us determine the underlying cause of physical un-wellness.
- It can help us determine the underlying cause of behavioural problems or unhappiness.
- It can give us a deeper understanding of their emotional state and how best to help them.
- They can communicate to us their likes and dislikes: *food, water, colours, sleeping arrangements, what's fun, other animals and/or people including your choice of mates!*
- We can learn to understand their true needs.
- We can feel how happy they are – dogs truly do love a lot of things including people.
- We can learn more about ourselves by understanding *their* perspective on *our* behaviours and lifestyles!
- We can appreciate a journey through the world of spirit.
- We can become enlightened on the art of unconditional love.

- We can understand and assist with the transition over the rainbow bridge.

In addition to the beautiful spiritual journeys that can be initiated by intuitive communications, dogs are also able to convey information important to their well-being. They can tell their people that their food is making them sick, that they are bored and need to get out more often, that they would like a companion, that their right leg is hurting, that they don't need to be walked with a leash or that they are still grieving over someone in their previous home. They might even tell you that they would like to sleep in the master bedroom and have your spouse sleep somewhere else! They can also express their talents as healers and help their people to alleviate guilt, lift sadness, calm anxiety, and understand their relationships better. And, perhaps most important of all, they can tell you how it is possible for them to experience unconditional love.

Dogs Just Want to Have Fun

One thing that a healthy dog knows is that they are here to have fun. Dogs are known to play right from puppyhood well into their senior years. So what motivates them to chase sticks, eat your shoes, learn tricks, slide down slopes, and jump into the air with sheer delight?

When puppies play, they learn important life skills, social skills, and other experiences that benefit physical and mental health, including coordination. Play also teaches puppies to communicate by reading and interpreting voice and body signals. Dogs who have never played with their own kind are not as adept at communicating with other dogs. But playtime for puppies is also a predatory instinct as they learn how to hunt and kill by pouncing on toys, tearing apart pillows, biting, jumping, running, body slamming other dogs, rumbling, growling and baring their teeth. All in the name of mock battle and truly fun to watch.

And then there is the "play bow" which is used by canines to signal that they want to play or continue to play. Studies indicate that the bow is used before and after "non-playful" actions to indicate to the play partner that the round isn't over. Both puppies and adult dogs use the play bow just before or after mock bites 75 percent of the time. Young wolves use it 79 percent of the time and young coyotes, 92 percent of the time. Clearly, our canines are coded to play!

But what about the adult dogs who presumably already have all their skills in place? Or puppies who like to toboggan down the snowy hill with the kids for the sheer thrill of it all? Is play for them a purposeless behaviour with no "utilitarian function" as the scientists would term it? Well, not exactly. Other species also display purposeless play behaviours. And what is becoming very clear is that play time is not just practice. It is a way of bonding with their partners – either their own species or other species including humans. Dogs who play with humans tend to be less competitive but are, nevertheless, forming important emotional bonds with their human friend, as is the human with the dog. Establishing and determining relationships is very important to all animals.

Play is analogous to a feel-good sport during which the brain and nervous system produce a variety of endorphins. Endorphins are opiate-like chemicals that lower stress levels, support the immune system and help us feel euphoric – no matter our age. Friends, love, laughter and sunshine are necessary ingredients for dogs too. Play on...

Sponging

What is it?

Sponging, or mirroring as it is sometimes known, is one of the most important concepts in our relationship and interaction with other species. Sponging is a process that occurs between a person and their pet when the bond or the attachment is very strong - as it is for most pet lovers. Dogs are sentient beings meaning that they feel, perceive, and sense things, just as we do. But their perceptions and senses, including intuition, are much deeper than what most people consciously experience. As a result, dogs are more connected to the universal flow and the "all is one" quantum energy field than we are. To a dog, the universe is just one big network within one compassionate space. A dog's capacity for empathy and unconditional love is immense, and not something that most of us humans have yet mastered - at least not to this degree. These virtues and excellence of character allow dogs to naturally identify and energetically assimilate all the blueprints in our energy field. These blueprints represent the events in our lives - mental, emotional and physical. Loyal dogs will then embody what they feel, see and sense, and take it on as their own.

What Does Sponging Look Like?

Your dog not only feels all your emotions and sees all your diseases, but she will actually absorb and retain them for you. This is why so many dogs have similar problems to their human counterparts. For example, if you have an arthritic knee, your dog will start limping. If you have a chronically sore shoulder, your dog may feel stiff in the same shoulder. If you have thyroid problems, your dog will end up with thyroid problems. If you gain weight your dog will likely gain weight. And, if you have cancer, or are at risk for cancer, your dog may take on the cancer. Some dogs will even exhibit the symptoms before you do or before your own diagnosis. More human disease syndromes have been observed in dogs than in any other domestic mammal. Coincidence?

If you are unhappy with your life, your dog will probably also feel bad. Or if you don't like your neighbour, your dog won't like your neighbour. If you are depressed, your dog will often be depressed. If you suffer from anxiety, you will have a nervous dog. If you sleep all the time, you will have a tired dog. If you are irritable and grumpy, your dog may start growling and perhaps even bite people (especially people that *you* don't like) and/or other dogs. And so on and so on.

Many animals will also sustain a physical injury or take on an accident in an effort to deflect the trauma from their human owner. Sometimes their actions will even predict an upcoming event – either literally or symbolically. And some very caring animals go beyond their pet parents and will actually start to mirror other family members, neighbours, friends, and acquaintances!

And why do some dogs start to look like their human owners? Because the identity of animals is more diffused, and less egocentric than a person's identity; ego is simply not as important to them. Therefore, when the dog and owner bond and the relationship integrates, the stronger identity will prevail and the dog will begin to display the characteristics of their stronger half. In other words, your dog can start to act like you, behave like you, have the same emotional and physical reactions that you do and begin to look like you. And, of course, they frequently experience the same physical problems.

In twenty-five years of animal practice, I have seen nearly every single problem, trauma, disease, and emotional imbalance taken on by the pets. I have even seen animals re-create personal dramas between their own species that mirror the same events within the human household. And the stronger the bond, the stronger the reflection. Our dogs just never seem to give up on us!

And be mindful of your addictions, including alcohol, tobacco (second-hand smoke can cause your dog pre-cancerous lesions), marijuana, prescription drugs, caffeine and street drugs since your dog will energetically and emotionally experience all of the same effects that you do, and more. And while you may not be concerned over your health, your dog is.

~~~~~~~ 🐾 ~~~~~~~

Your dog not only feels all your emotions and sees all your diseases, but she will actually absorb and retain them for you.

Is Sponging Beneficial?

Yes, it can be. Pets think nothing of taking on the problems of a loved one and will happily sacrifice themselves by carrying the burdens for another. When older pets, who are carrying physical conditions for their human, eventually pass over, the pet parent often notices that their own original health condition worsens. Not from loss or grief, but because they are carrying the full load of their own problems again.

Many people ask if there is anything they can do to stop their pets from sponging their issues since, very often, they see their pets suffering with their own problems and would like to reason with them. The answer is no. Dogs are incredibly loyal and dutiful, as they should be. You cannot stop the process of sponging; once a pet bonds with you it is natural law within the animal kingdom. Animals perceive the truth in all things; there are no filters.

Can people sponge their pets' problems? Yes, they can, but it is not as common since most people have not normally expanded their consciousness to the degree that is necessary for this depth of empathy.

Awareness

As of yet, few pet parents, animal health practitioners, or dog experts are aware of the remarkable transfer of energies between sentient beings. This is unfortunate because the health repercussions are enormous, and many animals cannot be helped or truly healed until their people have taken responsibility for healing themselves.

Clary & Margaret

Clary was a six-year-old German shepherd for whom I was asked to do a health assessment by distance. Clary lived in Ohio, and his pet parent's daughter, Ana was asked to contact me and give me the information for her mother Eva. Now when the pet parent is unwilling to communicate with me directly, it is usually an indication that they are nervous about the outcome – consciously or subconsciously. Clary was showing signs of fatigue, depression, stiffness and mobility problems, which his veterinarians felt was neurological and could be related to degenerative myelopathy which as a progressive disease of the spinal cord nerves that can cause paralysis in the hind end. It is common in German shepherds and is a result of indiscriminate breeding. I sensed that Clary also had a lot of numbness and tingling in his legs as well as a stiff "frozen" shoulder.

Clary was started on a nutrition program, which included improved diet choices and the correction of multiple nutrient deficiencies. But Clary's response was limited, and he showed very little improvement, which is not what I normally expect. So I examined the information more closely and asked more questions. I was told that Eva had suffered a stroke a few months ago, leaving her with numbness, tingling, mobility problems and an inability to move her left shoulder. She was feeling quite depressed over what had happened and had not or could not pursue a self-help program of any kind. Unfortunately, Clary was merely the reflection of Eva's health trauma. He could not recover on his own because he was fulfilling his duties to carry as much of the burden for her as he could. Unfortunately, the situation was stuck, and Clary passed over later that same year.

"An emotionally balanced human family is a healthy family with an emotionally balanced and healthy dog"

Anthropomorphism

This long technical word describes our behaviour when we give human characteristics to animals. It is often used in an uncomplimentary manner by many people who don't like those of us who treat our dogs as somewhat human. This is a particular mindset for more "cerebral" people who regard with disdain those of us who talk to, communicate with, play with, sleep with, hug, dress up, assign human thoughts to, or otherwise explain canine behaviour in human terms. Some opposers even deny that dogs (and all animals) have emotions! This belief is nothing short of dangerous because it gives people with a vested interest the rationale to abuse and/or profit from the unethical breeding and/or suffering of animals.

Anthropomorphism may be especially practiced by people who lack social connections. Thus we may see lonely, bored, childless, rich and/or stressed people replace human companionship with dogs and may even raise them like children. And while there is no harm in canine companionship of course, we must be cautious that our dogs do not become objects of entertainment or obsession.

Now, given the previous discussion of sponging and identity, it is clear that our dogs actually take on human qualities through observation, conditioning, osmosis and telepathic communications. Dogs listen to us, pick up our vocabulary and pay attention to all that we do. They tolerate us, read and mimic our body language, know our habits, read human facial expressions, and communicate various emotions learned from hundreds of people-like traits over thousands of years. The result? The adoption of particular characteristics that specifically mirror our own. And that, is the definition of anthropomorphism.

Anthropomorphism therefore, is a unique and fascinating evolutionary concept that is alive and well and perfectly explains why we love treating our dogs like people. And rightfully so. So long as our dogs live in our homes, they will increasingly absorb our traits and continue to be a part of our culture, which is now also their new culture. They no longer live in the world that they were genetically predisposed for. Dogs might be genetically unfamiliar with this relatively new and foreign human pack, but they are very familiar with love and bonding since these are also elements of survival – across all species and all cultures. As time goes on, anthropomorphism will continue to evolve between all interactive species. Here are two examples of what can be accomplished when the inter-species bond is beautifully connected.

~~~~~~ 🐾 ~~~~~~

So long as our dogs live in our homes, they will increasingly absorb our traits and continue to be a part of our culture…. They no longer live in the world that they were genetically predisposed for.

~~~~~~~~

Frosty & Georgia – Healing Together

When Frosty's pet mom, Georgia, brought him into the clinic, Frosty had a number of health issues including fatigue and depression. But his main problem was with a number of respiratory symptoms: sneezing, coughing, choking, congestion and trouble breathing. Frosty is a Sheltie and he felt so terrible. And the allergies were causing him behavioural changes as well; chronic allergies compromise adrenal function, over time interfering with cortisol production, which then results in fatigue, increased stress levels, and poor immunity. It wasn't difficult to determine that Frosty had immune problems – we also discovered that he had multiple inhalant allergies, especially feathers. After a discussion with Georgia, she realized that her house was full of feather pillows! And she told me that she had had allergy symptoms for herself for years and that her symptoms were the same as Frosty's. This was a typical case of sponging, and Georgia had to agree to start her own health program too otherwise the results with Frosty would be very limited.

So that's exactly what we did. We changed Frosty's diet and also started him on a homeopathic feathers remedy, homeopathic adrenal organ, homeopathic Lachesis, Riva's Allerg-Ease, and vitamin B5 (pantothenic acid). And we started Georgia on the same remedy program. Georgia also had to eliminate wheat and dairy products from her diet. And, of course, she had to remove all the feather pillows from the house.

Georgia writes:

"Dear Marijke,

Here is a photo of my best friend, Frosty.

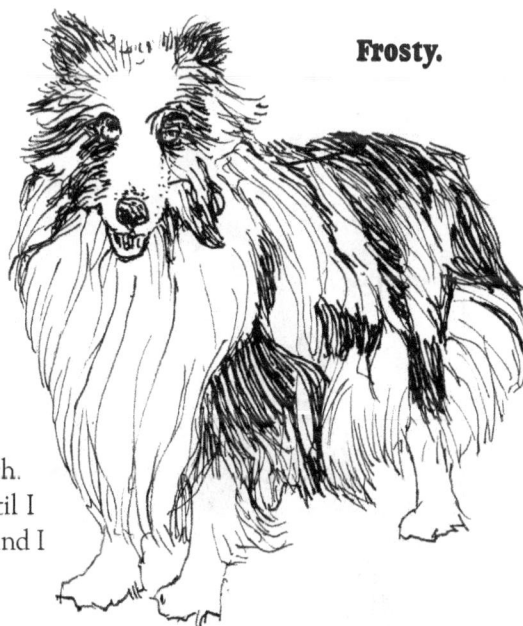

Frosty.

He is back to normal, thank heavens. I really was afraid that he wasn't going to be with me much longer. He had no life in him, his eyes were dead, and he had no interest in anything. If you went to pat him, he would duck and pull away. He looked as though his head would explode. His sneezing and choking was terrifying.

I thank you, Marijke, for identifying allergies, especially to feathers! And I thank you and Riva's Remedies for putting him on the road to health. Now he is my fun-loving, cuddly, fur-ball once again.

And a bonus!! You helped me with my own allergies so much. I never realized how many feathers we had in this house! Not until I started a room to room search. Now my sneezing is at a minimum and I have more energy, and at 70+ years old that really is a bonus!!

Thanks again,

Georgia and Frosty"

Harley's Miracle Healing

Harley is a beloved Chihuahua who had a very sore right eye with irritation, tearing, and light sensitivity. He was diagnosed with a corneal ulcer and treated with antibiotic and lubricant eye drops. However, Harley did not respond to the treatment and his eye continued to be very sore. I was asked to help Harley so his pet parent Lindsay sent me a picture for my assessment. I planned on reviewing his condition the next day to recommend an appropriate program including a diet change with natural remedies. However, about an hour after looking at his picture, my own right eye started to hurt and continued to be sore for several hours until I went to bed. Then, in the middle of the night I was suddenly awakened. The energy and a fuzzy visual of his eye ulcer came straight at me, somehow hit my right leg which I could physically feel on the outside of my lower right calf. It felt like the eye had embedded itself in my leg and I could sense the word "healing". I was somewhat bewildered until the next morning when Lindsay called to ask me what I had done! When she got up that morning Harley had experienced an instantaneous healing, and he was completely recovered. And my own right eye and leg were fine by then too. Although to this day, I don't know why he aimed for my leg! Some mysteries are never solved.

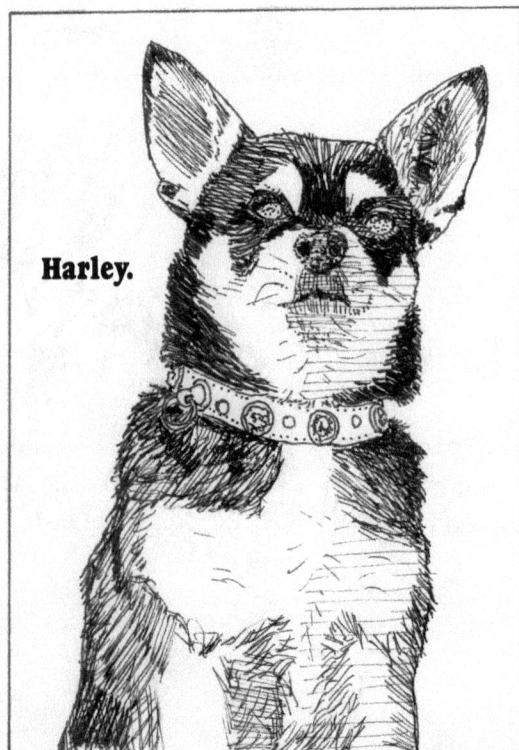

Harley.

A Word About Alpha

We have learned a lot here about our relationship with dogs: theories of domestication, why we own them, inter-species bonding, the emotional bond, the complex and incredible variety of two-way communications, the spiritual transfers of energies, and the profound empathy and love that our dogs are capable of. And yet, for the most part dog people are still mostly stuck in "alpha" mode. Convinced, by popular thought, that the biological relationship is the primary one, they are conditioned to believe that the only way to control or train a dog is to be an authoritative boss.

Unfortunately, the concept of the alpha-wolf is mostly a myth or a wildly flawed interpretation at the very least. Swiss behavioural scientist Rudolf Schenkel first proposed it in the late forties after extensive study of captive wolves in Basel, Switzerland. His work was influential and went unchallenged for years as he discovered that captive wolves and wolf packs in the wild don't function in the same way. Once people started studying wild packs the picture changed somewhat and it became clear that the "hierarchies" of wild packs were a lot more fluid.

Aggressive conduct is not how wolf packs maintain order. In fact, research shows that wolves are more likely to sustain peace within the pack without resorting to aggression and violence; relationships are frequently resolved through submissive and respectful behaviours by the subordinates, not by alpha threats and dominance. In addition, the concept of rank in the wolf pack is highly flexible and can change due to a number of factors: age, availability of food, the seasons, emotional maturity, play-fighting and/or repeated behaviour to test another wolf's abilities. Surprisingly, rank is also often frequently ignored during feeding times. Rank, it appears, is mostly demonstrated for breeding purposes.

What all this means is that rank order and rules of hierarchy are likely less important to wolves (and dogs) than perhaps they are to humans. The myth of the human alpha is not a particularly helpful paradigm when it comes to our dogs, and I predict it will become an out-dated training posture in time. Certainly, our relationship with dogs are much more complex than "I am superior, you are inferior and I have dominion." Our dominion over the animal kingdom has been a dismal failure so far.

I suggest then that it is now time to let our dogs, with their innate wisdom, do more of the training. And let us learn to be quiet, to listen, to comprehend and to understand the canine-human relationship on a much deeper level than we ever have before. Perhaps our own evolution depends on it.

And One Day the Rainbow Bridge...

Compassionate Euthanasia

One of the most frequent questions that I get asked is how will the pet parent know when it's time to let them go. Usually, if people are finding themselves asking the question at all, then it is not time. If there is any shred of doubt, it's better to wait for an hour, a day or a month. In most cases, however, the dog will almost always give you a sign, a feeling, or send you a dream at night to tell you that she is ready. But know too that if you have made the decision sooner than you thought you should have, no dog will ever judge you for sending her on the journey a little early. They don't have the same concept of time as we do; they care more about our emotional wellness. The only time that early euthanasia becomes a problem is when people euthanize an animal for personal convenience – lack of time, lack of money, lack of patience, and lack of love. And even then, an animal will seldom judge. They just don't have the same attachments to anger, resentment, guilt or blame that we do.

Once the decision is made, always have the grave ready before they pass, or make early arrangements for cremation. Spreading ashes can be ceremonial and therefore enjoyed by all those who knew your dog and would like to participate. Make it a sacred ritual and a celebration of life and transition.

If your dog has died in an accident or other kind of trauma, a part of the soul may have become disassociated and left behind at the time of death due to shock. Disassociation can hold the spirit back from fully crossing over and passing through the portals or result in a fragmented spirit even if it does pass. (This is similar with people as well.) If this is the case, you may have to get help from a spiritual professional or energy worker experienced with animals who can retrieve and heal the part of the soul which became separated during trauma. Once healed, the part will re-unite with the soul making it easier for the spirit to pass in a more whole state. Soul retrievals can also be performed at a distance. Disassociation can also occur with live animals (or people) who have experienced shock or trauma and may present itself as depression, anxiety, brain fog, confusion, detachment and/or unhealthy repetitive behavioural patterns. A healing is in order for these cases as well.

Letting Them Go

Most dogs naturally live between 10 and 12 years, although there is a lot of variation, of course with dogs living anywhere between 6 and 17 years. Thankfully, most dogs have become members of the household over the last decade or two, but the downside is that when they are ready to pass between the worlds, it can be a very difficult time for the humans. As it turns out, people are not nearly as comfortable at accepting the death transitions as animals are. Animals are very adept at passing back and forth over the veil because their energy field is of a higher vibration – the results of mastering the practice of oneness. Similar to us they experience the death transition as a re-birth and that in order for the energy field or "light body" to expand it must leave the denser and coarser aspects of the material physical body. However, they inherently know all of this beforehand and are, therefore, fully prepared to leave one journey and begin another. There is no resistance. The only problem they have is when the pet parent's do not want to let go of their beloveds.

People naturally like to own, possess or emotionally attach themselves to the things, people or animals that they love, and they want to keep them physically close for emotional security. They have not yet mastered the relationship between love and freedom and that true and unconditional love will set the beloved free. True love and compassion comes from detachment, not attachment. For most of us it is normal to mourn the loss of a beloved dog (or person) but when a dog's pet parent or human companion grieves and mourns a physical death beyond a reasonable amount of time, strong negative emotions are perpetuated which act like a magnet and keeps the dog's spirit attached to the person's energy field. This prevents the dogs from emotionally detaching and travelling completely into their next spiritual journey. Once we let go of our hold and/or if our love has evolved and expanded to a place of freedom and flow, the spirit shall be set free and the passage will be seen and experienced as a beautiful time.

What also holds some people back from facing death is a lack of understanding of the transition itself and that compassionate presence during a ritual or a ceremony is an important part of any new journey - human or animal. It is recommended, where possible, to always allow your pet to die in their own home with you and/or other family members at their side. The environment should be calm and peaceful. Once the spirit begins to open and expand and the physical body drops away, close your eyes and begin to breathe very slowly and deeply. As the animal's spirit begins to release, it will use your breath to carry itself up and onward with ease. The breath represents the new life and facilitates the spiritual journey. This can also be done at a distance during meditation as well - remember there are no boundaries in these spatial dimensions.

Either way, most animals will stay close for a week or two (in our time) as they slowly detach themselves to take the time necessary to protect you, to send final messages, to find the right "portal" into heaven or wait for their spiritual guide. Many times, there is an already deceased dog or person that they once knew, happily waiting at the end of the tunnel to show them the way.

If you stay energetically connected to them, you will be aware of how near or how far away they are over the next few days. And some of you may also become aware of other people, animals, and perhaps spirit guides across the veil. The day that my fifteen-year-old hound passed at home, his spiritual energy immediately appeared everywhere on the property as a thick yellow "drip". It was present in every single living thing on the farm - plants, flowers, trees, and leaf blades. It was stunning! He had

clearly become one, or always had been, with everything in his natural physical environment. The next day his spirit appeared in one of the apple trees where there were only three blossoms remaining - not yet opened in the month of May. And there his spirit stayed for three more days until one of those blossoms opened. And I stood on a ladder in that apple tree for much of that time holding my breath and taking pictures. Then one early morning, in a flash of rainbow light and astral speed, his spirit shot through the energy vortex that this precious little blossom had created, disappeared through the light tunnel, and into the "paws" of an old dog friend. It was tremendously joyful and full of colour, light and happiness. And even though his physical passing was a surreal moment - we never really thought that his time would ever come - I couldn't have been happier for him. As I shared with him his incredibly sacred journey the experience completely displaced any of my lingering attachments and profoundly transformed my heart and soul into the higher vibration of love and freedom. And for this final gift from him I will eternally be grateful.

The apple tree is the Tree of Life.

The apple blossom is the gateway and the apple is the spiritual fruit.

She upholds the Worlds above, below and in between.

And guides us through the veil with beauty, integrity and truth.

The next day his spirit appeared in one of the apple trees where there were only three blossoms remaining – not yet opened in the month of May.

Healing Dogs Their Way

Conclusion

There are two quotes here worth considering. The first from Abraham Maslow, the American psychologist who is most famous for articulating the human hierarchy of needs. Maslow once said, "If you only have a hammer, you tend to see every problem as a nail." The second quote comes from American journalist and satirist H.L. Menken who once pointed out that "For every complex problem there is an answer that is clear, simple, and wrong."

Clearly there is more to veterinary science than pharmaceuticals. That being said, when one considers just how quickly and how often practitioners turn to Big Pharma in search of clear, simple solutions to complex problems it boggles the mind—especially given the mixed results and sometimes tragic consequences of that professional reliance. Make no mistake, the pharmaceutical industry is massive, powerful, and influential. It wields a multi-billion-dollar hammer and is happy (indeed eager) to cast every ailment and disorder known to man or beast as nails.

But the reality behind many ailments is often complex enough that an adequate answer is not a pill or a shot away. Dogs, like humans, are complex creatures. These days, most people accept that inappropriate diet and lifestyle choices can have adverse even profound effects on their health. Most people accept that when something is bothering them there is often something behind it and that a deeper underlying problem prevails. These answers are not always obvious. It's the same with dogs. Why wouldn't it be? In the first chapter, I pointed out that dogs and wolves share 98.9 percent of the same DNA. Do you know what that percentage is when comparing dogs to humans? It's 84 percent. In the grand scheme of things, we are not that different after all.

Our choices affect our health and well-being. The same holds true with dogs except that, in the case of *Canis lupus familiaris*, we make many of those choices for them. This is a huge responsibility, one we need to take seriously. Our dogs rely on us - not just for their medical and nutritional needs, but for their social and emotional well-being as well. With that in mind I offer you my Twelve Canine Commandments.

The Twelve Canine Commandments

1. Ensure that all dogs get regular and high-quality meals

2. All dogs need exercise and quality play time - no matter the breed or the size.

3. Don't leave dogs alone for extended periods of time. Dogs hate being alone.

4. Don't yell. Keep your vocal cues and body language subtle. Dogs already get it - we don't!

5. Be patient - dogs don't always understand what you mean. This is our issue, not theirs. They are in a foreign world, remember?

6. Teach your dogs what to do, rather than what not to do. Use positive reward-based training programs.

7. Don't blame them for your bad day.

8. Give your dog a cushion and don't expect them to get comfortable on concrete, wood or hard floors. Wild canids don't sleep on these kinds of surfaces either.

9. Dogs that bite, chase cars, run away, have panic disorders or are hyperactive need your help. Punishment, force, confinement, tying or violence does not correct behavioural problems, or any other problems for that matter. We bred these behaviours, remember? Now let's take responsibility for them.

10. Don't sentence dogs to a lifetime left alone in a dog house or tied up on a chain. Find them another home instead. And take a look at your own lifestyle - are you feeling trapped, isolated or lonely yourself? Are you projecting that on to your pets?

11. Be the best role model to all the animals and people in your life by being emotionally fit, calm and patient.

12. Enjoy, absorb, and then pass forward the grace, respect, and unconditional love that all dogs are happy to share with us from the bottom of their hearts.

Appendices

Guideline to Feeding Supplements

Herbs, Nutrients, and Homeopathic Medicines

How to Administer

Herbs, herbal tinctures, vitamins, and minerals can be added to the food. Herbs and any of the specialized nutrients can be fed together. If using supplements in capsules, empty capsules into the food so that capsules are not ingested. Capsules may include artificial colouring, plasticizers and magnesium stearate, all of which are detrimental for the immune system.

Most products including the Riva's Remedies products are very palatable; however, for any stronger tasting herbs (or for finicky pets) start with one product at a time. Then start with a very small amount and increase the dosage gradually to the desired amount or until they refuse it – at which point you can decrease the dosage again. However, should your dog suddenly refuse a supplement after several weeks it is likely that the product is no longer necessary.

Homeopathic remedies (liquid or pellets) need to be administered directly into a clean mouth without food. Riva's Remedies liquid formulations come with a dropper, and the drops should be given into a clean mouth without food. They can also be dissolved into a small amount of clean water. Either way, it is convenient to use a medicine dropper or syringe. Follow it up with a little treat, and they will look forward to their medicines every day. If the animal is very difficult to handle, add the recommended drops or the water solution to their drinking water.

Homeopathic remedies in any form are completely safe for all animals, including dogs, puppies, cats, kittens, and even birds.

Course of Treatment

The obvious question, if not stated explicitly, is how long to keep administering a given treatment. Unfortunately, the answer is often not obvious. Like humans, animals are all unique and can have very different responses to their supplement programs. The duration of a health program not only depends on the health of the animal but also on the specific health condition, as well as the actual supplements. It is never advisable to keep animals (or people) on the same herbs, vitamins, minerals, or homeopathic remedies for long, indefinite periods of time. Health and wellness is in a state of constant change. If supplements are taken for too long, they will no longer be of benefit, or in some cases, they can begin to cause other problems or unbalance other nutrients. Many times, animals are fed a particular health product for several months or even years without the owners ever knowing if it is even helping.

Supplements should be used to resolve a specific health problem or to correct a deficiency, after which, they should be discontinued or reduced to a maintenance dosage. They can also be used as needed – in other words, if the symptoms disappear every time you add the supplement, then continue to feed it. Or if the general well-being of the animal is obviously improved while on a particular product, then it is beneficial to continue. But if there are no observable differences with or without the supplement, it is best not to continue. In any case, give all supplements a break from time to time, not only to determine the actual benefits, but also to *refresh* the response should that particular supplement ever be required again.

Here are some general guidelines for specific supplements and remedies:

Herbal Blends

It is advisable to feed the daily dosage on the label for up to one month. If the health condition has completely improved by that time, slowly discontinue the product. If the condition reappears, then resume giving the product as before. If after one month, the condition is still gradually improving (but not yet resolved), continue feeding the herbs. If there is no improvement after one month, then the herbs can be discontinued. Herbs used for cleansing or detoxification can be given for up to 6 to 8 weeks. Herbal blends used for nutritional purposes (e.g., Riva's Happy Pets, Happy Pets Senior and Vital Force) can be used indefinitely because the ingredients are blended to provide vitamins and minerals from plant food sources. In this case, they are considered more as functional supplements rather than therapeutic medicines.

Specialized Nutrients

Specific vitamins and minerals should be given at the recommended dosage for 4 to 6 weeks. After that time, if the condition has improved, continue to feed a maintenance dose of twice weekly, instead of daily. Maintenance dosages prevent both nutrient deficiencies as well as excesses. If the original health problem or condition reappears on the maintenance dosage, then resume the full dosage as recommended.

Homeopathic Remedies

The general rule of thumb is to give the remedy as per label instructions and discontinue the remedy as soon as the symptoms disappear. If symptoms reappear, resume the remedy. If the symptoms do not disappear within a few days, change remedies. Remedies of higher potencies are usually prescribed for a specific period of time by a homeopathic practitioner, so it is best to follow their instructions.

NOTE: As with any supplement or feed, if adverse effects are suspected, discontinue the product immediately. That said, barring a specific allergy or intolerance, negative reactions to good quality herbs and remedies are very uncommon, and if they do occur, they disappear almost immediately after discontinuing the product. With the appropriate diet and supplement program, positive results and changes are usually observed within one to two weeks if not sooner. However, chronic problems, such as metabolic problems, immune disorders, arthritis, and some skin conditions may take longer.

Table of Daily Recommended Dosages

I have organized the following tables to correspond to the natural treatment programs as laid out in the book. And so we have three tables: Nutrients, Herbal Remedies, and Riva's Remedies. In all three cases I have split the tables up into four weight classes. They are:

Small dogs	up to 10 kg (22 lbs)
Medium-sized dogs	10 to 24 kg (22 to 53 lbs)
Large dogs	24 to 50 kg (53 to 110 lbs)
Very large dogs	over 50 kg (110 lbs)

In cases where there is a range of dosages indicated for a given weight class, look to where you dog falls in their weight-class range. So for example: Marlowe is a 23 kg basset hound suffering from muscle cramps, and his pet parent wants to mix some magnesium citrate into his food. The chart indicates that for medium-sized dogs like Marlowe the dosage is 50 to 100 mg. Marlowe is at the upper end of his weight class and so 100 mg would be the correct dosage.

A few notes on units of measure.

- A milligram (mg) is a thousandth of a gram (g). Therefore 1 g = 1,000 mg.

- A microgram (µg) is a thousandth of a milligram (mg) and, therefore, 2000 µg is the same as 2 mg.

- A teaspoon (tsp) is approximately 5 millilitres (ml).

- A tablespoon (Tbsp) is approximately 15 millilitres (ml) or 3 teaspoons (tsp).

- A drop is .05 millilitres (ml) or the amount dispensed in a single drop of a dropper.

- A pinch is dry measure equal to a sixteenth of a teaspoon.

- UI (International Unit) is a specialized unit of measure for fat soluble vitamins.

- The Herbal Remedy table and Riva's Remedy table will rely on units such as teaspoons, tablespoons, and drops simply because most folks don't have delicate scales or pipettes to measure things out in grams and millilitres. If you are looking for a way to measure out fractional teaspoons you have but to go to a store that sells baking supplies.

Vitamins & Minerals

	Small Dogs	Medium Dogs	Large Dogs	V. Large Dogs
beta-carotene	2,000–3,000 IU	5,000–10,000 IU	25,000 IU	50,000 IU
biotin	500–1,000 µg	2,000 µg	5,000 µg	5,000 µg
calcium citrate	25–50 mg	50–100 mg	100–150 mg	150–200 mg
coenzyme Q10	25-30 mg	30-50 mg	100 mg	100–200 mg
creatine	0.5 g	1–2 g	3–4 g	5 g
digestive enzymes	¼ capsule	½ capsule	½ capsule	1 capsule
folic acid	250 µg	250–1,000 µg	1,000–2,000 µg	2,000–3,000 µg
iodine, liquid	Less than a drop	1 drop	1 drop	2 drops
iron gluconate	7–12 mg	12–15 mg	15–25 mg	25–50 mg
lysine	50 mg	200–250 mg	300–400 mg	500 mg
magnesium citrate	25–50 mg	50–100 mg	100–200 mg	200–300 mg
manganese	50 ug	250 ug	1 mg	2 mg
MSM (methylsulfonylmethane)	25–50 mg	100–200 mg	250–500 mg	500 mg
potassium citrate	25–50 mg	50–100 mg	100–125 mg	125–250 mg
selenium, organic	15–25 µg	25–50 µg	50–100 µg	100–200 µg
vitamin A, liquid	¼ drop/2–3 days	½ drop /2–3 days	½ drop	1 drop
vitamin B5	25 mg	100 mg	200 mg	300 mg
vitamin B6	10–15 mg	15–25 mg	25–50 mg	50–100 mg
vitamin B12	100 µg	250 µg	500 µg	1,000 µg
vitamin C	50–75 mg	75–250 mg	250–500 mg	500–1,000 mg
vitamin E	50 IU	100 IU	200 IU	400 IU
zinc citrate or picolinate	2–5 mg	5–10 mg	10–25 mg	25–30 mg

Herbal Remedies

Herbal Remedies	Small Dogs	Medium Dogs	Large Dogs	V. Large Dogs
aloe vera juice	2–3 ml	5 ml	5–10 ml	15 ml
black %walnut hulls (tincture)	1 drop	2–3 drops	3–5 drops	5–7 drops
cayenne pepper powder	pinch	pinch to ▯ tsp	▯ tsp	▯ tsp
chaste berry (tincture)	1 drop	2–3 drops	3–5 drops	5–7 drops
comfrey leaf, dried	¼ tsp	½ tsp	1 tsp	1–2 tsp
dandelion root (tincture)	1–2 drops	2 drops	5 drops	10 drops
Echinacea (tincture)	1 drop	2–3 drops	3–5 drops	5–7 drops
fenugreek seeds	▯ tsp	¼ – ½ tsp	½ – 1 tsp	1 tsp
flaxseed oil	½ tsp	1–2 tsp	2–3 tsp	1 Tbsp
ginger, fresh or powdered	¼ tsp	¼ – ½ tsp	½ tsp	1 tsp
grapefruit seed extract	10–25 mg	25–50 mg	50–100 mg	125 mg
hawthorn berry (tincture)	1–2 drops	2–3 drops	3–5 drops	5–7 drops
horsetail shavings	¼ tsp	½ tsp dulse	½ – 1 tsp	1 tsp
lemon juice, fresh	¼ tsp	½ tsp	½ – 1 tsp	1 tsp
licorice root powder	Pinch	¼ tsp	¼ – ½ tsp	½ tsp
maitake mushroom	¼ tsp	¼ – ½ tsp	½ – 1 tsp	1–2 tsp
milk thistle seed (tincture)	1–2 drops	2–3 drops	3–5 drops	5–10 drops
olive oil, light	1 tsp	2 tsp	1 Tbsp	1–2 Tbsp
parsley tea	1–2 tsp	2–3 tsp	1 Tbsp	1–2 Tbsp
passion flower (tincture)	1 drop	2–3 drops	3–5 drops	5–10 drops
Pau D'arco (taheebo) powder	¼ tsp	¼ – ½ tsp	½ tsp	½ – 1 tsp
peppermint leaf	1 tsp	2–3 tsp	1 Tbsp	1–2 Tbsp
psyllium seed powder	¼ tsp	¼ – ½ tsp	½ – 1 tsp	1 tsp
pumpkin seeds, crushed	¼ tsp	¼ – ½ tsp	½ – 1 tsp	1 tsp
red wine vinegar	1–2 ml	2–3 ml	3–5 ml	5 ml
reishi mushroom powder	¼ – ½ tsp	½ – 1 tsp	1–2 tsp	2 tsp
shiitake mushroom powder	¼ – ½ tsp	½ – 1 tsp	1–2 tsp	2 tsp
skullcap (tincture)	1 drop	2–3 drops	3–5 drops	5–7 drops
yellow dock (tincture)	1–2 drops	2 drops	5 drops	5–7 drops

Riva's Remedies has 3 different categories of natural products for dogs: Herbal Blends, Homeopathic Remedies and Specialized Nutrients. For product ingredients and more information please see: *www.rivasremedies.com*.

Riva's Remedies	Small Dogs	Medium Dogs	Large Dogs	V. Large Dogs
Allerg-Ease (homeopathic)	3-4 drops	5-10 drops	5-10 drops	5-10 drops
Arnica Rub (homeopathic)	Massage externally into affected areas as needed. Do not use on open sore or wounds.			
Bladder Drops (homeopathic)	3-4 drops	5-10 drops	5-10 drops	5-10 drops
Blood Sugar Formula (homeopathic)	3-4 drops	5-10 drops	5-10 drops	5-10 drops
Bone-Up (specialized nutrient)	¼ tsp	½ tsp	1 tsp	2 tsp
Calm & Cool (Herbal Blend)	¼ – ½ tsp	½ – 1 tsp	1-2 tsp	2-3 tsp
Calm-Aid (homeopathic)	3-4 drops	5-10 drops	5-10 drops	5-10 drops
Detox Dog (herbal blend)	¼ - ½ tsp	½ - 1 tsp	1-2 tsp	2-3 tsp
Digestive Drops (homeopathic)	3-4 drops	5-10 drops	5-10 drops	5-10 drops
Five Herb Digest (herbal blend)	¼ – ½ tsp	½ – 1 tsp	1 – 2 tsp	2-3 tsp
Flu-Ease (homeopathic)	3-4 drops	5-10 drops	5-10 drops	5-10 drops
Gastricol (homeopathic)	3-4 drops	5-10 drops	5-10 drops	5-10 drops
Happy Pets (herbal blend)	¼ – ½ tsp	½ – 1 tsp	1-2 tsp	2-3 tsp
Happy Pets Senior (herbal blend)	¼ – ½ tsp	½ – 1 tsp	1-2 tsp	2-3 tsp
Hormone Boost (herbal blend)	¼ – ½ tsp	½ – 1 tsp	1-2 tsp	2-3 tsp
Immune Boost (herbal blend)	¼ – ½ tsp	½ – 1 tsp	1-2 tsp	2-3 tsp
Infection Drops (homeopathic)	3-4 drops	5-10 drops	5-10 drops	5-10 drops
Injur-Ease (homeopathic)	3-4 drops	5-10 drops	5-10 drops	5-10 drops
Iron-Up (specialized nutrient)	1/8 tsp	¼ tsp	½ tsp	1 tsp
Joint-Clear (herbal blend)	¼ – ½ tsp	½ – 1 tsp	1-2 tsp	2-3 tsp
Kava's Healing Oil (herbal blend)	Spray or apply externally onto affected area twice daily.			
Kava's Primrose Oil (specialized nutrient)	¼ tsp	¼ - ½ tsp	½ – 1 tsp	1 tsp
Kidney Care (herbal blend)	¼ – ½ tsp	½ – 1 tsp	1-2 tsp	2-3 tsp

	Small Dogs	Medium Dogs	Large Dogs	V. Large Dogs
Magnesium citrate (specialized nutrient)	1/8 tsp	¼ tsp	½ tsp	1 tsp
Para+Plus (tincture)	1–2 drops	2–5 drops	5–10 drops	10 drops
Pro-Colon probiotics (herbal blend)	1/8 tsp	½ tsp	1–2 tsp	2 tsp
Pro-Dygest (herbal blend)	¼ – ½ tsp	½ – 1 tsp	1–2 tsp	2–3 tsp
Skin-Heal (herbal blend)	¼ – ½ tsp	½ – 1 tsp	1–2 tsp	2–3 tsp
Vac-Aid (homeopathic)	3–4 drops	5–10 drops	5–10 drops	5–10 drops
Vital Force (herbal blend)	¼ – ½ tsp	½ – 1 tsp	1–2 tsp	2–3 tsp
vitamin B6 (specialized nutrient)	1/8 tsp	¼ tsp	½ tsp	1 tsp
vitamin B12 (specialized nutrient)	1/8 tsp	¼ tsp	½ tsp	1 tsp
vitamin C (specialized nutrient)	1/8 tsp	½ tsp	1 tsp	2 tsp
vitamin E (specialized nutrient)	1/8 tsp	½ tsp	1 tsp	2 tsp

All About Homeopathy

Homeopathy is known as energy medicine and is the second most widely-used system of medicine in the world. It is available in most countries and is gaining in popularity every day. It is currently practiced around the world by homeopaths, pharmacists, medical doctors, and veterinarians.

What is Homeopathy?

Homeopathy is a natural yet sophisticated modality of medicine that uses highly diluted doses of substances to stimulate the body's own healing mechanism. Homeopathic medicine is based on the principle that natural substances are capable, in a diluted form, of curing the same symptoms they cause in a crude form when taken by a healthy person. This is known as the Law of Similars or "like cures like".

A homeopathic remedy is prepared by diluting the original substance down to the point that not even a single molecule of that substance remains in the homeopathic solution. When a substance, especially a toxic one, is administered in large crude dosages to a healthy body, it will produce specific symptoms of disease, but when this same substance is reduced and diluted to the point where only the "essence" of the substance remains, the new remedy will then stimulate the body's reactive forces to relieve the symptoms and overcome the condition. For example, crude arsenic causes symptoms of poisoning, diarrhea, restlessness and anxiety, but in homeopathic doses it will actually relieve symptoms of poisoning. Peeling an onion causes irritating eye and nose discharge, therefore homeopathic onion is a useful remedy for the common cold. Homeopathic remedies are prepared in laboratories and are commonly made from plants, minerals, animal products or even energy substances such as X-rays or radiation.

How Does It Work?

The vibrational pattern of the remedy transfers its information to the vibrational pattern of the disease or health condition. These symptom patterns then interact with one another, and the balanced healing vibration of the remedy quietly cancels out its unbalanced counterpart. It's really just a shift within the behaviour of the energy field. All diseases are first manifested in the energy field as a type of energetic "blueprint" before ever causing symptoms in the physical body. Interestingly enough, similar disease states have similar "energetic signatures". Experienced medical intuitives recognize these similar vibrations and are often able to identify the problems based on the "pattern". The physical body then absorbs the information in the blueprint and follows the instructions to create new activities at the cellular level. The physical body is a much denser energy field but nevertheless its behaviour is impelled to change by the information conveyed to it by the much lighter electromagnetic fields surrounding the body. Drugs or medications are also heavy energies; they initiate changes by crudely suppressing and/or replacing the body's functions and natural defense mechanisms. But unfortunately, because they depress many important physiological functions, they result in multiple side effects as well as nutritional deficiencies. In contrast, homeopathy gently creates a shift in the vibration of the imbalance by informing it to change its structure, function and/or physiology.

In addition, many homeopathic remedies are known as "polycrests", which are remedies which have multiple benefits or multi-purpose. This means that one single remedy can be used for various problems and affect various different systems in the body – physical, emotional or mental.

Why Homeopathy?

- Instead of suppressing symptoms, homeopathic remedies support the inherent ability of the body to heal by stimulating the body's natural defense mechanism

- Homeopathy treats the whole individual and improves general health, not just a specific problem.

- It is very gentle but the results can be very powerful and effective.

- Homeopathy has no harmful side effects, no withdrawal symptoms, and is non-invasive.

- For acute conditions the effects are fast-acting and can provide rapid relief for issues such as bruises, injuries, insect bites, anxiety, indigestion, and physical discomfort.

- It addresses both acute and chronic problems be they physical, mental, or emotional.

- Homeopathic remedies are not contraindicated with any medications; however, medications can limit the efficacy of homeopathic remedies.

- Homeopathic remedies are very cost-effective and usually provide many dosages per product.

- Homeopathic remedies are not tested on animals. They are only given to people to record their experiences with the remedies.

- Homeopathy does not negatively impact the environment. There are no animals killed, no trees cut down, no pollution generated, and no industrial or medical waste.

- Homeopathy is one of the safest health modalities that exists today. It can be used for both people and all animals – puppies, kittens, horses and wildlife.

Who Are the Skeptics?

For homeopaths and the millions of fortunate recipients who have benefited from the remarkable health effects of homeopathic remedies, it is hard to believe that some opponents are so outspoken. They have chosen to idolize evidence-based medicine, despite the fact that chemical medications of all kinds inadvertently harm and/or kill thousands of people and animals every year. Science has brought healthcare a long way, but it is definitely not foolproof, no matter what modality is being studied or what technique is being used to study it. And science doesn't know what to do with the concepts that it cannot yet measure, such as the energy fields produced by the dilution process of preparing a homeopathic medicine. But science always catches up, albeit sometimes slowly and with a lot of resistance. But we can't afford to wait.

It's very difficult to confront homeopathy with medical testing and clinical trials since homeopathic medicine, similar to other vibrational therapies work on the principle of energy fields. The results are determined by the response of the immune system to a specific vibration, i.e. the remedy, which contains a broad sphere of information capable of shifting disease patterns. However, because of the sensitivity of these energy fields, the remedy can be influenced by the dynamics of the study itself, as well as the people involved. The same is true in any chemistry lab actually which is why there is so much variation in the therapeutic results in the field of medicine. And need I remind you that many conventional medical procedures have not been supported by solid scientific studies with conclusive clinical trials?

However, several studies have found evidence that vibrational fields can indeed transfer their information. One study showed that the DNA from bacteria and viruses is capable of producing structural changes in water, which persist even when the DNA is highly diluted. These changes actually create electromagnetic signals that scientists can measure. These signals then imprint the DNA structure on other molecules, which project the information from one cell to another. And in another study, a test tube was prepared which contained fragments of DNA while the other contained nothing but pure water. They were placed in a copper coil that emanated a small electromagnetic field. A few hours later, testing indicated that there were DNA fragments in both tubes.

Energy-field studies are on-going but are often not publicized because the visionary and innovative scientists who conduct them are at risk of attacks against their professional integrity and credibility. In the 1980s, the eminent French immunologist Jacques Benviniste reported that white blood cells could be activated to produce an immune response by solutions of antibodies that were diluted so far that they contained none of the original biomolecules at all. The water molecules appeared to retain the memory of the antibodies that they had previously been in contact with. He explained that biomolecules can communicate with receptor cells by sending out low-frequency electromagnetic signals. He was vilified for his claims, of course, because he went against orthodox thinking, even though it was supported by a great deal of research.

But perhaps not surprisingly skeptics, particularly the vehement ones, are rarely educated in homeopathy other than studying the lack of studies or piggy-backing on other scientist's opinions. This unscientific attitude of making judgements on topics on which they have very little knowledge nor practice are frequently expressed by common sentiments like "Even if it were true, I wouldn't believe it" or "I haven't heard of it before; therefore, it doesn't exist" or "I don't understand how it could work, which means that it doesn't" or "My colleagues belong to an important medical association and they don't believe in it." A lack of understanding or experience in regard to any particular phenomenon is not a refutation of it; it's just lack of knowledge. Ignorance definitely breeds skepticism; and often a confrontational attitude which serves to deflect the attention off the inexperience. Just human nature really, isn't it?

Proponents and advocates of homeopathy understand that it is a specialized and sophisticated form of medicine that is frequently just as effective as pharmaceuticals without the side effects. And this is precisely what has them worried. Big Pharma is fighting hard to keep homeopathic medicines off the shelves; they have supported several lawsuits against homeopathic companies. To them, it matters not that homeopathy is a highly effective system of medicine that has safely helped millions of people and animals worldwide. First, do no harm...

When to Use

Homeopathic remedies can be used for virtually all health conditions, including injuries, inflammation, colic, flus, colds, fevers, skin conditions, respiratory problems, allergies, infections, colic, indigestion, hormonal imbalances, anxiety, and behavioural issues.

In acute conditions, homeopathic medicines are very fast acting. Often you will see results within one to two minutes of administering the correct remedy. As a rule, unless otherwise instructed, discontinue the remedy as soon as symptoms disappear; if symptoms reappear, repeat the remedy and use as needed.

Selecting & Administering Homeopathic Remedies

Homeopathic remedies are available in liquid as small white sugar tablets, granules, and pellets and in a liquid form which can be syringed, sprayed, or medicine dropped. Homeopathic medicines can also be used externally in the form of an ointment or liniment.

Pellets and liquids should be administered directly into a clean mouth without food, otherwise the vibration may be absorbed by the food. To administer homeopathic remedies, pellets can be put inside the lip or mouth, or offered on the bottom of a clean pail or dish. You may also dissolve the pellets in a small amount of water and syringe. For dogs give 2 to 3 pellets and for cats give 1 or 2 pellets. Liquids can be dropped directly into the mouth or added to a small amount of water and medicine dropped. Wait until the pellets have dissolved in the mouth, then follow it up with a little treat and they will look forward to their "medicines" every day. For very difficult animals, add to the drinking water.

Homeopathic remedies should be stored away from sunshine, strong electrical fields such as computers, refrigerators, stoves, or other appliances, and strong aromatic substances such as essential oils. It is also advisable to not store homeopathic remedies near your crystals as they both have strong vibrational fields.

Common Single Homeopathic Remedies Beneficial for Dogs

The following remedies are easily available at most health food stores or from homeopathic practitioners. Use in a 30C potency and repeat once or twice daily until symptoms have abated. If symptoms reappear you may resume as needed. If there is no improvement within 2 or 3 days, discontinue the remedy and choose another. Bear in mind however, that chronic or challenging conditions will require specific remedies and potencies. It is therefore recommended to seek help from a professional homeopath who works with animals.

Homeopathic pellets should be given directly into a clean mouth without food or dissolved into a small amount of water to medicine drop or syringe.

- **Aconitum** – Conditions due to long-term or previous unresolved emotional shock and trauma. Fears, panic and phobias. Rescue dogs.

- **Arnica montana** – Indicated for strains, sprains, muscles, stiffness, bruising, injuries, accidents, surgeries. Helps with trauma shock.

- **Arsenicum album** – Feelings of nervousness, restlessness, and worry. Conditions due to meat toxicity, food poisoning, diarrhea, thirst and vomiting.

- **Calc Carb** – Supports dogs with arthritic conditions, bone spurs, weakness of legs and/or back. Dogs with a tendency to obesity can be helped, as can stubborn and/or nervous dogs.

- **Chamomila** – Promotes calm in dogs with nervous tension, irritability, and/or whining. Ear infections. Hypersensitive to pain. Gas and bloating.

- **Ignatia** – Calm support for dogs who have suffered the loss of a loved one or is grieving. Indicated for dogs who suppress their emotions and for dogs who are easily hurt, reactive and/or offended.

- **Nux-vomica** – Supports liver stress and detoxification, plant poisonings, and reactions to medications and/or chemicals. Maintains a healthy digestive system in dogs with heartburn, indigestion, bloating, and gas, especially irritable dogs.

- **Rhus Tox** – Supports ligaments, tendons and muscles after injuries or trauma. Stiffness. Sore lower back. Sore dogs especially those who suffer in cold, wet weather.

- **Silicea** – Excellent remedy for abscesses. Use to expel foreign objects. Aids nutrient absorption, hair coat and brittle nails. Shy dogs who suffer from lack of confidence or experience anxiety from noise can be helped as can those suffering the adverse effects of vaccinosis.

- **Sulphur** – Indicated for liver congestion and fat metabolism. Promotes healthy skin in dogs with itching and burning skin, hot spots, and mange.

- **Thuja** – Helps to neutralize adverse reactions to vaccines in chronic conditions. A skin remedy for dogs with warts, growths, rashes, fungus and itching. General detoxifier.

Riva's Remedies Homeopathic Combinations

Give 5 to 10 drops once or twice daily as needed. Discontinue when symptoms improve and resume if symptoms reappear. Homeopathic liquid drops should be given directly into a clean mouth without food or added to a small amount of water to medicine drop or syringe. Follow it up with a little treat, and they will look forward to their "medicines" every day. For difficult dogs add to the drinking water. If using more than one homeopathic combination they can be given together.

- **Allerg-Ease** – Use to neutralize inhalant allergies and support respiratory conditions in dogs with allergies. Builds immunity. [alder, Canada pollens, molds, natrum sulph, thuja, thymuline]

- **Bladder Drops** – Incontinence, frequent urination, dribbling and urinary symptoms due to tension and anxiety. [causticum, equisetum, gelsemium, magnesium phosphate, stramonium]

- **Blood Sugar Formula** – Supports blood sugar levels and maintains metabolism. Balances appetite and promotes weight loss. [alfalfa, insulin, juniperus, syzigium]

- **Calm-Aid** – Promotes calm in dogs with nervousness, tension, agitation and various fears due to travel, noise, strangers and separation anxiety. [aconitum, arsenicum, chamomila, ignatia, passiflora, phosphorus]

- **Digestive Drops** – Promotes healthy digestion in dogs with painless and/or chronic diarrhea. Supports digestive processes and nutrient absorption. [aloe, cinchona, natrum mur, podophyllum, silicea]

- **Flu-Ease** – Promotes a healthy respiratory system in dogs with fevers, discharges, coughs, congestion, colds, flus. [aconitum, argentum, baptisia, bryonia, drosera, eupatorium, influenzum]

- **Infection Drops** – Supports dogs with infections, abscesses, pus, wounds and various discharges. Skin, ears and eyes. [lachesis, hepar-sulph, mercurious-v, silicea]

- **Injur-Ease** – Promotes recovery in dogs with sprains, strains, bruising, muscle soreness and stiffness due to injuries and traumas. [arnica montana, byronia, hypericum, rhus-tox, ruta-grav, symphytum]

- **Gastricol** – Supports a healthy digestive system in dogs with indigestion, bloating, gas, colic pains and liver and gallbladder ailments. [aconitum, argentum, chamomila, colchicum, colocynthis, lycopodium, magnesium phosphate, nux vomica, veratrum]

Flower Essences for Dogs

Flower remedies are vibrational substances pioneered by Dr. Edward Bach in the 1800s and are very beneficial for both people and animals. They are prepared from the blossoms of different flowers with unique properties and vital energies expressed in the flowering plant. They are not just an herbal extract, which holds the chemical properties of a plant, but rather, they are an alchemical or vibrational essence captured from the blossoms of the plant at the time of flowering. The effects of flower essences promote the balance and well-being of a variety of different emotional and spiritual conditions. To prescribe flower essences we put the emphasis on identifying the underlying issues or any life changes and then correlate that "portrait" with an essence which embodies the same qualities and processes. Flower essence therapy could be considered as a dialogue between the soul of nature and the soul of the animal or human.

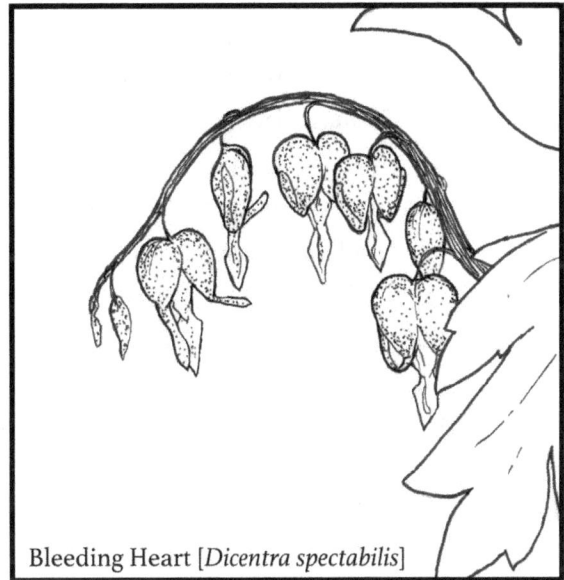

Bleeding Heart [*Dicentra spectabilis*]

With animals, emotional and/or soul imbalances are frequently expressed through behaviour. A dog may bite, growl, whine, cry, run away from home, get hyperactive, act skittish, or tremble with fear. It is important, therefore, to distinguish normal and instinctive behaviour from what is abnormal or unusual.

And, as we recall, domestic dogs are strongly influenced by their pet parent's health and life situations to the point where, it is often beneficial for the parent and the dog to take the same flower (or homeopathic) remedies. And the human parent, as well as their families, should reflect on how their own attitudes and behaviours are impacting on their dog. See Chapter 17 for extensive information on the human-canine relationship.

Give 2-4 drops of each flower essence twice daily as needed. Drops should be given directly into a clean mouth without food or added to a small amount of water to medicine drop or syringe into the mouth. You can also gently rub the essence on to the gums. Follow it up with a little treat, and they will look forward to their "medicines" every day. For difficult dogs add to the drinking water. If using more than one flower essence you can mix together and give them at the same time.

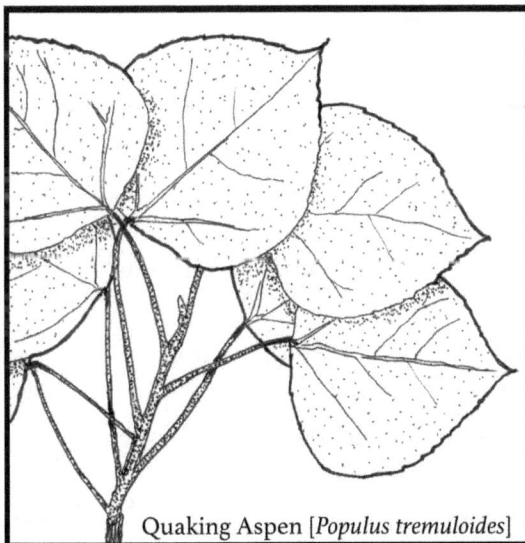

Quaking Aspen [*Populus tremuloides*]

- **Aspen** – hidden fears or fear of the unknown, anxiety and apprehension, trembling, nightmares; dogs who are easily startled or frightened.

- **Bleeding Heart** – grief and pain from a broken heart, loss of friends or family, emotional dependence and/or neediness, moping or whining; dogs who suffer from separation anxiety and over-attachment to their owner.

- **Borage** – heavy heart or discouragement from difficult circumstances or depression.

- **Chamomile** – relationship problems, emotional tension in the solar plexus; dogs who are easily upset and/or moody and irritable, teething puppies.

- **Cherry Plum** – fear of losing control, mental and emotional breakdown, acute tension and rigidity; dogs who display desperate or destructive impulses such as chewing, running away, biting.

- **Chestnut Bud** – learning from life's lessons; a good training remedy that addresses failure to learn, poor observation, and tendency to repeat the same mistakes.

- **Chicory** – dogs who are self-centred or selfish, emotionally demanding, and used to getting negative attention through negative behaviour.

- **Cosmos** – lack of focus, over-excited barking; dogs who are easily overwhelmed.

- **Dill** – overwhelmed and/or congested from excess stimulation; dog who are hypersensitive to the environment and outer activity.

- **Five Flower Remedy** – a first aid remedy for panic, disorientation, acute trauma or pain; Loss of consciousness or shock. Pre- or post-surgery.

- **Holly** – envy, suspicion and anger; jealous dogs, fighting for attention and struggling with "sibling rivalry".

- **Impatiens** – pain due to tension and resistance in the body; impatience, irritation, and hyper-activity; nervous, high-strung animals.

- **Larch** – self-doubt, poor self-esteem, and lack of confidence; shy dogs who suffer with feelings of unworthiness.

- **Lavender** – spiritually sensitive dogs with highly refined awareness; dogs who are easily over-stimulated from mental or spiritual forces; nervous, high-strung and/or "wired" dogs.

- **Mariposa Lily** – alienation; dogs abandoned by or taken from mother. Good for rescue puppies in a new home. Helps with surrogate mother situations.

- **Mimulus** – shyness and a tendency to hide from people; known fears of everyday life, such as thunder, strangers or loud noises.

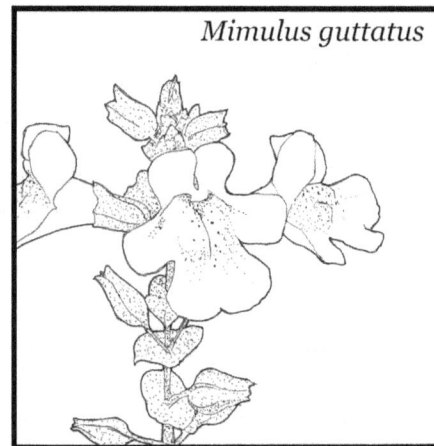

Mimulus guttatus

- **Olive** – mental/emotional/physical exhaustion from long-term stress due to fear, illness, or other ongoing struggle.

- **Penstemon** – for inner strength during illness, trauma or other adverse circumstances.

- **Pink Yarrow** – dysfunctional merging with *others*; dogs who overly sponge or mirror emotions from other animals or people. Dogs who lack emotional boundaries.

- **Poison Oak** – fear of intimate contact or bonding with other dogs or people; over protection of personal boundaries and territory; dogs who are hostile, distant, or aggressive.

- **Quaking Grass** – helps animals adjust and live together in a group; good for introducing a new dog, cat, or other animal to the household.

- **Red Clover** – dogs susceptible to mass hysteria and anxiety as caused by the whole group or pack; attacking and barking as a group; easily influenced by other animals.

- **Snapdragon** – verbal aggression, biting, and snarling; tension around the jaw; aggressive tendencies.

- **Star of Bethlehem** – dogs suffering from past abuse, injury, shock, or trauma; dogs in need of healing and comfort.

- **Tiger Lily** – excess "yang"; dogs who are overly aggressive, competitive, hostile, and uncooperative.

- **Vervain** – dogs who are overenthusiastic, striving for perfection, and/or suffering from nervous exhaustion from trying too hard.

- **Vine** – domineering behaviour; tyrannical pack-leaders who force their will on others and need to be in control.

- **Walnut** – dogs facing transition and change; use before and after moving locations. For letting go of past experiences.

- **Wild Rose** – giving up on life; dogs with broken spirits, who are joyless, indifferent and apathetic.

- **Willow** – resentment, anger, and attachment to negative emotions; dogs holding a grudge or feeling bitter and/or inflexible.

- **Yarrow** – dogs who are overly vulnerable to others and the environment and thus easily depleted; dogs overly absorbent of negative energies or psychic toxicity.

Yarrow [*Achillea millefolium*]

Kinesiology – Muscle Response Testing

What is Kinesiology?

Kinesiology is a type of muscle testing or energy testing used to evaluate health status as well as the energetic response by the dog to specific foods, remedies, supplements, or other substances. It can also be used to test different body functions and body systems including organs. Muscle testing animals is conducted by using a surrogate, i.e. another person whose arm strength is tested by the person doing the testing while both persons are touching the dog to complete the circuit.

How Does It Work?

When certain foods, nutrients, or other substances touch a subject's body, the energy field will either stay neutral, weaken, or gain strength. This is determined by how strong the surrogate's arm muscles are when pressure is applied at the same time that the substance is held close to the dog. A weak response means that the food or substance is not helpful or beneficial, a strong response means that it is beneficial, and a neutral response (where the arm strength doesn't change) means that it is neither good nor bad.

Energy testing is made possible by the understanding that anatomical body parts and systems including connective tissue, blood, the nervous system, the immune system, and all body organs are surrounded by an electromagnetic or energy field. This field is a fundamental force of nature. It is a physical field that is produced by electrically charged particles and is a combination of an electric field and a magnetic field. The interaction between these two fields is mediated by units of light: these photons and the fields themselves are subject to a number of variables that can and do induce change.

This energy field, when seen as a whole, surrounding a living organism (or an inanimate object for that matter), is commonly known as the aura. An aura surrounds every living thing, including all body systems and organs. When physical, mental or emotional health problems develop within these areas, the energy field becomes impeded and blocked and experiences a break in intercellular communications. Muscle testing opens a pathway of communication between the body's energy field(s) and the people doing the testing. Therefore, when testing specific substances, kinesiology works by checking the resonance of a particular substance, remedy, vitamin, or food against the resonance of the dog's electrical field. And when the two electrical fields (dog and substance) are disharmonic or dissonant (not beneficial), the surrogate muscle being tested will feel weaker. When the resonance is neutral, the muscle strength won't change. When the resonance is harmonic, indicating benefit, the surrogate muscle will feel stronger and have more resistance. If Vitamin C is going to be helpful for a particular dog's immune system, then holding Vitamin C close to the dog will make the surrogate arm very strong.

A weakness, blockage or sensitivity will show up as a weak muscle test. A weak and toxic liver for example will have a disturbed flow of energy that will, when touched, create an immediate weak response throughout the entire energy field, including the surrogate muscle.

Why Use Kinesiology?

Experienced kinesiologists can use muscle testing to "read" or "track" the body and many of its functions. It enables us to identify energy fields that are blocked or dysfunctional, to identify the underlying cause, and to then assess what is necessary to correct the imbalance. Underlying causes can include nutrient deficiencies and excesses, dietary indiscretions, toxins, organ stress, past injuries, shock, trauma and/or emotions. Kinesiology is often capable of detecting problem areas long before they are found with conventional medical tests. That is because all imbalances first manifest themselves in the energy or vibratory field before they manifest as physical problems.

Kinesiology can also easily be used by those dog parents who have little to no experience and is, therefore, a very valuable tool to identify food intolerances as well as remedies and supplements that are of benefit.

The Method

Sit near the dog that you are wanting to test and have your surrogate person facing you. You can both sit on the floor or couch with the dog or, if the dog is quieter and/or smaller, they may want to sit in your lap or stand up on a table or counter. Have your surrogate helper touch the dog with one hand while holding the other arm up in the air horizontally but not too high. Instruct your surrogate to just hold the arm in place without excessive pressure or weakness. Try to push your surrogate's hand down gently so you can reference how strong the arm is when it is neutral.

Hold a piece of chicken or other dog food in your hand and touch your dog with it. Then use the other hand to push your surrogate's arm. If the arm is weaker, then the food in question is not healthy for the dog. If the arm is stronger, then this food is beneficial for the dog. If the arm-strength is neutral, then it's neither positive nor negative.

Similarly, if you are testing a remedy, vitamin, or mineral hold the substance against the dog and test your surrogate's arm. A strong arm means that the dog will benefit from the product, and a weak arm muscle means that it is not likely to be of value, and may even cause a reaction.

Remember, that you are just testing the comparisons of the two energy fields – substance vs dog – strong or weak. Do not ask yes or no questions, such as, "Is this food good for my dog?" or "Will Vitamin B12 give my dog more energy?" and so on.

Hair Tissue Mineral Analysis

A hair analysis is a scientific test which accurately measures the mineral content of the hair using atomic absorption methods. It can be done for both people and animals including dogs, cats and horses. Mineral content of the hair reflects the mineral content of the body's tissues. If a mineral deficiency or excess exists in the hair, it usually indicates a mineral deficiency or excess within the body, although sometimes it can actually mean the reverse. It can also indicate whether that mineral is bioavailable to the cells and tissues.

Hair mineral analyses are also very accurate in determining the levels of toxic heavy metals - a problem which is becoming all too common in an ever-increasing toxic world. Toxic metals such as mercury, aluminum, arsenic and/or lead can have a profound impact on health and can be very destructive. Routine blood tests cannot detect chronic heavy-metal poisoning; however, tissue mineral analysis, using atomic absorption, is considered a legitimate method.

A mineral hair analysis can also reveal a variety of different nutritional and health problems as well as the status of many organs and glands, including the liver and kidneys; and thyroid, pituitary, and adrenal glands. It can detect adrenal dysfunction, digestive disturbances, thyroid and pituitary dysfunction, blood sugar imbalances, anemia, and inflammation.

A hair analysis can detect these imbalances and problems, where often conventional blood testing cannot. Nutritional physiology takes place at the cellular level, not in the blood. Blood levels of nutrients and minerals are kept within very narrow limits by the body and are slow to change; thus, blood levels are not a true reflection of the nutrient status within the tissues, organs and glands which are all often depleted before the blood is. In contrast, tissue mineral analysis provides information about cellular activity within the tissues and the metabolism of all nutrients throughout the body.

Common causes of a mineral imbalance are poor diet, mal-digestion of foods, nutrient deficiencies, medications, stress, and/or the accumulation of toxic or heavy metals.

The results of a hair tissue mineral analysis include a complete written report with a laboratory bar graph which shows the values of over 30 minerals and elements, 8 toxic heavy metals and 15 mineral ratios. Hair analysis is

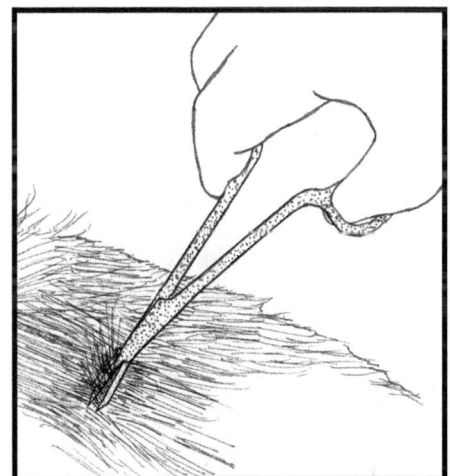

Hairs are collected with scissors.

an invaluable screening tool which guides diet choices and a recommended supplement program for optimum health and wellness. However, the analysis results can be very complex so ensure that the results are interpreted by a practitioner who is experienced in formulating nutritional programs based on hair tissue analyses. Too many times I have seen people arrange for a hair analysis test which is returned to them with very little explanation, an incomplete interpretation and no recommendations for correcting the imbalances.

A hair sample should be approximately 125 mg (about ½ Tablespoon). Take from the chest area as close to the skin as possible. The hair should be no longer than 1½ inches. For long-haired dogs cut the extra length off and keep the 1½-inch section which was closest to their skin. For outdoor dogs wash the testing area with rubbing alcohol and let dry completely before taking the sample. Place the hair sample in a paper envelope. Do not use plastic or zip-lock baggies and do not tape the sample to a piece of paper or put it in aluminum foil. Plastic, glue and aluminum will contaminate the hair sample.

See the Services page (page 230) to arrange a test for your pets or for yourself.

Recommended Reading

Genetics and The Environment

Dr. Jean Dodds W. Jean Dodds and Diana Laverdure. *Canine Nutrigenomics The New Science of Feeding Your Dog for Optimum Health.* 2015. DogWise E Books.

Lipton, Bruce. *The Biology of Belief.* Santa Rosa, California: Mountain of Love/Elite Books. 2005.

Nutrition

"Cancer Patients Should Not Eat Meat Here Are The Reasons Why". March 06, 2011. https://ejtcm.com/2011/03/16/cancer-patients-should-not-eat-meat-here-are-the-reasons-why/

"Meat Contamination." 2017. http://www.peta.org/living/food/meat-contamination/

Vaccines

"Schultz: Dog Vaccines May Not Be Necessary." March 14, 2003. news.wisc.edu/schultz-dog-vaccines-may-not-be-necessary/

"Duration of Immunity for Canine and Feline Vaccines: A Review. 2006 http://belbergere.com/documents/vaccinations/vaccinedurationShultz.pdf

"Canine Health Survey". http://www.canine-health-concern.org.uk/caninevaccinesurvey.html

"Vaccination of Dogs and Cats: No Longer So Controversial." http://www.wsava.org/sites/default/files/2011_VetRecord_EditorialVaccinati on.pdf

Deva Khalsa. *Natural Dog.* Irvine, California. i-5 Publishing, LLC. 2015.

Homeopathy

"Nobel Prize Winner Luc Montagnier Supports Science of Homeopathy." February 04, 2011. http://www.naturalnews.com/031210_Luc_Montagnier_Homeopathy.html #ixzz1duGOq7db

John Saxton and Peter Gregory. *Textbook of Veterinary Homeopathy.* 2005. Bucks, U.K.: Beaconsfield Publishers Ltd.

National Center For Homeopathy. http://www.homeopathycenter.org/research

Neutering

"Golden Retriever Study Suggests Neutering Affects Dog Health." February 13, 2013. http://news.ucdavis.edu/search/news_detail.lasso?id=10498

"Evaluation of the Risk and Age of Onset of Cancer and Behavioural Disorders in Gonadectomised Vizslas." 2014. http://mercola.fileburst.com/PDF/HealthyPets/61314_Pets_Lead%20Article_VizslaStudy.pdf

The Human Canine Relationship

Jessica Addams and Andrew Miller. *Between Dog and Wolf.* 2012. Wenatchee, Washington, Dogwise Publishing.

"Research Explores Close Prehistoric Relationship Between Humans and Dogs." March 02, 2016. http://phys.org/news/2016-03-explores-prehistoric-relationship-humans-dogs.html#jCp

Breeding

"One Hundred Years of Breed 'Improvement'." September 29th, 2012. https://dogbehaviorscience.wordpress.com/2012/09/29/100-years-of-breed-improvement/

"The Price of a Pedigree." 2006. http://www.onekind.org/uploads/publications/price-of-a-pedigree.pdf

"Selective Breed Problems." September 16, 2010. http://www.pbs.org/wnet/nature/dogs-that-changed-the-world-selective-breeding-problems/1281/

"We're Breeding Our Dogs To Death." May 27th, 2015. http://inthesetimes.com/article/17910/bred-to-death

Services

Dogs & Cats

www.rivasremedies.com

Health Consultations

Hair Mineral Analyses

Seminars

Online Courses

Riva's Remedies   *(Herbal Blends, Homeopathic Remedies, Specialized Nutrients)*

Horses

www.rivasremedies.com

Health Consultations

Hoof Assessments

Hair Mineral Analyses

Seminars

Online Courses

Riva's Remedies   *(Herbal Blends, Homeopathic Remedies, Specialized Nutrients)*

People: Marijke's Intuitive Healing Services

www.marijke.com

Online Courses

Destination Healing Retreats

Health Consultations

Hair Mineral Analyses

Healing Products

Index